MEDIEVAL TEXTS

GENERAL EDITORS

V. H. Galbraith, Sir Roger Mynors and C. N. L. Brooke

CHRONICA BURIENSIS

1212–1301

THE CHRONICLE OF BURY ST EDMUNDS

1212–1301

Chronica Buriensis
1212—1301

NELSON

The Chronicle of
Bury St Edmunds
1212—1301

Edited with Introduction, Notes
and Translation by

Antonia Gransden

NELSON

THOMAS NELSON AND SONS LTD
36 Park Street London W1
Parkside Works Edinburgh 9
117 Latrobe Street Melbourne C1
10 Warehouse Road Apapa Lagos
P.O. Box 25012 Nairobi

THOMAS NELSON AND SONS (AFRICA) (Pty) LTD
P.O. Box 9881 Johannesburg

THOMAS NELSON AND SONS (CANADA) LTD
81 Curlew Drive Don Mills Ontario

THOMAS NELSON AND SONS
Copewood and Davis Streets Camden 3, N.J.

SOCIÉTÉ FRANÇAISE D'ÉDITIONS NELSON
97 rue Monge Paris 5

Printed in Great Britain by
Thomas Nelson (Printers) Ltd, London and Edinburgh

CONTENTS

ACKNOWLEDGMENTS

I SHOULD like to thank the following who have helped me in the preparation of this volume : Professor V. H. Galbraith whose article on the chronicle of Bury St Edmunds first introduced me to it and who encouraged me to edit it ; Sir Goronwy Edwards who as my supervisor helped me edit the chronicle for a London Ph. D. degree ; Sir Roger Mynors who read my translation and made many useful suggestions; Professor C.N.L. Brooke to whose hard work on the proofs I am deeply indebted. I should also like to thank the Chapter of the College of Arms for placing Arundel MS 30 on temporary loan in the British Museum for my use, and the Museum and Libraries Committee of Bury St Edmunds for similarly lending the Moyses Hall manuscript. In addition I am grateful to Professor Bruce Dickins for allowing me to collate MS 92 in the library of Corpus Christi College, Cambridge. In addition I am grateful to Professor V. H. Galbraith, to the Editor of the *English Historical Review* and to Messrs Longmans Green and Co. Ltd for permission to reprint part of Professor Galbraith's article.

ABBREVIATIONS

Ann. Lond.	*Annales Londonienses* in *Chronicles of the Reigns of Edward I and II*, ed. W. Stubbs (RS, 1882–4), I, pp. 3–251
Ann. Mon.	*Annales Monastici*, ed. H. R. Luard (RS, 1864–9), 4 vols.
Arnold	*Memorials of St Edmund's Abbey*, ed. T. Arnold (RS, 1890–6), 3 vols.
Bliss	W. H. Bliss, J. A. Twemlow, C. Johnson, *Cal. of Entries in the Papal Registers relating to Great Britain and Ireland* (1893–1912), 10 vols.
Burton	*Annales Monasterii de Burton, 1004–1263*, in *Ann. Mon.*, I, pp. 181–510
CCR	*Calendar of Close Rolls*
CFR	*Calendar of Fine Rolls*
CPR	*Calendar of Patent Rolls*
Chron. Bur.	*Chronicon Buriensis 1020–1346*, in Arnold, III, pp. 1–73
Cotton	*Bartholomaei de Cotton Monachi Norwicensis Historia Anglicana 449–1298*, ed. Luard (RS, 1859)
De Ant. Leg.	*De Antiquis Legibus Liber: Chronica Maiorum et Vicecomitum Londoniarum*, ed. T. Stapleton (Camden Society, 1846)
Dunst.	*Annales prioratus de Dunstaplia 1–1297*, in *Ann. Mon.*, III, pp. 1–420
EHR	*English Historical Review*
Flores	*Flores Historiarum*, ed. Luard (RS, 1890), 3 vols.
Foedera	T. Rymer, *Foedera* (Record Commission, 1816–69)
Gerv. Cant.	*The Historical Works of Gervase of Canterbury*, ed. W. Stubbs (RS, 1879–80), 2 vols.

Grandes Chron.	*Les Grandes Chroniques de France,* ed. J. Viard (Société de l'histoire de France, 1920–37), 9 vols.
Guisborough	*Chronicle of Walter Guisborough, previously edited as the chronicle of Walter of Hemingford or Hemingburgh,* ed. Harry Rothwell (Camden Series, LXXXIX, 1957)
Jocelin	*Chronicle of Jocelin of Brakelond,* ed. H. E. Butler, with an English translation (Nelson's Medieval Texts, 1949)
Joinville	Jean de Joinville, *Histoire de S. Louis,* in M. Bouquet, *Recueil des Historiens des Gaules et de la France,* XX, pp. 191-304
Liebermann	extracts 1083–1130 from the Bury chronicle by F. Liebermann in *Mon. Germ. Hist. Scriptores,* XXVIII, pp. 584–98
Lobel	M. D. Lobel, *The Borough of Bury St Edmunds* (1935)
Matthew Paris, *Chron. Maj.*	*Chronica Majora,* ed. Luard (RS, 1872–83), 7 vols.
Liber Additamentorum	printed in *Chron. Maj.,* VII
Hist. Angl.	*Historia Anglorum sive Historia Minor,* ed F. Madden (RS, 1866–9), 3 vols.
Mon. Angl.	W. Dugdale, *Monasticon Anglicanum* (Caley's ed., 1817–30), 6 vols.
Oseney	*Annales Monasterii de Oseneia 1016-1347,* in *Ann. Mon.,* IV, pp. 1–352
Oxenedes	*Chronica Iohannis de Oxenedes,* ed. H. Ellis (RS, 1859)
Parl. Writs	*Parliamentary Writs and Writs of Military Summons* (Record Commission, 1827–34), 2 vols.
Potthast	A. Potthast, *Regesta Pontificum Romanorum* (Berlin, 1874-5) 2 vols.
Rishanger	*Willelmi Rishanger . . . Chronica et Annales,* ed. T. H. Riley (RS, 1865)
Rot. Parl.	*Rotuli Parliamentorum* (1767), 6 vols.

RS	Rolls Series
Tewk.	*Annales Monasterii de Theokesberia 1066–1263,* in *Ann. Mon.,* I, pp. 41–186
VCH	*Victoria County Histories*
Wav.	*Annales Monasterii de Waverleia 1–1291,* in *Ann. Mon.,* II, pp. 127–411
Wendover	*Rogeri de Wendover . . . Flores Historiarum,* ed. H. G. Hewlett (RS, 1886–9), 3 vols.
Wig.	*Florentii Wigorniensis monachi chronicon ex chronicis,* ed. B. Thorpe (1848-9) 2 vols.
William de Nangis, *Chron.*	*Chronique Latine de Guillaume de Nangis de 1113 à 1300 avec les Continuations de cette Chronique de 1300 à 1368,* ed. H. Geraud (Société de l'histoire de la France, 1843), 2 vols.
Vie de S. Louis	in M. Bouquet, *Recueil des Historiens des Gaules et de la France,* XX, pp. 313–465
Wint.	*Annales Monasterii de Wintonia 519–1277,* in *Ann. Mon.,* II, pp. 1–125
Wykes	*Chronicon vulgo dictum Thomae Wykes,* in *Ann. Mon.,* IV, pp. 6–319

INTRODUCTION

I   THE ABBEY OF BURY ST EDMUNDS

LITTLE remains today of the abbey of Bury St Edmunds except the gateway of the church with its fine Norman tower, the fourteenth-century gatehouse of the abbot's palace and the bridge over the river Lark. Yet once the abbey was one of the greatest in England. Herman, a monk of Bury, compared the presbytery of the church, completed in 1095 by Abbot Baldwin, to the Temple of Solomon.[1] The church was bigger than Durham cathedral.[2]

King Canute founded the abbey for twenty Benedictine monks from Ely and twenty from St Benet's Hulme, Norfolk, in honour of St Edmund, king of East Anglia, who was killed fighting the Danes on 20 November 870. The monks replaced a community of secular clerks which had served St Edmund's tomb since the ninth century. The abbey and its saint retained the affection and devotion of the kings of England throughout the Middle Ages. It was said that when Edward the Confessor visited the abbey he always walked the last mile on foot, as a pilgrim.[3] It was he who gave the abbot of Bury its Liberty of eight and a half hundreds and other privileges which were confirmed and augmented by his successors.

After the Norman Conquest the abbot became a tenant-in-chief of the king and a baron of the realm. He had to supply the king with forty knights in time of war, and was liable for the usual feudal aids. During a vacancy the king

---

[1] Arnold, I, p. 85. A good short history of Bury is by A. Goodwin, *The Abbey of St Edmundsbury* (1931).

[2] The whole length of the abbey church was between 480 and 502 ft. (M. R. James, *On the Abbey of St Edmund at Bury*, Cambridge Antiquarian Society, 8vo ser., XXVIII (1895), p. 166.) Durham cathedral is 411 ft. long (*Mon. Angl.*, I, p. 231).

[3] Arnold, I, p. 363

took the abbot's barony into his hands and received the revenues: this was the prime cause of the division of property between the abbot and convent which took place at Bury, as in many other religious houses, early in the reign of Henry I [1]; as a result of the division the king took only the abbot's portion during a vacancy and the convent remained in undisturbed possession of theirs.

Apart from the ' feudalisation ' of the abbey the continuity of its history was unbroken by the Conquest. This was partly because Abbot Baldwin (1065–97), the physician of Edward the Confessor, was a Frenchman and had the favour of William I.[2] Until the end of the twelfth century the king in practice chose the abbot and the convent accepted his nominee, provided he was suitable. Two abbots besides Baldwin were the king's friends: Abbot Anselm (1121–48), a Lombard and nephew of St Anselm of Canterbury, was often at Henry I's court [3]; Abbot Ording (1148–58) appears to have been Stephen's tutor, which may account for that king's generosity to the abbey.[4]

The affection of Henry III and Edward I for St Edmunds rivalled that which they showed for St Albans. Henry III named his second son Edmund after the saint.[5] Both kings frequently visited the house, often with their families.[6] Edward had his banner touched with St Edmund's relic and the mass for St Edmund celebrated over it before he set out for his Scottish campaign in 1300.[7]

The abbot exercised powers like those of a sheriff within

---

[1] For Henry I's confirmation of the division see D. Douglas, *Feudal Documents from the Abbey of Bury St Edmunds* (1932), p. 69

[2] Arnold, I, pp. 56, 345

[3] An account of Abbot Anselm's life is given by E. W. Williamson, *The Letters of Osbert de Clare, prior of Westminster* (1929), pp. 191–200. See also R. W. Southern in *Medieval and Renaissance Studies*, ed. R. W. Hunt, R. Klibansky and L. Labowsky, IV (1958), pp. 190–1, and E. Bishop, *Liturgica Historica* (1918), pp. 238–49.

[4] Arnold, I, pp. xxxv, 93

[5] Below, p. 13

[6] Below, p. xxxii–xxxiii

[7] Below, p. 157

St Edmund's Liberty,[1] which covered nearly a third of Suffolk. He held the view of frank-pledge, tried pleas of the crown, was responsible for the return and execution of royal writs, and imprisoned and hanged criminals, and within the *banleuca* of Bury, an area comprising the town and suburbs,[2] he appointed his own justices in eyre.

The abbot also had an extensive ecclesiastical franchise within the *banleuca* of Bury. Here he exercised the powers of an archdeacon, and no other cleric could celebrate mass or erect an altar without his consent.[3] The franchise originated with the grants of Anglo-Saxon kings, which asserted the abbey's independence of episcopal authority. It was defined and elaborated by a series of twelfth-century bulls which brought the abbey into direct dependence on Rome. Only a legate specially appointed by the pope could hold a visitation of the abbey, until the Fourth Lateran Council in 1215 decreed that such exempt houses should be visited by nominees of the Provincial Chapters of the Order.[4] The same council ordained that the abbots of exempt houses should go personally to Rome for papal confirmation of their election. The first pope to enforce this ruling was Alexander IV (1254–61), and the first English abbot to make the journey was Simon de Luton of Bury in 1257.[5]

II INTELLECTUAL LIFE AT BURY

With privilege went responsibility. The abbot and those monks who held official positions in the abbey spent much time administering the manors, Liberty and ecclesiastical

[1] The best modern account of the Liberty is by Professor H. M. Cam, ' The King's Government, as administered by the Greater Abbots of East Anglia,' in *Communications of the Cambridge Antiquarian Society*, XXIX (1928), reprinted in Professor Cam, *Liberties and Communities in Medieval England* (1944), pp. 183–204.

[2] A map of the *banleuca* of St Edmund is in Lobel at the end of the volume. For the exempt jurisdiction see ibid., pp. 41–4.

[3] *Pinchbeck Register*, ed. Lord F. Hervey (privately printed, 1925), I, pp. 16f.

[4] Decree XII

[5] Below, p. 21

franchise. The abbey had to defend its rights, often with expensive and protracted litigation, against encroachments by royal officials, the bishops of Norwich and others, throughout the Middle Ages.

Perhaps the most famous inmate of St Edmund's abbey was Samson (abbot 1182/3–1214), a Norfolk man with a genius for administration. His chaplain and biographer Jocelin of Brakelond wrote of him that he ' seemed to love the active life better than the contemplative; he had more praise for good obedientiaries than good cloister monks, and rarely did he approve of any man solely for his knowledge of literature, unless he were also wise in worldly affairs.' [1]

Nevertheless his election was, as Professor Knowles has pointed out,[2] to some extent a compromise, to satisfy those monks in favour of the new learning of the schools, and those opposed to it on the grounds that scholars are not good rulers. He was a man of some education. He had taken degrees at Paris and taught at Bury; he had composed verses for the paintings in the choir and written a work on St Edmund's miracles. Intellectual life at Bury was flourishing in the Middle Ages.

The abbey had one of the most productive monastic scriptoria and greatest libraries in the country.[3] The literary tradition apparently began in the last years of the eleventh century with Herman's book on the miracles of St Edmund.[4] From then until the end of the Middle Ages a quantity of hagiographical material relating to St Edmund, in Latin, French and English, in prose and verse, was composed in the abbey. Other saints were not neglected. A poem in Anglo-Norman on St Faith was written there early in the thirteenth century.[5] Bury played a part in spreading the cult of St Mary; Abbot Anselm (1121–48) seems to have been the first man to

[1] Jocelin, p. 40
[2] Dom David Knowles, *The Monastic Order in England* (1941), pp. 503–4
[3] N. R. Ker, *Medieval Libraries of Great Britain* (1941), pp. 10–14
[4] Arnold, I, pp. 26–92
[5] M. D. Legge, *Anglo-Norman in the Cloisters* (1950), pp. 9–10

celebrate the feast of the Immaculate Conception in England.[1]
Two poems about St Mary, one on her miracles and the other
on her Fifteen Joys, were written at Bury in Anglo-Norman
in the thirteenth century.[2]

Serious historical writing began in the thirteenth century,
when Jocelin wrote his biography of Samson. It is an intimate,
even gossipy work, and gives a picture of life in the cloister
and of the abbey's relationship with its neighbours. From the
early thirteenth century until the fifteenth many historical
tracts were compiled there. They describe important events
in the abbey's history, such as the disputed election of Abbot
Hugh in 1214,[3] the quarrel of the monks with the Grey friars
when they tried to establish themselves within the abbey's
banleuca (1257–63),[4] the revolt of the townsmen against the
abbey during the Barons' War,[5] and the dispute with the king
over the abbot's right to hold the assize of weights and
measures.[6] Some of the tracts are little more than collections
of documents; a few have the notary's attestation.[7] Probably
they were partly written for reference in case of future disputes.

Two thirteenth-century works were composed apparently
because the author had an antiquarian interest in the abbey's
past. The first is the *Gesta Sacristarum*,[8] a history of the sacrists
from the time of Abbot Baldwin (1065–97) to 1280, with a
continuation from 1294 to the early fourteenth century (the
years 1280–94 are omitted). The part to 1280 is mainly about
the sacrists' building activities. The other work is an archi-
tectural history of the conventual church and its chapels and
of the other churches at Bury, compiled probably early in
Edward I's reign.[9]

---

[1] Williamson, *Letters of Osbert de Clare*, pp. 11–14
[2] Legge, op. cit., pp. 13, 17
[3] Arnold, II, pp. 29–130
[4] ibid., II, pp. 263–85
[5] Below, p. xxiv
[6] Kempe register of St Edmund's abbey, B. M. MS Harley 645, f. 49
[7] For examples see Arnold, II, pp. 279, 314 and III, p. 99
[8] ibid., II, pp. 289–96
[9] James, *On the Abbey of St Edmund at Bury*, pp. 161–2

All these historical works are of local interest and not proper chronicles. The monastic chronicle, though it usually has notices of events concerning the house of its origin, is a general history, recording events in chronological order. Most begin at the Creation of the World, the Coming of the Saxons or the foundation of the house where it was written, and continue to times contemporary with their composition. A chronicle was compiled from literary sources till these ended, and then from other documents, personal observation and hearsay. A chronicler of Winchester describes one method of writing the contemporary section [1]: loose leaves were attached to the end of the book; rough notes were entered on them of current events and a specially appointed monk copied them in a literary form on to the end of the chronicle each year. The entries for the last years were often revised as fresh news arrived or attitudes changed, and year by year new annals were appended. A chronicle was often the work of more than one monk. The contemporary part is of value, for it may preserve facts not found elsewhere and it gives an insight into men's thoughts.

Two such chronicles were written at Bury. The first, the *Annales Sancti Edmundi*, was written in the first half of the thirteenth century.[2] It covers briefly the period from the Incarnation to 1212. The last few annals are of some interest for English history. The chronicle breaks off incomplete in the middle of the annal for 1212, owing to the loss of leaves from the only known manuscript. The other chronicle is more important. It is published here, complete for the first time.

III   THE BURY CHRONICLE

The Bury Chronicle was written in the second half of the thirteenth century and covers the period from the Creation

---

[1] *Ann. Mon.*, IV, p. 355. For the Winchester/Waverley chronicle see N. Denholm-Young in *EHR*, XLIX (1934), pp. 85f.

[2] Ed. F. Liebermann, *Ungedruckte Anglo-Normannische Geschichtsquellen* (1879), pp. 97–155. Excerpts are printed in Arnold, II, pp. 3–25.

to 1301. It is probably the work of three men. The first, John de Taxter, seems to have compiled the chronicle from the Creation to 1265: he relates under 1244 that he ' the writer of the present volume' assumed the monk's habit on St Edmund's day in that year. A second monk, whose name is unknown, apparently revised Taxter's work and continued it to 1296. A third monk, also anonymous, added a continuation to 1301. The chronicle is a valuable contemporary authority for the last years of Henry III's reign and for Edward I's reign to 1301.

Thomas Arnold did not print the chronicle in the *Memorials of St Edmund's Abbey* (Rolls Series, 1890–6, three volumes). He devoted over a third of his space to hagiographical material relating to St Edmund, printed Jocelin's *Life of Abbot Samson* (an excellent edition had appeared in 1840 by John Gage Rokewode, Camden Society publications, vol. XIII), and printed some of the short tracts about the abbey's history.

Benjamin Thorpe, the Anglo-Saxon scholar, printed a text for the period 1152 to 1294 in his edition of Florence of Worcester's chronicle (English Historical Society, 1848/9). He did so probably because this part of the Bury chronicle is appended to Florence's work in one manuscript, Corpus Christi College, Cambridge, MS 92. This is not, however, a good text of the Bury chronicle. Collation proves that it was copied directly from MS Arundel 30 (College of Arms), which was written at Bury and is the best text known. The Corpus manuscript was copied for Peterborough abbey: it contains extra passages relating to that house and omits others relating to Bury, and the annals for 1294 and 1295 differ from those in Arundel 30. It does not have the second continuation from 1296 to 1301, which is in Arundel 30. Apparently Thorpe did not collate his text with any of the others and took liberties in his transcription: he corrected words to improve the Latin and transposed passages to improve the chronological order. There are also a number of careless mistakes.

Extracts from the Bury chronicle about German history,

with a valuable introduction, were printed by F. Liebermann in *Monumenta Germaniae Historica: Scriptores*, xxviii (1888), pp. 584–600. He printed from Cotton MS Julius A i to 1265 and from Arundel 30 from 1266 to 1301, and collated these texts with Arundel 6 (College of Arms) and the Corpus manuscript. The second continuation, 1296 to 1301, in Arundel 30 was printed by Professor V. H. Galbraith in the *English Historical Review*, lviii (1942), pp. 51–74.

To 1212 the chronicle was compiled from well-known sources. The main source up to 1131 is Florence of Worcester. Probably the chronicler used the Bury version of his work (now Bodley MS 297), as he apparently cites some of its interpolated passages about St Edmund and the abbey.[1] From 1131 to the end of the twelfth century the principal sources are the works of Ralph de Diceto, and for the reign of King John till 1212 the *Annales Sancti Edmundi*.[2] Since the *Annales* end incomplete in the middle of the annal for 1212, it is impossible to say exactly when the chronicler stopped using them.

Quotations also occur from the following authors in the section from the Creation to 1212: (*a*) Late Roman: Lucius Apuleius, *De Deo Socratis*; Aulus Gellius, *Noctes Atticae*; Justin's epitome of Trogus Pompeius; Eutropius, *Historia Miscella*; (*b*) Early Christian: St Jerome's Latin translation of Eusebius's chronicle; St Augustine, *Confessions* and *City of God*; Orosius, *Historia*; Boethius, *De Consolatione Philosophiae*; (*c*) Medieval: Gildas, *De Excidio Britanniae*; Bede, *Historia Ecclesiastica*; Herman, *De Miraculis Sancti Edmundi*; the chronicles of Freculphus, Peter Comestor, Sigibert of Gembloux, Hugh of St Victor, William of Malmesbury (*Gesta Regum* and *Gesta Pontificum*), Symeon of Durham, Geoffrey of Monmouth, Henry of Huntingdon, Roger of Hoveden, the *Historia Eliensis* and John of Salisbury's *Policraticus*.

From 1212 to the end the chronicle is 'original,' that is

---

[1] The interpolations relating to St Edmund and Bury are printed in Arnold, I, pp. 340–56.

[2] For the relationship of Taxter, the *Annales S. Edmundi* and Wendover see Liebermann, op. cit., pp. 101–5

it copies no known literary source. The section from 1212 to 1264 is of little value (apart from a few entries about the domestic history of St Edmund's), because it is brief and written well after the events recorded. The last annal is fuller than the previous ones and was probably compiled in that year or soon afterwards: it contains what must surely be an eye-witness account of the storm and fog which followed the battle of Evesham; the fog was so dense, the chronicler relates, that people could not see their food at lunch.

The following evidence suggests that the chronicle to 1265, containing the passage recording that Taxter took the habit, is the earliest version and not a copy with variants of the version with continuations. The best manuscript of the ' Taxter ' version was written soon after 1265 and internal evidence indicates that it is the earliest text of the chronicle.[1] The version with continuations qualifies the statement which appears in the ' Taxter ' version that de Montfort's corpse worked miracles with the words ' ut plurimi asserebant '; it seems likely that this caution was a reviser's.[2]

There are other important differences between the ' Taxter ' version and the version with continuations. The latter does not have the entry stating that Taxter took the habit, nor two passages of chronological computation (one of about half a page and the other of about two pages) in the section before the Incarnation, nor an account under 1265 of the siege of the Lord Edward at Gloucester. On the other hand it has some material not in the ' Taxter ' version: about twenty-four passages (from a few lines in length to over two pages) relating to pagan history in the section before the Incarnation, a note ' hic attonsus fui ' under 1255, and a notice of the birth of John de Hastings in 1265. Also under 1265 is an additional paragraph [3] concerning the fine of 800 marks which, as the ' Taxter ' version records, was imposed on the abbey in the parliament of Winchester. This addition anticipates the

---

[1] Below, p. xxxvii   [2] Below, p. 33 and *n. b* cf. p. xxxvii
[3] Below, p. 32

interest in the abbey's financial burdens shown by the author of the first continuation (1265–96),[1] and suggests he was the reviser of the ' Taxter ' version.

The annals of the first continuation were probably compiled close to the events. The descriptions of storms (in the years 1277, 1284, 1287, 1288, 1295) read like those of an eye-witness. In 1287 the chronicler laments that the abbey lost the manors of Semer and Groton by judicial duel and never regained them: in fact it got them back in 1292, so the annal must have been written before that date. The text in Arundel 30 for the years 1285 to 1296 was written fairly close to the events.[2]

A change of authorship occurs in 1296. The principal evidence for this is a change in the chronological system.[3] To 1296 the chronicle has Marianus Scotus's system of dating. Each year begins with the date according to the Gospels (from which Marianus calculated that the birth of Christ was twenty-two years earlier than Dionysius had reckoned), the Dominical letter, and the date according to Dionysius. The author of the second continuation abandons Marianus's system; instead he begins each year with the Dominical letter, proceeds with the events till Easter, when he records the year according to Dionysius, the date of Easter, and again, the Dominical letter. This system starts at Easter 1296. Another feature distinguishes the second continuator from the first: he is not particularly interested in taxation.

The second continuation was probably written fairly close to events. Professor Galbraith[4] points out that the accounts of Edward I's visits to Bury appear to be by an eye-witness: Edward is referred to as ' rex noster ' and in places the present tense is used. It is probable that the panegyric on Edward's return from Scotland in 1296 was written before his later failures. In the same year the notice of the marriage of the Princess Elizabeth to the count of Holland was probably written before 1302, when, her husband having died, she

---

[1] Below, pp. xxvf.   [2] Below, pp. xlf.
[3] See V. H. Galbraith in *EHR*, LVIII (1942), p. 56   [4] ibid., pp. 55–6

married Humphrey de Bohun.   The narrative of the quarrel between the bishop and monks of Durham stops in 1300, though it continued till at least 1304.

The authors of the chronicle from 1212 to 1301 may not have used literary sources, but they used royal letters and other records, presumably preserved with the abbey archives.   One letter of Edward I concerning the case of the Scottish succession in 1291 is quoted in full.   Other letters and records supplied information: for example for the notice of the naming of Henry III's son Edmund after the king and martyr in 1245, the battle of Parma in 1248 and of Mansourah in 1250, the coronation of Richard, king of Germany, in 1257, the account of the Dictum of Kenilworth in 1267, the sentence on the rebellious citizens of Norwich in 1275, Edward I's settlement of Wales in 1283 and his seizure of the alien priories in 1294.[1]

The chroniclers profited from the abbey's position as a centre of affairs.[2]   Royal visits gave them chances to hear news. For example Edward I was at Bury during his negotiations with Philip of France in 1294 concerning his proposed marriage to Blanche, Philip's sister.   The chronicle gives details of the negotiations which do not occur in the other authorities.   In 1295 it mentions a fire in Windsor castle which is not recorded by the other chroniclers: the king issued instructions for the castle's repair while at Bury.   The news of the surrender of the Welsh rebel Rhys in 1296 reached the king when he was there, and was entered in the chronicle under that year.

The contemporary part of the chronicle is valuable to historians partly because there is no one chronicle of outstanding excellence for the period: Matthew Paris, whose great works are the chief source of information for three-quarters of Henry III's reign, stopped writing in 1259, and for the next thirty years but little history was written at St Albans. Historians have to turn to lesser works, including the Bury

[1] For chroniclers' use of letters see V. H. Galbraith, *Anonimalle Chronicle, 1333–81* (1927), pp. xxxiv–xxxvi
[2] cf. Matthew Paris's use of similar advantages; R. Vaughan, *Matthew Paris* (1958), pp. 11f.

chronicle. As the century nears its close the relative value of the Bury chronicle increases, for many other works end: Thomas Wykes in 1289, the chronicle of Waverley abbey in 1291, that of Dunstable priory in 1297, and Bartholomew Cotton, monk of Norwich, in 1298. For the crucial years of Edward I's reign there are few contemporary authorities. Besides the Bury chronicle the principal ones are those of Peter Langtoft, canon at Bridlington, the Dominican Nicholas Trivet, Walter, canon of Guisborough, the *Flores Historiarum* compiled at Westminster and the chronicle of Lanercost.

The Bury chronicle is the only known authority for a number of statements relating to general history. For example under 1269 it attributes the quarrel between the Lord Edward and the earl of Gloucester to Edward's love of Gloucester's wife, and in the same year asserts that Gloucester captured a man at Cardiff who had plotted to poison him. Under 1275 it tells the story of Robert of Reading, the Dominican who adopted the Jewish faith. Under 1277 and 1280 it notes embassies of the Tartars to Edward I. Under 1279 it alleges that the Jews crucified a boy at Northampton, and under 1282 that the bishop of Sidon celebrated mass in Jerusalem. Also under 1282 it notices the burial of Llewelyn's body at Cwmhir and describes the reception of his head in London, and notes the attacks by pirates in the neighbourhood of Yarmouth and Dunwich. Under 1285 it states that the relics of David (called in Welsh Dewi) were brought to Westminster. The death of John de Warenne at a tournament in 1286 is recorded, and the date and place of Archbishop Pecham's council under 1290. Under 1293 are details of a battle in the Channel.[1]

The chronicle has a good account of the Barons' War. Like most monastic chronicles it is pro-Montfortian. Taxter remarks that the bishop of Norwich would never have escaped from the barons in 1263 had he not fled to St Edmund's Liberty, which was 'precious in the sight of the barons.' He

---

[1] For the value of the second continuation see Professor Galbraith, below, pp. xxxiv–xxxv.

states that if the coasts had not been guarded against the queen, who planned an invasion from France to help Henry, England would have been overrun by foreigners. He records that Simon de Montfort's corpse worked miracles. Nevertheless his account is factual rather than partisan. Perhaps he was restrained from expressing sympathy with the barons' cause by fear of the king,[1] but probably he was less concerned with political issues than with the abbey's welfare, which was threatened by the troubles of the times. The abbey, as far as is known, only once actively helped the barons: in 1264 Taxter records that the abbey, with other clergy and the laity, contributed to the defence of the coasts against the queen, as commanded by the king (at that time the barons' prisoner) and the barons. His reviser adds that this contribution was the reason for the imposition on the abbey of the fine of 800 marks [2] in the Winchester parliament. He complains that the convent had to pay half the fine, though the abbot should have paid it all, since he and not the convent was accused in the king's court.

Disorder and lawlessness continued in East Anglia and St Edmund's Liberty till at least 1267. It is known from the records of the central government that the king took the Liberty into his hands on account of trespasses committed in it against him and his,[3] and that the abbot of Bury was held responsible for attacks on the property of two of his neighbours,[4] and was alleged to have bought wood from the Disinherited barons.[5] The chronicle records that in 1266 the Disinherited

---

[1] Below, p. xxxvii and n. 1

[2] Above, p. xix; *CPR, 1258–66*, p. 525

[3] *CCR, 1264–8*, p. 298; *CPR, 1266–72*, p. 45

[4] An action against the abbot of Bury and others by Robert de Tateshall for attacks on his manors in Norfolk and Suffolk first appears on the *Coram Rege* roll of 49/50 Henry III (PRO), K.B. 26, 175, membrane 9. The suit is noticed by E. F. Jacob, *Studies in the Period of Baronial Reform and Rebellion, 1258–67*, Oxford Studies in Social and Legal History, ed. P. Vinogradoff, VIII (1925), p. 293. A similar action by Henry de Caldecote is first enrolled on the *Coram Rege* roll of 49/50 Henry III, K.B. 26, 174, membrane 18.

[5] Assise Roll 83 (PRO), pleas before William of St Omer; the list, headed ' Isti sunt emptores de bosco,' is on membrane 21.

ravaged the countryside and hid at Bury before attacking Lynn. It relates that at Easter 1266 William de Valence and John de Warenne came to Bury to inquire about the king's enemies hidden there.[1] They accused the abbot and townsmen of favouring the Disinherited and allowing them to trade and store their booty in the town. The abbot cleared himself of the charges but the town was fined 200 marks.[2] As the burgesses could not raise the money the abbot helped them, but only after they had asked him ' tearfully,' as the chronicle puts it, and promised him 100 marks. The chronicle attributes the abbot's reluctance to the disputes between the abbey and the town.

In 1264, before the battle of Lewes, the young men of Bury, organised in the Guild of Youth, wrested control of the government of the town from the abbey.[3] The town submitted to the abbot in the autumn of the same year rather than risk a royal inquiry. But apparently opposition to the abbey's rule continued; it seems likely that the abbot and convent escaped the blame of Warenne and Valence by pleading that they had lost control of the town. A letter close [4] supplements the story in the chronicle: it reveals that Warenne and Valence summoned a jury to discover whether the abbot or townsmen should appoint the aldermen and gate-keepers; the jury found in the abbot's favour. The king ordered the abbot to appoint an alderman and gate-keepers, keep the peace in Bury and see that the king's enemies were not harboured.

The chronicle shows that Bury was still in a disturbed state in February 1267, when Ottobuono held a council to excommunicate the Disinherited and fled to London the next day, scared

---

[1] The *Coram Rege* roll of 1266/7 contains an account by the jurors of Ipswich of the imprisonment in the town of Bury by the Disinherited from the Isle of Ely of an Ipswich merchant who had helped the king besiege Ely; Jacob, op. cit., p. 238.

[2] *CPR, 1258-66*, p. 604

[3] *Pinchbeck Register*, I, pp. 53-7; Lobel, pp. 126-9; H. W. C. Davis in *EHR*, xxiv (1909), pp. 313-17; F. M. Powicke, *King Henry III and the Lord Edward* (1947), I, pp. 449-50

[4] *CCR, 1264-6*, p. 197

by ' secret rumours.' Under the same year the chronicle has
a story about the theft of horses belonging to ' certain men ' by
some ruffians from the Isle of Ely. The Disinherited of the
Isle (who held out till July) forced the thieves to return the
horses.

The amount of space devoted to taxation is remarkable.[1]
Scarcely a year passes without a notice of some royal or papal
tax. Under 1268 are details of the assessment of the abbey
for the tenth of clerical incomes, which had been granted by
Clement IV to Henry to help him in his financial straits after
the Barons' War. The assessment for the first year, 1267,
was based mainly on the ' Norwich ' valuation, made by
Walter de Suffield, bishop of Norwich, in 1254. This assessment did not prove satisfactory and the clergy were reassessed
by the king's clerks, in order to increase the ' Norwich '
assessment and include revenues omitted from it. The excess
of the new assessment on the old was to be levied for the first
year. The clergy opposed the new assessment and the legate
Ottobuono summoned a convocation at Bury to voice their
objections, without effect.[2]

The chronicle records that the bishop of Norwich, like
other bishops, compounded for the tax for the last two years;
that is, he paid a lump sum and recovered the money from his
diocese. The chronicle records that the abbot and convent
of Bury were, at their request, included in the bishop's composition. They thought that the bishop would give them more
time to pay and they could argue more easily with his assessors
than the king's. They arranged to pay the bishop a tenth for
three years according to the ' Norwich ' valuation (instead of
for two years according to the valuation of the king's clerks),
and to pay a tenth of income not included in the ' Norwich '
valuation according to the assessment of the king's clerks for
two years. The convent bribed the bishop's assessors with

---

[1] Arundel 30 is cited by Professor W. E. Lunt, *Financial Relations of the
Papacy with England to 1327* (1939), *passim*.
[2] Lunt, op. cit., pp. 291f.

20 marks to overlook the town, but the royal clerks found out, assessed the town and had to pay the convent £100.[1]

The chronicle gives the assessment of the convent: the total incomes and tenths from the manors, churches, etc., of the various obedientiaries are listed, and headings state whether the valuation was the 'Norwich' one or that of the king's clerks.

Under 1276 are details of the assessment of Bury according to the 'true value'[2] for the sexennial tenth granted in the Second Council of Lyons in 1274 to Edward I for his projected crusade.[3] The assessment of Bury was made by five of the monks on oath.[4] The chronicle gives the abbot's total income and tenth, the convent's total income and tenth, and the income of each obedientiary.

Under 1292 is information about the sexennial tenth granted by Pope Nicholas IV to Edward in 1291.[5] The collectors of the tenth were John de Pontoise, bishop of Winchester, and Oliver de Sutton, bishop of Lincoln, and the assessment was made by local assessors. The assessment gave rise to bitter opposition at Bury,[6] as elsewhere, and it was revised by the collectors. The chronicle gives the original assessment of the obedientiaries' revenues from spiritualities and of the revenues from temporalities of St Saviour's hospital at Bury, and the revised assessment of the obedientiaries' temporal revenues.

The details of taxation are out of proportion to the scale of the chronicle. They are a reminder that the chronicle, like many others, was written as a monastic record as well as for the general edification of posterity.

---

[1] ibid., p. 300
[2] The 'true value' was the estimated average annual yield; ibid., p. 353.
[3] ibid., pp. 311f.
[4] ibid., p. 319 and n. 7
[5] ibid., pp. 346f.
[6] ibid., pp. 350-2 and W. E. Lunt, *Papal Revenues in the Middle Ages* (1934), I, pp. 191-3

From 1212, when the *Annales Sancti Edmundi* end, to 1301
the chronicle is the chief literary authority for the abbey's
history. It gives the succession of the abbots and priors in the
thirteenth century. It also notices, for example, a fire in the
abbey in 1215, the division of the debts of the house between
the abbot and convent in 1260/1, the demolition of St
Edmund's chapel and the construction of a new one in 1275,
the succession of William de Hoo as sacrist in 1280, and his
presentation of Richard de Lothbury as moneyer of the Bury
mint at the Exchequer in 1287. Under 1238, 1257 and 1263
it gives details of the abbey's dispute with the Grey friars who
tried to settle in the *banleuca* of the town.[1]

The chronicle has information about the abbey's relations
with Henry III and Edward I. Besides mentioning twelve
royal visits it records, for example, the action taken by the
royal justices in the town against debasers of the coinage in
1278 and 1279, the king's seizure of the convent's property as
well as that of the abbot in the vacancy of the abbacy in 1279,
the royal confirmation of the separation of the abbot's and
convent's property in 1281, and the dispute between the abbot
and king in 1285 over the abbot's right to hold the assize of
weights and measures.[2] Much, but not all, of the information
about Bury is also in the abbey's registers and in the public
records, but there it is, generally speaking, less readable and
less easy to find.

The value of the chronicle was recognised in its own time.
It was apparently the only chronicle compiled at Bury to be
used by other houses. Bartholomew Cotton has citations from
it for the years 1258 to 1263,[3] and at second hand for the years
1279 to 1284, for which period he draws on the chronicle
compiled at St Benet's Hulme. The Hulme chronicle cites
from the Bury chronicle from 1030 to 1169 and from 1259 to

---

[1] For a tract written at Bury on this dispute see above, p. xv
[2] For a tract on the same subject see above, p. xv
[3] For the relationship between Cotton's chronicle and the Bury chronicle
see H. R. Luard's edition of Cotton, pp. lii–lviii

the end in 1292.[1] As has been seen, a copy of the Bury chronicle covering the years 1152 to 1294 was made for Peterborough abbey.

The chronicles of Norwich, Hulme and Peterborough did not always copy the Bury chronicle word for word, but adapted it to suit their interests. They wrote more and more independently as they neared their own time, altering facts from their own knowledge and working in other material. The Bury chronicle itself was being constantly revised. Its plunderers do not always seem to have drawn on the chronicle itself but on the same or similar sources; for example Cotton's account of the 1272 riots at Norwich is like, but not the same as, that in the Bury chronicle.

Quotations from the Bury chronicle occur in the *Chronica Buriensis*, a history of St Edmund's abbey from its foundation to 1327 (with additions), probably compiled in 1327 at Hulme, where some Bury monks took refuge during the revolt of the town. The chronicle of Spalding priory in Lincolnshire has citations under 1265, 1267, 1269 and 1271.[2] Late in Edward II's reign a copy was made for the abbey of St John at Colchester.[3] In the middle of the fourteenth century an

---

[1] Luard, op. cit., collates part of 'Oxenedes' with Cotton and the Bury chronicle. Sir H. Ellis, in his edition of 'Oxenedes,' quotes 'Cont. Flor. Wig.' (i.e. Thorpe's edition of the Bury chronicle) in a few footnotes, but he does not appear to have realised that this was the Bury chronicle. Nor did he realise how much 'Oxenedes' was indebted to it, for he overlooked Arundel 30, which contains many passages borrowed by 'Oxenedes' and which are not in the Peterborough text provided by Thorpe.

[2] The chronicle of Spalding priory is printed as 'Chronicon Johannis abbatis S. Petri de Burgo' in J. Sparke, *Historiae Anglicanae Scriptores Varii* (1723), reprinted as *Chronicon Angliae Petriburgense* by J. A. Giles (Caxton Society, 1845). Its provenance is discussed by F. Liebermann, 'Ueber Ostenglische Geschichtsquellen des 12., 13., 14. Jahrhunderts, besonders den falschen Ingulf' in *Neues Archiv der Gesellschaft für ältere deutsche Geschichtskunde*, xviii (1893), pp. 235–6.

[3] Described and the additions to the Bury chronicle printed by F. Liebermann, *Ungedruckte Anglo-Normannische Geschichtsquellen*, pp. 158–65. Liebermann did not notice that where the text of this chronicle (B. M. Harley MS 1132) uses the Bury chronicle it is probably copied from Arundel 30; this is suggested by the fact that it incorporates in its text seven passages which are in the margins of Arundel 30 (see the annals for 846, 849, 852, 1060, 1062 and 1170).

abstract was with the Grey friars at Lynn,[1] and in Richard II's reign a copy was in the library of John Erghome, Austin friar of York.[2]

IV   HISTORICAL SETTING OF THE CHRONICLE

by V. H. Galbraith

(reprinted from EHR, LVIII (1943), pp. 57–61)

In the thirteenth century the abbey of Bury St Edmund's was still at the height of a reputation that had always owed less to fervour and austerity than to the solid merits of vast wealth, age and royal patronage.   Henry III had done a great deal for the cult of St Edmund, and Edward I showed his 'special' affection by visiting the abbey at least fifteen times, often accompanied by his wife and children.   The same test, if applied to the abbey of St Albans, whose history in so many ways presents a close parallel, would probably reveal an equally warm sentiment towards that house.   For these great abbeys, in addition to their religious uses, fulfilled a social purpose. There were not so many monasteries which could house a king and his court for weeks together, and provide accommodation for a parliament.[3]   Edward I, moreover, never forgot the importance of the regulars, whose establishments were centres of local loyalty: the means by which the king became personally known to the generality of his subjects.   As the price of great possessions the Bury monks were cumbered with much serving: condemned in practice to the part of Martha, though in theory dead to the world.   The management of great estates; the catering required for so large a household of monks, servants and guests; the exercise of its jurisdiction over

[1] B. M. Additional MS 47214, printed by A. Gransden in *EHR*, LXXII (1957), pp. 273–8

[2] Below, p. xxxvii

[3] Arnold, II, p. 338.   In 1327 the insurgent villeins destroyed, besides the queen's chamber, 'quandam mansionem solempnem, vocatam Brade-field, cum aula et cameris et coquina ubi rex multotiens se recepit.'   The list of monastic buildings destroyed, the foundations of which can still be traced among the ruins of the abbey, is a long one.

the eight and a half hundreds of West Suffolk; the maintenance
of its privileges against king, pope, archbishop, friars, the town
of Bury and the subinfeudated military tenants—these things
produced the rather ' Boeotian '[1] community described in
Jocelin's famous chronicle. We have no such living picture
of the monks at the close of Edward's reign. The evidence,
such as it is, suggests that though perhaps less liberal in their
outlook, and more on the defensive in a world that was leaving
them behind, they were not greatly changed.

The abbot of St Edmund's at the close of the thirteenth
century was John of Northwold (1279–1301), of whom all that
is known—and it is not much—is good.[2] To him we owe the
anonymous ' history of the knights ' fees of St Edmund's
drawn up in 1300 at the command of ' my lord abbot '[3]; and
he was gratefully remembered by the convent for his brave
protest in parliament against the king's financial extortion.
He died in the very year at which our chronicle ends, and the
names of the chief obedientiaries are preserved in the official
account of the election of his successor. The most important
were Thomas of Tottington, the subprior, who now became
abbot, and John of Eversden, the cellarer, who took a prominent part in the election. There is an interesting reference
in the text to his successful arrangements at Warkton (co.
Northampton) extracted from the precentor's register,[4] and it
is on this unlikely evidence alone that Eversden has been so
often described as author of the Bury chronicle from 1265–95.[5]
Of the sacrist, Richard of Brunne, who had only recently
assumed office, we know nothing, for the *Gesta Sacristarum*,

[1] Knowles, *The Monastic Order in England*, p. 311
[2] One of his first acts as abbot was to revise the *consuetudines*. An
agreement was drawn up between abbot and convent defining the ancient
division of revenues between the two, and carefully specifying the rents
and duties assigned to each of the monastic offices. This was inspected
and confirmed by Edward I in 1281 and enrolled on the Charter Roll
(below, p. 73). It is printed in *Mon. Angl.*, III, p. 156.
[3] *Pinchbeck Register*, I, pp. 271ff.
[4] Which has not survived
[5] Below, p. xli

our best evidence for conventual history, ends with this account of his immediate predecessor, William of Luton:

Huius tempore concessa est regi medietas omnium bonorum temporalium et spiritualium. . . . Qui tam in contributione illa quam in aliis casibus fortuitis et infortunatis multipliciter est molestatus et vehementer afflictus. Hic primus cultum dei in ecclesia, et circa sanctum Edmundum, sanctum Botulphum, aliaque sanctuaria, in cereis et luminaribus diminuit, et plusquam dimidiavit: quod sibi in prosperum cessisse non arbitror. Et quamvis in aliis honestus homo fuit et modestus, in his tamen quae conventui facere tenebatur, utpote pitantiis, misericordiis et huiusmodi, superrigidus fuit et austerus. . . .[1]

The abbey was clearly hard hit financially, and retrenchment was the order of the day. Among the ' unfortunate incidents ' referred to above must certainly be included the loss of the manors of Semer and Groton, after a lawsuit in which the abbot's champion perished in a duel; and there is perhaps also a reference to the long and costly litigation with the town of Bury which had been going on since 1292. The medieval monastery was accustomed to debt; and the records suggest that at all times Bury St Edmunds was more often and more deeply insolvent than most. There had been difficulties when Samson became abbot in 1182, and again in 1234 when the papal commissioners had hard things to say about its finances.[2] But it seems likely that by the crisis of the very last years of the thirteenth century its economic position was impaired permanently and beyond the possibility of complete recovery. The good old days perhaps ended with the last major addition to the fabric, the new Lady Chapel built by

---

[1] Arnold, ii, p. 296

[2] See Rose Graham, ' A Papal Visitation of Bury St Edmunds and Westminster in 1234 ' in *EHR*, xxvii (1912), pp. 728–39. In the next century there are traces of the *treasurers* and of an abbey exchequer at Bury; cf. R. A. L. Smith, ' The *Regimen Scaccarii* in English Monasteries,' *Trans. Roy. Hist. Soc.* (1942) [repr. in Smith, *Collected Papers* (1947), pp. 54–73].

Abbot Simon in 1275.[1] All lines of inquiry suggest that Abbot John fought a losing battle against excessive taxation, aggravated by deeper causes that still await examination. The abbey had been taxed to the bone, and John's successor, Abbot Thomas, was so loaded with debt that he had to disperse his household and horses among his manors for the sake of economy.[2]

Against this gloomy background our chronicler draws a vivid picture of the masterful king, who never lost the respect and even the loyal affection of the religious. Both sides contrived to keep politics separate from personalities, and social relations with the king, if strained, were never interrupted. Between 1296 and 1301 Edward visited the monastery six times, four of which are mentioned below. He was there from 16 to 20 January 1296 when he entertained the convent ' laute et copiose,' and again for nearly three weeks in November when he held a parliament. The quarrel with the Church was then becoming acute, and this probably explains why Edward stayed in the house of Henry of Lynn, a merchant. The chronicler tells us that this defiance of the conventions gave offence:

Quod quidem hospicium multis cessit in offendiculum tamquam regie excellencie inhonestum et regibus preteritis temporibus inusitatum.[3]

After brief visits in 1297, 1298 and 1299, of which only that in 1298 is mentioned in our chronicle,[4] the king, accompanied by his son, stayed at the abbey from 9 to 11 May 1300 on his way to Scotland.[5] It was a great event in the life of the monks, fully recorded below, and proves that king and abbey were

---

[1] Below, p. 58
[2] Arnold, III, p. 37. [In 1268 a royal licence was given for the abbot to go abroad for the relief of himself and his church, and to stay beyond the sea with a moderate household, *CPR, 1266–72*, p. 238.—A.G.]
[3] Below, p. 134
[4] Below, p. 148
[5] Gough, *Itinerary of Edward I* (1900), II, p. 189; below, p. 156

once more on the best of terms. Again the king ' dined ' the convent, granted them a charter and specially charged his justices to respect their privileges. Prayers were offered to St Edmund for success against the Scots, and the chronicler, surely an eye-witness, notes that the king, as he rode away, turned in the saddle to look again on the church and bowed his head. If anything was still needed to gain the hearts of the monks it was supplied by the young Edward, who stayed on for a time with the monks, living the common life as one of themselves. ' Frater vero noster factus est in capitulo,' says the chronicler; and it was only on the twelfth day that he dragged himself away to rejoin his father, saying in effect that he had never enjoyed himself more in his life. Beside this account we may set just such another of a visit which Edward had paid to St Albans in the previous year. Special prayers were offered for success in Scotland, and special masses conceded to the royal family. The king's particular devotion to St Alban is noted by the local chronicler: while the queen soon after stayed at the abbey for three weeks, leaving at last, we are told, with the greatest reluctance! Edward I showed something of Elizabeth's genius in the handling of his subjects. William Rishanger,[1] the contemporary St Albans writer, calls Edward I ' devotissimus ecclesie,' [2] a title at least partly earned by his unfailing capacity in all personal relations to do and say the right thing.

The sufferings of the Church are succinctly related by our chronicler year by year. He speaks out, glossing over nothing, but always with restraint or at least good temper. He treats the struggle broadly as one between the king and the whole of

---

[1] Rishanger, pp. 398, 401. The royal households could be a great burden on the countryside. The Dunstable chronicler complains bitterly of a long visit paid to St Albans by Prince Edward in 1294. More than 200 dishes (*fercula*) were needed daily, and the Dunstable market was ruined, the prince's servants taking all the cheese, eggs, etc. without payment; *Dunst.*, p. 392.

[2] Rishanger, p. 411. Similarly the Worcester annalist says of Edward I (*sub* 1298), ' in praesenti meruit amari, et futuris temporibus benedici '; *Ann. Mon.*, IV, p. 536.

the clergy, solidly ranged behind their archbishop.[1] The trials of his own abbey are compressed into a single sentence:

Memorandum quod die Cinerum confiscata sunt omnia bona et omnia maneria seisita abbatis et conventus sancti Edmundi unacum burgo sancti Edmundi.[2]

His story, while independent and original, is in close general agreement with the longer narrative of Bartholomew Cotton, so far as that goes; and he accurately summarises the ecclesiastical council at London in June 1298,[3] which is not in Cotton, though his chronicle includes the battle of Falkirk in July of that year. Like all the chronicles of the time he is interested in Langton's election to the bishopric of Ely, and his journey to the papal curia; and he describes in verse the early stages of a famous dispute between the bishop of Durham and his monks.[4] Less near to his heart, but more valuable, are the notices of the struggle between Edward I and his barons. Here he writes with a certain reserve, dictated either by prudence or (more probably) faint sympathy with their cause. The facts are impartially stated and no morals are drawn. The most important of these passages, the account of the *Confirmatio Cartarum* (1297), differs in several of its details from all other sources, though in general it supports the version of Guisborough. Attention should be called to the ' baronial ' parliament at Northampton on 21 September 1297,[5] which is mentioned without comment and seems to be new: and also to an attempt to evade military service by the barons at the parliament of York (1300) which was defeated by reference to the chronicles of Marianus Scotus, Henry of Huntingdon,

---

[1] Except for the inevitable time-servers. Below, p. 138: he notes especially in this class the ' regis secretarii et aulici.'

[2] Below, p. 139: 27 February 1297

[3] Below, p. 149; cf. Wilkins, *Concilia*, II, p. 236

[4] Below, pp. 161–3 (1300)

[5] Below, pp. 141–2. The date is significant: the battle of Stirling was fought on 11 September and the ' confirmation of the charters ' took place on 10 October.

William of Malmesbury and Roger Hoveden.[1]   The evidence
for this decision had no doubt been supplied by the extracts
from monastic chronicles collected in 1290–1.[2]   It is interesting
to note that Edward again applied to the monasteries for
information regarding Scotland later in this very year.[3]   Very
different from these colourless entries is the chronicler's
reference to the other great baronial grievance—the reform
of the forests.   In this matter the abbey was an interested
party, for the perambulation undertaken in accordance with
the *articuli super cartas* (1300) resulted in the disafforestation of
the conventual manor of Warkton.[4]   This was in practice
accomplished, the writer tells us, 'donis et epulis preciosis,'
but he is careful to add the argument advanced to prove that
Warkton had never been of ancient demesne.   It was simply
a legend of a pre-Conquest grant (apparently built round
an old East Anglian drinking-custom [5]) and is doubtless a
characteristic sample of the 'evidence' upon which the
commissioners had to make their decisions.

v   The Manuscripts

There are two manuscripts known of John de Taxter's
chronicle, and four of the revised version of Taxter's chronicle
with continuations.

John de Taxter's Chronicle

COTTON MS JULIUS A i (British Museum), ff. 3–43^v
is Taxter's chronicle from the Creation to 1265.   The leaves
were slightly damaged in the fire of 1731 in the Cotton library:

[1] Below, p. 156; cf. Rishanger, p. 123, where the same list of 'standard
authors' is given, with the addition of Ralph of Diceto.

[2] *Foedera*, I, p. 769; F. Palgrave, *Documents illustrating the History of
Scotland* (1837), I, p. xcv

[3] Rishanger, p. 455.   The information was to be sent to the January
parliament of 1301.

[4] Below, p. 160

[5] A daily toast drunk after dinner in honour of the glorious martyr
'quam plenum sive plenitudinem sancti Edmundi vocabant' (below,
p. 160).

they are charred at the edges and apparently shrunk. They now measure approximately $8'' \times 5\frac{1}{2}''$. The writing is a good book hand, dating from late in Henry III's reign, and is in one column of thirty-four lines. There is a medieval pagination from 1 to 82 in Arabic numerals, besides the modern foliation. The text was probably written at Bury, as there are three contemporary marginal notes about St Edmund and his abbey. It ends on folio 43^v, leaving two lines blank at the bottom of the page. The scribe wrote the letters 'c,' 'b' and 'a' one under the other at the beginning of the blank lines and below: possibly these were reminders for the next three annals, as they are the Dominical letters for 1266, 1267 and 1268. A medieval note in pencil, partly illegible, is at the foot of the page.[1]

The leaves were mounted and bound, with other chronicles, etc., in 1848. The volume is described in J. Planta, *Catalogue of MSS in the Cottonian Library* (1802). None of the other items has anything to do with Bury, except folio 71, royal genealogies from Charlemagne to the children of Henry III, which is written in the same hand as the Bury chronicle and should precede it.[2]

The text of the Bury chronicle is copied from another manuscript, now lost. This is proved by an error in the arrangement. To 1249 most of the annals are undated, having only their Dominical letter. About half-way down each page and in the margin a hand contemporary with the scribe's has dated one of the annals. The same date, deleted with a red line, is at the top of the page in the hand of the scribe of the text. The scribe must have set out his pages from the exemplar, heading each page with the date of the first annal on the

---

[1] The following words are legible: '. . . miles . . ./. . . exhibitio operis . . ./. . ./. . . nec (? n^o) in (? i) aduersis in (? i) sua iustitia defe (?) . . ./. . . socialem exhibeat cum ergo tota militare . . ./. . . minori ut R (?) miles se fiducie . . . deberet (?) . . ./. . . et mirificam socialem conuersacionem qui (?) armis strum . . ./. . . libere obedientiam mand . . . et confiduciam (confiducī) deuocionis med . . ./. . . iustitie in concilii per . . ./. . .'

[2] It precedes the chronicle in the description of Julius A i in T. Smith, *Cat. Librorum Manuscriptorum Bibliothecae Cottoniae* (1696).

exemplar's page. But, after copying the text, it was realised that the first annal on each page of the copy was not the same as that in the exemplar. So the dates at the top of the pages were crossed out and rewritten beside the correct annal.

The copy was probably made soon after 1265, the date of the last annal. It is almost certainly the earliest text of the chronicle known. This is suggested by the many marginal additions in the hand of the original scribe: the names of ten of the popes, and five passages (one of nearly a hundred words) on folios 13, 17ᵛ, 20, 23 and 38ᵛ. All these marginalia are incorporated in the text in the other copies of the chronicle.

The statement under 1265 that Simon de Montfort's body worked miracles has been carefully erased by scratching. The erasure, of course, cannot be dated, but it might well be early. The Dictum of Kenilworth, issued in October 1266, chapter 8, prohibited de Montfort's cult. The chronicle of Furness records that stories about the miracles were hushed up for fear of the king.[1] A somewhat similar erasure occurs in the City of London chronicle, in a passage about the baronial parliament at Oxford in 1258: ' hoc anno fuit insigne parliamentum apud Oxoniam.' An apparently contemporary hand has changed ' insigne ' to ' insane '; and so the ' Mad ' parliament slipped into history.[2]

ARUNDEL MS 6 (College of Arms), ff. 109–24ᵛ. This volume belonged to John Erghome, Austin friar of York,[3] and was written in Richard II's reign. It is textually valueless because it almost certainly descends directly from Julius A i. This is suggested by an error in the annal for 1239. Like Julius A i it refers the reader for the genealogy of the kings of

---

[1] The chronicle of Furness, printed in *Chronicles of the Reigns of Stephen, Henry II and Richard I*, ed. R. Howlett, (RS, 1885–90), ii, p. 548; and see H. O. Halliwell, *Chronicle of William de Rishanger of the Barons' War: the Miracles of Simon de Montfort* (Camden Society, 1840), p. xxix

[2] R. L. Poole in *EHR*, xl (1925), p. 402 and C. Bémont, *Simon de Montfort*, ed. and translated by E. F. Jacob (1930), p. 155, *n.* 1

[3] Arundel 6 is noticed by M. R. James, ' Catalogue of the Library of the Augustinian Friars at York ' in *Fasciculus Ioanni Willis Clark dicatus* (privately printed, 1909), p. 36.

England from Adam to Alfred to ' p. 44 above ': the genealogy is not on p. 44 in Arundel 6 (which is not paginated), but it is on p. 44 of the medieval pagination of Julius A i.

Another error proves that the text is not copied directly from Julius A i. Under 874 (f. 117^v) it reads: ' Lodowicus imperator [obiit] nis muneribus imperator factus est. Karolus senior imperator. Karolus Romam perveniens datis Johanni pape mag.' The passage is absurd and the scribe must have been misled by the following arrangement in his exemplar:

Lodowicus imperator obiit.   nis muneribus imperator factus est.
Karolus senior imperator.   Karolus Romam perveniens datis Johanni pape mag-

The words in the exemplar, ' nis muneribus imperator factus est,' were meant to follow ' pape mag ' but were written above the line for want of space. This arrangement does not occur in Julius A i.

The Revised Version of Taxter's Chronicle with Continuations

ARUNDEL MS 30 (College of Arms), ff. 97–205 is the Bury chronicle from the Creation to 1301, with additional annals for 1313, 1316, 1319, 1329, 1334, 1335. The volume has two hundred and sixteen leaves, measuring 9″ × 5½″. Besides the chronicle it contains miscellaneous historical and ecclesiastical pieces, listed by [W. H. Black], *Catalogue of the Arundel Manuscripts in the Library of the College of Arms* (1829, privately printed). It was written for St Edmund's abbey. Some of the fly-leaves relate particularly to Bury, viz: notes on the demolition of St Edmund's chapel in 1275, f. 8^v (see M. R. James, *On the Abbey of St Edmund at Bury*, Publications of the Cambridge Antiquarian Society, oct. ser., xxviii (1895), p. 188); verses which decorated the abbey church, ff. 9–10, 209–12^v (ibid., pp. 186–203); the assessment of the abbey in 1273 for the papal tenth (see R. Graham in *EHR*, xxiii (1908), p. 449, and W. E. Lunt, *Financial Relations of the Papacy with England to 1327*, p. 319, *n.* 7); and the measurements of the cloisters at Bury, f. 214 (see James, op. cit., p. 203).

The volume was owned after the Dissolution of the monasteries successively by Nicholas Bacon (1509–79), the Lord Keeper,[1] John Bale (1495–1563), the antiquary, Matthew Parker, archbishop of Canterbury (1559–75) [2] and Lord William Howard of Naworth (1563–1640).[3] It was acquired, together with other books from Naworth, by Thomas Howard, second earl of Arundel 1586–1646. Part of his library, including this volume, came into the possession of the College of Arms in 1678.[4]

The text of the chronicle from the Creation to 1268 is in one book hand, with thirty-two lines to a page. The annals for 1260, 1262 and from 1265 to 1295 are divided from each other by one or two blank lines, which were probably intended for additions (cf. the Moyses Hall MS described below). One of the spaces (at the end of the annal for 1262) has an addition,

---

[1] Nicholas Bacon (see *DNB*), second son of Robert Bacon, of Drinkstone, Suffolk, sheep-reeve of St Edmund's abbey. Nicholas obtained by royal grant various lands previously belonging to the abbey; *Letters and Papers, Foreign and Domestic, Henry VIII*, xx, pt i, art. 620 (53). His ownership of the volume now Arundel 30 is suggested by the fact that the Bury chronicle and other items all included in Arundel 30 are listed in John Bale's *Index* (compiled 1549–57) as being in the possession of 'master Bacon'; *Index Britanniae Scriptorum*, ed. R. L. Poole and M. Bateson (1902), pp. 94, 200, 293. The *Index*, pp. 200, 293, stated that the volume was kept at the Charterhouse, which was at that time owned by John Bridges and Thomas Hales in consideration of keeping the king's tents; L. Hendriks, *The London Charterhouse* (1889), p. 244. Bacon, who in 1546 became an attorney in the Court of Wards and in 1550 a bencher of Gray's Inn, may have had a room there.

[2] The titles from John Bale's *Catalogue* are inscribed above the appropriate items in Arundel 30 in the rust-coloured chalk found in many a Parker book: for these chalk annotations in Parker's books see C. E. Wright, 'The Dispersal of the Monastic Libraries and the Beginnings of Anglo-Saxon Studies' in *Transactions of the Cambridge Bibliographical Society*, III (1951), p. 228; see also the front fly-leaf of B.M. MSS Harley 550 and Arundel 288, f. 5.

[3] His lion rampant is on folio 10ᵛ and his handwriting is in the margins of some pages (e.g. on f. 202). The hands of John Stow the antiquary (who used the volume for his *Chronicles of England from Brute unto . . . 1580*) and of Sir Simonds Dewes (ff. 5, 11, 30, etc.) also occur.

[4] The volume was no. 157 in the library of Thomas Howard, 2nd earl of Arundel (see the fly-leaf). For the acquisition of part of the Arundel library by the College of Arms see Black, *Catalogue of the Arundel Manuscripts*, pp. v–ix.

a notice of the birth of John de Hastings, inserted in another hand: this entry does not occur in the first recension of the chronicle and is incorporated in the texts of the other manuscripts of the second recension. From 1267 to 1295 some passages are marked 'vacat' in the margin in pencil, as though the text had been prepared for a copyist who was to omit these passages.

In the middle of the annal for 1268, at the head of folio 157, a new hand begins and writes to 1285, with thirty-three lines to a page. This scribe draws some quite good grotesques of men and of a griffin in the bottom margins of folios 161, 165^{v}, 166, 170. From 1270 there are signs of revision: mistakes are erased and the letters rewritten, and the correct reading is in the margin in pencil. These corrections were probably made before 1295, as they are incorporated in the text of Corpus Christi College, Cambridge, MS 92 (see the description below), which was copied from Arundel 30 in about 1295.

From 1286 to 1296 there are many changes of hand. That this part of the text is very nearly a first draft can be seen, for example, by the copying of the letter of Edward I about the case of the Scottish succession, in the middle of the annal for 1291, before the part of the annal which precedes it had been written: the last nine words in front of the letter are written in the margin for lack of space.

The text from 1286 to 1296 was obviously written close to events. The scribe leaves spaces for news he is expecting and late news is added in various contemporary hands in the margins. Thus after the notice of Pope Nicholas V's death in 1292 half a line is left blank for the length of the vacancy, which is noted in pencil in the bottom margin, ' mensibus tribus et diebus ix.' In the same year the death of Robert Burnell, bishop of Bath and Wells, is mentioned; the succession of William March, elected three months later, is noted in the margin. The death of John de Sanford, archbishop of Dublin, is recorded in 1294; William de Hothum's succession, which took place eight months later, is noted in the margin. Half a

line is left blank after the notice of the death of Roger, bishop of Coventry and Lichfield, in 1295, and the succession of Walter de Langton, which took place after just over two months, is inserted in another hand.

The second continuation, 1296 to 1301, with additions, is a fair copy, written in one book hand soon after 1334, the date of the last additional annal. It begins on a new page, but in the same gathering as the preceding text.

The annal for 1300 has a passage on the successful expedition of John de Eversden, cellarer of Bury, to Warkton, near Northampton, to get the manor disafforested. In the margin the scribe of the text has written ' nota ' and there is a sketch in red ink of a rustic's head. John Bale attributed the chronicle to 1301 (plus the additional annals), to John de Eversden. He also attributed to him four other works, all in Arundel 30.[1] As Bale owned the volume,[2] he probably had it before him when writing his entry on Eversden in the *Catalogue*. Unless he had other evidence, now lost, for Eversden's authorship, he jumped to this conclusion from the passage on Warkton, the ' nota ' and the sketch of the rustic's head, which presumably he mistook for that of the monk Eversden.[3] H. R. Luard was the first man to point out that there is no evidence that Eversden wrote the chronicle.

[1] J. Bale, *Scriptorum Illustrium Maioris Britannie . . . Catalogus* (1557/9), p. 410

[2] Bale wrote at the beginning of the chronicle in pink ink ' Ioannes Everesden celerarius Buriensis presens chronicon edidit.' The entry ' Joannes Everisdeni series temporum cum aliis ' (almost certainly a reference to Arundel 30) is in the list of Bale's books made in 1553, printed in his *Catalogue*, pp. 159f. and in H. MacCusker, *John Bale, Dramatist and Antiquary* (1942), pp. 32–47. Miss MacCusker identifies some volumes which have survived, but omits Arundel 30. Bale's library was scattered when he fled from Dublin in 1553. The fate of most of his books is unknown, but he recovered a few, some of which he gave to Archbishop Parker.

[3] Bale's statement (*Catalogue*, p. 410) that Eversden ' flourished until 1336 and was buried at St Edmund's ' has proved impossible to substantiate. Possibly Bale took the last date in the chronicle in Arundel 30 as the date of Eversden's death: the date is in fact 1335, but Bale might have misread the roman numerals: indeed Bale says that the chronicle ends in 1336, which no known version does.

Possibly the reviser of Taxter's chronicle and author of the first continuation, or the author of the second continuation, was tonsured in 1255. Even this, however, is doubtful, as the note 'hic attonsus fui' under 1255 is not in the hand of the scribe in Arundel 30, the best text (it is in the scribe's hand in the Moyses Hall MS and in CCCC. 92).

MOYSES HALL MUSEUM MS (Bury St Edmunds), ff. 30–104^v is the chronicle from the Creation to 1283. Scholars have not known of this text since the time of John Stow, who wrote at the top of folio 30, 'Johannes Eueresdene monacus de buri S. Edmondi.'

The volume has a hundred and four leaves, measuring $8\frac{1}{4}'' \times 5\frac{1}{2}''$, and with thirty-six lines to a page. Besides the chronicle it has other historical material (ff. 1–29^v), all of which is also in Arundel 30, ff. 11–21, 25^v–32. It is a fair copy throughout, in one book hand. Possibly it was written after 1288, for the chronicle calls Pope Nicholas III by mistake Nicholas IV, who was elected in February 1288. It was written in the Bury scriptorium, for the same scribe wrote the chronicle from 1268 to 1285 in Arundel 30.[1] There are grotesques on folios 46^v, 49, 60^v, 72^v, 73, 84, 84^v, similar to those in Arundel 30. The detailed assessment of the Bury obedientiaries for the papal tenth, which is in Arundel 30 s.a. 1268, has been removed by erasing half a page and cutting out a page.

The volume belonged in the sixteenth century to William Fleetwood, recorder of London and a friend of John Stow. In the eighteenth century it was owned by Edward Browne, M.A.,[2] and by Thomas Somers Cocks, 1737–96 [3]; in the

---

[1] The same scribe wrote a copy of Peter Lugdunensis for the Bury library, now MS 32 in the library of Pembroke College, Cambridge. He may also have written the Pembroke College MSS 43, 87 (ff. 97–109), 101 (ff. 94f.) and 104.

[2] His book-plate is pasted inside the front cover. Possibly he was the sizar of Clare College, Cambridge and rector of Halton listed by J. A. Venn, *Alumni Cantabrigienses*, I, pt i, p. 232.

[3] His book-plate is pasted inside the front cover. For him and his descendants see Burke's *Peerage* (1890), p. 1271.

nineteenth century by Charles Lygon Cocks of Treverbyn Vean, Cornwall.[1] It was lot 22 at Sotheby's sale on 9 February 1948, when it was purchased for the Moyses Hall Museum at Bury.

The text of the chronicle is closely related to that in Arundel 30. Thus like Arundel 30 it describes Socrates's wife as ' ad modum morora ' in error for ' morosa ' and carelessly writes ' auxilium ' twice under 1274. It is not, however, copied from Arundel 30, nor is it Arundel 30's exemplar. Thus it says that Hubert de Burgh's wife fled ' ad auxilium sancti Edmundi ' in 1232, while Arundel 30 reads ' ad asilum.' Variants from Arundel 30 become important after 1268. Under 1274, 1275 and 1277 it has four sentences not in Arundel 30 (one of them is also in the ' Oxenedes ' chronicle). In 1282 there is a space left for the name of Queen Eleanor's daughter born at Rhuddlan. Arundel 30 gives her name as Elizabeth. The ' Oxenedes ' chronicle gives Elizabeth but the name is written on an erasure. Cotton calls her Walkiniana. It looks as if the surviving texts of the chronicle all descend from some draft which was constantly altered and revised.[2]

The annals from 1265 to the end in 1283 are divided from each other by spaces, some of as many as nine blank lines. They are not meant to be decorative, as two spaces are at the head of the page (ff. 93^v, 102^v). Obviously they are intended for additions though none have been used. Similar spaces, which have been used for additional matter, occur in the thirteenth-century chronicles of Worcester cathedral priory (Cotton MS Caligula A x) and Melrose abbey (Cotton MS Faustina B ix),[3] and in the fourteenth-century chronicle of Croxden abbey (Cotton MS Faustina B vi).

HARLEY MS 3977 (British Museum), ff. 55^v-9 is the

---

[1] Died 1885, descendant of the above. His book-plate is pasted inside the front cover.

[2] cf. the manuscripts of Ralph de Diceto: two are from the author's scriptorium and each has some original features; W. Stubbs, *The Historical Works of Master Ralph de Diceto* (RS, 1876,), I, pp. xciii–xcvi.

[3] Facsimile edition by A. O. Anderson and M. O. Anderson (1936)

part of the Bury chronicle for 1267 and 1268, preceded by the assessment of the abbey for the papal tenth, which follows the annal for 1268 in Arundel 30. The volume was written at Bury early in the fourteenth century and contains customs, etc. The text of the chronicle has a few small variants from the other two texts, which suggests that it is not copied from them. For example under 1269, after the account of Edward's treaty with France, it mentions that King Louis set sail for Jerusalem on 16 March [1269/70]. Arundel 30 and the Moyses Hall MS put this entry under 1270, but at the point in the text where the entry occurs in Harley 3977, Arundel 30 has two blank lines, and the entry itself is erased in the Moyses Hall MS.

CORPUS CHRISTI COLLEGE, CAMBRIDGE MS 92, ff. 175^v-203 is the Bury chronicle from 1152 to 1294, written for Peterborough, as mentioned above (p. xvii). The fact that it follows Arundel 30 exactly, even reproducing its mistakes (for example both texts carelessly write ' applicuit ' twice *s.a.* 1230), proves that it was copied from Arundel 30. The address of Edward I's letter about the case of the Scottish succession, transcribed under 1291, is altered from ' abbati et conventui sancti Edmundi ' to ' abbati et conventui sancti Petri de Burg' ': in the margin of Arundel 30 at this point ' Sancti Petri de Burg' ' is written in pencil in a contemporary hand; this must have been done as a reminder to the scribe of the Peterborough copy.

VI THIS EDITION

A   British Museum MS Cotton Julius A i
H   British Museum MS Harley 3977
M   Moyses Hall Museum MS
MS   College of Arms MS Arundel 30 (MS²: contemporary corrections by another hand)
P   Corpus Christi College, Cambridge, MS 92

The text of this edition is based on MS Arundel 30 and begins in 1212, where this chronicle becomes independent of other known chronicles. Important variant readings are given in the footnotes from Julius A i, the Moyses Hall Museum MS and Harley 3977. Contemporary corrections to the text (see above, p. xl) and marginalia not in the hand at the text are indicated as MS². Where the scribe has indicated a name by a letter, the name is usually supplied in square brackets. Other words and letters omitted by the scribe are also supplied in square brackets. In passages in French the accents, apostrophes and division of words are the editor's. The annals are dated in Arabic numerals, according to Dionysius, in the normal way, and the double system of dating and the Dominical letters at the beginning of the annals, which occur in the chronicle to 1296 (see above p. xx), are left out.[1]

Some of the footnotes from Professor Galbraith's edition of the second continuation in *EHR*, LVIII have been borrowed with his permission: those of any length are initialled V. H. G.

---

[1] The text of the whole chronicle from the Creation, with a full collation of all the known texts and full details of marginalia and corrections in the MSS, is in the typed copy of my Ph.D. thesis in the Institute of Historical Research, Senate House, London, W.C.1.

LATIN TEXT

and

ENGLISH TRANSLATION

CHRONICA BURIENSIS

1212

f. 143 Burgenses sancti Edmundi permiserunt quamuis [1] inuiti
per manum monachi collectam inter eos fieri. Rex fecit
suspendi obsides Walensium apud Notigham. Religiosi
et clerici scripserunt domino pape ad instanciam regis
Anglie omnem iniuriam eis illatam ab eo uel a suis ex
bona et mera uoluntate remisisse. Rex Philippus [a]
magnam classem congregauit ut ad debellandam Angliam
transfretaret; quedam a regis Anglie primoribus in
littore combusta est. Hiis diebus contigit in Anglia
quidam dictus Petrus sapiens qui predixit regi Io[hanni]
infausta futura sibi, que post patuerunt, quam ob rem
iussus est apud Coruiam suspendi. Sauaricus de Malo
Leone insurgens in Pictauia contra regem Anglie cepit
omnia infra paucos dies, sola Rupella uiribus suis
resistente. [2]

1213

Nicholaus cardinalis episcopus Tusculanensis legacionis
officium exercet in Anglia. Hugo [3] monachus sancti
Edmundi electus est in abbatem eiusdem monasterii
communiter ab omnibus fratribus [4]; sed non multo post
scisma in conuentu propter electionem factum est.

---

[a] + post A

[1] Here the annals of Bury St Edmunds break off in the middle of a
sentence owing to the loss of leaves from MS Harley 447, the only known
text of the annals; see Introduction, pp. xvi, xvii.

[2] Apparently a reference to Arthur, duke of Brittany's invasion of
Poitou in 1202, led by Savari de Mauléon.

I

THE CHRONICLE OF BURY ST EDMUNDS

1212

The burgesses of Bury St Edmunds allowed, though [1] reluctantly, a monk to collect money from them. The king had some Welsh hostages hanged at Nottingham. The members of the religious orders and the secular clergy wrote to the pope, on the instruction of the king of England, to say that they forgave from genuine good-will all the wrongs done them by the king and his subordinates. King Philip [II] assembled a large fleet to invade and defeat England. The fleet was burnt by the king of England's captains while it lay on the coast. At this time a man called Peter the Wise came to England and prophesied to King John the misfortunes which afterwards befell him. Because of this he was ordered to be hanged at Corfe. Savari de Mauléon revolted in Poitou against the king of England. Within a few days he captured the whole country except La Rochelle, which withstood his onslaught.[2]

1213

Nicholas, cardinal-bishop of Frascati, took up his office of legate in England. Hugh,[3] a monk of Bury St Edmunds, was elected abbot of Bury by all the monks together.[4] Soon after, however, there arose a dispute

---

[3] Hugh II, de Northwold, abbot of Bury St Edmunds 1215–29.
[4] According to *Electio Hugonis* (Arnold, II, p. 33), Hugh de Northwold was unanimously elected abbot by seven electors in 1213, by the method of compromise.

Nicholaus apostolice sedis legatus fuit in die Natiuitatis
ad sanctum Edmundum.

1214

Rex Io[hannes] perrexit in Pictauiam circa Purificacionem beate Marie.[1] Bellum in Flandria gestum
prope Bouins die dominica inter regem Francie et
magnates regis Anglie, in quo capti sunt de Flandria et
de Bolonia comites et Willelmus comes de Salisber'[2] ex
parte regis Anglie. Oto eciam imperator ibi prope
existens uiso belli euentu fugam iniit. Interdictum
generale relaxatum est in Anglia vi. Non. Iulii mandato
domini pape Innocentii quod iam durauerat annis vi.
ebdomadis xiiii. dies iii.[3]

1215

Eustachius episcopus Elyensis obiit ii. Non. Februarii.
Otoni imperatori Fredericus rex Sicilie, filius Henrici
quondam imperatoris, successit. Hugo electus sancti
Edmundi confirmatus est [a] iudicibus a domino papa
delegatis v. Idus Marcii et accepit benedictionem a
Benedicto Rofensi episcopo. Hoc anno incipit guerra
circa Pascha inter [b] Io[hannem] et barones. Iohannes
de [c] Grey episcopus Norwicensis obiit [4]; Pandulfus sub-
diaconus domini pape electus est. Ignis succensus iii.
f. 143ᵛ Non. Iunii / magnam partem uille sancti Edmundi consumpsit. Innocentius papa celebrauit concilium Lateranense mense Nouembri in quo fuerunt cccc.xii.

---

[a] +a A   [b] + regem A   [c] le A

[1] 2 February
[2] Ferrand, count of Flanders 1206-33, Reginald, count of Boulogne
1191-1216, and William Longespée, 3rd earl of Salisbury 1196-1225/6

in the convent over the election.   Nicholas the papal
legate was at Bury St Edmunds on Christmas day.

1214

King John reached Poitou about Candlemas.[1]   The
king of France and the king of England's nobles met in
battle at Bouvines in Flanders on a Sunday.   On the
king of England's side the count of Flanders, the count
of Boulogne and William, earl of Salisbury, were
captured.[2]   The Emperor Otto [IV], who had taken
his stand near by, fled when he saw the outcome of the
battle.   On 2 July by order of Pope Innocent [III]
England was released from the general interdict, which
had already lasted for six years, fourteen weeks and
three days.[3]

1215

Eustace, bishop of Ely, died on 4 February.   Frederick,
king of Sicily, the son of the former Emperor Henry [VI],
succeeded the Emperor Otto.   On 11 March Hugh,
the abbot-elect of Bury St Edmunds, was confirmed by
the papal judge-delegates and blessed by Benedict,
bishop of Rochester.   In this year about Eastertide the
war between King John and the barons began.   John
de Gray, bishop of Norwich, died [4] and Pandulf, the
pope's subdeacon, was elected bishop.   On 3 June a
fire broke out and burnt a great part of the town of
Bury St Edmunds.   Pope Innocent held the Lateran
Council in November; it was attended by four hundred
and twelve bishops, over eight hundred abbots and

---

[3] Wendover, II, p. 103, reads incorrectly six years, three months and
fourteen days.
[4] He died on 18 October 1214 according to *Tewk.*, p. 61.

episcopi, abbates et priores plusquam dccc., nuncii eciam Frederici *ᵃ* eciam *ᵇ* plures alii. *ᶜ*

1216

Galo presbiter cardinalis tituli sancti Martini in Angliam uenit xiii. Kal. Iunii. Datis obsidibus Philippo regi Francie a baronibus Anglie, Lodowicus filius regis Francie Angliam est ingressus, cui ciuitas London' statim tradita est. Dominus papa excommunicauit barones et Angliam interdixit in eorum presencia quia regi rebelles erant. Innocentius papa obiit xvi. Kal. Augusti [1]; successit Honorius papa. Iohannes rex obiit xv. Kal. Nouembris; sepultus est Wigorn'. Successit filius eius Henricus qui apud Bristowe coronatus est a Galone cardinali et legato v. Kal. Nouembris. Iste fuit xxii. rex Anglie Alfredo qui fuit post Britones primus monarchus Anglorum. *ᵈ*

1217

In conflictu apud Lincolniam interfectus est comes de Pertico [2] et multi alii ex Francis xiii. Kal. Iulii.[3] Barones uero et Franci ab obsidione castri fugati sunt per milites regales. Exercitus ueniens de Francia in auxilium Lodowici pene submersus est ix. Kal. Septembris ab Huberto de Burgo aliisque regis fidelibus nauali prelio in ostio fluminis Tamensis. Iohannes abbas de Fontibus electus est in episcopum Elyensem.[4] Lodowicus a

---

ᵃ + electi *A*
ᵇ *Corr. to* et *MS*
ᶜ Concilium Lateranense *MS*²
ᵈ iste fuit . . . Anglorum *om. A*

[1] He died on 16, not 17, July.
[2] Thomas, count of Perche 1202–17

priors, ambassadors of the Emperor Frederick [II] and
many others.

1216

Guala, cardinal-priest of St Martin, arrived in England
on 20 May. After the barons of England had given
hostages to King Philip of France, his son Louis came
to England. The city of London was immediately
made over to him. The pope excommunicated the
barons and laid an interdict on England in their
presence, because they had rebelled against the king.
Pope Innocent died on 17 July [1] and was succeeded by
Pope Honorius [III]. On 18 October King John died
and was buried at Worcester. He was succeeded by
his son Henry [III], who was crowned by the Cardinal-
legate Guala at Bristol on 28 October. Henry was the
twenty-second king of England since Alfred, who had
been the first monarch of the English after the time of
the Britons.

1217

The count of Perche [2] and many other Frenchmen were
killed in the battle at Lincoln on 19 June.[3] Knights of
the royal army put the barons and the French to flight
from the besieged castle. In a naval battle in the
estuary of the Thames on 24 August, Hubert de Burgh
and other supporters of the king sank almost the whole
army sailing from France to help Louis. John, abbot
of Fountains, was elected bishop of Ely.[4] Louis,

---

[3] The correct reading would be *Iunii*, as the battle of Lincoln was on
20 May 1217.

[4] John of Fountains was elected bishop of Ely in the winter of 1219/20,
not in 1217; *CPR, 1216–25*, p. 224.

sententia excommunicacionis a Galone legato absolutus redit in Gallias. Deinde post duos annos et dimidium guerre pax optata redit circa Natiuitatem beate *a* Marie.[1]

1218

Ranulfus prior Norwicensis consecratus est in episcopum Cicestrensem. Galo recessit ab Anglia xii. Kal. Decembris. Pandulfus Norwicensis electus fit domini pape legatus in Angliam. Ciuitas Damieta in Egypto, que secundum quosdam dicitur Memfis, a Christianis post Pascha est obsessa, que obsidio durauit magis quam per annum et dimidium, in qua nunc Christiani nunc Saraceni diuersa sorte uictores fuerunt.

1219

Non. Nouembris feria iii. ciuitas Damieta capta est a Christianis, in qua die xl. millia uiris armatis cum tot mulieribus in principio obsidionis deputatis ad tutelam / f. 144 ciuitatis uix l. in captione sunt inuenti uiui; nam omnes diuino strati gladio sub loco cinctorii sunt putrefacti. Fredericus coronatur in Romanum imperatorem ab Honorio papa.

1220

Beatus Thomas Cantuariensis archiepiscopus Non. Iunii est translatus. Herebertus prior sancti Edmundi obiit iiii. Idus Septembris; successit ei Ricardus de Insula.

---

a sancte *A*

[1] 8 September

absolved from the sentence of excommunication by the legate Guala, returned to France.   After this, about the time of the Nativity of the Blessed Virgin Mary,[1] the great gift of peace was granted once more after two and a half years of war.

1218

Ranulf prior of Norwich was consecrated bishop of Chichester.   Guala left England on 20 November. Pandulf, the bishop-elect of Norwich, became the legate of the pope in England.   The city of Damietta in Egypt, which some people call Memphis, was besieged by the Christians after Easter.   The siege lasted for more than a year and a half; sometimes, through changing fortunes, the Christians were victorious and sometimes the Saracens.

1219

On Tuesday, 5 November the Christians took Damietta. On that day when the city was captured scarcely fifty people were found alive of the forty thousand armed men and as many women to whom the defence of the city had been entrusted at the beginning of the siege; for everyone, smitten by the sword of the Lord, had mortified from the waist downwards.   Frederick was crowned Roman emperor by Pope Honorius.

1220

The blessed Thomas, archbishop of Canterbury, was translated on 5 June.   Herbert, the prior of Bury St Edmunds, died on 10 September and was succeeded by Richard de Insula.

1221

Pandulfus Norwicensis electus a legationis officio reuo-
catur. Damieta Sarracenis est tradita, Christianis
omnibus inde expulsis.

1222

Ranulfus Cicestrensis episcopus quondam prior Nor-
wicensis obiit. Pandulfus consecratus est in episcopum
Norwicensem. Ricardus de Insula electus est in abbatem
Burtonie, cui successit Henricus in prioratu ii. Kal. Iunii.
Stella cometes apparuit mense Iunio. Stephanus
Cantuariensis archiepiscopus celebrauit concilium apud
Oxoniam cum suffraganeis suis.

1223

Circa tale tempus cepit peregrinatio apud Bromholm.[1]
Philippus rex Francie obiit; sepultus est apud sanctum
Dionisium. Successit Lodowicus. [a]

1224

Castrum de Bedeford obsessum mense Iulio et xix. Kal.
Septembris captum est suspensique sunt omnes fere qui
in eo sunt inuenti.

1225

Iohannes episcopus Elyensis obiit ii. Non. Maii; successit
ei Galfridus frater Huberti de Burgo iusticiarii. Ordo

---

[a] + filius eius *A*

[1] Bromholm, Norfolk. References, excluding this notice, relating to
the rood at Bromholm have been collected by F. Wormald in the *Journal
of the Warburg Institute*, I (1937), pp. 31–45.

1221

Pandulf, the bishop-elect of Norwich, was recalled from his position of papal legate. Damietta was surrendered to the Saracens and all the Christian inhabitants expelled.

1222

Ranulf bishop of Chichester, formerly the prior of Norwich, died. Pandulf was consecrated bishop of Norwich. Richard de Insula was elected the abbot of Burton and was succeeded as prior of Bury St Edmunds by Henry on 31 May. A comet appeared in June. Stephen, archbishop of Canterbury, held a council at Oxford with his suffragans.

1223

About this time pilgrimages to Bromholm began.[1] King Philip of France died and was buried at St Denis. Louis [VIII] succeeded him.

1224

Bedford castle was besieged in July and captured on 14 August. Nearly everyone who was found there was hanged.

1225

John, bishop of Ely, died on 6 May and was succeeded by Geoffrey, brother of Hubert de Burgh, the justiciar. The order of the Friars Minor and the order of the

Minorum et Predicatorum locum primitus occupat in Anglia.[a]

1226

Willelmus comes Salisb' obiit. Pandulfus episcopus Norwicensis obiit in Italia xvii. Kal. Septembris[1]: successit ei Thomas de Blunuile, consecratus xii. Kal. Ianuarii. Lodowicus rex Francie apud Auinun[2] obiit; sepultus est apud sanctum Dionisium. Successit ei Lodowicus filius eius.

1227

Honorius papa obiit; successit Hostiensis episcopus dictus Gregorius IX. Scisma inter papam et imperatorem oritur. Vnde papa eundem imperatorem excommunicauit.

1228

Franci crucesignati in pectore Abigeos inuadunt. Stephanus Cantuariensis archiepiscopus vi. Idus Iulii obiit. Eustachius de Faucunberge episcopus Londoniensis obiit. Galfridus de Burgo episcopus Elyensis obiit xvi. Kal. Ianuarii.

1229

Ortum est scisma inter scolares Parisienses et ciues causa rusticorum sancti Marcelli.[3] Vnde magistri legere per totum annum cessabant et scolares persecucionem f. 144ᵛ legati, tunc in Gallia existentis, et regine / non ferentes

[a] Ordo Minorum et Predicatorum *in margin in red MS*

[1] Cotton, p. 394, gives 16 September, not 16 August.
[2] Louis VIII died at Montpensier, Auvergne.
[3] A suburb of Paris

Preaching Friars established themselves for the first time in England.

1226

William, earl of Salisbury, died. Pandulf, bishop of Norwich, died in Italy on 16 August.[1] Thomas de Blundeville succeeded him and was consecrated on 21 December. Louis, king of France, died at Avignon [2] and was buried at St Denis. His son Louis succeeded him.

1227

Pope Honorius died and was succeeded by the bishop of Ostia, who took the name Gregory IX. A dispute arose between the pope and the emperor, on account of which the pope excommunicated the emperor.

1228

The French, with the sign of the cross on their breasts, attacked the Albigensians. Stephen, archbishop of Canterbury, died on 10 July. Eustace de Fauconberg, bishop of London, died. Geoffrey de Burgh, bishop of Ely, died on 17 December.

1229

A dispute arose between the scholars and the citizens of Paris on account of the common people of St Marceau.[3] Because of this the masters stopped lecturing for almost a whole year and nearly all the scholars left; they were unable to bear the persecution of the legate, who was then in France, and of the queen. Concerning the

pene omnes recesserunt. De legati[1] et regine[2] nimia familiaritate dixit quidam;

> Eu morimur strati, cesi, mersi, spoliati;
> Scortum legati nos facit ista pati.[a][3]

Magister Ricardus Magnus electus Cantuariensis et magister Rogerus Niger Londoniensis et Hugo abbas sancti Edmundi, electus in episcopum Elyensem, consecrati sunt iiii. Idus Iunii. Ricardus abbas de Burton' electus est in abbatem sancti Edmundi Non. Iunii.

1230

Henricus rex cum exercitu transfretauit in Britanniam. Reimundus de Burgo[4] et Gilebertus de Clare comes Glouern' obierunt. Rex Henricus rediens de Britannia[b] applicuit apud Portesmu mense Octobris et Kal. Nouembris fuit Wintonie.

1231

Ricardus Cantuariensis archiepiscopus obiit Non. Augusti. Thomas episcopus Norwicensis interfuit festo sancti Edmundi[5] et Ricardus abbas eiusdem loci[6] in uigilia post uesperas dedit benedictionem presente episcopo capa seculari indutus. Willelmus Marescallus iunior obiit.

1232

Ranulfus comes Cestrie obiit. Hubertus de Burgo

---

^a *The verses are unspaced and* uersus *is written in the margin MS.*
^b + applicuit *deleted MS and expunged P*

[1] Romano Bonaventura, cardinal-deacon of S. Angelo 1212
[2] Blanche of Castile, formerly Louis VIII's queen
[3] Another version of the verse is in Matthew Paris, *Chron. Maj.*, III, p. 169.

excessive intimacy of the legate [1] and queen [2] someone wrote:

> Alas we die; slaughtered, despoiled and drowned,
> To such fates by the legate's harlot bound.[3]

On 10 June Master Richard Magnus, the archbishop-elect of Canterbury, Master Roger Niger, the bishop-elect of London and Hugh, abbot of Bury St Edmunds, who had been elected bishop of Ely, were consecrated. Richard, abbot of Burton, was elected abbot of Bury St Edmunds on 5 June.

1230

King Henry crossed into Brittany with an army. Raymund de Burgh [4] and Gilbert de Clare, earl of Gloucester, died. King Henry landed at Portsmouth in October on his return from Brittany and was at Winchester on 1 November.

1231

Richard, archbishop of Canterbury, died on 5 August. Thomas, bishop of Norwich, attended the feast of St Edmund [5] and Richard, abbot of that place,[6] vested in a secular cope, gave the blessing on the vigil after vespers in the presence of the bishop. The younger William the Marshal died.

1232

Ranulf earl of Chester died. Hubert de Burgh, earl of

---

[4] Raymund de Burgh of Dartford, Kent, nephew of Hubert de Burgh; G.E.C., *Complete Peerage*, v, p. 133
[5] 20 November
[6] Richard de Insula, abbot of Bury St Edmunds 1229–33.

comes Cancie offensam regis incurrens incarceratur; cuius uxor [1] ad asilum *a* sancti Edmundi fugiens illuc securior permansit donec pax formaretur.

1233

Episcopi per Angliam uisitauerunt domos religionis. Magister Edmundus de Abingdone electus est in archiepiscopum Cantuariensem. Ricardus abbas sancti Edmundi iiii. Kal. Septembris obiit in Pontiua.[2] Henricus prior sancti Edmundi electus est in abbatem in die sanctorum Cosme et Damiani.[3]

1234

Henricus electus sancti Edmundi suscepit benedictionem ab Hugone Elyensi apud Hadfeld Episcopi in die Purificacionis. Eodem tempore Gregorius factus est prior sancti Edmundi. Edmundus Cantuariensis electus consecratus est iiii. Non. Aprilis. Ricardus Marescallus occisus est in Ybernia xviii. Kal. Maii. Hubertus de Burgo reconciliatur regi apud Gloucestriam x. Kal. Iunii.[4] Fredericus imperator duxit Isabell', sororem regis Anglie mense Iunii.[5]

1235

Hugo episcopus Lincolniensis obiit; successit magister Robertus Grosseteste. Elyensis et Herefordensis episcopi

a auxilium *M*

[1] Margaret, eldest daughter of William the Lion, king of Scotland 1165–1214. A mandate on the Close Rolls (*CCR, 1231–4*, p. 161) of 16 October 1232 orders that Margaret should be captured when she left St Edmund's Liberty.

[2] According to Matthew Paris, *Chron. Maj.*, III, p. 239, Abbot Richard went abroad to appeal to the pope against the 1232 episcopal visitation.

[3] 27 September. The royal licence to elect is dated 17 September and the signification to the pope of the king's assent to the election is dated 10 October; *CPR, 1232–47*, pp. 26, 27.

Kent, was imprisoned because he had incurred the king's displeasure. His wife [1] fled for sanctuary to Bury St Edmunds; she remained there safely until peace was made.

1233

Throughout England bishops held visitations of religious houses. Master Edmund de Abingdon was elected archbishop of Canterbury. Richard, abbot of Bury St Edmunds, died on 29 August in Ponthieu.[2] Henry, the prior of Bury St Edmunds, was elected abbot on the feast of SS. Cosmas and Damian.[3]

1234

Henry, the abbot-elect of Bury St Edmunds, was blessed by Hugh, bishop of Ely, at Candlemas at Bishop's Hatfield. At the same time Gregory was made prior of Bury St Edmunds. Edmund, the archbishop-elect of Canterbury, was consecrated on 2 April. Richard the Marshal was killed in Ireland on 14 April. Hubert de Burgh made his peace with the king at Gloucester on 23 May.[4] In June the Emperor Frederick married Isabel, the king of England's sister.[5]

1235

Hugh, bishop of Lincoln, died and Master Robert Grosseteste succeeded him. The bishops of Ely and

---

[4] This date, 23 May, is a few days too early; Bracton's *Note Book*, ed. F. W. Maitland (1887), II, p.665, no. 857, dates the reconciliation 27 May, and Hubert's safe conduct to come to Gloucester to seek the king's grace is dated 25 May; *CPR, 1232–47*, p. 48.

[5] Isabel's marriage took place on 15 July 1235; J. L. A. Huillard-Bréholles, *Historia Diplomatica Frederici II* (Paris 1852-61), IV, pt ii, p. 728.

transfretauerunt in Gallias ut adducerent filiam comitis
f. 145 Prouencie [1] quam rex / Anglie in uxorem duceret. [a]

1236

Henricus rex Anglie traduxit Alianoram filiam comitis
Prouincie, quam desponsauit apud Cantuariam Idus
Ianuarii die dominica.[2] Rex H[enricus] et regina
coronati sunt Londonie xiii. Kal. Februarii. Thomas
de Blunuile episcopus Norwicensis obiit xvii. Kal.
Septembris.

1237

Oto diaconus cardinalis tituli sancti Nicholay in Carcere
Tulliano uenit in Angliam vi. Idus Iulii [3] fungens
legacionis officio. Ortum est iterum scisma inter papam
Gregorium et Fredericum imperatorem.

1238

Celebratum est concilium Oxonie Otone legato presidente post Pasca, ubi orta est seditio inter scolares et
familiam legati de qua quidam uulnerati ceciderunt.
De scolaribus uero per ministros regis plures incarcer-
antur. Dominus papa Fredericum imperatorem propter
diuersas causas excommunicauit et excommunicari
precepit. Oto legatus [b] uenit ad sanctum Edmundum
ad quem Fratres Predicatores accedentes rogauerunt
instanter ut eis locus daretur ad inhabitandum infra
limites libertatis eiusdem ecclesie, contradicentibus uero

---

[a] deduceret A
[b] nota in margin MS²; fratres Predicatorum in margin in red A

[1] Hugh, bishop of Ely 1229–54, and Ralph, bishop of Hereford 1234–9,
fetched Eleanor, daughter of Raymond Berengar IV, count of Provence.

Hereford sailed to France to fetch the count of Provence's daughter,[1] whom the king of England was to marry.

1236

Henry, king of England, married Eleanor, daughter of the count of Provence, to whom he had been betrothed on Sunday, 13 January, at Canterbury.[2] King Henry and the queen were crowned in London on 20 January. Thomas de Blundeville, bishop of Norwich, died on 16 August.

1237

Otto, cardinal-deacon of the title of St Nicholas in Carcere Tulliano, came to England on 10 July [3] to be papal legate in England. A dispute arose again between Pope Gregory [IX] and the Emperor Frederick.

1238

A council was held at Oxford after Easter over which the legate Otto presided. On this occasion a dispute broke out between the scholars and members of the legate's retinue. Some people were wounded and killed and many scholars were imprisoned by the king's officials. For various reasons the pope excommunicated the Emperor Frederick and ordered the excommunication to be pronounced. The legate Otto arrived at Bury St Edmunds. The Preaching Friars came to him and earnestly asked him, in spite of the opposition of the monks, to give them somewhere to live within the boundaries of the Liberty of St Edmund's church. The

---

[2] The marriage was on Monday, 14 January; *Foedera*, I, p. 222.

[3] The chroniclers do not agree about the date of Otto's arrival. See also *CCR, 1234–7*, p. 540.

monachis. Legatus personaliter ad predictos limites cum maxima multitudine accessit et inspectis mona-chorum priuilegiis peticionem tam Minorum quam Predicatorum irritam fore diffiniuit.[1] Acta sunt hec viii. Idus Iunii in octauis sancte Trinitatis.

1239

Willelmus de Ralleia electus est in episcopum Norwicensem iiii. Idus Aprilis. Gens nefanda dicta Tartarins que nuper de insulis ebulliens superficiem terre impleuerat Hungariam cum adiacentibus regionibus deuastat. Alienor regina Anglie peperit xiiii. Kal. Iulii Edwardum filium suum primogenitum, eius pater Henricus, cuius pater Io[hannes], cuius pater Henricus, cuius mater Matildis imperatrix, cuius mater Matild' regina Anglorum, cuius mater Margareta regina Scot-torum, cuius pater Edwardus, cuius pater Edmundus Ferreum Latus, qui fuit filius Ethelredi, qui fuit Edgari, qui fuit Edmundi, qui fuit Edwardi senioris, qui fuit Alfredi. Genealogia autem ab Alfredo usque ad Adam primum hominem supra texitur. *[2]*

1240

Apud Norwic' iiii. Iudei propter diuersa scelera sunt equis distracti et demum suspensi, maxime quia puerum f. 145ᵛ quemdam Christianum secundum ritum / Iudeorum circumciderant. Ricardus comes Cornubie frater H[enrici] regis Anglie cum multis Anglie proceribus iter

---

a + 44 *A*

[1] A royal mandate on the Close Rolls orders the sheriff of Suffolk to adjourn the inquest which was to decide whether the place granted by Hawisia, countess of Oxford, to the Preachers was within St Edmund's Liberty or not, until the abbot of Bury had recovered from his illness;

legate went personally with a crowd of people to inspect the boundaries. When he had examined the monks' privileges he gave judgment that the petition of both the Friars Minor and the Preaching Friars was null and void.[1] These events took place on 6 June, the octave of Trinity Sunday.

1239

William Raleigh was elected bishop of Norwich on 10 April. That horrible race of men known as the Tartars, which had once come swarming from remote fastnesses and overrun the face of the earth, laid waste Hungary and the neighbouring territories. On 18 June Eleanor, queen of England, gave birth to her eldest son Edward. His father was Henry; Henry's father was John, whose father was Henry, whose mother was the Empress Matilda. Her mother was Matilda, queen of the English, the daughter of Queen Margaret of Scotland. Margaret's father was Edward, son of Edmund Ironside, son of Ethelred, son of Edgar, son of Edmund, son of Edward the Elder, son of Alfred. Alfred's genealogy back to Adam is written above.[2]

1240

At Norwich four Jews were drawn apart by horses and then hanged for various crimes, but mainly because they had circumcised a Christian boy according to the Jewish rite. Richard, earl of Cornwall, brother of King

---

CCR, *1237–42*, p. 127.   Another notice of the Preachers at Bury is in *Gesta Abbatum Monasterii S. Albani*, ed. H. T. Riley (RS, 1867–9), I, p. 386.   Pope Gregory confirmed the spiritual monopoly of St Edmund's abbey within the *banleuca* in a bull of 16 April 1239; Bliss, I, p. 127.

[2] The genealogy is on f. 128ᵛ under the year 849.

arripuit uersus Ierosolem iii. Idus Iunii. Dominus papa
misit literas post festum Omnium Sanctorum ad omnes
ecclesie prelatos ut uenirent ad sequentem Pascam ad
sedem apostolicam, sine aliqua excusatione, uel eorum
nuncii, super arduis ecclesie negociis tractaturi.
Edmundus Cantuariensis archiepiscopus migrat a seculo
xvi. Kal. Decembris.

1241

Oto legatus de Anglia Romam rediturus egressus mense
Ianuarii, sed ipse et alii duo legati, scilicet Francie et
Italie,[1] cum multis ecclesie prelatis a Ianue mare
intrantes in manus imperatoris Frederici v. Non. Maii
inciderunt, quos per diuersa loca custodie mancipauit.
De quibus quidam sic ait;

Omnes prelati, papa mandante uocati,
Et tres legati ueniant hucusque ligati. [a]

Gregorius papa obiit xi. Kal. Septembris; successit
Galfridus cardinalis, consecratus v. Kal. Nouembris
dictusque [b] Celestinus IIII uixitque in pontificatu xvii.
dies obiitque iii. Idus Nouembris. Vacauit sedes post
obitum eius anno i. mensibus vii. diebus xiii. Bonefacius
de Sauueia natus hoc anno electus est in archiepiscopum
Cantuariensem Kal. Februarii. Alienor filia Galfridi
comitis Britannie soror Arturi obiit. Regina Alienor
peperit filiam que uocata est Margareta.[2]

---

[a] The verses are unspaced MS.
[b] + est A

[1] Jacopo de Pecoraria, cardinal-bishop of Palestrina 1231–45, legate in
France, and Gregory de Romagna, legate in Italy
[2] According to Matthew Paris, *Chron. Maj.*, IV, p. 48, Margaret was
born on 29 September 1240. She was born before 30 May 1241, as she is
mentioned in an entry on the Patent Rolls of that date; *CPR, 1232–47*,
p. 252.

Henry of England, left for Jerusalem on 11 June accompanied by many English magnates. After the feast of All Saints the pope wrote to all the prelates of the Church ordering them, without exception, to come or send representatives to the Apostolic See next Easter to discuss important business relating to the Church. Edmund, archbishop of Canterbury, died on 16 November.

1241

The legate Otto left England in January to return to Rome. When he and two other legates, namely those of France and Italy,[1] and many other dignitaries of the Church, set sail from Genoa, they fell into the hands of the Emperor Frederick on 3 May. He imprisoned them in various places. Someone said about them:

> All prelates, summoned as the pope ordained,
> And legates three, to come, all now are chained.

Pope Gregory died on 22 August; he was succeeded by Cardinal Geoffrey, who was consecrated on 28 October and took the name Celestine IV. He was pope for seventeen days and died on 11 November. The Holy See was vacant after his death for a year, seven months and thirteen days. Boniface, a Savoyard by birth, was elected archbishop of Canterbury on 1 February in this year. Eleanor, the daughter of Geoffrey, duke of Brittany, and sister of Arthur, died. Queen Eleanor gave birth to a daughter, who was named Margaret.[2]

1242

Ricardus comes Cornubie ab imperatore Frederico et rege Francie ceterisque principibus transmarinis plurimum *a* honoratus rediit a Terra Sancta et *b* applicuit apud Doueram xi. Kal. Februarii. Gregorius prior sancti Edmundi obiit ix. Kal. Maii; successit Daniel. *c* Rex Anglie H[enricus] posuit scutagium in Anglia xl. solidorum super scutum. Rex Anglie cum regina et magnatibus suis transfretauit in Gasconiam ii. Non. Maii.

1243

Alienor regina peperit filiam que Beatrix est uocata. Sinebaldus presbiter cardinalis tituli sancti Laurencii in Lucina consecratus est in summum pontificem vii. Kal. Iulii et dictus est Innocentius IIII. Rex H[enricus] cum regina rediens de Gasconia applicuit apud Portesmu f. 146 vii. Kal. Octobris. Hubertus de Burgo comes Cancie / obiit iii. Idus Maii.[1] Ricardus comes Cornub' duxit filiam comitis Prouencie sororem regine Anglie.[2] Willelmus episcopus Norwicensis postulatus in Wintoniensem episcopum, transtulit se Winton' mandato domini pape quamuis contra regis uoluntatem.

1244

Discordia orta est inter reges Anglie et Scocie. Defuncto Daniele priore sancti Edmundi, Ricardus de Bosco monachus successit eidem ii. Non. Iunii. Turbo magnus arbores et edificia prostrauit plurima iii. Idus Iunii.

---

a plurimis *M*   *b* sanctaque *MS*   *c In margin A*

[1] According to Matthew Paris, *Chron. Maj.*, iv, p. 243, he died on 12 May.
[2] Sanchia, third daughter of Raymond Berengar IV, count of Provence

1242

Richard, earl of Cornwall, returned from the Holy Land greatly honoured by the Emperor Frederick, the king of France and the other foreign princes. He touched Dover on 22 January. Gregory, the prior of Bury St Edmunds, died on 23 April and was succeeded by Daniel. Henry, king of England, imposed a scutage in England of 40s. on each knight's fee. He sailed to Gascony on 6 May with the queen and his magnates.

1243

Queen Eleanor gave birth to a daughter, who was named Beatrix. Sinibaldo, cardinal-priest of St Lawrence in Lucina, was consecrated pope on 25 July and called Innocent IV. King Henry and the queen returned from Gascony and landed at Portsmouth on 25 September. Hubert de Burgh, earl of Kent, died on 13 May.[1] Richard, earl of Cornwall, married the daughter of the count of Provence, the queen of England's sister.[2] William, bishop of Norwich, was nominated bishop of Winchester; he was translated by the pope's order against the king's wishes.

1244

A dispute arose between the king of England and the king of Scotland. On 4 June, after the death of Daniel, the prior of Bury St Edmunds, the monk Richard de Bosco succeeded him. On 11 June a storm blew down a great many trees and buildings. On 13 August peace

Pax inter reges Anglie et Scocie reformatur Idus Augusti
apud Nouum Castrum. Innocencius papa uenit in
Gallias, apud Lugdunum moratus est. Mirabilis *a*
conflictus habitus est vigilia sancte Lucie [1] inter Christianos et Cosmerinos prope Gazam, in quo omnis milicia
de regno Syrie cum multitudine Christianorum a dictis
Cosmerinis interfecta est. *b*

1245

Alienor *c* regina peperit filium *d* qui ex nomine gloriosi
regis et martiris Edmundi Edmundus appellatur; domino
rege per litteram suam domino H[enrico] abbati hoc
demandante ut inter eos condictum fuit xviii. die
Ianuarii anno regni regis H[enrici] xxix.[2] Bonefacius
electus Cantuariensis consecratur a summo pontifice.
Walterus electus Norwicensis consecratur xi. Kal. Marcii.
Rex Henricus duxit in Walliam exercitum post Pentecosten. Innocentius papa celebrauit concilium apud
Lugdunum in quo Fredericum Romanorum imperatorem priuauit sentencialiter imperio. Rogerus de
Weseham decanus Lincolniensis consecratur *e* in
episcopum Couentrensem.

1246

Innocencio papa existente apud Lugdunum Henricus
landegrauius electus est a principibus Alemannie in
regem eorum et in futurum imperatorem Romanorum
xi. Kal. Maii,[3] feria iii. Eodem [anno] *f* landegrauius

---

a miserabil' *A*

b + hoc anno scriptor presentis uoluminis habitum suscepit monachicum
dictus I. de Taxter (Taxt' *A*; Tayster *Arundel 6*) die sancti Edmundi *A*

c On erasure MS   *d* + Henr' regi *A*

e consecratus *A*   *f* Supplied from *A*; om. MS, M

was made between the kings of England and Scotland at Newcastle. Pope Innocent went to France and stayed at Lyons. An amazing battle was fought near Gaza between the Christians and Khorazmians on the vigil of the feast of St Lucy [1]; the Khorazmians exterminated the complete army of the kingdom of Syria together with numerous Christians.

1245

Queen Eleanor gave birth to a son, who was named Edmund after the glorious king and martyr Edmund; King Henry, in a letter dated 18 January in the twenty-ninth year of his reign [1245], instructed Henry, abbot of Bury St Edmunds, to announce this to his monks.[2] Boniface, the archbishop-elect of Canterbury, was consecrated by the pope. Walter, the bishop-elect of Norwich, was consecrated on 19 February. King Henry led an army to Wales after Pentecost. Pope Innocent held a council at Lyons and formally deprived Frederick, emperor of the Romans, of the empire. Roger de Weseham, dean of Lincoln, was consecrated bishop of Coventry.

1246

On Tuesday, 21 April,[3] while Pope Innocent was at Lyons, the princes of Germany elected the Landgrave Henry as their king and future emperor of the Romans. In the same year the landgrave fought and defeated

---

[1] 12 December

[2] See Introduction, p. xii.   The letter is printed in Arnold, III, p. 28.

[3] The correct reading would be *Iunii*, as Henry Raspe, landgrave of Thuringia 1227–47, was elected anti-king on 22 May.

habuit conflictum cum Conrado filio Frederici quondam imperatoris qui Conradus deuictus est ab ipso. Capti sunt autem ex parte Conradi dc. milites m. et cc. armigeri preter pedites et mortuos quorum numerus non habetur. Archiepiscopi Colonie ¹ et Maguncius ² et episcopus Metensis ³ cum suis adherentes dicto landegrauio mandato domini pape dictam pugnam uicerunt f. 146ᵛ apud Straburh ⁴ / in principio mensis Augusti. Fuerunt autem capti preter predictos comites et magni barones xvi. Beatus Edmundus Cantuariensis archiepiscopus canonizatur.

1247

Terremotus magnus factus est Kal. Marcii per plura loca in Anglia. Landegrauius,⁵ anno precedenti electus in imperatorem, obiit. Beatus Edmundus Cantuariensis archiepiscopus v. Idus Iunii est translatus. Fredericus quondam imperator obsedit Parmam. Hoc anno facta est [mutacio] ᵃ monete in Anglia. Quo tempore Henricus rex concessit sancto Edmundo unum cuneum noue incisionis ita libere utendum cum excambio, sicut ipse rex utitur suis cuneis.⁶

1248

Magna tempestas uenti facta est in nocte Circumcisionis.

ᵃ *Supplied from A, om. MS, M*

¹ Conrad von Hochstadt, archbishop of Cologne 1238–61
² Siegfried von Eppstech, archbishop of Mainz 1230–49
³ James of Lotharingia, bishop of Metz 1239–60
⁴ Probably ' Straburgh ' is an error: the battle was fought near Frankfurt on 5 August 1246.
⁵ Henry Raspe
⁶ The mandate dated 6 December 1247 for the delivery of a new die to St Edmunds is on the Close Rolls; *CCR, 1247–51*, p. 12. A copy of a royal mandate dated 28 December 1247 to the abbot and convent, en-

Conrad, son of the former Emperor Frederick. Of Conrad's army six hundred knights and one thousand, two hundred men-at-arms (excluding the foot-soldiers and the slain whose number is unknown) were captured. This battle was won at the beginning of August at Strasbourg [4] by the archbishop of Cologne,[1] the archbishop of Mainz [2] and the bishop of Metz [3] and their men, who had allied themselves to the landgrave at the pope's command. Besides those mentioned above, sixteen counts and important barons were captured. The blessed Edmund, archbishop of Canterbury, was canonised.

1247

A severe earthquake shook many places in England on 1 March. The landgrave,[5] who had been elected emperor in the preceding year, died. On 9 June [the body of] the blessed Edmund, archbishop of Canterbury, was translated. Frederick, the former emperor, besieged Parma. There was an alteration in the coinage in England and King Henry granted a newly cut die to Bury St Edmunds. The new die was to be used freely with the right of exchange, just as the king himself used his dies.[6]

1248

On the night of the Circumcision there was a terrible

---

joining them to use the liberty of striking coins like the City of London and other cities, is in Brit. Mus. MS Harley 645, f. 79ᵛ. The Memoranda Rolls (P.R.O.), L.T.R., 32 Henry III, for Michaelmas 1247, membrane 4ᵈ, record that Edmund de Walpole and Thomas, monks of St Edmunds, came before the barons of the Exchequer, armed with charters, to protest that the abbot of St Edmunds had the right to a mint and exchange. A specimen of the new coin struck at Bury is in the British Museum; see *Brit. Mus. Quarterly*, xxi (1957), no. 1, p. 18 and plate iii (12).

Exercitus Frederici a Parmensibus est deuictus, multis interfectis, ipso Frederico fugato, per uexillum cum forma gloriose uirginis Marie [1] quod Parmenses portabant. Acta sunt hec xii. Kal. Marcii. Henricus abbas sancti Edmundi obiit xiii. Kal. Iulii [a]; post cuius obitum magister Edmundus de Walepol electus est in abbatem Non. Iulii.[2] Hic non stetit in religione per biennium a suscepcione habitus ante diem electionis; qui accepit benedictionem ab Hugone Elyensi v. Kal. Octobris. Eodem anno Lodowicus rex Francie crucesignatus cum uxore sua exit a Francia post Pentecosten [3] uersus Terram Sanctam et ueniens Lugdunum a domino papa est absolutus[b]; benedictione percepta nauigando uenit Cyprum citra festum sancti Michaelis et ibidem hyemauit.

1249

Die Ascensionis Domini[4] rex Francie exiit a Cypro et in ebdomada Pentecosten nauigando uenit ante Damietam quam pene uacuam inueniens feria v. in eadem ebdomada [5] et eam cum omnibus que in ea inuenta sunt occupauit; ciues enim Damiete uersus Alexandriam tenderant credentes regem Francie illo uenire. Eodem anno xx. die Nouembris dictus rex cum suis arripuit iter a Damieta uersus Mossoram quo deuenerunt die martis ante Nathale Domini,[6] in quo itinere graues a Sarracenis tulerunt oppressiones, ibique castra metati sunt iuxta Mossoram iuxta fluuium qui [c] dicitur

[a] Iunii *M*   [b] est absolutus *om. A*   [c] que *MS, M*

[1] *per uexillum . . . uirginis*: possibly the chronicler used the same letter which Matthew Paris copied into *Liber Additamentorum*, p. 146.
[2] The royal assent to the election is dated 17 September; *CCR, 1247–51*, p. 87.
[3] 7 June   [4] 13 May

hurricane. The army of Frederick was defeated by the men of Parma with heavy loss, and Frederick himself put to flight, by reason of the banner bearing the figure of the glorious Virgin Mary [1] which the men of Parma carried. This happened on 18 February. Henry, abbot of Bury St Edmunds, died on 19 June. On 7 July Master Edmund de Walpole was elected abbot.[2] He had not been two years in religion from the day when he professed to the day of his election. He was blessed on 27 September by Hugh, bishop of Ely. After Pentecost [3] in the same year Louis, king of France, left France with his wife for the Holy Land as a crusader. When he reached Lyons he received absolution and blessing from the pope. He arrived in Cyprus by sea before Michaelmas and spent the winter there.

1249

On Ascension day [4] the king of France left Cyprus. In Whitweek he sailed to Damietta and arrived on the Thursday [5] to find it almost deserted, so he took possession of the town and all that was in it; the citizens of Damietta, indeed, had gone out in the direction of Alexandria, believing that the king of France would arrive there. On 20 November of the same year King Louis and his army left Damietta for Mansourah, which he reached on the Tuesday [6] before Christmas. On the journey they suffered badly from attacks by the Saracens. They pitched camp outside Mansourah by the river

---

[5] 27 May. Joinville, *Histoire de S. Louis*, p. 213 (and see *n.* 16), also gives 27 May, but most authorities including Nangis, *Vie de S. Louis*, p. 370, and Paris, *Liber Additamentorum*, p. 153, give 4 or 5 June.

[6] 21 December

Thaneos[1] in Egypto. Manserunt autem ibi facientes passagium ut transirent ad pugnandum contra Sarra-
f. 147 cenos, statuentes / machinas ad protegendum passagium quas Sarraceni combusserunt.

1250

Die carnipriuii[2] rex Francie, habito cum suis consilio, statuit transire fluuium quodam Sarraceno demonstrante eis propter mercedem bonum passagium. Sed Templarii, Robertus comes Attrabacensis,[3] dominus Willelmus Longespeie,[4] dominus R[adulfus] de Cusci[5] et alii plures, dictum fluuium transeuntes et non expectato domini regis exercitu usque *a* Mossoram incaute ulterius, ut dicitur de consilio comitis Attrabacensis, sparsi et sine balistariis procedentes a paganorum infinita multitudine superantur; ipso rege nullum eis succursum prebente, eo quod ipse undique ex paganorum multitudine circumdaretur. Illo igitur die et in illo congressu magna pars milicie Templi, comes Attrabacensis, Willelmus Longesp[eie], R[adulfus] de Cusci cum multis aliis Christianis occubuerunt. Mansit autem rex ibidem cum exercitu per totam Quadragesimam in magna infirmitate et inedia et frequenti paganorum inuasione. Igitur die martis post octauas Pasce[6] rex, uidens multa pericula sibi iminere, uersus Damietam reuertitur quod paganos per quosdam Christianos renegatos non latuit. Vnde factum

---

a + ad M

[1] The Aschmoun-Thenah or Thanis canal, Egypt
[2] 9 February, Ash Wednesday. The first battle of Mansourah was fought on Shrove Tuesday (*Burton*, p. 286; Paris, *Chron. Maj.*, v, pp. 147–69, and *Liber Additamentorum*, p. 192). Paris records that it began in the middle of the night. *Carniprivium* can also mean the first days of Lent, or Septuagesima Sunday, or Sexagesima Sunday.
[3] Robert I, count of Artois 1237–50

which is called Thanis [1] in Egypt. They stayed there to build a crossing to pass over and fight the Saracens, and erected engines-of-war to protect it, but the Saracens burnt them.

1250

On Ash Wednesday [2] the king of France, after he had consulted his followers, decided to cross the river. They had been shown a good way over by a Saracen for a bribe. But the Templars, Robert, count of Artois,[3] William Longespée,[4] Raoul de Coucy [5] and many others did not wait for the royal army. They crossed the river and incautiously advanced farther, as far as Mansourah, on the advice, it is said, of the count of Artois. They went forward in scattered formation without the crossbowmen, and were overcome by a great host of the heathen enemy; the king could offer no help because he was totally surrounded by innumerable Saracens. In the battle fought on this day most of the knights of the Temple, the count of Artois, William Longespée, Raoul de Coucy and many other Christians perished. The king himself remained there with his army for the whole of Lent. He suffered from great sickness and want and frequent attacks by the heathen. On Tuesday after the octave of Easter [6] the king, realising the many dangers which threatened him, returned towards Damietta. His movements, however, were not concealed from the infidels, thanks to some apostate Christians. And so it happened that on the

---

[4] Sir William de Longespée (1212?–50), called earl of Salisbury, eldest son of William Longespée, the 3rd earl

[5] Raoul II de Coucy (d. 1250), son of Raoul I de Coucy, killed at Acre in 1191

[6] 6 April

est quod pagani die mercurii sequente Christianos tam
audacter inuaserunt quod ipsum regem et fratres suos
et totum exercitum ceperunt et apud Mosoram incar-
cerauerunt. Vbi rex per mensem detinebatur, id est
usque ad diem Ascensionis Domini.[1] Die igitur
Ascencionis rex a carcere liberatur, tali conditione quod
redderet Damietam et liberaret captiuos. Insuper pro
redemptione sua dampnis et expensis c. libras stirling-
orum uel cccc. libras turon[enses] et ipsi Sarraceni omnes
captiuos redderent et sic date sunt treuge per decennium.
Rex uero recedens ac concredens hanc conuencionem
impleri quam Sarraceni tenere non curantes nam
captiuos non nisi pro parte reddiderunt. Willelmus
Wintoniensis episcopus obiit, Kal. Septembris sepultus
Tur' in ecclesia sancti Martini. Fredericus quondam
imperator obiit; Willelmus comes Holondie eligitur.[a]
Eodem anno die Nathalis Domini in aurora audita sunt
fulgura et tonitrua.

1251

f. 147ᵛ Dominus papa recessit a Lugduno in ebdomada Pasce
feria iiii.[2] Eodem anno uenit quidam seductor in
Gallias,[3] collecta secum pastorum multitudine, dicens se
esse Pastorem et a beata Dei genitrice missum et sibi
dictum per tales pastores scilicet Terram Sanctam posse
adquiri. Qui circuiens uniuersas pene Gallie ciuitates,
predicans et fallaciter crebro fingens miracula tandem
uenit Aurelianis cum suis; ubi per sedicionem inter eos
et clerum multi quidem ex clero, sed multo plures ex
pastoribus, Idus Iunii occisi sunt. Sequenti uero feria

---

a Fredericus . . . eligitur *after* tonitrua A

[1] 5 May   [2] 19 April

following Wednesday the heathen attacked the Christians so boldly that they captured the king, his brothers and the whole army and imprisoned them at Mansourah. The king was detained for a month, that is until Ascension day.[1] On Ascension day the king was freed from prison on condition that he handed over Damietta and freed the captives. He was, moreover, to pay a ransom of £100,000 sterling or 400,000 livres tournois for damages and costs. The Saracens were to return all prisoners. Thus a truce was concluded for ten years. The king departed, thinking that the Saracens would observe this agreement. But they did not trouble to do so and returned only some of the captives. William, bishop of Winchester, died and was buried on 1 September in the church of St Martin at Tours. Frederick, the former emperor, died. William, count of Holland, was elected emperor. In the same year at dawn on Christmas day there was lightning, and thunder was heard.

1251

The pope left Lyons on Wednesday in Easter week.[2] In this year an impostor arrived in France.[3] He was accompanied by a great crowd of shepherds whom he had collected together. He claimed to be the Good Shepherd and said that he had been sent by the blessed mother of God, who had told him that the Holy Land could be won by such shepherds. He visited nearly all the cities of France, preaching and often pretending to perform miracles. He came at length to Orleans with his followers. There on 13 June, during a clash between

---

[3] Roger, ' the master of Hungary '; Nangis, *Vie de S. Louis*, pp. 382–3, and *Hist. Paris.*, p. 605

vi.[1] ipse magister pastorum occiditur, reliquis omnibus dispersis. Eodem anno die Nathalis Domini Alexander rex Scocie accinctus est militaribus apud Eboracum a rege Anglie Henrico et in crastino duxit in uxorem Margaretam filiam eiusdem regis Anglie.

1252

Hoc anno immoderatus calor estiuus plures extinxit; horrida eciam tonitrua in crastino Assumpcionis beate Virginis sunt audita.[2] Bellum [3] gestum est inter Alemannos et Flandrenses in quo multa milia Flandrensium ceciderunt. Eodem anno dedicata est noua ecclesia Elyensis xv. Kal. Octobris. Ricardus prior sancti Edmundi obiit x. Kal. Nouembris. Successit Symon de Lutone prior. Iste Symon prior fuit primus qui per scrutinii electionem, abbate Edmundo et duobus monachis uno per abbatem altero per conuentum electis et una cum abbate uota singulorum audientibus, in priorem ecclesie sancti Edmundi electus fuit.[4]

1253

Henricus rex cepit auxilium, scilicet xl. solidos de quolibet feodo militari, ad suum filium primogenitum militem faciendum. Eodem anno idem rex H[enricus], cupiens promouere filium suum secundo genitum, scilicet Edmundum, procurauit a domino papa per quin-

---

[1] 16 June. The date of Roger's death does not appear to be mentioned by the other authorities. Paris, *Chron. Maj.*, v, p. 249, says that the ' Pastoureux ' reached Orleans on 11 June.

[2] 16 August

[3] This seems to refer to the battle of Walcheren, which was fought on 4 July 1253, not in 1252.

[4] Election by scrutiny (i.e. the formal taking of individual votes) was one of the ways of election decreed by the Fourth Lateran Council, 1215 (cap. 24). Under 1287 below, p. 89, the chronicle notices the election

them and the clergy, many of the clergy, but even more of the shepherds, were killed. On the following Friday [1] the master of the shepherds himself was killed and the remainder of his followers dispersed. In this year on Christmas day Alexander, king of Scotland, was knighted at York by King Henry of England and on the next day he married Margaret, the king of England's daughter.

1252

In this year an exceptionally hot summer killed many people, and alarming thunder was heard on the day after the Assumption of the Blessed Virgin.[2]   A battle [3] was fought between the Germans and the Flemings in which many thousands of the men of Flanders fell. In the same year the new church of Ely was dedicated on 17 September. Richard, prior of Bury St Edmunds, died on 23 October and was succeeded by Simon de Luton. This prior, Simon, was the first to be elected prior of St Edmund's church by the method of scrutiny; it was done by the Abbot Edmund and two monks (one chosen by the abbot and the other by the convent), who together with the abbot took the vote orally of each monk.[4]

1253

King Henry took an aid, that is of 40s. from each knight's fee, for knighting his eldest son. In the same year King Henry, wishing to promote the interests of his second son Edmund, obtained from the pope a tenth

---

of William de Rockland as prior by scrutiny. The appointment of important conventual officials in Benedictine monasteries belonged to the abbot, but at the end of the twelfth century many convents disputed the abbot's control (Knowles, *Monastic Order in England*, pp. 414–15); it looks as if St Edmund's convent gained some control over the prior's appointment.

quennium¹ decimam omnium prouentuum, tam de
uiris religiosis quam ecclesiasticis, quasi in subsidium
Terre Sancte; et hoc factum est ut posset facere filium
suum Edmundum regem Cicilie et Apulie. Eodem
anno H[enricus] rex concessit Anglicis libertatem, tam
per cartas de foresta quam de aliis libertatibus olim
f. 148 concessam, in contradicentes ᵃ / eisdem libertatibus
uinculum excommunicacionis procurando. Eodem
anno idem rex viii. Idus Augusti intrauit mare apud
Portesmu ut transfretaret in Gasconiam ad domandos
rebelles in ea, quod et fecit. ᵇ Robertus episcopus
Lincolniensis obiit Non. Octobris. Mare proprium
litus egressum plura loca maritima submersit. Alienor
regina peperit filiam que dicta est Katerina. Henricus,
filius Frederici imperatoris, nepos regis Anglie, obiit.

1254

Conradus, filius Frederici imperatoris, obiit die Ascen-
cionis.² Hugo Elyensis episcopus migrat a seculo viii.
Idus Augusti; magister Willelmus de Kilkenni domini
regis cancellarius electus est in episcopum. Lodowicus
rex Francie rediit de Terra Sancta et in festo beate
Marie uirginis, scilicet Natiuitate, ᶜ³ uenit Parisius.
Edwardus, filius regis Anglie, accinctus est militaribus
in Hyspania a rege Castelle die Translacionis sancti
Edwardi ⁴ et non multo post duxit sororem ⁵ eiusdem
regis in uxorem.

Henricus rex et regina cum multis Anglie proceribus

ᵃ contradicentibus *MS, M*
ᵇ + eodem aut' *A*
ᶜ scilicet *om. and* Natiu' *above after* festo *A*

¹ Innocent IV extended the period of the tenth from three to five years
on 23 May 1254, not in 1253; *Foedera*, i, pt i, p. 303.
² 21 May

for five years [1] of all the revenues of both the monks and the secular clergy, nominally to help the Holy Land. This was done so that he could make his son Edmund king of Sicily and Apulia. In this year the same king granted to the English the liberties which had previously been conceded to them both in the charters of the forest and in the charters of other liberties. He obtained sentence of excommunication on those who disputed these liberties. In the same year the king sailed from Portsmouth on 6 August for Gascony to defeat the rebels there, which he succeeded in doing. Robert, bishop of Lincoln, died on 7 October. The sea flooded its shores and submerged many coastal districts. Queen Eleanor gave birth to a daughter, who was named Katherine. Henry, son of the Emperor Frederick and nephew of the king of England, died.

1254

Conrad, son of the Emperor Frederick, died on Ascension day.[2] Hugh, bishop of Ely, died on 6 August and Master William de Kilkenny, the king's chancellor, was elected bishop. King Louis of France returned from the Holy Land and reached Paris on the feast of the Nativity of the Blessed Virgin Mary.[3] Edward, the king of England's son, was knighted in Spain by the king of Castile on the feast of the Translation of St Edward.[4] Soon afterwards he married the king of Castile's sister.[5]

King Henry and the queen and many English

---

[3] 8 September
[4] 13 October
[5] Eleanor of Castile (d. 1290), daughter of Ferdinand III, king of Castile 1217–52, and sister of Alfonso X, king of Castile 1252–84

recesserunt a Gascon' mense Nouembris, illis ad pacem
dispositis. Qui postquam uisitauit regem Francie
Parisius et reginam, a quibus honorifice suscipiebantur,
perrexit apud Pontiniacum gratia uisitandi sanctum
Edmundum confessorem,[1] a quo discendens uenit
Boloniam ibique Nathale Domini celebrauit. Innocencius papa obiit; successit Alexander IIII. Henricus
rex Angliam rediens nocte sancti Iohannis apostoli [2]
mare intrauit.

1255

Petrus episcopus Herefordensis, procurante rege
H[enrico] et, ut dicebatur, aliquibus prelatis consencientibus, falso et prodiciose fingens se procuratorem [a] tocius
cleri Anglie in curia Romana obligauit pene [b] omnes
domos religionis Anglie, exemptas et non exemptas,
mercatoribus tam Senensibus quam Florentinis, minores
ad c. uel ad cc. marcas, maiores ad iii.c. uel cccc., non
nullas ad quingentas, ecclesiam uero beati Edmundi
regis et martiris ad dcc.[3] obligauit, et tamquam uerus
procurator publica instrumenta confecit; sed et assensum
prebuit per omnia summi pontificis auctoritas, utinam
circumuenta. Et hec tota pecunia collecta fuit ad
expugnandum Manfredum filium Frederici imperatoris
f. 148ᵛ / de terra Apulie et Sicilie quam dominus papa contulit
Edmundo filio regis Anglie quam numquam consecutus
est.[4] Hic attonsus fui. [c]

---

[a] procurante rege . . . curia Romana *marked* uacat *in margin in pencil.
From here until 1296 the MS has many passages marked* uacat *in pencil: it looks
as if the MS was being prepared for a scribe to copy.*
[b] *Corr. from* penes *MS*
[c] hic attonsus fui *MS²*, *in text M*

[1] Edmund Rich, archbishop of Canterbury 1234–40, canonised 1247.
Buried at Pontigny.

nobles left Gascony in November after they had pacified the inhabitants. Afterwards they visited the king and queen of France in Paris, who received them honourably, and went on to Pontigny to visit the shrine of St Edmund the Confessor.[1] From there the king went to Boulogne, where he celebrated Christmas. Pope Innocent died and was succeeded by Alexander IV. King Henry set sail for home on the night of the feast of St John the Apostle.[2]

1255

Peter, bishop of Hereford, at the instance of King Henry and, it was said, with the approval of some other prelates, falsely and traitorously claimed to be the procurator of the English clergy at the Roman court. He made nearly all the religious houses of England, both exempt and non-exempt, liable for certain debts to Sienese and Florentine merchants. He made the small religious houses liable for 100 or 200 marks, the larger for 300 or 400 marks and some for 500 marks, while the church of the blessed Edmund, king and martyr, was made liable for 700 marks.[3] He executed official documents just like a true procurator, and what is more, the Holy Father himself confirmed everything by his authority—would that one could say he had been mis-led. All this money was collected to drive Manfred, son of the Emperor Frederick, from the land of Apulia and Sicily, which the pope had given to the king of England's son Edmund and of which he never gained possession.[4] I was tonsured at this time.

---

[2] 27 December   [3] *CPR, 1247–58*, p. 516
[4] Urban IV finally revoked the grant of Sicily to Edmund in 1263; Potthast, II, no. 18603. Possibly the entry was written after that date.

1256

Willelmus comes Holandie occiditur mense Februarii. Willelmus episcopus Elyensis *a* obiit. Die sanctorum Innocencium apud Westmonasterium fulgura et tonitrua horribilia sunt audita. Edmundus abbas sancti Edmundi diem clausit extremum ii. Kal. Ianuarii.

1257

Ricardus comes Cornubie frater regis Anglie eligitur in regem Alemannie mense Ianuarii. Qui, ueniens per sanctum Edmundum apud Gernemu die Translacionis eiusdem [1] mare intrans, die apostolorum Philippi et Iacobi [2] in Alemanniam applicuit et in die Ascensionis [3] ab archiepiscopo Colonie in regem coronatur.[4] Eodem anno Symon prior sancti Edmundi electus est in abbatem eiusdem monasterii xix. Kal. Februarii, pro cuius confirmationem directi sunt nuncii [5] ad sedem apostolicam; sed eis infecto negocio redeuntibus, eo quod statutum fuit de nouo omnes exemptos ad curiam Romanam in propria persona uenire,[6] idem electus iter arripuit uersus dictam curiam iii. Kal. Augusti. Qui consecutus est munus benedictionis ab Alexandro papa apud Viterbium xi. Kal. Nouembris. Et memorandum quod *a* dictus Symon abbas sancti Edmundi fuit primus qui curiam Romanam adiuit pro confirmatione et benedictione sua ex omnibus abbatibus Anglie exemptis, curia in duobus

---

a de Ely *A*

[1] 29 April   [2] 1 May   [3] 17 May
[4] *apud Gernemu . . . coronatur*: possibly the chronicler used the letter which Matthew Paris copied into the *Liber Additamentorum*, p. 366.
[5] The messengers were Alexander de Brewrth, a servant, and Richard de Frostenden, a clerk; Arnold, II, p. 257.
[6] The Fourth Lateran Council decreed (cap. 26) that pastors should come to Rome for confirmation; in practice most obtained dispensations

1256

William, count of Holland, was killed in February.
William, bishop of Ely, died.   On the day of the Holy
Innocents there was terrible lightning, and thunder
was heard at Westminster.   Edmund, abbot of Bury
St Edmunds, died on 31 December.

1257

Richard, earl of Cornwall, the king of England's
brother, was elected king of Germany in January.   He
travelled to Yarmouth via Bury St Edmunds and set
sail on the day of the Translation of St Edmund.[1]   He
landed in Germany on the feast of SS. Philip and James [2]
and was crowned king on Ascension day [3] by the archbishop of Cologne.[4]   Simon, prior of Bury St Edmunds,
was elected abbot of this monastery on 14 January and
messengers [5] were sent to the Holy See to obtain his
confirmation.   But they were unsuccessful and returned
because it was newly enacted that the abbots of all
exempt houses should go to the Roman court in person.[6]
So on 30 July Simon set out for Rome and was blessed
by Pope Alexander at Viterbo on 22 October.   It should
be remembered that this Simon, abbot of Bury St
Edmunds, was the first abbot from any of the exempt
abbeys of England to go to the Roman court for confirmation and blessing, and that this visit to the curia

---

(F. Tenckhoff, *Papst Alexander IV* (Paderborn 1902), p. 267).   On 3 August
1257 Alexander revoked all such indulgences; Potthast, II, no. 16958.

milibus *a* sterlingorum *b* uisitata.[1] Eodem anno rex duxit exercitum in Walliam. Eodem anno Fratres Minores intrauerunt clamdestine burgum sancti Edmundi x. Kal. Iulii et in domo Rogeri de Herdeber' militis, a latere porte aquilonis contra orientem, missas, clam conuentu sed in audiencia omnium confluencium, alta uoce celebrarunt. Symone, priore et tunc electo, cum subpriore et sacrista et multis aliis proelecti ad dominum regem representacione euntibus, sed nichilominus eodem die oratorium eorum cum omnibus domibus in curia illa existentibus, dicto milite cum fratribus predictis iam prandere incipientibus, solo tenus prostrata sunt. Walterus episcopus Norwicensis obiit; successit magister Symon de Wauton'. Hoc anno /

f. 149 immoderata sepe extitit pluuia sed et tanta inundacio erupit Idus Iulii ut domos, muros et arbores prosterneret et fena, impetu aquarum sullata, pontes innumerabiles fregerunt.

1258

Penuria omnium bonorum sequitur precedentis anni inundacionem; nam quartarium frumenti, quod raro inueniebatur, ad xv. solidos et eciam usque xx. solidos uendebatur. Vnde tanta fames orta est ut pauperes carnem equinam, cortices arborum, uel quod deterius est, comederent; innumerabiles fame defecerunt. Eodem anno omnia farris genera copiose terris data per pluuiam autu[m]pnalem pene sunt perdita et ultra festum Omnium Sanctorum blada in pluribus locis in

---

a + marcarum *A*   *b* On erasure *MS*

[1] 'Visitata' as used here is related to the term 'uisitatio,' which in the thirteenth century signified money paid for papal confirmation of elections; towards the end of the century it was replaced by the term 'service tax';

cost £2,000 sterling.[1]   In this year the king led an
army into Wales.   On 22 June the Friars Minor entered
the town of Bury St Edmunds by stealth.   They cele-
drated mass in an audible voice in the house of Roger
de Harbridge, knight, on the east side of the north gate,
in the presence of all comers but unknown to the
convent.   Simon, the prior and at this time the abbot-
elect, together with the subprior, the sacrist and many
others representing the point of view of the abbot-elect,
went to the king.   But nevertheless, on the same day,
when the above-mentioned knight and the friars had
just begun their dinner, the friars' oratory and all the
buildings belonging to that house were razed to the
ground.   Walter, bishop of Norwich, died and was
succeeded by Simon de Walton.   In this year there was
much heavy rain and on 15 July such a flood that
houses, walls and trees were washed away, and hay
swept down by the force of the water broke many
bridges.

1258

There was a great shortage of everything because of the
floods of the previous year, and corn, which was very
scarce, cost from 15s. to as much as 20s. a quarter.
Famine resulted so that the poor had to eat horsemeat,
the bark of trees and even more unpleasant things.
Many died of hunger.   In the same year all kinds of
grain grew abundantly in the fields but were ruined by
the autumn rains.   In many places the corn remained

W. E. Lunt, *Financial Relations of the Papacy with England to 1327* (1939),
pp. 463–4, and Lunt, *Papal Revenues in the Middle Ages* (1934), II, p. 238.

campis iacebant; plurimi eciam diebus dominicis et aliis diebus festis que sereniores habebantur blada sua in horrea ducebant. Hiis diebus regina Anglie et eciam *a* fratres regis Pictauenses at parentes regine Sauuerenses unusquisque ubi dominabantur tyrannides regias intollerabiliter exercentes, proceres regni contra eos exacuerunt. Vnde post Pasca,[1] conuenientibus cunctis proceribus Anglie apud Oxoneford, promulgata sunt statuta quedam ut dicebatur ad exaltacionem ecclesiastice libertatis et regie corone et eciam ad utilitatem totius regni Anglie, presente domino rege et eius filio primogenito Edwardo, qui dictis statutis sigilli regii et sacramenti auctoritate assensum prebuerunt, licet inuiti. Proceres eciam *b* regni sacramento et obligacione inter se condixerunt quod pro dictorum statutorum obseruacione, *c* si necesse foret, morti se exponerent et in eos qui ea nollent obseruare cursuros. Vnde ad dictum parlamentum [2] Audomarus electus Wintoniensis, Willelmus de Valence et ceteri fratres regis Pictauenses et Sauueienses a regno Anglie expulsi sunt; quibus expulsis paulatim *d* predicte tortuose exactiones cessare ceperunt. Robertus dictus Russel electus est in priorem sancti Edmundi. Eodem anno Fratres Minores intrusi sunt potestate regia et ui armata per Gillebertum de Preston', iusticiarium domini regis,[3]

a et eciam regina Anglie *after* Sauuerenses *A*
b enim *A*
c inter se . . . obseruacione *om. M*
d Del. *and written below after* exactiones *A*

[1] 24 March
[2] The chronicler has conflated three events: the barons demanded the expulsion of the aliens at the London parliament in April 1258; the aliens fled from the Oxford parliament in June; they were besieged in Winchester castle in July and exiled.
[3] See above, p. 22, under 1257. On 22 April 1258 King Henry appointed Gilbert de Preston his attorney to receive seisin of land in

in the fields after the feast of All Saints. Many brought
their corn into the barns even on Sundays and feast days
if the weather was fine. At this time the great men of
the land were exasperated with the queen, and also with
the king's Poitevin brothers and the queen's Savoyard
kinsmen, because wherever they held sway they behaved
unbearably, like tyrants. The magnates, therefore, met
at Oxford after Easter [1] and made public certain provisions ostensibly to preserve the dignity of the Church
and Crown and the well-being of the whole kingdom.
The king and his eldest son Edward were present and
reluctantly approved the provisions and gave them
authority by oath and royal seal. The magnates bound
themselves to each other under solemn oath to risk
death if necessary in defence of the provisions and to
hunt down those who would not observe them. At this
parliament [2] Aymer, the bishop-elect of Winchester,
William de Valence and the rest of the king's Poitevin
and Savoyard relatives were exiled from the realm of
England. Soon after their expulsion the above-
mentioned despotic oppressions and demands began to
stop. Robert, surnamed Russel, was elected prior of
Bury St Edmunds. On 25 April of this year the Friars
Minor made a forcible entry into the town of Bury
St Edmunds with royal authority and armed force, led
by Gilbert de Preston, justice of the King's Bench. [3]

St Edmund's and to assign it to the Friars Minor; *CPR, 1247–58*, p. 623.
The story of the dispute between St Edmund's abbey and the Friars
Minor, 1257–63, is told by A. G. Little, *Studies in English Franciscan History*
(1917), pp. 96–8. Paris, *Chron. Maj.*, v, p. 688, writes under 1258 that
the Friars Minor at Bury ' introducti sunt et instituti uiolenter per laicorum
manum, uidelicet comitis Glouerniae, quem constat esse dictorum abbatis
et conuentus aduersarium, et Gileberti de Prestone.'

in burgo sancti Edmundi contra iura et priuilegia eiusdem loci septem Kal. Maii. Eclipsis lune facta est / f. 149ᵛ totalis xiiii. Kal. Iunii. Eodem anno nocte sancti Andree [1] uentus magnus prostrauit domos, arbores et turres plurimas. Quo tempore fuit rex apud sanctum Edmundum. Scutagium xl. solidorum Anglis est impositum propter exercitum in Walliam. Et sciendum quod post coronacionem Henrici regis, filii regis Iohannis, undecies positum est scutagium subscriptis temporibus:

SCUTAGIUM

In recessu Lodowici	ii. mar'	anno secundo.
Biham	x. sol'	anno v.
Mungomeri	ii. mar'	anno vii.[a]
Bedeford'	ii. mar'	anno viii.
Kerri	ii. mar'	anno xiii.
Britannia	xl. sol'	anno xiiii.
Pictauia	xl. sol'	anno xv.
Elweyn	xx. sol'	anno xvi.
Gasconia	xl. sol'	anno xxvi.[b]
Gannoc	xl. sol'	anno xxix.
Wallia	xl. sol'	anno xlii.

1259

Rex Ricardus Alemannie rediit in Angliam circa Purificacionem. Eodem anno Fulco Londoniensis episcopus obiit xii. Kal. Iunii. Concordia facta est inter Ricardum de Clare comitem Glouernie et conuentum sancti Edmundi de placito terre Mide[n]hale et Ikeligham,[3] quod durauit ix. annis et v. diebus, in crastino sancti Leonardi.[2] Eodem anno H[enricus] rex transfretauit

---

[a] viii. *MS, A, M* [b] xxii. *MS, A, M*

[1] 30 November [2] i.e. 8 November
[3] For the fine see *Cal. Ancient Deeds*, v, p. 509, no. 13425. For the suit

This was a violation of the rights and privileges of the Liberty of Bury St Edmunds. On 19 May there was a total eclipse of the moon. In the same year on the night of the feast of St Andrew [1] a gale blew down many houses, trees and towers. The king was staying at Bury St Edmunds at the time. A scutage of 40s. was imposed on the English on account of the Welsh campaign. It is worth noting that since the coronation of King Henry, son of King John, a scutage was imposed eleven times in the following years:

SCUTAGE

On the retreat of Louis	2 mks	In the second year
Bytham	10s.	In the fifth year
Montgomery	2 mks	In the seventh year
Bedford	2 mks	In the eighth year
Kerry	2 mks	In the thirteenth year
Brittany	40s.	In the fourteenth year
Poitou	40s.	In the fifteenth year
Elfael	20s.	In the sixteenth year
Gascony	40s.	In the twenty-sixth year
Gannoc	40s.	In the twenty-ninth year
Wales	40s.	In the forty-second year

1259

King Richard of Germany returned to England about Candlemas. In the same year on 20 May Fulk, bishop of London, died. On the morrow of the feast of St Leonard,[2] Richard de Clare, earl of Gloucester, and the convent of Bury St Edmunds reached an agreement in the suit, which had lasted for nine years and five days, relating to lands in Mildenhall and Icklingham.[3] In

---

between the abbot of St Edmund's and the earl of Gloucester see Arnold, II, pp. xxxi, 295; Paris, *Chron. Maj.*, v, p. 297, and *Hist. Angl.*, III, p. 119.

circa festum sancti Martini et Nathale Domini Parisius celebrauit. Quo tempore [reddidit] *a* regi Francie Normanniam, Pictauiam et Andegauiam et fere omnes *b* terras transmarinas preter Aquitanniam. *c* Eodem eciam tempore rex Anglie mutauit sigillum suum pro gladio sceptrum. Vnde quidam sic:

> Est m.c. bis l.ix. utinam concordia felix;
> Andegauis, Pictauis, Neustria gente relicta
> Anglorum, cedunt tibi, France, sigilla mutantur,
> Nomina tolluntur, fugit ensis, sceptra geruntur.[1]

1260

Lodowycus primogenitus regis Francie obiit. Rex Anglie rediit in Angliam. Discorda orta est inter regem et magnates propter statuta Oxonie minime obseruata. f. 150 Symon de Munford bar/onum extitit. Isto anno partita sunt debita abbatis et conuentus sancti Edmundi circa Purificacionem beate Marie,[2] scilicet v. millia marcarum. Ita utrim *d* cedebant ii. millia marcarum quingente. *e*

1261

Eclipsis solis facta est Kal. Aprilis in fine quarti mensis Arabum,[3] feria vi. hora diei iii. Alexander papa obiit octauis Kal. Iunii,*f* uacauitque sedes mensibus tribus

---

a reddidit *supplied from A*; *om. MS, M*
b *Om. M*; + alias *A*
c + concessit *in margin with tie-marks* P²; + resignauit *Oxenedes*; + carta sua confirmauit *Cotton*
d + que *A*
e *Lacuna of 3 lines A, MS (4 M)*
f Iu *and a final minim illegible* A; Iulii *Arundel 6*

[1] The reference is to King Henry's third seal; W. de G. Birch, *Cat. of Seals in the Dept. of MSS in the British Museum* (1887–1900), I, p. 18. The verses are quoted by Birch.
[2] Division of debts between the abbot and convent (another example

the same year King Henry sailed across the Channel
about Martinmas and kept Christmas in Paris.   At this
time he returned to the king of France, Normandy,
Poitou, Anjou and nearly all his continental territory
except Aquitaine.   At the same time the king of England
changed his seal, replacing the sword by a sceptre.   On
this subject someone said:

> Would that the treaty of 1259 had been a favourable one.
> But Anjou, Poitou, Normandy and the English left behind
> Are ceded, France, to you.   The seals are changed,
> The names removed, the sceptre replaces the sword.[1]

1260

Louis, the eldest son of the king of France, died.   The
king of England returned to England.   A quarrel broke
out between the king and the magnates because the
Provisions of Oxford had been very little observed.
Simon de Montfort emerged as the leader of the
baronage.   In this year about Candlemas [2] the debts
of the abbot and convent of Bury St Edmunds, which
amounted to 5,000 marks, were divided so that 2,500
marks fell to the lot of each.

1261

There was an eclipse of the sun on Friday, 1 April at
the end of the fourth month of the Hegira,[3] in the third
hour of the day.   Pope Alexander died on 25 May.
The Holy See remained vacant for three months because

---

occurs below, pp. 31–2, under 1265) was a result of the division of the property
of St Edmund's monastery between abbot and convent; for this division,
dating at least from the early twelfth century, see above, p. xii.

   [3] i.e. Rabia II of the Hegira

propter discidium cardinalium. Tandem elegerunt
magistrum Iacobum de Trecis, patriarcham Ierosolem
iiii. Kal. Septembris et dictus _a_ est Vrbanus IIII. Senchia
regina Alemannie obiit._b_ Vrbanus papa canonizauit
beatum Ricardum Cicestrensem episcopum et constituit
sollempnizari diem depositionis eius iii. Non. Aprilis.

1262

Henricus rex transfretauit in Gallias xiiii. Kal. Augusti [1]
et ueniens Parisius post non multum tempus infirmabatur
cum tota fere familia sua, ubi plures eciam magnates
mortui sunt, reliqui uero mortem uix euaserunt. Inde
rediens per Campaniam in Flandriam transfretauit in
Angliam _c_ in uigilia sancti Thome apostoli [2] et apud
Cantuariam Natale Domini celebrauit. Ricardus de
Clare comes Glouernie obiit xi. Kal. Augusti.[3] Henricus
episcopus Londoniensis obiit xi. Kal. Augusti, post quem
Ricardus Talebot eligitur, qui statim post confirma-
cionem suam obiit; cui successit Henricus de Sanwich.
Iohanna uxor Henrici de Hasting' peperit Iohannem
filium suum apud Aleste die sancti Iohannis ante
Portam Latinam. _d_ [4]

1263

Ignis succensus in furore cameram regis minorem aulam
capellam et alias domos consumpsit apud Westmonasterium vii. Idus Februarii. Orta est dissencio inter

---

_a_ et dictus] dictusque _A_   _b_ + eodem anno _A_   _c_ in Angliam _om. A_
_d_ Iohanna uxor . . . Latinam _MS²_; _in hand of text M, P_; _om. A_

[1] Henry reached France before 19 July; letters close were dated at
Boulogne on 16 July; _CCR, 1261–4_, p. 140.
[2] 20 December
[3] This date, 22 July, is wrong; it is the date given below for the bishop
of London's death. Richard de Clare died on 15 July; G.E.C., _Complete
Peerage_, v, p. 700. cf. a similar error below, p. 71, _n._ 2.

the cardinals could not agree. At last on 29 August they elected Master James of Troyes, patriarch of Jerusalem, and he took the name Urban IV. Sanchia, queen of Germany, died. Pope Urban canonised the blessed Richard, bishop of Chichester, and ordered the feast of his deposition to be celebrated on 3 April.

1262

King Henry sailed to France on 19 July.[1] He reached Paris, where soon he and nearly all his household fell ill; many nobles perished and the others only just escaped with their lives. The king then returned through Compiègne to Flanders and set sail for England on the vigil of the feast of St Thomas the Apostle.[2] He kept Christmas at Canterbury. Richard de Clare, earl of Gloucester, died on 22 July.[3] Henry, bishop of London, died on 22 July. Richard Talbot was elected his successor but died directly after his confirmation and was succeeded by Henry de Sandwich. Joanna, the wife of Henry de Hastings, gave birth to her son John at Allesley on the feast of St John before the Latin Gate.[4]

1263

A terrible fire raged in the king's chamber, the lesser hall, the chapel and other buildings at Westminster on 7 February. The king and the barons quarrelled because the king, advised by the queen and others,

---

[4] 6 May. An inquisition 'post mortem' confirms that this was the birthday of John de Hastings, 1st baron Hastings 1290–1312/13; *Cal. Inq. Post Mortem, Henry III*, v, p. 229, no. 719. The Hastings were hereditary stewards of St Edmund's Liberty from the twelfth century to 1389; L. J. Redstone, ' The Liberty of St Edmund,' in *Proceedings of the Suffolk Institute of Archaeology and Natural History*, xv (1915), pp. 207–9.

regem et barones, eo quod rex, consilio regine et quorundam aliorum et maxime alienigenarum, absolui impetrauit a domino papa ab obseruacione statutorum Oxonie et a sacramento. Vnde missis predonibus a baronibus per uniuersam Angliam, omnia bona regine et consiliariorum *a* regis, quorum instinctu dictam f. 150ᵛ absolucionem impetrauit, nullo habito respectu / ordinis aut dignitatis, depredabant. Nam episcopum Herefordensem,[1] ab ecclesia abstractum, incarcerabant. Episcopus Norwicensis,*b*[2] nisi ad sancti Edmundi libertatis cicius confugisset presidium, nusquam tutum sibi inuenisset auxilium, *c* tunc enim in conspectu baronum ualde preciosa fuit libertas sancti Edmundi. Romanorum eciam bona ubicumque inuenta, ipsis ab Anglia expulsis, diripiebant et ecclesias eorum uel conferebant uel cui uolebant tradebant, et similiter de alienigenis faciebant.

Vigilia sancti Edmundi [3] Fratres Minores locum quem infra uillam eiusdem sancti per intrusionem domini regis et contra libertatem dicte ecclesie per v. annos, mensibus vi., diebus xxiiii. [sic] occupabant, relinquentes disposicioni abbatis et conuentus eiusdem loci absolute se subdiderunt; sed ad hoc faciendum inducti erant quadam litera papali,[4] a conuentu sancti Edmundi impetrata, que eos in uirtute obediencie a dicto loco recedere precipiebat. Vnde ne ui expellerentur, sponte decesserunt palam omni populo contestantes se iniuste

---

a consiliorum MS, M, A; *corr. to* consiliariorum *A*²; consiliariorum *Arundel 6, Oxenedes and Cotton*
b Episcopum Norwicensem MS, A, M, P; Episcopus Norwicensis *Oxenedes and Cotton*
c asilum A

[1] Peter d'Aigueblanche, bishop of Hereford 1240–68
[2] Simon de Walton, bishop of Norwich 1257–65/6.   cf. Wykes, p. 135.

principally aliens, obtained absolution from the pope from his oath and obligation to observe the Provisions of Oxford. So the barons sent out men to plunder England. Without regard for rank or dignity they despoiled the property of the queen and of the counsellors who had advised the king to obtain absolution. They even dragged the bishop of Hereford[1] from his church and incarcerated him. The bishop of Norwich [2] would have found no safe asylum had he not hastily fled to the security of St Edmund's Liberty; for at this time the Liberty of St Edmund was exceedingly precious in the eyes of the barons. They seized the property, wherever it was to be found, of the Roman clergy who had been driven from England, and conferred or gave their churches to whomsoever they chose. They treated aliens in the same way.

On the vigil of the feast of St Edmund [3] the Friars Minor gave up the place within the town of this same saint which they had obtained by the king's order and in violation of the liberties of St Edmund's church. They had lived there for five years, six months and twenty-four days. The friars submitted themselves absolutely to the will of the abbot and convent of Bury St Edmunds. They were induced to do this by a papal letter [4] which the convent had obtained, ordering them in virtue of their obedience to leave the said place. They left, therefore, voluntarily to avoid being expelled by force, and made a public declaration before all the people

---

[3] 19 November
[4] Calendared by Bliss, I, p. 391; dated 28 May 1263. For other documents and a narrative about the expulsion of the Friars Minor from Bury see Arnold, II, pp. 271–85.

locum predictum possedisse. Ex mutuo assensu Henrici
regis Anglie et baronum dictorum provisionum
[carta(?)] Oxonie posita est super arbitrium regis
Francie.

1264

Edwardus primogenitus regis Anglie statim post Nathale,
ante regis Francie sententie [a] promulgacionem, multo
adunato exercitu depredacionibus et combustionibus
operam dedit multis potentibus qui prius parti baronum
fauebant sibi copulatis. Rex Francie regem Anglie a
predictorum prouisionum Oxonie obseruacione abso-
lutum sentencialiter decreuit. Guerra statim secuta est
per totam Angliam, regalibus in barones, baronibus in
regales miserabiliter seuientibus. [b] Rex Anglie cum rege
Alemannie, fratre suo, et Edwardo, primogenito suo,
Norhamtonam multo milite munitam cepit sabbato ante
Passionem Domini.[1] Barones cum Londoniensibus
milites arcem Rouecestrie munientes et sibi ad prelian-
dum obuiantes turrim reintrare compulerunt, pluribus
ex suis interemptis. [c] Barones cum Londoniensibus
Iudaismum London' spoliauerunt, multis Iudeis inter-
f. 151 fectis. Post multas / et flebiles molestias hinc inde
illatas apud Lewes dicti duo reges cum baronibus bellum
satis durum commiserunt ii. Idus. Maii, [d] ubi barones
uictoriam optinuerunt. Regem Anglie licet ceperunt,
tamen non quasi captum sed curialiter tanquam
dominum custodierunt. Regem Alemannie captiuum

---

[a] sentem *MS, M, P (and Cotton)*; sentē *A*
[b] + Edwardus apud Glouerniam cum se comprehendi comperit ubi
dimicandum foret prudenter obside dato pacem promisit sed obside ob
curialitem sibi remisso quod prius ceperat exequebatur *A*
[c] barones . . . interemptis *after* interfectis *A*
[d] bellum de Lewes *in margin MS²*; *rubric in text after* victoriam *P*

that they had occupied the place unlawfully. The Provisions of Oxford were submitted to the arbitration of the king of France with the mutual consent of Henry, king of England, and the barons.

1264

Edward, the king of England's eldest son, did not wait for the award of the king of France. After Christmas he collected a large army and devoted himself to plunder and arson, joined by many important men who had before been on the barons' side. The king of France formally pronounced that the king of England was completely free from any obligation to observe the Provisions of Oxford. War immediately broke out all over England; the king's men raged bitterly against the barons and the barons against them. On the Saturday before Passion Sunday [1] the king of England with his brother, the king of Germany, and his eldest son Edward, captured Northampton, which was strongly defended by knights. The barons, with the Londoners, met the knights who were defending Rochester castle in battle, and forced them to take refuge in the tower after many of the barons had been killed. The barons, with the Londoners, ransacked the London Jewry and killed a number of Jews. After many regrettable incidents had happened in various places, the above-mentioned kings met the barons in a fierce battle at Lewes on 14 May. The barons were victorious. They captured the king of England. They did not, however, guard him like an ordinary prisoner, but treated him courteously as their lord. They also took the king of Germany captive.

---

[1] 5 April

duxerunt. Edwardus pro suorum liberacione obsidem se dedit. Omnes dictas prouisiones Oxonie se fore obseruaturos iurauerunt. Deinceps autem rex quo barones pergebant perrexit et quod faciendum decreuerant diligenter et libenter faciebat. Edicto regis pax proclamata est per uniuersam terram.

Regina Anglie in partibus transmarinis existens et audiens rem gestam sic indoluit conducensque exercitum infinitum Angliam inuadere arbitrata est. Sed mare littoreque marino per preceptum regis et baronum [1] copioso exercitu Anglorum custodito transfretare aduersarii formidabant, thesauroque regine consumpto, singuli ad propria non sine labore et rubore reuersi sunt. Quo audito custodia marina cessauit. Memorandumque quod, nisi mare sic custoditum fuisset, Anglia ab alienigenis capta fuisset. Memorandum eciam quod omnes burgi, ville et *a* campestres et ecclesiastice persone taxati fuerunt ad inueniendum secundum suum posse ad custodiam marinam et uiros pugnaturos *b* et eis expensas sufficienter quam diu ibi morabantur.

Cometa apparuit in parte *c* orientali ante auroram diei per totum mensem Augusti plumbei coloris radium dirigens uersus austrum.

Gwydo Sabinensis episcopus cardinalis et apostolice sedis legatus uenit in Franciam uolens transire in Angliam; qui, quia in fauorem regis et regine uenire a baronibus arbitrabatur, in Angliam non est permissus applicare. Vrbanus papa obiit apud Perusium Kal. Octobris,[2] uacauitque sedes mensibus *d* iiii.

---

a que *A*   *b* pugnatores *A*   *c* Om. *A*
d Fran[ciam] . . . ba[ronibus] . . . men[sibus] *charred and imperfect A*

[1] *CPR, 1258–66,* pp. 160–1

Edward gave himself as a hostage for the liberation of his men. They all swore to observe the Provisions of Oxford in future. Thereafter the king went wherever the barons went, and of his own free will did whatever they had decided should be done. Peace was declared throughout the land by royal edict.

Meanwhile the queen of England, who was abroad, grieved to hear the course events had taken. So she collected an enormous army and decided to invade England. As, however, the sea and coasts were strongly guarded by an English army by order of the king and barons,[1] the enemy was afraid to sail. When the queen's money ran out everyone went home, not without discomfort and disgrace. When this was known the coastal guard was disbanded. It should be remembered that England would have been captured by foreigners if the seas had not been protected. It should also be remembered that every borough and town and all the countryside and the clergy were taxed according to their means to provide for the coastal defences and men to fight, and to pay them adequately for as long as they remained there.

A comet of a leaden colour with its tail pointing south appeared throughout August in the eastern sky before the dawn of the day.

Guy, cardinal-bishop of St Sabina and legate of the Apostolic See, entered France, intending to cross to England. But because the barons thought that he favoured the king and queen they would not let him land in England. Pope Urban died in Perugia on 1 October [2] and the Holy See remained vacant for four months.

---

[2] He died on 2, not 1, October.

1265

Gwido, quondam Narbonensis archiepiscopus, cardinalis episcopus Sabinensis, apostolice sedis legatus, factus est papa Non. Februarii et dictus est Clemens. Gilebertus f. 151ᵛ de Clare comes Glouernie et alii / plures cum eo recesserunt a comite Leycestrie ob uarias causas, et maxime quod post bellum Lewense particio castrorum et possessionum non fuit inter eos recte diuisa, ut aiebant, secundum quantitatem sumptuum et laborum. Karolus comes Andegauie in regem Sicilie et Apulie electus est, senatoria eciam dignitate sublimatus, Romanam urbem vigilia Pentecosten intrauit.[1] Eo tempore Edwardus filius regis Anglie de custodia eductus, cum rege et comite Leycestrie circumcirca deducitur, tandem uenerunt Herfordiam; ubi dictus Edwardus de custodia dicti comitis declinans, ad comitem Glouernie et marchiones prope existentes euasit v. Kal. Iunii. Rege in partibus Wallie cum comite Leycestrie in angustia magna et penuria degente, eo quod comes Glouernie et qui cum eo erant non permittebant eos uersus Angliam declinare. Interim Symon de Monte Forti filius S[ymonis] comitis Leycestrie ui et armis Wintoniam ingressus circa festum sancti Swithwni,[2] multam pecuniam et spolia inde detulit; et non multum post dictus Si[mon], filius comitis Leycestrie, comes Oxonie,[3] Willelmus de Monte Caniso[4] et multi alii nobiles, dum presidium S[ymonis] comitis Leycestrie facere uellent, apud Keligwrthe adunantur. Sed

[1] 23 May
[2] The feast of the Translation of St Swithun, 15 July, must be intended; cf. *Wav.*, p. 363, *Wint.*, p. 102, *Wig.*, p. 454. The feast of St Swithun falls on 2 July.
[3] Robert de Vere, earl of Oxford 1263–96

1265

Guy, formerly bishop of Narbonne, the cardinal-bishop
of St Sabina and papal legate, was made pope on 5
February and took the name Clement [IV]. Gilbert de
Clare, earl of Gloucester, and many others deserted the
earl of Leicester for various reasons, but mainly because
after the battle of Lewes the division of castles and
property among the victors was not fairly proportioned,
as they said, in accordance with their expenditure of
money and manpower. Charles, count of Anjou, was
elected king of Sicily and Apulia and raised to the
dignity of senator. He entered Rome on the vigil of
Pentecost.[1] At this time Edward, the king of England's
son, was brought out of prison and taken around with the
king and the earl of Leicester. At length they reached
Hereford. There Edward escaped from the earl's
custody and on 28 May joined the earl of Gloucester and
the Marcher lords, who were in the neighbourhood.
The king, who was in Wales with the earl of Leicester,
suffered great hardship and privation because the earl
of Gloucester and his followers prevented their return
to England. In the meantime, about the feast of St
Swithun,[2] Simon de Montfort, the son of Simon, earl of
Leicester, entered Winchester by force and carried off
much money and booty. Soon afterwards the same
Simon, the son of the earl of Leicester, with the earl of
Oxford,[3] William de Munchensy,[4] and many other
nobles, met at Kenilworth in order to help Simon, earl

---

[4] William de Munchensy of Norfolk (d. 1287); G.E.C., *Complete Peerage*,
IX, pp. 422ff.

Edwardus, comes Glouernie et qui cum eis erant clam
superuenientes, ipsos incautos et inermes ceperunt,
spoliauerunt et per diuersa Anglie loca custodie manci-
pauerunt; factum est istud Kal. Augusti, die sabbati.
Dum hec sic agerentur istius facti ignari Symon comes
Leycestrie et qui cum eo erant, ducentes regem, transier-
unt flumen Sabrinum, uenerunt usque Euesham; quo
Edwardus, G[ilbertus] de Clare comes Glouernie et
marchiones cum magna insequentes multitudine comi-
serunt cum eis prelium extra Euesham ii. Non. Augusti,
die Martis; in quo ceciderunt S[imon] comes *a*
Leycestrie, Henricus, filius eius primogenitus, Hugo
Dispensator, iusticiarius Anglie, et fere omnes alii nobiles
ex parte regis existentes. Walenses uero et alios ad
f. 152 ecclesiam fugientes, tam intra ecclesiam / quam extra
horribiliter trucidauerunt rege et aliis ministris regalibus
captis et sic uolentibus. Eodem die circa horam diei
terciam tanta pluuie inundacio, tanta tonitrua et
coruscacio et tam dense tenebre extiterunt ut cum esset
hora prandii uix cibum appositum *b* potuerunt come-
dentes uidere. *c* Hoc bello sic peracto, rex qui quasi in
custodia nuper fuerat, familiam suam collegit et multo
numerosiorem quam prius, pacem proclamans et parlamentum suum in Natiuitate beate Marie [1] apud
Wintoniam denuncians, ubi magnam pecuniam ab
omnibus fere Anglie prelatis, tam pater quam filius
ceterique curiales, extorserunt. Vnde et de ecclesia
sancti martyris Edmundi fere dccc. marcas habuerunt. [2]

---

a Bellum de Euesham *in margin MS*[2]; *rubric in text after* Euesham *P*
b + percipere, *and* corus[catio] . . . [app]ositum *charred and imperfect A*
c *In margin MS*[2]; *in text after* potuerunt *M*

[1] 8 September
[2] *CPR, 1258–66*, p. 525. See above, p. xxiii, and notes; below, p. 35

of Leicester. But Edward and the earl of Gloucester with their followers made a surprise attack and caught them unawares and unarmed. They despoiled them and sent them for imprisonment to different parts of England. This took place on Saturday, 1 August. While all this was happening Simon, earl of Leicester, and his men were ignorant of events. They crossed the river Severn, bringing the king with them, and reached Evesham. There outside Evesham on 4 August, which was a Tuesday, they met in battle Edward, Gilbert de Clare, earl of Gloucester, and the Marcher lords, who came with a great army. Simon of Leicester, Henry his eldest son, Hugh Despenser, the justiciar of England, and almost all the nobles on the king's side were killed. The Welshmen and others fled to a church, but both within and without it they were brutally slaughtered with the approval of the king and of the royal officials, who had been taken [by the victors]. On that day about three o'clock there was such a downpour of rain, such thunder and lightning, and the darkness was so profound, that though it was dinner-time those who sat down to eat could scarcely see the food before them. When the war was thus concluded the king, who formerly had been virtually a prisoner, gathered together an even larger household than before, proclaimed peace and summoned his parliament at Winchester on the Nativity of the Blessed Virgin Mary.[1] At that parliament both the father and son and all the courtiers extorted huge sums of money from nearly all the prelates of England. They took almost 800 marks from the church of Bury St Edmunds.[2] The convent, though unwillingly, had

Istius pecunie dimidiam partem conuentus, licet inuite, reddidit quia tam homines conuentus quam abbatis ad custodiam maris fuerunt contra reginam, ne cum excercitu suo Angliam intraret. Verumtamen in curia regis solummodo persona abbatis de transgressione calumpniabatur et ideo durius conuentus particionem pecunie predicte tollerabant et propter similitudinem consequencie.[a] Imponebat uero rex singulis qui cum Simone comite contra eum tenuerunt. Inde in festo sancti Michaelis usque ad [b] Windeshoram parlamentum protractum est a quo quidam regales Londoniam transmittuntur; qui, sagacium uerborum colore, inter ipsos et regem fedus federantes immo fedantes, tandem maiorem ciuitatis cum pluribus ciuibus ad Windeshoram secum adduxerunt; quo cum peruenissent statim capti incarcerabantur. Municione ciuitatis a regalibus occupata, qui repagula et cathenas ferreas quibus omnes platee et uiculi ciuitatis mirabiliter muniebantur funditus auellentes eam regi subiugauerunt, et pluribus ciuibus exheredatis ceteri uiginti milibus marcarum sibi pacem redimebant.[1] Rex pro libito suo contulit tam alienigenis quam Anglis omnes terras et possessiones eorum qui in bello apud Lewes et Ewesham contra ipsum fuerunt uel apud Norhamtonam et Kenilword' inuenti fuerunt, exceptis terris G[ilberti] de Clare comitis Glouernie, consilio regis sentenciante sic licet aliqui huic sentencie non consentirent. Castrum / de Douera Edwardo redditum est. Et postea Alienor regina cum Edmundo, filio suo, applicuit in Angliam iiii. Kal. Nouembris. Eodem eciam tempore Ottobonus diaconus

f. 152ᵛ

[a] istius pecunie dimidiam partem . . . consequencie *om. A*
[b] *Om. A*

[1] cf. *CPR, 1258–66*, p. 530; *De Ant. Leg.*, pp. 78–80

to pay half this sum, because the convent's men as well
as the abbot's had guarded the coasts against the queen
lest she might invade England with her army. But in
the king's court only the abbot was personally charged
with the offence; which made the convent all the more
indignant at the division of the fine, because the
results were the same for them. The king oppressed
everyone who had supported Earl Simon against him.
On Michaelmas day he adjourned his parliament to
Windsor. From there he sent some of his courtiers to
London. Under colour of wise words, negotiating a
treaty between the Londoners and the king (but in fact
dishonouring it), they brought back the mayor of the
city and some of the citizens to Windsor, but immediately
on arrival they were seized and imprisoned. The king's
men occupied the fortifications of London, tore up all
the barriers and iron chains, which were remarkably
effective for the defence of every open space and narrow
street of the city, and put London at the king's mercy.
After many of the citizens had suffered confiscation the
others paid 20,000 marks for the king's peace.[1] The
king at his royal pleasure gave to aliens and Englishmen
all the land and property of those who had fought
against him at Lewes and Evesham and who had been
found at Northampton and Kenilworth; the lands,
however, of Gilbert de Clare, earl of Gloucester, were
excepted on the advice of the king's council, though
some of the counsellors did not agree with this decision.
Dover castle was returned to Edward. Later, on 29
October, Queen Eleanor and her son Edmund landed
in England. At the same time Ottobuono, cardinal-

cardinalis sancti Adriani, apostolice sedis legatus, uenit in Angliam. Qui, conuocans omnes Anglie prelatos, celebrauit concilium circa festum sancti Nicholai [1] apud Nouum Templum London'; in quo denunciauit excommunicatum Symonem de Monte Forti comitem Leycestrie omnesque fautores et complices suos. Dictus tamen Simon comes Leycestrie multis diuinis coruscauit miraculis, [a] ut plurimi asserebant. [b]

Eodem anno in nocte uigilie Natalis Domini feria v., circa mediam noctem facta est generalis eclipsis lune sanguinei coloris per tres horas noctis, sole in capite luna existente in cauda draconis,[2] in anno Alligere 664, die xv. mensis tercii [3] Arabum. Iste annus Arabum sumpsit exordium iiii. Idus Octobris, feria ii. [c]

Symon filius S[ymonis] comitis Leycestrie post bellum de Euesham castrum de Kenilword' egressus cum quibusdam exheredatis insulam de Oxholm intrauit, quod cum rex comperit, copioso exercitu dictam insulam uallauit. Dictus uero S[ymon] et sui cum percepissent se in breui comprehensuros si restitissent pacem cum rege pepigerunt, Symone in custodia Edwardi retento. Necnon absolutionis beneficium dictus Symon et qui cum eo erant a legato optinuerunt. [d]

1266

Symon iunior apud London' euasit de custodia Edwardi post Nathale et festinanter transfretauit in Galliam. Multi exheredatorum castrum de Kenilword' intra-

---

[a] multis diuinis . . . miraculis *totally erased by scraping* A
[b] ut plurimi asserebant *om.* A
[c] *Here ends the text in* A *with the letters* c.b.a. *each written at the beginning of the next three lines. At the foot of the page in* A *is a mainly illegible note of ten lines in pencil.*
[d] *Lacuna of 2 lines MS (3 M)*

deacon of St Adrian's and papal legate, came to England. He summoned all the prelates of England and held a council about the time of the feast of St Nicholas [1] at the New Temple in London. He pronounced the excommunication of Simon de Montfort, earl of Leicester, and all his supporters and accomplices. Numerous people, however, said that the body of Simon, earl of Leicester, worked many miracles.

In this year, about midnight on Christmas eve, which was a Thursday, there was a total eclipse of the moon; it was blood-coloured for three hours in the night. This happened when the sun was on the Dragon's head and the moon on its tail,[2] in the year 664 of the Hegira, on the fifteenth day of Rabia,[3] the third month. This year of the Hegira began on Monday, 12 October. Simon, the son of Simon, earl of Leicester, left Kenilworth castle after the battle of Evesham and occupied the isle of Axholme with some of the Disinherited. When the king learnt this he surrounded the island with a large army. Simon and his men, seeing that they would soon be captured if they resisted, sought peace from the king. Simon was kept a prisoner under Edward's guard. Nonetheless he and his followers obtained absolution from the legate.

1266

Simon de Montfort the younger escaped in London from the custody of Edward after Christmas and hastily crossed to France. Many of the Disinherited occupied Kenilworth castle, fortified it energetically and laid

---

[1] 6 December
[2] The Dragon: a northern constellation. The Dragon's head and the Dragon's tail: respectively the ascending and descending node of the moon's orbit with the ecliptic.   [3] Rabia I of the Hegira

uerunt et, patriam in girum deuastantes, studiose
munierunt. Quidam exheredati, qui apud sanctum
Edmundum latitabant, in crastino Palmarum,[1] cum
magno apparatu, dictam uillam exierunt et Mersland
inuadentes eciam insultum contra Len in septimana
Pasce [2] fecerunt, sed illis uiriliter resistentibus uoto
frustrati abcesserunt. [a] Vigilia Pentecosten [3] cum exheredati in unum collecti in opido de Cestrefeld se
f. 153 recepissent et timore nudi alii se minuerunt, / alii
uenatum issent, subito superuenit exercitus regalium et
impetum in eos facientes, quosdam occiderunt, alios
ceperunt, ceterisque fugatis, cum uictoria et spoliis
multis abscesserunt. Iterum qui remanserant de exheredatis per turmas se recolligentes per nemora latibulis
apta in diuersis locis sibi lustra parabant et durius erat
eis quam urse raptis fetibus obuiare. Nam rapiebant
undique omnia que sibi uidebantur utilia.

Accidit hoc anno vi. Kal. Iunii ut I[ohannes] comes
Warennie et W[illelmus] de Valence frater regis cum
turba multa causa perquirendi inimicos regis apud
sanctum Edmundum inopinate uenirent, qui abbatem
et burgenses uille durius conuenientes imponebant
eisdem quod inimicis regis fauebant quia barones
exheredati ibidem predas [b] suas et roberias sine aliquo
obstaculo condebant et uendebant.[4] Et quoniam abbas
pro se et conuentu suo satis sufficienter respondit,
intorquebant pondus criminis in burgenses qui indiscrete
et sine consilio abbatis respondentes per proprium
responsum culpam suam regalibus manifestabant. Erat

---

[a] recesserunt M
[b] [Waren]nie . . . c[ausa perqui]rendi . . . [inopina]te . . . [durius] . . .
r[egis] . . . p[re]das *imperfect from a tear* M

[1] 22 March   [2] 28 March to 3 April

waste the neighbouring countryside. Some of them, who were lying hidden in Bury St Edmunds, on the morrow of Palm Sunday[1] marched from the town in battle order and invaded the Marshland. They even attacked Lynn in Easter week,[2] but retreated, their plans frustrated by the manful resistance of the townsmen. On the vigil of Pentecost,[3] when the Disinherited had met together and withdrawn to the town of Chesterfield and, free from fear, some were being bled and others were out hunting, a force of the king's men was suddenly upon them. It attacked, killing some, capturing others and putting the rest to flight, and left victorious with much booty. Those of the Disinherited who survived collected in bands in the woods, which were suitable hiding-places, and made hide-outs in various places. They were more dangerous to meet than she-bears robbed of their cubs and seized everything they wanted from anywhere.

On 27 May Earl John de Warenne and William de Valence, the king's brother, came unexpectedly to Bury St Edmunds with a great band of retainers to seek out the king's enemies there. They summoned the abbot and burgesses and accused them of favouring the king's enemies, because the Disinherited hid and sold their booty and stolen goods in the town without hindrance.[4] As the abbot cleared himself and the convent to their satisfaction, the burden of the crime was thrown on the burgesses, who replied thoughtlessly, without the abbot's advice, and showed their guilt to the king's men by their

---

[3] 15 May
[4] The abbot of Bury is listed on a schedule headed ' Isti sunt emptores de bosco . . .'; see above, p. xxiii and *n.* 5.

eciam tunc *a* discordia inter abbatem et conuentum et
burgenses eo quod dicti burgenses eis rebelles et balliuis
suis iamdiu extiterant [1] et, quia tunc pecunia pacem sibi
redimere necesse habebant, nec hoc sine consilio et
auxilio abbatis et conuentus ad debitum finem perducere
poterant, eos lacrimabiliter rogauerunt ut ipsis mediantibus pecunia offerretur et fine facta per manus conuentus
pecunia regalibus traderetur, ut sic libertas eorum et
conuentus illibata conseruaretur. Quod et factum fuit,
dederunt enim regi statim cc. marcas,[2] abbati autem et
conuentui c. libras promiserunt. Circa festum sancti
Iohannis Baptiste rex castrum de Kelinword' obsedit.
Deinde legatus admonicione premissa obsessos cum
complicibus excommunicauit. Obsessi regalibus uiriliter restiterunt necnon plurima grauamina intulerunt
eisdem. Tandem treuge inter regem et obsessos capte
f. 153ᵛ erant / a festo sancti Martini usque in quadraginta dies
sequentes, in quo spacio multi de castro potu uenenato
inficiati mortui sunt.[3] Deficiebant eciam eis uictualia
nec defectus eorum aliquo signo regalibus patebat.
Erant eciam inter eos quidam regalibus fauentes et
consilium eorum occultis signis propalantes eisdem ita ut
numquam prout uellent et poterant exire contra regales
ualebant. Qui tandem *b* de proditione conuicti sus-

---

a discordia inter burgenses et conuentum *in margin MS²*
b tan[dem] . . . [vigil]ia . . . red[ditum] . . . circumexisten[tibus] . . .
indul[genc]iam . . . [quod] . . . [An]glie *imperfect from a tear M*

[1] For the revolt of the town of Bury St Edmunds against the abbey in
1264 see above, p. xxiv and note.
[2] The fine was for having the king's goodwill and for the restoration of
the liberty of the abbot, forfeited for transgressions: *CPR, 1258-66*, p. 604;
Fine Rolls (P.R.O.), 51 Henry III, membrane 6. See above, p. 31.
[3] This poisoning of the people in Kenilworth castle does not seem to be
mentioned by the other authorities.

own reply. Moreover at this time there was a dispute
between the abbot and convent and the burgesses
because the burgesses had for a long time defied them
and their bailiffs.[1]   Now, because they were compelled
to redeem their peace with money and were unable to
raise the money for the fine they owed without the advice
and help of the abbot and convent, they tearfully
besought them that the money should be offered by
their mediation and, when the fine had been made, the
money handed to the royal officials by the convent.
In this way their liberty and that of the convent would
be preserved unimpaired.   This was done; they straight
away gave the king 200 marks [2] and promised £100 to
the abbot and convent.   About the time of the feast of
St John the Baptist the king laid siege to Kenilworth
castle.   The legate, having issued a warning, excommunicated the besieged and their accomplices.   The
besieged resisted the king's army bravely and not without
inflicting some heavy losses on it.   At length the king
and the besieged made a truce for forty days from
Martinmas.   During this interlude many people in the
castle were made ill by poison in their drink and died.[3]
They also lacked food, but their plight was not betrayed
to the royal army by any sign.   But among them were
certain men who favoured the royal side and by secret
signals divulged that the besieged were not strong
enough to come out and attack the king's men as they
wished and had once been able to do.   These men were
finally convicted of treachery and hanged in the castle.

pensi erant in castro. Vigilia sancte Lucie castrum de Kenileword regi redditum fuit.[1]

Interim rex presente legato et circumexistentibus quampluribus magnatibus et prelatis Anglie indulgenciam domini pape ostendit. In qua continebatur quod dominus papa decimas omnium ecclesiasticorum prouentuum Anglie secundum uerum ualorem per triennium regi concessit exceptis bonis Hospitalariorum, Templariorum et Cisternensium.

Preterea tempore treugarum electi fuerunt xii. magnates tam clerici quam laici qui de exheredatis captis in bello captiuis et obsessis sic prouidebant: uidelicet quod aliqui carerent terris suis per annum, alii per biennium, nonnulli per triennium, plurimi per quadriennium, plerique per quinquennium et ultimi per septennium. Darentque singuli regi infra triennium ualorem terre eorum per septennium et, si possent infra dictos tres annos terciam partem dicte taxationis soluere, possiderent terciam partem terre eorum; si dimidiam partem dicte pecunie, dimidiam partem terre eorum; si totum persoluerent, totam terram suam recuperarent; et si infra dictos tres annos totum non persoluissent exheredati perpetuo remanerent.[2] Secundum hanc legem magnates qui apud Kenilword' ante bellum Eueshamense et in bello de Euesham capti fuerant et obsessi in castro de Kenilword' libere abire permissi sunt. Quinto Idus Augusti exheredati qui, ut dictum est, in siluis *a* latitabant, insulam Elyensem caute ingredientes ceperunt, quam episcopus in presencia

---

a Insula Elyensis capta ab exheredatis *in margin MS²*; *rubric in text after* permissi sunt *P*

[1] 12 December. The chronicles disagree on the date of the surrender; Powicke, *Henry III and the Lord Edward*, II, p. 539, accepts 14 December.
[2] cf. the Dictum of Kenilworth, cap. 12, *Statutes of the Realm*, I, pp. 12–17

On the vigil of the feast of St Lucy, Kenilworth castle was surrendered to the king.[1]

Meanwhile the king, in the presence of the legate and surrounded by many magnates and prelates of England, announced an indulgence of the pope; it said that the pope had granted the king a tenth of all ecclesiastical revenues in England according to their true value for three years, with the exception of the goods of the Hospitallers, Templars and Cistercians.

In the meantime during the truce, twelve notables were chosen, both clerks and laymen, who made the following provisions relative to the Disinherited, both those captured in battle and those in the siege: some were to lose their lands for one year, others for two years, some for three years, many for four years, most for five years and a last group for seven years; each was to give to the king within three years the value of his land for a seven-year period, and if within the three years they managed to pay a third of the sum they would regain possession of a third part of their land, if they paid half the sum, half their land, if all, all their land; but if they paid nothing during the three years they would remain disinherited for ever.[2] According to these conditions the magnates who were captured at Kenilworth before the battle of Evesham or in the battle of Evesham, and those besieged in Kenilworth castle, were allowed to go free. On 9 August those Disinherited who, as has been mentioned, lay hidden in the woods, stealthily entered the Isle of Ely and took it; the bishop of Ely, who had undertaken in the king's presence to guard the

regis antea presumpsit custodiendam sed casu accidente sic inde recessit et insulam suspendit.¹ Isti totam

f. 154 patriam in girum depredauerunt. Sed et / ultro procedentes xvii. Kal. Ianuarii uillam Norwic' ui ceperunt, vii.xx. curribus et aurigis, ut dicebatur, de preda onustis et secum abductis. ^a ²

1267^b

Octauo Idus Februarii uidelicet dominica post Purificationem uenit rex Henricus apud sanctum Eadmundum et die sequenti Ottobonus legatus uenit ibidem, cunctis prelatis et proceribus regni ex utroque edicto ad locum prelibatum conuocatis. Legato siquidem [die] sancti Petri in Cathedra ibidem concilium celebrante, ^c ³ exheredatos ^d insulam Elyensem occupantes cum complicibus et fautoribus ammonitionibus premissis puplice excommunicauit, rege ibi presente, nisi infra quindenam sequentem regie paci se supponerent. Nocte autem proxima sequente quidam occulti rumores legatum et suos uehementer terrentes ipsum in crastinum quasi inopinate iter uersus London' arripere fecerunt. Quo die eciam dominus rex, oppidum beati martiris Eadmundi relinquens, apud Cantebrig' cum excercitu suo castra metauit. Ibique totum ieiunium Quadragesimale in insule Elyensis obsidione consumauit. Interim elaboratum est ut dicta obsidio frustraretur; unde G[ilbertus] comes Glouernie uigilia Palmarum ⁴ London'

<hr>

^a Lacuna of 1 line MS (2 M)   ^b The text for years 1267–9 is also in H.
^c Supplied from H; om. MS, M, P   ^d celebrauit exhereditatos H

¹ Hugh Balsham, bishop of Ely 1258–86. For the meaning of 'suspendit' see J. H. Baxter and C. Johnson, Medieval Latin Word-List (1934), p. 418, sub 'Suspendiculus'.

² Wykes, p. 193, quotes a popular estimate that over 2,000 marks' worth of goods were taken.

³ 22 February. The chronicles disagree on the dates of the king's and

Isle, had by a coincidence gone away and abandoned it.[1] The Disinherited ravaged all the neighbouring country-side. They went farther afield and on 16 December seized Norwich by force, carrying off a hundred and forty carts and wagons laden with booty.[2]

1267

On 6 February, that is on the Sunday after Candlemas, King Henry came to Bury St Edmunds. On the next day the legate Ottobuono arrived there. All the prelates and magnates of the realm had been summoned by a twofold edict to the place aforesaid. The legate held a council on the feast of St Peter in Cathedra.[3] He publicly, in the king's presence and after due warning had been given, excommunicated the Disinherited who were occupying the Isle of Ely, together with their supporters and accomplices, unless they submitted to the king within fifteen days. But on the night following the council certain rumours so scared the legate and his household that on the next day they departed un-expectedly for London. On the same day the king left the town of the blessed martyr Edmund and pitched camp with his army at Cambridge. He spent the whole of Lent there besieging the Isle of Ely. In the meantime efforts were made to render the siege fruitless; Gilbert, earl of Gloucester, advanced with a great retinue on London on the vigil of Palm Sunday.[4] Supported by

---

legate's arrival and of the convocation. Lunt decides in favour of the dates in our chronicle; 'The Consent of the English Lower Clergy to Taxation during the reign of Henry III,' in *Persecution and Liberty: Essays in honor of George Lincoln Burr* (New York [1931]), pp. 156–7 and *n.* 206.
   [4] 9 April

ingrediens cum magno apparatu ciuitatis municiones, ciuibus sibi fauentibus, continuo occupauit, qui eciam legato in Turri existenti exitum uersus ciuitatem omnino preclusit. Quod rex mox comperiens, obsidionem insule relinquens, post octauas Pasche apud Stratford se recepit London' obsessurus.[1] Quo comes sancti Pauli,[2] comes Bolon'[3] et comes de Gysnes[4] cum magno apparatu uenerunt auxilium regi pro uiribus prestaturi.

Dum hec agerentur quibusdam curiose interuenientibus de pace inter eos reformanda tractauerunt et citra festum sancti Iohannis Baptiste[5] pax inter eos reformata est, comite in presencia legati super altare sancti Pauli iurante se arma contra dominum suum regem, nisi se defendendo, numquam portaturum. Londoniensibus comiti fauentibus uitam et membrum rex concessit, f. 154ᵛ aliis / auxilium dicto comiti ferentibus secundum dictum de Kenilewrth' in pace receptis. Hiis peractis rex London' ingressus est xiiii. Kal. Iulii nullo exceptis ciuibus ultra triduum in urbe remanere permisso.

Ribaldi quidam de municione Elyensi egredientes,[a] equos quorundam uirorum qui in secretioribus locis curie beati martiris Eadmundi occultabantur per medium infirmarie deducentes in insulam secum duxerunt. Quos cum quidam monachus eiusdem loci insequeretur, magnatibus insulanis rem gestam luculenter exposuit. Tandem, dictis insulanis sentenciantibus, dicti ribaldi cum dictis equis arbitrio dicti monachi committebantur. Quos uidelicet equos cum ad altare

[a] expedientes H

[1] 24 April. The London chronicles give 8 April: De Ant. Leg., p. 90; Ann. Lond. p. 77.
[2] Guy III, count of St Pol 1248–89
[3] Robert V, count of Boulogne 1260–77

the citizens he immediately occupied the city's defences and completely blocked the access towards the city of the legate, who was in the Tower. The king soon learnt this, abandoned the siege of the Isle and after the octave of Easter proceeded to Stratford to besiege London.[1] The count of St Pol,[2] the count of Boulogne [3] and the count of Guînes,[4] with many followers, came to lend the king help according to their strength.

In the meantime, after painstaking mediation on the part of certain people, they negotiated for the restoration of peace, which was concluded between them before the feast of St John the Baptist.[5] The earl swore on the high altar of St Paul in the presence of the legate that he would never bear arms against his lord the king unless in self-defence. The king granted life and limb to the Londoners who had favoured the earl, after the other accomplices of the earl had been received in peace according to the Dictum of Kenilworth. This done, the king entered London on 18 June. No-one except the citizens was allowed to remain in the town for more than three days.

Some ruffians came out of the stronghold of Ely and took certain men's horses which were hidden in the most secret places within the precincts of the blessed martyr Edmund. They led them through the middle of the infirmary and carried them off to the Isle. As a certain monk of this place followed them, he related clearly to the magnates of the Isle what had happened. Finally by judgment of the aforesaid islanders, the ruffians with the above-mentioned horses were committed to the decision of the monk. After bringing back their horses

---

[4] Arnulf III, count of Guînes 1245–83
[5] Peace was made on 16 June; *Foedera*, I, p. 472.

sancti Eadmundi reduxissent, in signum presumpcionis
gladios suos quos irreuerenter contra sancti libertatem
erexerant martyri optulerunt.[1]

Edwardus domini regis primogenitus quibusdam
insulanis ipsum ducentibus v. Idus Iulii insulam
Elyensem intrauit, cui statim insula reddita fuit, ipsis
in forma dicti de Kenilewrth' pacem recipientibus. [a]

1268

Ciuitas Antiochie capta est a soldano Babilonie [2] Iudeis
qui ibidem morabantur hoc procurantibus [b] die Ascensionis Domini qui fuit xvi. Kal. Iunii. [c][3]

Ottobonus legatus celebrauit concilium apud
London' post Pascha dominica [4] qua cantatur ewange-
lium, ' Ego sum pastor bonus ' [5]; in quo absoluit
Symonem de Monte Forti comitem Leycestrie et alios
quos prius excommunicauerat ratione perturbacionis
antedicte. Iterum celebrauit concilium apud Norhampton' rege ibidem cum proceribus parlamentum
tenente, in quo concilio idem legatus dominum
Edwardum, G[ilbertum] comitem Glouernie et quamplures alios nobiles crucesignauit. Concilioque peracto
licenciam repatriandi deuote postulauit et tercio Idus /
f. 155   Iulii [6] mare ingrediens transfretauit.

Karolus rex Sicilie et frater regis Francie pugnauit
contra Conrad' [7] apud Beneuent' in Apulia et consecutus

---

[a] Insula Elyensis reddita *in margin MS*[2]; *rubric in text after* forma dicti *P*;
lacuna of 2 lines MS (3 M)
[b] proiurantibus *H*
[c] Iudeis qui . . . Iunii *marked* uacat *MS*[2]

[1] *Ribaldi quidam de municione Elyensi . . . optulerunt*: the same passage
with a little verbal embellishment is in MS Bodley 240, p. 667 (printed
Arnold, II, p. 362).
[2] i.e. Cairo. Du Cange, *sub* Babilonia. The sultan was Bibars, 4th
sultan of the Mamlouks-Baharytes 1260–77.

to St Edmund's altar, as an acknowledgment of their impiety they offered the holy martyr the swords which they had rashly drawn in defiance of his Liberty.[1]

Edward, the king's eldest son, entered the Isle of Ely on 11 July, led by some men of the Isle. The Isle was immediately surrendered to him, and the defenders were granted peace according to the terms of the Dictum of Kenilworth.

1268

The Sultan of Babylon [2] captured the city of Antioch, through the connivance of the Jews living there, on Ascension day, which was on 17 May.[3] The legate Ottobuono held a council in London on the Sunday after Easter,[4] when the gospel ' Ego sum pastor bonus ' is sung.[5] There he absolved Simon de Montfort, earl of Leicester, and the others whom he had previously excommunicated for their part in the revolt. He held a council again at Northampton while the king was there holding a parliament with his magnates. In this council the legate made the Lord Edward, Gilbert, earl of Gloucester, and many other nobles crusaders. When the council was over the legate earnestly asked for permission to return home. He set sail on 13 July.[6]

Charles, king of Sicily, the brother of the king of France, fought against Conradin [7] at Benevento in Apulia

---

[3] Antioch fell probably on 19 or 27 May; R. Grousset, *Histoire des Croisades et du Royaume franc de Jérusalem* (Paris 1934–6), iii, p. 641.

[4] 15 April

[5] John 10: 11–16; the antiphon sung on the second Sunday after Easter (22 April). The same date is given by Wykes, p. 215, as the date of Ottobuono's council; see Wilkins, *Concilia*, ii, p. 1.

[6] The chronicles disagree on the date of Ottobuono's departure.

[7] Conradin (1252–68), son of Conrad IV, king of Germany

est uictoriam uigilia sancti Bartholomei,[1] in quo conflictu
habuit Conradus xvi. millia loricatorum et Karolus vii.
millia. [a]

Hoc anno auctoritate regia diriguntur clerici per
omnes episcopatus Anglie ad taxandum omnia bona
temporalia et spiritualia tocius cleri Anglie secundum
uerum ualorem [2] exceptis bonis Templariorum, [b] Hospitalariorum et Cisternensium, per estimacionem plebey-
orum ad hoc uocatorum. [c] Quo peracto omnes episcopi
singuli pro episcopatu suo cum rege composuerunt.
Vnde episcopus Norwicensis [3] pro episcopatu suo cum
rege componente pro decima duorum annorum finalium
monasterium eciam beati martyris Eadmundi in pactione
sua recepit. Abbate tamen et conuentu super hoc prius
requisitis et licet hoc contra libertatem dicti monasterii
uideretur existere, tamen propter dilacionem temporis
quam possent consequi et eciam quia liberius contra
episcopales exactores quam contra regales ualerent
cauillare, pocius episcopalibus quam regalibus tunc
temporis preelegerunt respondere. Et licet non nisi per
biennium clerus de decimis respondere deberent quia de
primo anno decimacionis iam satisfecerunt, tamen ultro
se optulerunt episcopo decimas suas se daturos eciam de
tercio anno post biennium prius concessum tali pacto ut
in decimando secundum taxacionem Walteri quondam
Norwicensis episcopi decimas suas possent contribuere,
quod et factum est. Et propter hanc causam conuentus

---

[a] *This paragraph* (*from* Iterum celebrauit) *marked* uacat *MS²*.
[b] + et *M*   [c] ad hoc uocatorum *om. M*

[1] The battle of Tagliacozzo, not Benevento.   23 August.
[2] For the meaning of ' uerus ualor ' see above, p. xxvi.
[3] Roger de Skerning, bishop of Norwich 1266–78.   For the bishop's
composition with the king for the city and diocese of Norwich and for
St Edmund's abbey see *CPR, 1266–72*, pp. 354, 410; Lunt, *Financial
Relations*, p. 300.   See above, p. xxv.

and on the vigil of St Bartholomew he was victorious.[1]
Conradin had sixteen thousand men in armour in the
battle and Charles seven thousand.

In this year clerks were dispatched to all the
bishoprics in England by authority of the king to tax
all ecclesiastical revenues, both temporal and spiritual
(except those of the Templars, Hospitallers and Cistercians), at their ' true value,' [2] by the assessment of
common people summoned for the purpose. When this
had been done each bishop settled with the king to pay
a lump sum for his bishopric. The bishop of Norwich,[3]
who was compounding with the king for his bishopric
for the tenth for the final two years, admitted the
monastery of the blessed martyr Edmund in his agreement. The abbot and convent had previously been
questioned about this, and although it seemed to be
against the liberty of the monastery, nevertheless they
chose on this occasion to be answerable to the bishop's
men rather than the king's, because of the delay in payment which they might thus be able to secure and also
because they could argue more forcibly and freely with
episcopal assessors than royal ones. Although the
clergy ought to have been answerable for the tenth for
only two years (because they had already paid the tenth
for the first year), all the same they offered to pay the
bishop in addition the tenth for the third year, after the
two years already conceded, with an agreement to the
effect that in the assessment for the tenth they could
pay their tenths according to the assessment of Walter,
formerly bishop of Norwich. And thus it was done.

sancti Eadmundi bona sua a dicto episcopo prius taxata triennaliter decimauerunt et eas episcopo Norwicensi contulerunt. Cetera autem bona sua a dicto episcopo W[altero] numquam taxata secundum taxacionem dictorum clericorum regis biennaliter decimata pariter contribuerunt. Exemplar taxacionis et decimacionis omnium bonorum temporalium et spiritualium porcionis conuentus sancti Eadmundi secundum formam prescriptam. *a*

f. 155ᵛ   TAXATIO CLERICORUM REGIS

Maneria et redditus forinseci celerarii	*Secundum taxationem istam decimatum est biennaliter*		
	li.	*s.*	*d.*
Berton	xxv.	xiii.	iiii.
Pakenham	xl.*b*	xiii.	ix.
Rutham	xx.	xvii.	i.
Bradef'	xx.		
Newton'	viii.	xiii.	ix.
Horningesh'	xix.	xv.	ii.ob.
Wepstede	xix.	xviii.	ix.
Ryseby	ix.	iiii.	ii.*c*
Herningewelle	xi.	vi.	iii.ob.*d*
Fornham	viii.	xvi.	ob.
Ingham, Tymewrth'	xii.	xiii.	i.ob.
Cokefeld, portio conuentus *e*	xi.	xvii.	vi.
Chebenhale	x.		
De redditibus in Saham		vii.	i.
De redditibus in Gnateshale		ii.	vi.

a Taxacio Ricardi persone de Snailwell' et Ricardi socii sui

Mildenhale	xlv. m.
Pakenham	xxxii. m.
Vicaria	xv. m.
Berton'	xxx. m.
Vicaria	xv. m.

at the foot of page MS²

b xi. *H*
c ii. d.] ob. *H*

For this reason the convent of Bury St Edmunds paid the tenth for three years on their property which had been assessed before by the said bishop, and handed the tenth to the bishop of Norwich. The rest of their property, which had never been assessed by the said Bishop Walter, contributed equally, having been assessed for the tenth for two years according to the assessment of the aforesaid king's clerks. Here is an example of the assessment and the tenths of all temporal and spiritual revenues of the portion of the convent of Bury St Edmunds according to this arrangement:

Assessment of the King's Clerks [1]

The cellarer's manors and forinsec revenues	This assessment for the tenth was for two years		
	£	s.	d.
Barton	25	13	4
Packenham	40	13	9
Rougham	20	17	1
Bradfield	20		
Newton	8	13	9
Horningsheath	19	15	2½
Whepstead	19	18	9
Risby	9	4	2
Herringswell	11	6	3½
Fornham	8	16	½
Ingham and Timworth	12	13	1½
Cockfield (the convent's portion)	11	17	6
Chepenhall	10		
From revenues in Saham		7	1
From revenues in Knettishall		2	6

d The sum is om. and Heringewell' *written below after* Fornham . . . ob. *H.*
e mon' *H*

[1] The assessments on the last half of this page and the first half of the next are erased and one leaf cancelled in M. (see p. 45, *n. a*).

Ista taxauit W[alterus] quondam Norwicensis episcopus secundum quam taxacionem ut ceteri de episcopatu decimatum est triennaliter.

	li.	*s.*	*d.*
Manerium de Mildenhal'	xxx.		
Portio conuentus in ecclesia ibidem	xx.		
Parua Berton	x.		
Elueden'		c.	
Suthereya	x.		
Ecclesia sancti Laurentii in Norwyc'		xx.	
Ecclesia de Pakenham	xx.		
Vicaria	viii. *a*		
SUMMA			

Certe pensiones   *Taxacio clericorum* *b*

	li.	*s.*	*d.*
De ecclesia de Berton'	iiii.	xiii.	iiii.
De ecclesia de Rucham	iiii.		
De ecclesia de Wlpet	xiii.*c*		
De ecclesia de Parua Horningh'		xiii.	iiii.
De ecclesia de Rudham		xx.	
SUMMA	xxiii.	xiii.	iiii.*d*
Decima		xlvi.	iiii.

f. 156 *Maneria sacriste*   *Taxacio clericorum.* *e*

	li.	*s.*	*d.*
Aldehahe		lxxii.	xi.
Aylesham	xx.		
Westle	vi.	xiii.	iiii.
Semere	xvi.		
Grotene	vi.	xiii.	iiii.
Porcio sacriste in Ikelingham		xxvi.	viii.
Dunham. *W[alterus] episcopus.*			
Decima triennalis		c.	
SUMMA	lix.	vi.	iii.
Decima		cxviii.	vii.ob.*f*

---

a Vicaria . . . li. *MS²*; *om. H*   *b* + regis *H*
c + vi. s. viii. d. *H*   *d* iiii. d. *om. H*

This is the assessment of Walter, formerly bishop of Norwich, according to which the tenth was assessed for three years like the rest of the bishopric.

	£	s.	d.
The manor of Mildenhall	30		
The convent's portion of the revenues of the church			
at Mildenhall	20		
Little Barton	10		
Elveden		100	
Southery	10		
The church of St Lawrence in Norwich		20	
The church at Pakenham	20		
The vicarage	8		
TOTAL			

Certain pensions	*The king's clerks' assessment*		
	£	s.	d.
From the church at Barton	4	13	4
From the church at Rougham	4		
From the church at Woolpit	13		
From the church at Little Horningsheath		13	4
From the church at Rougham		20	
TOTAL	23	13	4
The tenth		46	4

The sacrist's manors	*The king's clerks' assessment*		
	£	s.	d.
Oldhall		72	11
Aylsham	20		
Westley	6	13	4
Semer	16		
Groton	6	13	4
The sacrist's portion in Icklingham		26	8
Downham. *Bishop Walter's assessment for*			
the triennial tenth		100	
TOTAL	59	6	3
The tenth		118	7½

---

e + regis *H*   *f Om. H*

Redditus forinseci sacriste [a]

	li.	*s.*	*d.*
De redditibus de Laki[n]ghey		ii.	xi.
de Mernigthorp		ii.	xi.
in Totington' et Baningh'	x.		
in Reppes et Plumstede		xiii.	ix.
in Thorp' et Frennes		ii.	vi.

SUMMA

Maneria camerarie   *Taxatio W[alteri] episcopi.*
                                Decima triennaliter

	li.	*s.*	*d.*
Hildercle	x.[b]		
Portio camerarie in ecclesia de eadem		xx.	
Stanton'	iiii.		
Castre	vi.	xiii.	iiii.
Broch manerium	xx.		
Portio camerarie in ecclesia de eadem	xxii.	vi.	viii.
Scotisham		xl.	
In Wyrlingwrth'		xx.[c]	

Beccles. *Clerici regis*   xxvi.

          SUMMA   iiii.xx. et xiiii.
          Decima   ix.   viii.

Redditus forinseci elemosinarii

	li.	*s.*	*d.*
Portio elemosinarii in Hildercle		xl.	
Portio eiusdem in Liuermer'			x.
Portio eiusdem in Rathlesden'		xiii.	iiii.
Portio eiusdem in Wlpet		xv.	
Portio eiusdem in ecclesia de Pa[n]keham		xx.	
f. 156ᵛ Portio eiusdem in Redgraue		xl.	
Portio eiusdem in Stanton'		xiii.	iiii.

          SUMMA   vii.   ii.   vi.
          Decima   xiiii.   iii.

---

[a] *Om. H*   [b] ix. *H*   [c] + Taxacio W[alteri] *in margin in red H*

The sacrist's forinsec revenues

	£	s.	d.
Revenues from Lakenheath		2	11
from Morningthorpe		2	11
from Tottington and Banningham	10		
from Northrepps and Plumstead		13	9
from Thorpe and Frenze		2	6
TOTAL			

The chamberlain's manors   Bishop Walter's assessment *for the triennial tenth*

	£	s.	d.
Hinderclay	10		
The chamberlain's portion from the church at Hinderclay		20	
Stanton	4		
Caister St Edmunds	6	13	4
Brooke manor	20		
The chamberlain's portion from the church at Brooke	22	6	8
Shottisham		40	
Worlingworth		20	
Beccles. *Assessment of the king's clerk*	26		
TOTAL	94		
The tenth	9	8	

The almoner's forinsec revenues

	£	s.	d.
The almoner's portion in Hinderclay		40	
His portion in Livermere			10
His portion in Rattlesden		13	4
His portion in Woolpit		15	
His portion in the church at Pakenham		20	
His portion in Redgrave		40	
His portion in Stanton		13	4
TOTAL	7	2	6
The tenth		14	3

Taxatio bonorum pertinencium ad
hospitalem sancti Saluatoris

	li.	s.	d.
Herningewell'		xl.	
Elmeswell'		xiii.	iiii.
Eluedene		xx.	
Coleford		x.	
Redgraue		xl.	
Stanton'		xiii.	iiii.
Haregraue		xiii.	iiii.
Hornigeshth'		xv.	
Newton		xl.	
Cheleswrth'		xxx.	
Meleford		xxxi.	
Cokefeld		xl.	
Saham		xxvi.	viii.
Wyrlingwrth'		liii.	iiii.
Rungeton'		vi.	viii.
Thiuethesal'		xx.	
Tilneye		xvi.	
Ikeli[n]gham	xii.		
Pakenham		xxvi.	viii.
SUMMA	lxv.	iiii.	iiii.
Decima	vi.	x.	v.qu.[a]

	li.	s.	d.
SUMMA taxationis portionis conuentus per omnes obediencias	vi.c.lxv.		ix.ob.
Summa decime	lxvi.	x.	i.
Summa uicesime	xxxiii.	v.	ob.

Singuli obedienciarii prout taxatum erat decimas suas
contribuerunt, excepto camerario quia ipse tunc de
exitu camerarie respondebat conuentui pro qua eciam
f. 157 cum celeraria conuentus decimas persoluit. Dictus [b] /
eciam conuentus monasterii beati martyris Eadmundi,

[a] Summa . . . qua om. H
[b] Change of handwriting, henceforth 33 lines to a page instead of 32 MS

Assessment of the revenues
  belonging to St Saviour's Hospital

	£	s.	d.
Herringswell		40	
Elmswell		13	4
Elveden		20	
Culford		10	
Redgrave		40	
Stanton		13	4
Hargrave		13	4
Horningsheath		15	
Newton		40	
Chelsworth		30	
Melford		31	
Cockfield		40	
Soham		26	8
Worlingworth		43	4
Runcton		6	8
Tivetshall		20	
Tilney		16	
Icklingham	12		
Pakenham		26	8
TOTAL	65	4	4
The tenth	6	10	$5\frac{1}{4}$

	£	s.	d.
The TOTAL of the assessment of the convent's portion including all the obedientiaries' offices	665		$9\frac{1}{2}$
The total tenth	66	10	1
The total twentieth	33	5	$\frac{1}{2}$

Each obedientiary contributed to the tenth according to the assessment except the chamberlain, because at this time he was liable to the convent for the income of the chamberlain's office, so the convent paid his tenth with that of the cellarer. The convent of the monastery

ne bona eorum infra limites uille eiusdem constituta taxarentur, episcopali exactori et decimarum collectori xx. marcas clam conferri procurauit. Taxatores tamen regales sub signo sacriste taxacionem antedictorum bonorum optinuerunt, uidelicet c. libre, vnde porcio sacriste fuit l. libre, porcio celerarii xvi. libre, porcio elemosinarii xxxiiii. libre. *a*

Isto anno die apostolorum Symonis et Iude[1] completus est lii. annus regni regis Henrici filii regis Iohannis. Clemens papa obiit uigilia sancti Andree[2] uacauitque sedes annis duobus, mensibus nouem, ebdomadis tribus diebus quatuor. *b*

1269

Eadmundus filius Henrici regis filiam et heredem comitis Aubemarlie[3] duxit in uxorem, domino rege apud Westmonasterium nupcias celebrante v. Idus Aprilis. Orta est discordia inter Eadwardum filium regis et G[ilbertum] comitem Glouernie ob nimiam [amoris] *c* familiaritatem quam idem Eadwardus erga uxorem dicti comitis dicebatur habere. Comes Glouernie cepit quemdam apud Kairdif qui ipsum ueneno moliebatur extinguere.[4] Rex Henricus transtulit sanctum Eadwardum in nouum presbiterium quod sibi opere mirifico preparauerat, ipsum in nouo loculo recondens die antique*d* translacionis eiusdem.[5] Rex exegit decimam cleri eciam de quarto anno; contra quam quia episcopi noluerunt ab uniuersitate cleri

---

a Taxacio clericorum regis (above, p. 41) . . . libr' *erased and cancelled M.*
b Clemens papa . . . quatuor om. H; *lacuna of 1 line MS (2 M)*
c *Supplied from M (also Oxenedes)*; amore H; *om. MS*
d antiqua *MS, H, M, P;* antique *Oxenedes and Cotton*

[1] 28 October   [2] 29 November   [3] Aveline de Forz (1258/9–74)

of the blessed martyr Edmund arranged for 20 marks to be given secretly to the episcopal assessor and collector of the tenth so that its possessions within the boundaries of the town of Bury St Edmunds should not be assessed. The royal assessors, however, obtained the assessment of these possessions under the sacrist's seal. The assessment was for £100; the sacrist's share was £50, the cellarer's £16 and the almoner's £34.

In this year on the feast of the apostles Simon and Jude [1] the fifty-second year of the reign of King Henry, son of King John, was completed. Pope Clement died on the vigil of the feast of St Andrew [2] and the Holy See remained vacant for two years, nine months, three weeks and four days.

1269

Edmund, son of King Henry, married the daughter and heiress of the count of Aumâle.[3] The king attended the marriage at Westminster on 9 April. A quarrel broke out between Edward, the king's son, and Gilbert, earl of Gloucester, because of the excessive intimacy which Edward was said to have with the earl's wife. At Cardiff the earl of Gloucester caught a man who was attempting to destroy him with poison.[4] King Henry translated Saint Edward [the Confessor] to the new presbytery which he had had built with great splendour for him, and there he was interred in a new grave on the day of his previous translation.[5] The king demanded the tenth from the clergy for a fourth year; the whole clergy appealed against this because the bishops were

---

[4] These last two remarks about Gilbert de Clare do not seem to be mentioned by any other authority.

[5] 13 October

appellatum est. Eadwardus et comes Glouernie multis magnatibus interuenientibus in osculum pacis se receperunt.

f. 157ᵛ   Eadwardus *a* transfretans ad colloquendum cum rege Francie super negocio eundi ad Terram Sanctam sic ferunt inter eos pactum fuisse, uidelicet ut rex Francie accommodaret domino Eadwardo lxx. millia marcas,[1] cunctis terris Eadwardi transmarinis regi Francie obligatis.*b* Quam summam pecunie nisi infra triennium persolueret dicte terre Eadwardi perpetuo*c* regi Francie remanerent et quia una cum rege Francie proficisceretur in Terram Sanctam eidem regi quasi unus de propriis baronibus fideliter obtemperaturus. Super quo filium suum Henricum nomine eidem misit obsidem *d* qui statim qua nescitur de causa remittebatur.*e* [2]   Ciuitas de Nuchers reddita fuit Karolo regi Sicilie uigilia sancti Bartholomei [3] in qua erant neci tradita iii. millia Sarracenorum reliqua multitudine in ciuitate sub tributo remanente. Iusticiarii itinerantes in Norf' et Suff' fuerunt Nicholaus de Turr', Henricus de Monte Forti et Henricus de Wlhamton'.*f*

1270

Vigilia et die Palmarum [4] conuenientibus Christianis et paganis inter Acon et Saphran cesis primo octo admiralis necnon paganorum xviii. aciebus non sine maxima

----

a + filius regis *interlin. MS²*
b Eadwardus transfretans . . . obligatis *seems to be marked* uacat *MS²*
c perpetue *M*
d obsidē *MS*; obsidem *M (and Oxenedes)*; obsidione *H*
e Lacuna of 2 lines MS; 3 lines erased M; + Lodowycus rex Franc' iter arripuit uersus Terram Sanctam xvii. Kal. Aprilis *H; the same passage is below under 1270 MS, M.*
f Lacuna of 1 line MS (3 M)

[1] *Foedera*, I, p. 481, gives 70,000 livres tour

unwilling to. Edward and the earl of Gloucester exchanged the kiss of peace after many magnates had intervened.

Edward set sail in order to discuss with the king of France the proposed expedition to the Holy Land. It is said that the following bargain was struck between them: the king of France was to pay the Lord Edward 70,000 marks,[1] and all Edward's continental possessions were pledged to the king of France as security for repayment; if the money was not repaid within three years these lands to be forfeited forever to the king of France; and that Edward would set out for the Holy Land with the king of France, being prepared to obey him faithfully like one of his own barons. Edward therefore sent his son called Henry to the king of France as a hostage; he was immediately sent back for no known reason.[2] The city of Lucera was surrendered to Charles, king of Sicily, on the vigil of the feast of St Bartholomew.[3] When it had been handed over three thousand Saracens were slaughtered and the many who remained stayed there as tributaries. The justices in eyre in Norfolk and Suffolk were Nicholas de Turr', Henry de Montfort and Henry de Woolhampton.

1270

On the vigil and on the day of Palm Sunday [4] the Christians and the infidels met in battle between Acre and Safed. First eight emirs and eighteen columns of infidels were killed, then eventually the infidels were

---

[2] cf. *Flores*, III, p. 18.
[3] 23 August was the date of the battle of Tagliacozzo (p. 40 above) in 1268. Lucera fell on 27 August.
[4] 6 April

suorum amissione uictoria tamen potiti sunt pagani.
Cesi sunt Christiani usque ad internicionem et hoc per
sedicionem Templariorum ubi eciam cecidit flos milicie
frater Iohannes de Merlawe de Hospitali. Ludowicus
rex Francie xvii. Kal. Aprilis iter arripuit uersus terram
Ierosolimitanam, qui die sancti Iacobi apud Aquam
Mortuam mari se commisit Mediterraneo.[1]

f. 158   In octauas sancti Iohannis [2] [Iohannes] [a] comes
Warrenn' insultum faciens in dominum Alanum la
Thuche in aula Westmonasterii ad Bancum coram
iusticiarios ipsum quidem crudeliter uulnerauit, qui die
sancti [b] Laurencii diem clausit extremum.[3] Filius uero
eius primogenitus Rogerus fuga sibi consulens, uix
tamen euasit. [c] Alienora uxor domini Eadwardi [d] regis
primogeniti peperit filiam apud Wyndleshores quam
uocauit Alienoram. Die Translacionis sancti Martini [4]
obiit Rogerus Bigod comes Norf' et Suff' marescallus
Anglie apud Cuhahe; sepultus [e] est apud Theford
Monachorum vigilia Translacionis sancti Benedicti.[5]
Qui sine prole decedens successorem habuit in hereditate
et dignitate Rogerum filium Hugonis Bigod, fratris
eiusdem defuncti. [f] Edwardus regis Anglie primogenitus, Henricus de Alemannia, ceterique Anglie
magnates non nulli in crastino sancti Laurentii [6] apud
Douere nauigio se commiserunt per Gasconiam tendentes
Ierosolimam. Qui die sancti Michaelis mare con-
scenderunt Mediterraneum et una cum Francie et
Sicilie regibus non nullis eciam singularum illarum

---

[a] *Supplied from M (and Oxenedes); om. MS*
[b] *Added MS²; in text M (and Oxenedes)*
[c] Vigilia et die Palmarum . . . euasit *seems to be marked* uacat *MS²*
[d] + domini *M*   [e] + que *M (and Oxenedes)*
[f] *Space for paragraph marks MS; paragraph mark M*

victorious, but not without very great loss of men. The Christian army was nearly wiped out because of the sedition of the Templars. Even Brother John de Marlow, a Hospitaller and a flower of knighthood, fell. Louis [IX], king of France, set out for the land of Jerusalem on 16 March and embarked on the Mediterranean at Aigues-Mortes on the feast of St James.[1]

On the octave of St John's day[2] Earl John de Warenne attacked Alan de la Zouche in Westminster hall before the justices of the King's Bench and badly wounded him; he died on the feast of St Lawrence.[3] Alan's eldest son Roger took refuge in flight but hardly escaped. Eleanor, wife of the Lord Edward, the king's eldest son, gave birth at Windsor to a daughter, whom she named Eleanor. On the feast of the Translation of St Martin,[4] Roger Bigod, earl of Norfolk and Suffolk and marshal of England, died at Cowhaugh; he was buried at Thetford on the vigil of the Translation of St Benedict.[5] As he died without children the heir to his inheritance and dignity was Roger, the son of Hugh Bigod, the brother of the deceased. Edward, the king of England's eldest son, Henry of Germany and some of the other English nobles, on the morrow of the feast of St Lawrence[6] sailed from Dover for Gascony on their way to Jerusalem. On Michaelmas day they embarked on the Mediterranean, and with the kings of France and Sicily and several nobles of their countries turned aside

---

[1] 25 July. According to Nangis, *Vie de S. Louis*, p. 442, Louis embarked on
1 July.
[2] 1 July   [3] 10 August   [4] 4 July   [5] 10 July
[6] 11 August. The chronicles disagree on the date.

nacionum *a* proceribus a recto deuiantes itinere Affricam tendentes terram regis Tunicie, *b* 1 ubi sita est famosissima ciuitas illa Cartaginensis, intrauerunt. Ibique cum rege supradicto pagano componentes *c* treugas cum eo inierunt quindecennales. Dominus autem Eadwardus ab Affrica rediens in Sicilia aliquandiu commoratus *d* est. In illo itinere *e* obiit Ludowycus rex Francie relinquens Philippum filium suum et heredem, sepultusque est apud sanctum Dionisium. Bonefacius Cantuariensis archiepiscopus obiit xv. Kal. Augusti apud Baleys castellum suum in Prouincia,2 electusque est in successorem eiusdem Adam de Chilenden' eius loci prior natus in Cancia, cui rex eiusque primogenitus se opposuerunt. Quapropter necessitate cogente curiam adiit Romanam. Guido de Monte Forti duxit in f. 158ᵛ uxorem Viterbii filiam / et heredem comitis Rubei 3 die sancti Laurencii.4 Adam de Wich abbas de Waltham obiit die sancti Lamberti,5 sepultusque est apud Waltham in crastino. Facta est eclipsis lune nocte primum diem Octobris precedente. *f*

1271

In octauis Epiphanie obiit Walterus de la Wile episcopus Sar',6 cui successit Robertus eiusdem loci decanus, uacante tunc sede Cantuariensi ab eiusdem loci capitulo confirmatus. Eadmundus filius regis Anglie mare transiit tam loca sancta quam fratrem suum primo-

---

a -nū *corr. MS*²   *b* -cie *corr. MS*²   *c* pepigentes *M*
d qui die sancti Michaelis . . . commoratus *seems to be marked* uacat *MS*²
*e Corr. MS*²
f Guido . . . precedente *marked* uacat *MS*²; *lacuna of* 1 *line MS* (*4 M*)

1 Emir Abû 'Abd Allâh al-Mostansir billâh (1249–77)
2 Now Savoy. He died at Sainte Hélène in Savoy; J. Le Neve, *Fasti ecclesiae Anglicanae* (ed. T. D. Hardy, 1854), I, p. 14, *n.* 88; continuator

to sail to Africa and disembarked in the land of the king
of Tunis,[1] where the renowned city of Carthage is.
There they concluded a truce of fifteen years with this
infidel king. Edward returned from Africa and stayed
for a while in Sicily. King Louis died on the journey,
leaving his son Philip as his heir, and was buried at
St Denis. Boniface, archbishop of Canterbury, died on
18 July at his castle of Belley in Provence.[2] Adam de
Chillenden, prior of Christ Church, Canterbury, who
had been born in Kent, was elected to succeed him.
But the king and his eldest son opposed him. For this
reason it was necessary for him to go to the Roman
court. Guy de Montfort married the daughter and
heiress of Count Rosso[3] at Viterbo on the feast of St
Lawrence.[4] Adam de Wich, abbot of Waltham, died
on the feast of St Lambert[5] and was buried on the next
day at Waltham. There was an eclipse of the moon on
the night preceding the first day of October.

1271

On the octave of the Epiphany Walter de la Wyle,
bishop of Salisbury, died.[6] He was succeeded by
Robert, dean of Salisbury. As the see of Canterbury
was then vacant his election was confirmed by the
chapter of Canterbury. Edmund, the king of England's
son, crossed the sea to visit both the Holy Land and his

Gervase of Canterbury, ed. W. Stubbs (RS, 1879–80), ii, p. 250.
  [3] Margaret, daughter of Ildebrandino, the first count of Soana and
Pitigliano, universally known as Rosso; F. M. Powicke, ' Guy de Montfort,'
in *Transactions of the Royal Historical Society*, 4th series, xviii (1935), p. 13.
  [4] 10 August. The date and place do not seem to be given by any
other authority.
  [5] 17 September
  [6] 13 January. According to *Oseney*, p. 238, *Wig.* p. 460, he died on
3 January.

genitum uisitaturus. Quinto Kal. Februarii cecidit
turris ecclesie beate Marie de Arcubus London'
multosque sub ipsa ecclesia commorantes oppressit et
extinxit. Dominus Henricus regis Alemannie primogenitus per *a* Viterbium ab Affrica transitum faciens, in
ecclesia sancti Siluestri [1] ibidem diuinorum celebracioni
deuote intendens, a dominis S[ymone] et G[uidone] de
Monte Forti, comite Rubeo,[2] necnon aliis *b* nonnullis
superuenientibus, in crastino sancti Gregorii [3] crudeliter
interemptus est. Cuius reliquias Anglie sui reportarunt
et apud Hayles xii. Kal. Iunii recondiderunt. *c*[4] Quinto-
decimo Kal. Augusti apud Norwycum celebratum est
diuorcium inter G[ilbertum] comitem Glouernie et
Aliciam comitissam eiusdem coniugem. Sexto Idus
Augusti traditus fuit sepulture apud Westmonasterium
dominus I[ohannes] de Wyncestr' primogenitus domini
Eadwardi domini H[enrici] regis Anglie primogeniti.
Philippus rex Francie coronatus est Remis die
Decollacionis sancti Iohannis Baptiste.[5] Duodecimo
Kal. Decembris natus est Henrico de Lacy comiti
Lincoln' filius quem *d* de nomine sancti Eadmundi
Eadmundum duxit nominandum. Apud Cantuariam
f. 159 tercio Idus Septembris descendit quasi / subito quedam
nubes integra circa horam uespertinam super ciuitatem
et super patriam adiacentem, ita ut maxima ciuitatis
pars aquis subito precipitaretur, durauitque illius aque
defluxus usque ad horam primam diei sequentis. *e*
Kalendis Septembris Theodaldus archidiaconus Leodiensis cum domino Eadwardo regis Anglie primogenito

---

a in *M*   *b Exp. M*
  c Quinto Kal. Februarii . . . recondiderunt *seems to be marked* uacat *MS*[2]
  d quam *before corr. MS*[2]; quam *M*
  e Duodecimo Kal. Decembr' . . . sequentis *marked* uacat *MS*[2]

eldest brother. The tower of the church of St Mary le Bow in London fell on 28 January and crushed to death a number of people living next to the church. Henry, the king of Germany's eldest son, passing through Viterbo on his way from Africa, while he was piously attending divine service in the church of St Silvester,[1] was attacked and brutally murdered by the lords Simon and Guy de Montfort, Count Rosso[2] and some others on the morrow of St Gregory.[3] His body was carried to England and buried at the abbey of Hayles on 21 May.[4] On 18 July the divorce took place at Norwich of Gilbert, earl of Gloucester, and his wife, the Countess Alice. On 8 August John de Winchester, the eldest son of the Lord Edward, the king of England's first-born, was buried at Westminster. Philip [III], king of France, was crowned at Rheims on the feast of the Decollation of St John the Baptist.[5] A son was born to Henry de Lacy, earl of Lincoln, on 20 November, who was named Edmund after St Edmund. At Canterbury on 11 September about nightfall an entire cloud burst over the city and the surrounding country-side, so that most of the city was swept away by the sudden downpour of rain; the cloud-burst lasted until the first hour of the next day. On 1 September Theodald, archdeacon of Liège, who was with Edward, the king of England's eldest son, in the region of Acre,

---

[1] Though authorities differ as to the scene of the murder, the church of St Silvester (now the Chiesa del Gesù) is the generally accepted place; Powicke, art. cit. p. 16.

[2] Guy's father-in-law.   [3] 13 March

[4] Richard, earl of Cornwall, was founder of the Cistercian abbey of Hayles; Mon. Angl., v, p. 686–8. He was buried there: below, p. 50.

[5] 29 August. He was crowned on 15 August; Grandes Chron., VIII, pp. 38, 39 and n. 1.

in partibus agens Acconensibus in summum pontificem
est electus, dictusque est Gregorius decimus. Ante
cuius eleccionem uacauit sedes apostolica annis duobus,
mensibus nouem, ebdomadis tribus, diebus quatuor.
Vigilia Omnium Sanctorum [1] dominus Philippus Basset
apud Weldam [2] diem clausit extremum. Obiit eciam
Fulco Dublinensis archiepiscopus. [a]

1272

Vigilia sancti Cuthberti [3] Theodaldus Leodiensis archidiaconus genere Piacentinus, nuper in Petri successorem
electus, in sacerdotem est consecratus et in crastino
dominica uidelicet secunda Quadragesime [4] ad summum
sacerdocium est prouectus et in cathedra summi pontificatus solempniter est cathedratus, dictusque est
Gregorius decimus. Ricardus Alemannie rex iiii. Non.
Aprilis apud Berhamstede diem clausit extremum;
sepultusque est apud monasterium de Hayles, quod ipse
a fundamentis construxit et honoribus pluribus ditauit,
cuius exequie solempniter sunt ibidem celebrate Idibus
Aprilis. Die Apostolorum Petri et Pauli [5] apud Norwicum conuentu ad primam existente subito fulminis
ictu uersus aquilonem percussa est ecclesie turris
principalis, in tantum ut tempestatis illius uiolencia non
nulli lapides euulsi ad loca remotiora uiolenter sunt
f. 159ᵛ transportati,[b] / quod quidem non sine prodigio uniuersis
sancte matris ecclesie filiis stupendo liquet contigisse.
In crastino enim sancti Laurencii [6] anno eodem, post

---

[a] *Lacuna of 1 line MS (3 M)*
[b] *A line in pencil runs down the margin from* ua- *written above, opposite*
sepultusque est apud monasterium, *but no* -cat *is visible MS²*.

[1] 31 October. *Ann. Lond.*, p. 82, agrees with this date, but *Oseney*, p. 247,
gives 29 October.

was elected pope and took the name Gregory X.
Before his election the Apostolic See had been vacant
for two years, nine months, three weeks and four days.
On the vigil of All Saints [1] Philip Basset died at Weldon.[2]
Fulk, archbishop of Dublin, also died.

1272

On St Cuthbert's eve [3] Theodald, archdeacon of Liège
and a native of Piacenza, who had previously been
elected successor of St Peter, was consecrated as a priest
and on the morrow (which was the second Sunday in
Lent)[4] promoted the head of the priesthood and solemnly
enthroned as supreme pontiff. He took the name
Gregory X. Richard, king of Germany, died at
Berkhampstead on 2 April and was buried at the
monastery of Hayles, which he had built from its
foundations and lavishly endowed. His obsequies were
celebrated there solemnly on 13 April. On the feast of
the Apostles Peter and Paul [5] at Norwich, when the
convent were at prime, a sudden flash of lightning struck
the main tower of the church towards the north so hard
that the force of the storm sent stones flying great
distances. This happened, it is clear, as a miraculous
portent for all the sons of Holy Mother Church. For in
the same year, on the morrow of the feast of St
Lawrence,[6] after many assaults had been made on the

---

[2] ? Weldon, Northants. He was buried at Stanley, Wilts., according
to *Oseney*, p. 247, *Wig.*, p. 461.

[3] 19 March

[4] 20 March. This is wrong for he was consecrated on 27 March;
Potthast, II, p. 1653.

[5] 29 June

[6] 11 August. cf. Cotton, pp. 146–8, for a similar account of the attack
on Norwich abbey.

insultus non nullos in prioratum sepius numero factos, post ianuas conuentus ab eorum emulis uiolenter confractas, necnon alias iniurias enormes sepius illatas, statim post conuentus refectionem ad sanctam matrem suam ecclesiam accesserunt eiusdem sancte matris filii spurcissimi, tota uidelicet communitas ciuitatis Norwic' numero ut creditur xxxii. millia strenuissime armatorum. Qui una cum ciuitatis mulieribus ignem per loca diuersa prioratus apponentes ecclesiam totumque prioratum preter tria uel quatuor edificia inter cetera uix numeranda, opere tantum lapideo sed nec hoc penitus exceptato in cineres redigerunt. Monachos uero fere omnes fugarunt. De eorum quoque seruientibus triginta uel eo circa diuersis suppliciorum generibus hos in gremio materno neci tradiderunt, illos a gremio eodem tanquam a matris abstractos uberibus et ante tribunal proprium adductos *a* nulli parcentes etati aut ordini eadem sentencia dampnauerunt. Omnia eciam preciosa tam in thesaurario, uestiario, refectorio, quam eciam in ceteris ecclesie illius officinis et almaria ea minutim confringentes et depredantes asportarunt. Monachi uero unus post alium clam fugientes uix uita comite recesserunt. Conuocato igitur die Decollationis sancti Iohannis Baptiste[1] apud Eyam tocius episcopatus concilio tam episcopus quam uniuersus episcopi clerus ibidem congregatus in dictum facinus perpetrantes f. 160 omnes eciam fauore auxilio aut / consilio eisdem consencientes aut contractu qualicumque cum eisdem communicantes, pulsatis campanis, accensis luminariis, sentenciam excommunicacionis puplice et solempniter tulerunt. Que quidem sentencia habito London' episco-

---

a abductos *before corr. MS²*; abductos *M*

[1] 29 August

priory, the convent gates broken down forcibly by
the rebels and much other outrageous damage done,
immediately after the convent had dined some vile
sons of Holy Mother Church, that is the whole
commonalty of Norwich city, numbering it is believed
thirty-two thousand men armed to the teeth, marched
on their holy mother church herself. Together with the
women of the city they set fire to various parts of the priory
and reduced the church and whole priory to ashes except
for three or four buildings hardly worth mentioning
among all the rest ; only the stone-work was saved and
even that not wholly. Nearly all the monks were driven
out. Some thirty or so of their servants, after tortures of
various kinds, were either done to death in the bosom of
their mother church or torn from the church as from a
mother's breast, dragged before a special tribunal and
condemned with the same sentence, without respect for age
or rank. The townsfolk smashed to pieces and plundered
all the valuables in the treasury, vestry and refectory as
well as in the other offices of the church and in the
cupboards. The monks fled secretly one after another
and scarcely escaped with their lives. Because of these
events a council of the whole diocese was held at Eye
on the feast of the Decollation of St John the Baptist.[1]
There both the bishop and all his clergy met in order to
pronounce publicly and solemnly, with the ringing of
bells and with lighted candles, the excommunication of
those guilty of this crime and all those who had supported
them with approval, help or advice, or had had anything
whatever to do with them. When a council of bishops

porum Anglie consilio die sancti Luce [1] ab eis renouata est et confirmata.[2] Ad cuius enormitatis scelus in transgressoribus refundendum motus dominus rex uersus partes Norwicenses die sancti Egidii [3] apud sanctum Eadmundum accessit. Ibidemque super negocio memorato consulendus uniuersos tocius Anglie proceres uocauit et magnates. Mora igitur ibidem per xi. dies facta, die sanctorum Proti et Iacincti [4] uersus Norwicum pro uindicta de tanto scelere capienda iter arripuit. Qui moram ibidem per dies xiii.[5] faciens uindicte de tanto scelere quamuis non ad plenum faciende aliquantulum indulsit. Triginta namque et quatuor uiri unaque mulier de tanta multitudine, reliquorum marsupiis a curialibus emunctis, quidam quidem per uicos ciuitatis distracti, quidam suspensi, quidam combusti, non nulli eciam eorum singularum penarum ipsarum mulctati [a] supplicio, penas luerunt ceterorum.

Eadmundus de Alemannia, comes Cornubie, duxit in uxorem Margaretam, sororem Gileberti comitis Glouernie, in crastino sancte Fidis.[6] Qui una cum Henrico de Lacy comite Lincoln' die Translacionis sancti Eadwardi [7] accinctus est militaribus. Adam de Chilenden' electus Cantuariensis in curia Romana pro beneficio confirmacionis sue optinenda [sic] constitutus animaduertens se propter emulos sibi uehementer infestos in negocio suo minime proficere immo si staret, quod in nominis sui uerecundia redundaret non modica, cassaturum se fore, cessit eleccioni pariter et dignitati.[b]

---

[a] *Om. and a lacuna* ⅔ *in. long M*
[b] Eadmundus de Alemannia . . . dignitati *marked* uacat *in margin MS*[2]

[1] 18 October
[2] Reference to this council in London does not seem to occur elsewhere.
[3] 1 September   [4] 11 September
[5] Probably an error for ' xvii,' as Henry was still at Norwich on 24

was held in London on the feast of St Luke [1] the sentence of excommunication was renewed and confirmed.[2] Determined to visit this monstrous outrage on its perpetrators the king set out towards Norwich, and on St Giles's day [3] came to Bury St Edmunds. There he summoned all the great men and nobles of all England to consult about the matter. After staying at Bury for eleven days he left for Norwich on the feast of SS. Prothus and Hyacinth [4] to take vengeance for so great a crime. He remained at Norwich for thirteen days [5] but compromised a little, doing only partial justice for the outrage: thus thirty-four men and one woman from the great multitude paid the penalty for the rest (the others had their purses emptied by the royal officials); some were dragged through the streets of the city; some were hanged; some burned and not a few of them subjected to the torment of each penalty in turn and paid the penalty for all the rest.

Edmund of Germany, earl of Cornwall, married Margaret, the sister of Gilbert, earl of Gloucester, on the morrow of St Faith's day.[6] He was knighted with Henry de Lacy, earl of Lincoln, on the feast of the Translation of St Edward.[7] When Adam de Chillenden, archbishop-elect of Canterbury, was staying at the Roman court to obtain the benefit of confirmation, he realised that because of the bitter enemies who surrounded him he was having little success in his quest, and that on the contrary if he persisted his election would be quashed, which would bring considerable disgrace on his name;

September (*CCR, 1268–72*, p. 526) and left on 26 September, according to Cotton, p. 149.

[6] 7 October   [7] 13 October

f. 160ᵛ / Pro quo dominus papa fratrem Robertum de Kilwardeby priorem prouincialem ordinis Fratrum Predicatorum in Anglia auctoritate apostolica subrogauit. Rex die sancti Calixti [1] synagogam Iudeorum in uilla London' fratribus de Penitencia contulit Iesu Christi. Qui quidem locus ad maiorem Iudeorum confusionem a quodam ad hoc uocato dedicatus est episcopo. Felicis memorie Henricus rex Anglie [a] filius regis Iohannis cum regnasset annis lvi., diebus xxix., die sancti Eadmundi Cantuariensis [2] archiepiscopi, Eadwardo primogenito suo in partibus agente transmarinis, apud Westmonasterium uite terminum fecit. Qui die sancti Eadmundi regis et martyris proximo sequente [3] honeste ibidem traditus est sepulture. Et quia, ut dictum est, dominus Eadwardus in partibus tunc agebat remotis, pacis regalitatisque cura usque [b] ad eiusdem domini Eadwardi aduentum seruande, communi procerum assensu Eadmundo Cornubie et Gileberto Glouernie comitibus est commissa. Alienora uxor domini Eadwardi peperit filiam apud Acconem quam uocauit Iohannam. Eadmundus filius regis Anglie rediit a Terra Sancta relinquens in partibus illis dominum Eadwardum fratrem suum. Qui a quondam Assisino in dolo nuper fere usque ad mortem fuerat uulneratus. Sed ab Eo qui humiles respicit uisitatus perfecte in breui fuit sanitati restitutus. Contigit autem hoc die sancti Botulphi.[4] Rogerus abbas sancti Augustini Idibus Decembris [5] diem clausit extremum. Dominus papa generale cele-

---

[a] obiit Henricus III ᵘˢ rex *in margin MS*
[b] *Corr. MS²*

[1] 14 October. The royal mandate to the mayor and sheriffs of London to give the Penitentiary friars seisin of the synagogue is dated 6 September 1272 at Bury St Edmunds; *CCR, 1268–72*, p. 522.
[2] 16 November   [3] 20 November   [4] 17 June

so he resigned his election and also the office. The pope, therefore, appointed in his place by apostolic authority Brother Robert de Kilwardby, the prior-provincial of the Friars Preachers in England. On the feast of St Calixtus [1] the king transferred the Jews' synagogue in London to the Brothers of Penitence in the name of Jesus Christ. The place was dedicated by a bishop summoned for the purpose, to the utter confusion of the Jews. Henry, king of England of happy memory, the son of King John, after he had reigned for fifty-six years and twenty-nine days, died at Westminster on the feast of St Edmund of Canterbury [2] while his eldest son Edward was abroad, and was honourably interred there on the following feast of St Edmund, king and martyr. [3] Because the Lord Edward, as has been mentioned, was in distant lands at the time, the keeping of the peace and care of the royal authority were committed, by the common consent of the leaders of the realm, to Edmund, earl of Cornwall, and Gilbert, earl of Gloucester, until Edward's return. The Lord Edward's wife Eleanor gave birth to a daughter at Acre, whom she named Joan. Edmund, the king of England's son, returned from the Holy Land leaving his brother Edward there. Edward was so badly wounded by the guile of an Assassin that he nearly died, but he was visited by Him who cares for the humble and quickly restored to perfect health. This happened on St Botulph's day. [4] Roger, abbot of St Augustine's [Canterbury], died on 13 December. [5] The pope

---

[5] This date is confirmed by W. Thorn, *Chronica de rebus gestis abbatum S. Augustini Cantuarie*, ed. R. Twysden, *Scriptores*, x (London 1652), p. 1920.

brari constituit concilium post biennium in capite Kal. Maii.*

1273

f. 161 Marcius ad modum uentosus et ultra quam nulla meminit etas pluuiosus. Sed et penultimo die Marcii uidelicet iii. Kal. Aprilis fere nocte dieque continuata inundacio tanta erupit quod parum ab inundacione [anni] *b* Domini m.cc.lviii. facta distare uidebatur. Sed et in quibusdam locis per Angliam supradictam inundacionem pre sui uiolencia transire uidebatur. Pontem enim Grantebrigie quinque pedum altitudine transcendit. Necnon eciam apud Norwycum tante fuit uiolencie quod nec insulanorum rapine nec regalium ibidem nuper facta discussio eidem uix possent equiparari infortunio. Dominus Eadwardus die sancti Valentini cardinalibus per v. dietas sibi occurrentibus apud Vrbem Veterem cum honore incredibili et antea inaudito a domino papa et populo uniuerso solempniter est susceptus. Comes Rubeus [1] coram domino papa dominoque E[dwardo] cum numerosa manu militari de morte domini H[enrici] de Alemannia prestito sacramento quod eius neci non consensisset se excusauit. *c* Dominus papa concessit domino E[dwardo] decimam omnium prouentuum ecclesiasticorum tam temporalium quam spiritualium de uno anno *d* et eius fratri de alio in recompensacionem expensarum factarum in Terra Sancta. Ad cuius negocii execucionem magister [2] Rey-

---

a *Lacuna of 1 line MS (3 M)*
b *Supplied from M (and Oxenedes); om. MS*
c Marcius ad modum . . . excusauit *seems to be marked* uacat *MS²*
d uno anno *on erasure MS*

[1] See under 1271, above p. 48, and n. 3. For the count's trial see

ordained that a general council would be held in two years' time on 1 May.

1273

March was very windy, and rainy beyond all memory. On the last day but one in March (that is on 30 March) rain poured almost without stopping night and day and a flood rose which seemed to be nearly as great as that of 1258. In some places in England it even appeared to exceed in violence that inundation, for the flood rose five feet above the bridge at Cambridge, and at Norwich the strength of the flood was such that neither the ravages of the men of the Isle nor the havoc wrought there recently by the king's officials could equal this catastrophe. The cardinals went a five-day journey to meet the Lord Edward, who was solemnly received at Orvieto on St Valentine's day by the pope and all the people with extraordinary and previously unheard-of honour. Count Rosso,[1] in the presence of the pope and the Lord Edward, with numerous knights excused himself from responsibility for the death of Henry of Germany, taking an oath that he had not consented to his murder. The pope granted the Lord Edward a tenth of all ecclesiastical revenues from both temporalities and spiritualities for one year. He granted Edward's brother a similar tenth for another year in return for the expenses he had incurred in the Holy Land. To dispatch this business Master Raymond de Nogaret,[2]

---

no. 217 in *Registres de Grég. X (1272–6)*, ed. Jean Guiraud (Bibliothèque des Écoles françaises d'Athènes et de Rome, série 2, XII).

[2] Master Raymond de Nogaret, canon of St Caprais, Agen, papal chaplain and nuncio, general collector in England 1272–7; Lunt, *Financial Relations*, p. 618.

mundus de Nogeriis prior sancti Caprasii Agennensis
uenit in Angliam. Vnde conuentus sancti Eadmundi
finem fecit pro decimis omnium bonorum *a* de uno anno
in communi cum abbate, de uno anno pro c. libris et
similiter pro secundo, abbate l. marcas et conuentu c.
marcas de ipsa pecunia contribuente, addita insuper
decima spiritualium ad conuentum spectancium de
primo anno sed non de secundo. Adam quondam
electus Cantuarie Angliam rediens prioratui / suo est
restitutus.

f. 161ᵛ

Quidam malignus spiritus in pago Rathomagensi in
uilla que Trobbleuill dicitur multos terruit parietes *b*
malleis prout audiebatur et hostia pulsando et loquebatur
humana uoce sed non uidebatur et uocabatur prout ipse
dixit Willelmus Ardens. Frequentabat autem domum
cuiusdam boni hominis cui multa mala inferebat et
similiter uxori et familie sue. Nec fugari potuit aut
crucis signo aut aque benedicte aspersione. Immo
quando coniurabant eum sacerdotes in nomine Domini *c*
ut recederet respondit, ' Non recedam immo si uoluero
omnes uos occidam. Ego bene noui crucem et aquam
benedictam non timeo.' Conuersabatur autem idem
spiritus in manerio et domo supradictis a festo Omnium
Sanctorum usque post Purificacionem et multos
sermones lasciuos et scuriles protulit. Tandem autem
Septuagesima recessit dicens se reuersurum in Pascha,
quod non fecit. *d*

Henricus de Sandwich' episcopus Londoniensis apud
Horseth' manerium suum post totum prelacionis sue
tempus in maxima angustia¹ consummatum diem

---

a + suorum *M* (*and Oxenedes*)
b parites *MS*; parietes *M* (*and Oxenedes*)
c -e do- *on erasure MS*
d Quidam . . . fecit *marked* uacat *MS*²

prior of St Caprais at Agen, came to England. The convent of Bury St Edmunds, instead of the tenth of all their revenues for one year, paid a fine in common with the abbot of £100 for one year, and similarly for the second year: the abbot contributed 50 marks and the convent 100 marks from their own money, and to these sums was added a tenth of the spiritualities belonging to the convent for the first year, but not for the second. Adam, formerly the archbishop-elect of Canterbury, returned to England and was restored to office as prior.

A certain evil spirit terrified many people in the town called Trouville in the district of Rouen, beating walls and doors (to judge by the sound) with a hammer; it spoke with a human voice but was not seen, and said it was called Blazing William. It haunted the house of a worthy man and did much harm to him, his wife and household. Neither the sign of the cross nor the sprinkling of holy water could drive it away. Indeed when priests conjured it in the name of the Lord to leave, it answered, ' I will not go but if I wish I could kill you all. I am fully acquainted with the cross and holy water and do not fear them.' The spirit remained with the family in the manor house from All Saints' day until after Candlemas and said many lascivious and scurrilous things. At length it left on Septuagesima, saying that it would return at Easter, but it never did. Henry de Sandwich, bishop of London, whose whole period of office had been spent in great distress,[1] died at his manor of Orsett on the octave of the Nativity of

---

[1] Henry de Sandwich, bishop of London 1262–73, was suspended in 1266 for supporting Simon de Montfort. He went to plead his cause in the Roman curia and had only a small pittance from his see to live on.

clausit extremum in octavis Natiuitatis beate Marie,[1]
cui successit magister Iohannes de Chishille, eiusdem
loci decanus, electus in crastino sancti Nicholai.[2]
Dominus papa uenit Lugdun' xi. Kal. Decembris.[3]
Henricus de Bauns prior Elyensis obiit die Natalis
Domini, cui successit Iohannes de Hemmingestone,
eiusdem loci claustralis. Domino Eadwardo natus est
filius apud Baunam in Gasconia nocte subsequente diem
sancti Clementis,[4] quem de nomine regis Hyspanie
sancti Iacobi [5] et Portugalensis Aldephonsum [6] nominauit.[a] Rodulphus comes Hauekesburgensis electus est
in regem Alemannie. [b]

1274

f. 162 Dominus papa celebrauit concilium [c] Lugdun' Gallie
quod quidem durauit a festo apostolorum Philippi et
Iacobi [7] usque xvi. Kal. Augusti; in quo concilio
concesse sunt decime in subsidium Terre Sancte ab
omnibus personis ecclesiasticis cuiuscumque condicionis,
status aut ordinis, de omnibus redditibus, fructibus et
prouentibus ecclesiasticis. Obierunt [d] Robertus Dunelmensis, Laurencius Rofensis, Willelmus Bathoniensis et
Wellensis episcopi. Dunelmensi Robertus de Halieylaund, eiusdem ecclesie monachus et prior de Finchale,[8]
Rofensi [e] dominus Walterus de Mertone, domini regis
cancellarius, Bathoniensi et Wellensi dominus Robertus
Burnel successerunt. Obiit eciam Adam de Chilendene,

---

[a] Henricus de Bauns . . . nominauit *marked* uacat *MS*[2]
[b] *Lacuna of 1 line MS* (*3 M*)   [c] *Added MS*[2]; *in text M*
[d] obiit *MS*; *corr. to* obierunt *MS*[2]
[e] Robertus de Halieylaund . . . Rofensi *marked* uacat *MS*[2]

[1] 15 September. Authorities disagree slightly on the date of his death.
[2] 7 December

St Mary.[1]   He was succeeded by Master John de
Chishull, dean of London, who was elected on the
morrow of the feast of St Nicholas.[2]   The pope arrived
at Lyons on 21 November.[3]   Henry de Bauns, prior of
Ely, died on Christmas day and was succeeded by John
de Hemingstone, a cloister monk of Ely.   A son was
born to the Lord Edward during the night following the
feast of St Clement [4] at Bayonne in Gascony; he was
named Alfonso after the king of Spain, Santiago [5] and
Portugal.[6]   Rudolf, count of Hapsburg, was elected
king of Germany.

1274

The pope held a council at Lyons in France, which
lasted from the feast of the Apostles Philip and James [7]
until 17 July.   At this council a tenth was granted in
aid of the Holy Land, from all ecclesiastical persons of
whatever condition, rank or dignity, from all ecclesiastical
rents, profits and revenues.   Robert, archbishop of
Durham, Lawrence, bishop of Rochester, and William,
bishop of Bath and Wells, died.   Robert of Holy
Island, a monk of Durham and prior of Finchale,[8]
became bishop of Durham, Walter de Merton, the king's
chancellor, bishop of Rochester, and Robert Burnell
bishop of Bath and Wells.   Adam de Chillenden, the

---

[3] He was there on 20 November; Potthast, II, nos. 20759–60.

[4] 23 November

[5] Santiago de Compostella, in Galicia, ruled by the king of Castile.

[6] Alfonso X, the Wise, king of Castile, and Leon 1252–84.   Queen
Eleanor had just returned from a visit to Alfonso X, her half-brother;
F. M. Powicke, *The Thirteenth Century 1216–1307* (1953), p. 226 and *n.* 2.
Alfonso III was king of Portugal 1248–79.   The chronicler must have
included Portugal in the title of Alfonso X by mistake.

[7] 1 May

[8] Prior 1260–74 of Finchale upon the Wear, Benedictine priory.

prior et quondam electus Cantuariensis.*ª* Dominus Henricus, domini Eadwardi filius, apud Westmonasterium xiii. Kal. Nouembris est sepultus et Auelina uxor domini Eadmundi regis filii comitissa Aubemarlie.*ᵇ* Pacificata discordia inter dominum E[dwardum] regis *ᶜ* Anglie primogenitum et comitissam Flandrie ¹ dudum habita. Idem dominus E[dwardus] in crastino sancti Petri ad Vincula ² apud Doueram applicuit in Angliam. Qui die sancti martiris Magni proximo sequente ³ apud Westmonasterium a Roberto Cantuariensi archiepiscopo in regem Anglie solempniter, una cum regina uxore sua, est coronatus.*ᵈ* Rex Francie duxit in uxorem filiam ducis Brabancie,*ᵉ*⁴ sorore regis eiusdem uice uersa eidem duci in matrimonium coniuncta.*ᶠ*

1275

Alienora uxor regis, regina Anglie, peperit filiam apud Windlesores quam uocauit Margaretam. Margareta regina Scocie et Beatrix comitissa Britannie, filie regis Henrici, diem clauserunt extremum. Dominus rex et f. 162ᵛ regina uenerunt apud / sanctum Eadmundum peregrinacionis causa xv. Kal. Maii prout in terra uouerunt Ierosolimitana. Qui dominus rex consilio suo hoc approbante post munimentorum ecclesie sancti Ead-

---

ᵃ Obiit eciam Adam . . . Cantuariensis *at end of annal, Oxenedes*
ᵇ Obiit eciam Adam . . . Aubermarlie *marked* uacat *MS²*
ᶜ -is *on erasure MS*
ᵈ in curia regis [. . .] *in margin in pencil MS²*; + in curia regis Francie foris iudicatus est rex Anglie de tota terra de Limozin et Prouincia uice comitisse eiusdem Prouincie adiudi\ata *in text M (and Oxenedes)*
ᵉ Burgundie *MS*; Brabancie *M (and Oxenedes)*
ᶠ A lacuna of 1 line and Rex Hyspan *in margin MS²*; *in pencil* + rex Hyspanie opposuit se electioni regis Alemann' et Romanorum imperatoris Ianuensibus et Marchione de Monte Ferrato sibi consencientibus *followed by a lacuna of 5 lines M*

prior and once the archbishop-elect of Canterbury, also died. Henry, Edward's son, was buried at Westminster on 20 October. Avelina, countess of Aumâle and wife of King Henry's son Edmund [died]. Peace was made between the Lord Edward, the king of England's eldest son, and the countess of Flanders,[1] who had long been at strife. The Lord Edward landed in England at Dover on the morrow of the feast of St Peter ad Vincula.[2] On the following feast of St Magnus martyr[3] he was solemnly crowned king of England, together with the queen, his wife, at Westminster by Robert, archbishop of Canterbury. The king of France married the duke of Burgundy's daughter[4] and the king of France's sister was joined in marriage to the duke of Burgundy.

1275

Eleanor, the king's wife and queen of England, gave birth to a daughter at Windsor, whom she named Margaret. Margaret, queen of Scotland, and Beatrix, countess of Britanny, daughters of King Henry [III], died. The king and queen came to Bury St Edmunds on a pilgrimage on 17 April in accordance with a vow made in the Holy Land. When the king had freely inspected the archives of St Edmund's church he granted to the convent of Bury, with his council's approval, the

---

[1] Margaret of Constantinople, countess of Flanders 1244–80.
[2] 2 August
[3] 19 August
[4] The reading in M is correct; on 21 August 1274 Philip III married Mary, daughter of Henry III, duke of Lower Lorraine and Brabant 1248–61. Philip's sister Agnes was betrothed in 1272 to Robert II, duke of Burgundy 1272–1305; they married in 1279.

mundi inspectionem liberam uisus faciendi de mensuris
et ponderibus absque aliquo ministrorum suorum
interesse eiusdem loci conuentui concessit facultatem. [a][1]
Obiit Iohannes Herefordensis episcopus, cui successit
magister Thomas de Cantilupo, eiusdem loci canonicus.
Deposita est capella sancti Eadmundi [b] et in eodem loco
capella sancte Marie est constructa. [c][2] Vbi sub terra
inuenti fuerunt muri cuiusdam ueteris ecclesie rotunde,[3]
que quidem multo latior fuit quam capella et ita
constructa quod altare capelle quasi in medio eius fuerat.
Et credimus illam fuisse que ad opus sancti Eadmundi
primo fuit constructa. Positus fuit primus lapis a
Roberto priore conuentu ibidem existente et antiphonam
'Aue regina celorum' modulante primo die mensis
Iulii. [4]

Londoniis quidam [d] de ordine Predicatorum dictus
frater Robertus de Redingge predicator optimus
linguaque Hebrea eruditissimus apostauit et ad Iudaismum conuolauit atque Iudeam ducens uxorem se
circumcidi atque Aggeum fecit [e] nominari.[5] Quem
accersitum et contra legem Christianam audacter et [f]
puplice disserentem rex archiepiscopo commendauit
Cantuariorum. [g] Tercio Idus Septembris factus est
terremotus magnus London' et fere per totam Angliam

---

[a] Dominus rex et regina uenerunt . . . facultatem *marked* uacat *MS*[2]
[b] + apud Sanctum Ædmundum *Oxenedes and Chron. Buriensis*
[c] nota de capella Marie *in margin MS*[2]
[d] + frater *M*   [e] + se *M*   [f] in *M*
[g] sedata est [. . .] *in margin in pencil MS*[2]; + sedata est discordia inter
Hispanie [*sic*] et imperatorem de nouo electum domino papa se
intromittente *in text M*

[1] A payment of 100 marks by the prior and convent of St Edmund's
'for a certain confirmation' is enrolled on Pipe Roll 3 Ed. I, m. 17.
[2] For the pulling down of the chapel of St Edmund and the building of
the Lady Chapel see M. R. James, *On the Abbey of St Edmund at Bury*, pp.

right to hold the view of weights and measures without any of his officials being present.[1] John, bishop of Hereford, died and was succeeded by Master Thomas de Cantilupe, a canon of Hereford. The chapel of St Edmund was pulled down and the Lady Chapel built on its site.[2] Under the earth were found the walls of an ancient round church[3]; this was much wider than the chapel of St Edmund and so built that the altar of the chapel was, as it were, in the centre. We believe that this was the chapel first built for the service of St Edmund. The foundation-stone [of the Lady Chapel] was laid on 1 July by Prior Robert in the presence of the convent, who sang the antiphon ' Ave regina celorum.' [4] In London a certain member of the order of Preachers called Brother Robert de Reading, who was a famous preacher and very learned in the Hebrew language, apostatised and embraced the Jewish faith; he even married a Jewess, had himself circumcised and changed his name to Haggai.[5] The king sent for him, and when he held forth brazenly in public against Christianity he handed him over to the archbishop of Canterbury. On 11 September there was a great earthquake in London

---

188–9, and G. M. Hill, ' Antiquities of Bury St Edmunds,' in *Journal of the British Archaeological Assoc.*, XXI (1865), pp. 51, 112–13.

[3] A. W. Clapham, *English Romanesque Architecture before the Conquest* (1930), p. 149, suggests that this old round church was the tomb-chapel built for St Edmund's body in 903. Possibly, however, it was Ailwin's chapel built in 1032 of stone; the chapel of 903 was wooden (Abbo and Herman in Arnold, I, pp. 19, 84–5), though it may have had stone foundations.

[4] For the ceremony of laying the foundation-stone of a church see M. Andrieu, ' Le Pontifical Romain au Moyen-Age ', *Studi e Testi*, nos. 86–8 (1940), II, pp. 420–1, III, pp. 451–5.

[5] Our chronicler is the only authority for this story, which may be true; *Transactions of the Jewish Historical Soc. of England*, VI (1912), pp. 256–9.

circa horam diei terciam. Magnates Anglie concesserunt
regi quintumdecimum denarium.[1] Liwelinus princeps
Wallie fit rebellis regi Anglie. *a* Inhibitum est Iudeis per
totum regnum Anglie ne de cetero pecuniam suam
alicui darent ad usuram sed uiuerent mercaturis suis
f. 163 le/gem in emendo et uendendo Christianorum habentes
mercatorum et quod quilibet eorum, cuiuscumque etatis,
status aut sexus, regi pro capite suo tres denarios daret
annuatim. Et qui hac condicione stare nollet ante
Pascha proximo sequens Angliam sua presencia
uacuaret.[2]

Dominus rex protulit sentenciam contra burgenses
Norwic' quod uidelicet pro iniuria corpori Christi illata
quoddam uas aureum ad corpus Christi recondendum
precii c. librarum sumptibus suis facerent. Et quod pro
iniuria conuentui illata tria milia marcarum contri-
buerent *b* eisdem infra sexennium soluenda, uidelicet
quolibet anno quingentas marcas. Et quod episcopus
sumptibus burgensium una cum eis ad curiam mitteret
Romanam de pace taliter ordinata testimonium per-
hibiturus. Et quod conuentus ianuam suam qua
uellent parte aque [3] dumtaxat excepta mutarent,
remanente uilla quoad libertatum burgalium priuaci-
onem in eo statu quo fuit die quo rex pater regis uiuus
fuit et mortuus.[4]

Dedicata est capella prioris in honore sanctorum
martyrum Eadmundi et Stephani a domino Willelmo

---

a Wallie *M*   *b* On erasure MS

[1] The fifteenth is mentioned again below under 1276 (p. 62), 1277
(p. 63) and 1278 (p. 65).
[2] cf. *Statutum de Judeismo*, in *Statutes of the Realm*, i, pp. 221–2; *CCR,
1272–9*, pp. 108, 259
[3] In the next year, on 27 July 1276, the king issued a licence to the
prior and convent of Norwich to erect gates towards the water of Norwich;
CPR, 1272–81, p. 157. 'Aqua' may mean here a stream or primitive

and throughout most of England at about three o'clock. The magnates of England granted a fifteenth penny to the king.[1] Llewelyn, prince of Wales, rebelled against the king of England. The Jews throughout England were forbidden henceforth to lend money at interest to anyone, but were to live by trade, buying and selling according to the laws of the Christian merchants. Moreover every Jew of whatever age, position or sex was to pay a poll-tax of threepence to the king annually. If a Jew refused to observe these regulations he was to leave England before the next Easter.[2]

The king pronounced sentence against the burgesses of Norwich: because of the damage they had done to the Body of Christ they were to have made at their own expense a golden pyx worth £100 for keeping the consecrated bread; they were to pay the convent 3,000 marks within six years (500 marks a year) because of the injury they had inflicted on the convent; the bishop and citizens jointly were to send evidence of the settlement to the Roman court at the burgesses' expense; the convent was to move its gate to wherever it wished (but not in the region of the water)[3]; and with respect to the deprivation of the burgesses' liberties, the town was to remain in the same condition as on the day when the king's father was alive and dead.[4]

The prior's chapel [at Bury St Edmunds] was dedicated in honour of the holy martyrs Edmund and

---

water-channel along which water flowed to the river Wensum; see *The Streets and Lanes of the City of Norwich: a Memoir by John Kirkpatrick*, ed. W. Hudson with an introduction by W. T. Bensly, with maps (1889), p. 99.

[4] This account of Edward I's sentence against the burgesses of Norwich is confirmed by entries on the Close and Patent Rolls; *CCR, 1272–9*, pp. 217–18, *CPR, 1272–81*, p. 157. See also the king's letter; Cotton, pp. 152–3.

Ragusie[1] Medorum archiepiscopo die sanctorum Innocencium.

Grauis et intollerabilis facta est exaccio super decimis in concilio Lugdunensi concessis. De nulla enim alicuius taxacione contenti fuerunt dictarum decimarum collectores. Immo sacramento corporaliter prestito ad uerum omnium prouentuum suorum ualorem eis ore proprio insinuandum omnes fere et singulos compellebant. Vnde decima porcionis conuentus sancti Eadmundi fuit cc.xli. marce iii. solidi vi. denarii[a] et hoc per sacramentum quinque monachorum ad hoc specialiter iuratorum.[2] Decima porcionis abbatis fuit c. libre.[b]

f. 163ᵛ   Abbatis porcio taxata fuit ad m. libras
          unde decima sua fuit c. libras.

	m.	s.	d.
Celerarius	m.ccc.xxxvii.	iiii.	x.
Sacristia	ccc.lviii.	xi.	viii.
Camerarius	ccc.vii. et dim.		
Elemosinarius	c.xxi.	v.	iiii.
Pitancerius	xxiii.	iii.	
Infirmarius	xx.		
Hostilarius	vii.		
Feretre	c.iiii.xx.		
Reliquie	x.		
Cripte	xii.		
Altare sancti Roberti	v.		
Capella prioris	vi.		
Vestiarius	vii. et dim.		
Precentor		xl.	
Sanctus Leodegarus		xxx.	
Sanctus Michael		x.[c]	

[a] + preter hospitale sancti Saluatoris *M, Chron. Buriensis*
[b] *Erasure* 1½ *in. long to the end of the line MS*
[c] + Sanctus Botulphus x. s. *Chron. Buriensis*

[1] William or Geoffrey, archbishop of Edessa, or Rages, in Media, a suffragan bishop ' in partibus ': W. Stubbs, *Registrum Sacrum Anglicanum*

Stephen by William of Rages,[1] archbishop of the Medes,
on the feast of the Holy Innocents.

The assessment for the tenth granted at the council
of Lyons was heavy and burdensome, for the collectors
of the tenth were not satisfied with any previous assessment. They preferred to compel nearly everyone to
swear personally, by corporal oath, to the ' true value ' of
all their revenues. The tenth due from the convent of
Bury St Edmunds amounted to 241 marks 3s. 6d.,
according to the assessment made on oath by five
monks especially sworn.[2] The abbot's tenth was £100.

The abbot's portion was assessed at   £1,000
of which the tenth was   £100

	mks	s.	d.
The cellarer	1,337	4	10
The sacrist	358	11	8
The chamberlain	307½		
The almoner	121	5	4
The pittancer	23	3	
The infirmarer	20		
The hostiller	7		
The shrines	180		
The relics	10		
The crypts	12		
The altar of St Robert	5		
The prior's chapel	6		
The vestry	7½		
The precentor		40	
St Leger		30	
St Michael		10	

(1897), p. 195; CCR, 1272-9, pp. 30, 370, 573. Brit. Mus. MS Harley
1005, f. 218ᵛ, has a similar account of the dedication of the chapel, reading
' Rages ' for ' Ragusie.' In 1261 and 1274 the archbishop of the Medes
granted indulgences to those visiting St Edmund's tomb; James, op. cit.,
p. 188.
[2] The cellarer, sacrist, chamberlain and two other monks of St Edmund's
swore to the ' true value ' of temporalities and spiritualities before the
collectors, Raymond de Nogaret and John de Darlington; Arundel 30,
f. 213. See above, p. xxvi and n. 4.

	m.	*s.*	*d.*
SUMMA omnium istorum	mm.cccc.xii.	viii.	ii.
Summa *a* decime	cc.xli.	iii.	vi.

Taxatio hospitalis sancti		
Saluatoris est	c.l.	
Decima	xv. *b* 1	

Eiecti sunt Iudei a Cantebr[igia] per reginam matrem regis.[2] Fratres laici de Furniuall'[3] de ordine Cisterciensi plures de monachis interfecerunt.[c]

1276

Dominus Aymericus de Monte Forti una cum sorore sua Alienora Liwelino principi Wallie maritanda per mare Walliam tendentes insidiante illis quodam milite dicto Thoma Archidiacono capti sunt et domini regis custodie mancipati.[d] Gregorius papa qui decimas inposuit decimo die mensis Ianuarii diem claudens extremum decimatus est apud ciuitatem Reatinam, seditque annis quatuor, mensibus quatuor, diebus xix. Successit Petrus Hostiensis episcopus de ordine Predicatorum dictusque est Innocencius quintus, qui dominica prima Quadragesime consecratus, uigilia[4] sancti Iohannis Baptiste defungitur. Successit Ottobonus tituli sancti Adriani diaconus cardinalis, dictusque f. 164 est / Adrianus. Quo statim infra octauas Assumpcionis

a Botulphus x. s. *in margin in pencil MS*[2]
b *M omits this paragraph (from* abbatis porcio taxata fuit).
c Lacuna of 1 line MS (6 M)
d va- *is written in margin by* deposita est capella sancti Eadmundi *above and another at head of* f. 163, *either of which may connect with* -cat *in margin by* mancipati *MS*[2].

[1] The Cellarer, etc.: the sums represent the total assessment of each obedientiary etc., not the tenth. The assessment of the separate sources of revenue of each obedientiary is in Arundel 30, f. 213, 213[v].

	mks	s.	d.
TOTAL of these items	2,412	8	2
The tenth	241	3	6
The assessment of the hospital of St Saviour is	150		
The tenth	15 [1]		

The Jews were expelled from Cambridge by the queen, mother of the king.[2] The lay brothers of the Cistercian house of Furnivall [3] killed many of the monks.

1276

Amauri de Montfort was sailing to Wales with his sister Eleanor, who was to marry Llewelyn, prince of Wales, when they were both captured by a certain knight called Thomas the Archdeacon, who was lying in wait for them, and were sent to the king for imprisonment. Pope Gregory X, who had imposed and reckoned up the tax of a tenth, died on the 10th day of January at Rieti and so himself met his day of reckoning. He had been pope for four years, four months and nineteen days. He was succeeded by a member of the order of Preachers, Peter, bishop of Ostia, who took the name Innocent V. He was consecrated on the first Sunday in Lent but died on the vigil of the feast of St John the Baptist.[4] Ottobuono, cardinal-deacon of St Adrian, succeeded him and took the name Adrian. He died soon afterwards in the octave of Assumption day and was

---

[2] The king granted to Eleanor, 12 January 1275, that no Jew should stay in her dower towns; *CPR, 1272–81*, p. 76.

[3] ? Francae Vallis (now Franquevaux), Languedoc, France, or ? Furness, Lancashire. For dissatisfaction of Cistercian lay-brothers see R. H. Snape, *English Monastic Finances in the Later Middle Ages* (1926), pp. 8–10.

[4] 23 June 1276. 22 June is the correct date; Potthast, II, p. 1710.

defuncto, successit eidem Petrus de Spineto Tusculanus
episcopus, nacione Hyspanus, uigilia *a* sancte Crucis
electus,[1] dictusque est Iohannes uicesimus secundus.
Magna pars Cantebreg[ie] una cum ecclesia sancti
Benedicti igne consumpta est. In itinere iusticiariorum
apud Turrim London' Michael Toui [2] quidam de
maioribus ciuitatis suspensus est. *b* Eadmundus comes
Lancastrie, domini regis frater, desponsauit reginam
Nauarre.[3] Alienor regina peperit filiam quam uocauit
Berengariam. Sanctus Ricardus quondam Cicestrensis
episcopus uigilia sancti Botulphi [4] domino rege et regina
una cum aliis Anglie magnatibus non nullis astantibus,
cum magna gloria est translatus. Collecta est medietas
quintedecime anno superiori domino regi concesse.
Francie Hispanieque reges discordes facti sunt adinuicem.
Rex igitur Francie contra regem Hispanie excercitum
mouens copiosum inpudenter omni penitus infecto
rediit negocio. Facta est eclipsis lune uniuersalis nocte
sancti Clementis [5] luna per duarum fere horarum
spacium in summa obscuritate ita quod uix aliquod sui
reliquid uestigium perdurante. Mortalitas ouium hoc
anno incepit in Lindeseia et per plures durans annos per
totam fere Angliam dispergebatur. *c*

1277

Rex Anglie excercitum copiosum misit in Walliam cui
prefecit H[enricum] de Laci comitem Lincoln'. Ipse
uero rex excercitu uersus Walliam proficiscente ad

---

a + exaltacionis *M* (*and Oxenedes*)
b dictusque est Innocencius quintus . . . est *marked* uacat *MS*²
c Collecta est medietas . . . dispergebatur *marked* uacat *MS*²; *lacuna of*
1 line MS (3 M)

[1] 13 September. John was elected probably on 15 or 16 September.

succeeded by Peter de Spineto, bishop of Frascati, a Spaniard; he was elected on the vigil of the feast of the Holy Cross [1] and took the name John XXII.

A great part of Cambridge, including St Benet's church, was burnt down. Michael Tovi,[2] a prominent citizen of London, was hanged at the Tower by the justices in eyre. Edmund, earl of Lancaster, the king's brother, married the queen of Navarre.[3] Queen Eleanor gave birth to a daughter, whom she called Berengaria. St Richard, formerly bishop of Chichester, was translated with great glory on the vigil of St Botolph's day [4] in the presence of the king and queen and other magnates of England. Half the tax of a fifteenth which had been granted to the king in the previous year was collected. The king of France and the king of Spain quarrelled with each other, so the king of France rashly marched a large army against the king of Spain; but as the enterprise was a complete failure he returned home. There was a total eclipse of the moon on the night of the feast of St Clement [5]; the moon was so completely eclipsed for nearly two hours that scarcely a trace of it remained visible. In this year a deadly disease began to afflict the sheep in Lindsey; it lasted many years and spread over most of England.

1277

The king of England sent a large army to Wales with Henry de Lacy, earl of Lincoln, in command. The king himself, while his army was setting out for Wales,

[2] Michael Tovi the younger; *Croniques de London*, ed. C. J. Aungier (Camden Soc., 1844), pp. 7, 14. He took part against the king in the Barons' War: *Dunst.*, p. 267; *CPR, 1266–72*, p. 237, *CCR, 1264–8*, p. 543.
[3] Blanche, widow of Henry, king of Navarre 1270–4.
[4] 16 June   [5] 23 November

partes interim Suff' et Norf' declinans, apud Norwic'
Pascha [1] celebrauit, per loca maritima Suff' et Esexie
London' reuersurus. Qui statim post festum sancti
Iohannis totam fere Anglie miliciam secum duxit in
f. 164ᵛ Walliam. [a] / Abbas et conuentus sancti Eadmundi
finem fecerunt de quintadecima bonorum suorum pro
quatuor uiginti et x. libris, trigenta per abbatem et lx.
per conuentum libris appensis. Idem eciam abbas et
conuentus finem fecerunt pro uillata sancti Eadmundi
pro c. libris de ipsa uilla leuandis et per conuentum
predictum pro libertate uille conseruanda domino regi
soluendis. [2]

A magno Tartarum rege [3] qui dicuntur Moal ab
orientalibus uidelicet mundi partibus circa festum
Pasche directi sunt ad regem Anglie sex nuncii solempnes
de maioribus tocius gentis illius cum suo interprete
excusantes illorum regem quod rege Anglie in partibus
nuper Acconensibus agente non occurrit insuper et ab
eodem contra crucifixi inimicos paganos scilicet auxilium
flagitantes. [b] Dominus papa sexto Idus Maii [4] apud
Viterbium diem clausit extremum. A quo die uacauit
sedes usque ad diem sancte Katerine. [5] Quo quidem
die dominus Iohannes Gaietanus tituli sancti Nicholai
in Carcere Tulliano diaconus cardinalis in summum
pontificem est electus, dictusque est Nicholaus tercius. [c]
Soldanus Babilonie habens in excercitu totam pene
miliciam tocius imperii sui electam circa xvi. Kal.

---

[a] *Illegible scribbles in margin MS²*; + idem rex in curia regis Francie
foris iudicatus fuit de castello de Funtsac *M*
[b] Abbas et conuentus Sancti Eadmundi . . . flagitantes *marked* uacat *MS²*
[c] rubrica *in margin MS*; quartus *M*

[1] 28 March
[2] For the royal licence to St Edmund's abbey to tax itself and the
burgesses of St Edmund's see *CPR, 1272–84*, pp. 132, 138. For the quit-

turned aside to visit Suffolk and Norfolk; he kept
Easter [1] at Norwich and then returned to London along
the coast of Suffolk and Essex. Immediately after St
John's day he went to Wales at the head of an army
comprising nearly all the knights of England. The
abbot and convent of Bury St Edmunds paid a fine of
£90 instead of the tax of a fifteenth of their revenues;
the abbot paid £30 of the fine and the convent paid £60.
The abbot and convent also paid a fine of £100 on
behalf of the town of Bury St Edmunds; this sum was
raised from the town and, in order to preserve the town's
liberties, handed by the convent to the king.[2]

The great king of the Tartars,[3] who are called
Mongols in the East, about Easter time sent six important
ambassadors, some of the most distinguished men of his
race, with an interpreter, bearing apologies that their
king had not visited the king of England recently when
he was in the region of Acre and, moreover, asking for
his help against the infidel enemies of the Cross. The
pope died on 10 May [4] at Viterbo. The Holy See
remained vacant from that day until St Katherine's
day,[5] when John of Gaeta, cardinal-deacon of St
Nicholas in Carcere Tulliano, was elected pope. He
took the name Nicholas III. The sultan of Cairo, with
an army of nearly all the picked soldiers of his empire,

---

tance to the abbey from the fifteenth on account of the composition of a
£100 see *CPR, 1281–9,* p. 165; *Rotulorum originalium in curia scaccarii abbreviatio*
(Record Commission, 1805–10), I, p. 27; Pipe Rolls, 4 Edward I, m. 8ᵈ.

[3] Abaqa, Khan of the Mongols 1265–81. For this embassy, which
does not seem to be noticed elsewhere, see Powicke, *Henry III and the Lord
Edward,* II, p. 602.

[4] The date is wrong: Pope John died on 20 May 1277; Potthast, II,
p. 1708.

[5] 25 November

Augusti inter Armeniam et fluuium Eufraten occurrens excercitui Tartarorum cum uniuersis copiis suis fere usque ad internicionem cesus est.[1] In quo conflictu de Agarrenis xlii. et de Tartarorum multitudine xv. millia hominum usque ad internicionem cesa sunt. Facta est pluuia magna et intollerabilis vi. Idus Octobris continuata pluuia per duos dies et unam noctem. Cuius quidem pluuie inmoderanciam tanta secuta est aquarum inundacio quod homines per loca boues et oues et alia quedam pecora campi tempestate f. 165 nocturna / intercipiendo submersit. Domos eciam muros et arbores sed et nonnulla edificia sibi obstancia penitus prostrauit. Hec quoque tempestas maxime circa sanctum Eadmundum, Esexiam et comitatum Cantebrig' suam precipue exhibuit uehemenciam. In ceteris Anglie partibus aut nulla aut perexigua fuit tempestatis illius pestilencia.[a] Walterus de Merton' Rofensis episcopus diem clausit extremum, cui successit Iohannes eiusdem loci monachus et precentor. Post dampna non nulla utrimque habita Liwelinus princeps Wallie submisit se uoluntati et disposicioni domini regis de uita et membris terreno honore et omnibus aliis omni penitus condicione submota. Quem dominus rex habita deliberacione aliquantula suscepit in osculo pacis secumque London' adduxit de pacis forma et confirmacione tractaturus. Liwelinus uero celebrato Dominico Natali cum domino rege apud Westmonasterium ad propria remeauit.[b]

[a] Soldanus Babilonie . . . pestilencia *marked* uacat *MS*[2]
[b] *Lacuna of 1 line MS (2 M)*

[1] Possibly this is a confused reference to the battle fought near Ablastyn in April 1277: 'L'Éstoire de Éracles Empereur,' in *Recueil des Historiens des Croisades Occidentaux*, II (1859), pp. 479–80; Makrizi, *Histoire des Sultans Mamlouks de l'Égypte*, translated into French by M. Quatremère (1837), I, pp. 139–41.

met the Tartar army in battle about 17 July between Armenia and the river Euphrates; the sultan was killed and his forces almost exterminated.[1] Forty-two thousand Hagarenes and fifteen thousand men from the Tartar horde were slaughtered in the battle.

There was a terrific downpour of rain on 10 October, which lasted continuously for two days and one night. Such a flood followed this cloud-burst that in some places men and cows, sheep and other domestic animals in the fields were overcome at night by the storm and drowned. Houses, walls, trees and some buildings which stood in the way of the flood were completely overthrown. The storm was at its most violent mainly in the region of Bury St Edmunds and in Essex and Cambridgeshire. Other parts of England were either spared the catastrophe of this storm or suffered little. Walter de Merton, bishop of Rochester, died, and was succeeded by John, monk and precentor of Rochester. After both sides had suffered considerable loss Llewelyn, prince of Wales, submitted unconditionally his life, limbs, worldly honours and everything else to the will and judgment of the king, who after a short consultation gave Llewelyn the kiss of peace and brought him to London to negotiate the terms of the peace and its confirmation. Llewelyn kept Christmas with the king at Westminster and then returned home.

1278

Rogerus episcopus Norwicensis die sancti Vincencii martyris [1] apud Suthelmham manerium suum diem clausit extremum, sepultusque est apud Norwicum in octauis sancte Agnetis,[2] cui successit magister Willelmus de Middeltone archidiaconus Cantuarie die sancti Mathie apostoli [3] electus. Collecta est alia medietas quintedecime domino regi concesse; pro qua quintadecima finem fecerunt abbas et conuentus sancti Eadmundi cum domino rege de iiii.xx. et x. libris, ipso abbate xxx. atque conuentu pro porcione sua lx. libris contribuentibus. [a] Robertus Cantuarie archiepiscopus ad curiam Romanam a domino papa uocatus factus [est] [b] episcopus Hostiensis [4] tituli sancte Rufine / episcopus cardinalis, quo sic uocato Robertus Burnel Bathoniensis et Wellensis episcopus domini regis cancellarius a conuentu Cantuarie mox ad archiepiscopatum fuit postulatus.

f. 165ᵛ ᶜ

Mirabilis factus est conflictus Aquisgrani in Teutonia ubi comes de Golc [5] et cum eo ccc. de sequacibus suis generosis cum tota fere familia eorum non tam humano quam diuino occubuerunt iudicio. Rex Boemie [6] factus rebellis Radulpho regi Alemannie post pacis confracta federa ab eodem a predicto Alemannie rege una cum l. millibus numero de suis usque ad internicionem cesus est.

Liwelinus princeps Wallie desponsauit Alienoram

---

[a] Collecta est alia medietas . . . contribuentibus *marked* uacat *MS*
[b] *Supplied from* M (*and Oxenedes*); *om.* MS
[c] *Grotesque of a man crouching at the foot of the page in pen and ink* MS

[1] 22 January. *Oseney*, p. 275, gives 25 November. The place of death and date of burial do not seem to be mentioned by any other authority.
[2] 28 January   [3] 24 February
[4] This is wrong. He was cardinal-bishop of Porto and Santa Rufina.

1278

Roger, bishop of Norwich, died at his manor of South Elmham on the feast of St Vincent the martyr [1] and was buried at Norwich on the octave of St Agnes [2]; he was succeeded by Master William de Middleton, archdeacon of Canterbury, who was elected on the feast of St Matthias the Apostle.[3] The other half of the tax of a fifteenth granted to the king [by the pope] was collected. Instead of paying this fifteenth the abbot and convent of Bury St Edmunds paid the king a fine of £90; the abbot contributed £30 and the convent £60 for its portion. The pope summoned Robert, archbishop of Canterbury, to the Roman court and made him bishop of Ostia,[4] cardinal-bishop of the title of St Rufina. Soon after he had been summoned, Robert Burnell, bishop of Bath and Wells, the king's chancellor, was postulated to the archbishopric by the convent of [Christchurch] Canterbury.

An amazing battle was fought at Aachen in Germany. In it the count of Jülich [5] and with him three hundred nobles of his retinue and most of their followers fell by divine rather than human judgment. The king of Bohemia [6] rebelled against Rudolf, king of Germany; after he had broken the peace treaty he was killed by the king of Germany and fifty thousand of his followers exterminated.

Llewelyn, prince of Wales, married Eleanor, the

---

[5] William IV, count of Jülich 1218–78
[6] Przélmilas-Ottokar II, king of Bohemia 1253–78.

filiam Symonis de Monte Forti quondam comitis
Leicestrie apud Wygorn' die Translacionis sancti
Eadwardi,[1] Anglie et Scocie regibus ibidem tunc
existentibus.[a] Rex et regina uenerunt apud sanctum
Eadmundum die sancti Clementis[2] tendentes uersus
Norwicum ad dedicacionem ecclesie factam iiii. Kal.
Decembris, existente ibidem tunc cum rege maxima
magnatum Anglie multitudine. Robertus Carleolensis
episcopus obiit, cui successit Radulphus prior Giseburn'.
Facta est itineracio iusticiariorum domini Iohannis de
Wallibus et sociorum sibi assignatorum apud Carleol'
in comitatu Cumberl' et domini Rogeri Loueday cum
sibi assignatis in comitatu Herefordie.[b] Omnes Iudei
Anglie cuiuscumque condicionis, etatis aut sexus in
octabis sancti Martini subito capti sunt et per diuersa
Anglie castella salue sunt deputati custodie; quibus sic
retentis eorum[c] interim diligenter scrutatis domiciliorum
penetralibus inuenta sunt apud plerosque retonsionis
monete signa atque instrumenta facti ipsius euiden-
tissima.[d] Capti sunt eciam subito per totam Angliam
omnes aurifabri et monetarie ministri in crastino sancti
Nicholai[3] atque sub salua positi / custodia atque eorum
domicilia diligenter perscrutata. Iuxta mandatum
igitur regium quo nulli quantum ad hoc pepercit
libertati, ducti sunt London' v. aurifabri atque tres alii
de uilla sancti Eadmundi per manum tamen balliui uille

f. 166

---

[a] Mirabilis factus est ... existentibus *marked* uacat MS[2]
[b] Facta est itineracio ... Herefordie *marked* uacat MS[2]
[c] + -que M (*and* Oxenedes)   [d] Corr. MS[2]

[1] 13 October
[2] 23 November. This visit is not mentioned in H. Gough, *Itinerary of
Edward I* (1900).
[3] 7 December 1278. The chronicler's authority for this date is not
apparent. Possibly it is the result of a confusion with a royal mandate of

daughter of Simon de Montfort, formerly earl of
Leicester, at Worcester on the feast of the Translation of
St Edward [1] in the presence of the king of England and
the king of Scotland. The king and queen arrived at
Bury St Edmunds on St Clement's day [2] on their way
to Norwich for the dedication of the church, which was
performed on 28 November in the presence of a great
crowd of the nobles of England, who were there with the
king. Robert, bishop of Carlisle, died and was succeeded by Ralph, prior of Guisborough. An eyre was
held by justice John de Vaux and his associates at Carlisle
in the county of Cumberland and by justice Roger
Loveday and his associates in the county of Hereford.
All the Jews in England, of whatever condition, age
or sex, were unexpectedly seized on the octave of
Martinmas and sent for imprisonment to various castles
throughout England. While they were thus imprisoned
the innermost recesses of their houses were ransacked
and in many very obvious proofs were found that they
had been clipping coins, including the tools used. On
the morrow of the feast of St Nicholas [3] the goldsmiths
and officials of the mints were also suddenly seized all
over England, put in safe custody and their premises
thoroughly searched. In accordance with the royal
mandate, which stipulated that no liberty whatsoever
was exempt in this respect, five goldsmiths and three
others were taken to London from the town of Bury
St Edmunds, but by the town bailiff. Many people

---

7 December 1278, forbidding the export of coin (*Foedera*, I, p. 564). Wykes,
p. 278, notes that soon after the imprisonment of the Jews on 17 November
the goldsmiths were arrested.

supradicte, in dicte libertatis ut plerisque uidebatur lesionem. Quod cum domino regi innotuisset omnet predictos iussit remitti iudicium ibidem prout merueruns siue bonum siue malum ibidem subituros. Tartari regnum occupant Ierosolimitanum.^a Rex iussit ut omnes habentes xx. libratas terre militaribus accingerentur.^b

1279

Dominus rex cepit scutagium pro expedicione Wallie positis xl. solidis super scutum. Alienora regina Anglie uigilia sancti Gregorii[1] apud Windleshores filiam peperit quam uocauit Mariam.^c Rex omnes Iudeos et quosdam Christianos de retonsura aut alia monete falsacione conuictos fecit suspendi. Vnde London' xiii.xx. et vii. Iudei mortis iudicium subierunt, quidam autem relegati, quidam eciam eorum perpetuo sunt carceri adiudicati, et quidam in Anglia remanserunt. Escambiatores quoque aut manucapi permisit aut salue per loca sua deputauit custodie qui redempcione facta liberi permissi sunt abire. In illius discussionis examine accesserunt apud sanctum Eadmundum domini Iohannes de Cobeham et Walterus de Heliun[2] missi a domino rege et contra libertates ecclesie rem agentes antea inauditam, nulli munimento papali regaliue deferentes, de aurifabris uille et aliis indictatis uel per suspicionem arestatis apud la Gildhalle iusticiam ulterius tenuerunt et amerciamenta inde prouencia regio fisco addixerunt. Ipsum eciam sacristam ad redempcionem

---

^a Iuxta mandatum igitur . . . Ierosolimitanum *marked* uacat *MS²*
^b *Lacuna of 1 line MS (6 M)*   ^c *Lacuna of 1 line MS (5 M)*

[1] 11 March
[2] John de Cobham and Walter de Heliun were justices appointed to

regarded this as an infringement on the liberty of Bury; when the king was notified of this he ordered all the prisoners to be sent back to Bury to be tried there according to their deserts, whether for good or ill.

The Tartars occupied the kingdom of Jerusalem. The king of England ordained that everyone holding twenty librates of land should be knighted.

1279

The king raised a scutage of 40s. on each knight's fee for his expedition to Wales.   Queen Eleanor gave birth at Windsor to a daughter on the eve of the feast of St Gregory,[1] whom she called Mary.   The king caused all the Jews and some Christians who had been convicted of clipping and otherwise falsifying coins to be hanged. Two hundred and sixty-seven Jews were condemned to death in London.   Some others were exiled, some condemned to life imprisonment and some remained in England.   Money-changers were either released on bail or committed to safe custody in their own localities and allowed to go free when they had paid a fine.   In the course of this investigation John de Cobham and Walter de Heliun,[2] sent by the king, came to Bury St Edmunds. They flouted in an unheard-of way the liberties of St Edmund's church, without regard for either papal or royal privileges; they even held a court at the Guildhall to try the goldsmiths of the town and others indicted or arrested on suspicion, and assigned the amercements accruing from the court to the royal treasury.   Even the sacrist of Bury was compelled to pay 100 marks as a

---

hear and determine pleas of trespass of money;   *CCR, 1272–9*, p. 529, *CPR, 1272–81*, pp. 297, 312.

f. 166ᵛ c. marcarum compulerunt. *¹ Cassa/ta postulacione *
de R[oberto] Burnell' Bathoniensi et Wellensi episcopo
facta dominus papa archiepiscopatum Cantuariensem
contulit fratri Iohanni de Peccham de ordine Minorum.
Symon abbas sancti Eadmundi v. Idus Aprilis dominica
uidelicet in albis apud Meleford manerium suum diem
clausit extremum. Quo ad patres suos apposito uigilia
sancti Iohannis ante Portam Latinam ² electus est
Iohannes de Northwold eiusdem loci monachus et
hostilarius interior.³ Qui assensu regio celeriter im-
petrato statim pro confirmacionis et benedictionis sue
beneficio consequendo curiam adiit Romanam habens
potestatem obligandi ᶜ conuentum quibuscumque credi-
toribus ad summam d. librarum. Dominus papa contulit
archiepiscopatum Dublinensem fratri I[ohanni] de
Derlingt' de ordine Predicatorum. Mortuo Symone
abbate sancti Eadmundi, dominus rex tam porcionem
conuentus quam baroniam occupauit,⁴ quod quidem
hactenus fuit inauditum. Que ᵈ conuentus porcio nec
prece nec precio ab eius manibus potuit extorqueri.
Sed omnia, facta sufficienti exhibicione conuentui talli-
atisque ad opus regis homagiis maneriorum conuentus,
tam infra uillam sancti Eadmundi quam extra, per
manum Iohannis de Berewich ⁵ regis attornati sunt
disposita.

a Escambiatores quoque . . . compulerunt *marked* uacat *MS²*
b + facta *del MS and not del. M*
c ligandi *M*   *d Corr. MS²*

¹ The sacrist was in charge of the mint at Bury; Lobel, p. 53.
² 5 May
³ The ' interior ' guestmaster, or the guestmaster ' of the monks ' (see
p. 112 below), at Bury St Edmunds was responsible for receiving guests of
the Benedictine order. The ' exterior ' guestmaster was responsible for
receiving secular guests and monks of other orders. See the late-thirteenth-
century customary of Bury St Edmunds in Brit. Mus. MS Harley 1005,
f. 108ᵛ.

fine.[1]   When the postulation of Robert Burnell, bishop
of Bath and Wells, [to the see of Canterbury] had been
quashed, the pope conferred the archbishopric on
Brother John de Pecham, a member of the order of
Friars Minor.   Simon, abbot of Bury St Edmunds, died
on 9 April, which was Low Sunday, at his manor of
Long Melford.   When he was laid with his fathers on
the vigil of the feast of St John before the Latin Gate,[2]
John de Northwold, a monk and the ' interior ' [3] guestmaster of Bury, was elected abbot.   After he had
quickly obtained the king's consent he set out at once
for the Roman court to obtain the papal confirmation and
blessing.   He was empowered to pledge the credit of the
convent to any money-lenders of his own choice up to a
total of £500.   The pope conferred the archbishopric of
Dublin on Brother John de Darlington, a member of
the order of Preaching Friars.   On the death of Simon,
abbot of Bury St Edmunds, the king took over the
convent's property as well as the barony [4]; such a thing
was unheard of before.   The convent's property could
not be wrung from his grasp either by prayer or price.
The convent was allowed enough for its sustenance,
but everything else, both within the town of Bury
St Edmunds and outside it, was disposed of by the
king's agent, John de Berwick,[5] and the tenants on
the convent's manors were tallaged for the king's profit.

---

[4] As the property of St Edmunds was divided between abbot and the
convent (p. 25, *n.* 2 above) the king had the right to take only the abbot's
portion into his hands during a vacancy.

[5] For the commission appointing Berwick to be the keeper of the abbey
during the vacancy see *CFR, 1272–1307*, p. 110.   For evidence that the
burgesses of St Edmunds were tallaged during the vacancy see *CCR, 1279–88*,
p. 17.

Regina Hyspanie, domina *a* Pontiui, mater Alienore regine Anglie, uite terminum fecit.[1] Rex igitur Anglie circa principium Maii facturus homagium regi Francie pro comitatu Pontiui, qui eum racione regine uxoris sue, filie et heredis regine *b* supradicte iam defuncte contingebat, transfretauit. Habito igitur Ambian' Francie parlamento conuenientibusque ibidem Francie atque Anglie *b* regibus necnon regionis utriusque plerisque magnatibus, rex Anglie quietumclamauit Normanniam regi Francie imperpetuum, recepturus tamen annuatim f. 167 de *b* scaccario Rotho/magensi in sempiternum xxx. millia libras Parisiacenses. Recepit eciam pro quietaclamancia supradicta Agenoys', Limozin, Perigoz atque Seintoyne[2] et hiis factis Anglie reuersus est.

Facta est itineracio iusticiariorum post Pascha in comitatu Eboracensi sub dominis I[ohanne] de Vallibus et R[ogero] Loueday et sociis suis; et in comitatu Cancie, Suthereye et Suths' sub dominis I[ohanne] de Reygate, R[icardo] de Boylund et sibi associatis. Iohannes archiepiscopus Cantuarie conuocatis *c* cunctis iurisdiccionis sue *d* episcopis die sancti Iacobi apostoli concilium suum apud Rading' celebrauit.*e*[3] Walterus Eboracensis archiepiscopus diem clausit extremum, cui successit magister Willelmus de Wikewane eiusdem loci cancellarius. Apud Norhamton' die Crucis Adorate[4] puer quidam a Iudeis crucifixus est, ipso tamen puero non tunc penitus interfecto. Cuius quidem rei pretextu multi de Iudeis statim post Pascha[5] London' equis

a + Iohanna *in margin in pencil with a tie-mark* MS²
b *Added* MS²; *in text* M   *c* + -que M
d *Added* MS²; *in text* M (*and Oxenedes*)
e Facta est itineracio . . . celebrauit *marked* uacat MS²

[1] Joanna, wife of Ferdinand III, king of Castile 1217–52, and countess of Ponthieu 1251–79

The queen of Spain, the lady of Ponthieu and mother of Eleanor, queen of England, died.[1] The king of England, therefore, about the beginning of May set sail to do homage to the king of France for the county of Ponthieu, which appertained to him by right of his wife, the daughter and heir of the queen of Spain, who was now dead. So a parliament was held at Amiens in France, attended by the king of France and the king of England and many magnates of both nations. There King Edward abandoned all claim forever to Normandy in favour of the king of France; in return he was to receive forever 3,000 livres parisis a year from the exchequer of Rouen. He also obtained for this quit-claim Agenais, the Limousin, Périgord and Saintonge.[2] When this business was concluded the king returned to England.

John de Vaux, Roger Loveday and their associates held an eyre in the county of York after Easter, and John de Rogate, Richard de Boyland and their associates held one in the county of Kent and in Surrey and Sussex. John, archbishop of Canterbury, having summoned all the bishops of his province, held a council at Reading on the feast of St James the Apostle.[3] Walter, archbishop of York, died and was succeeded by Master William de Wickwane, chancellor of York. At Northampton on the feast of the Adoration of the Cross[4] the Jews crucified a boy, who was not, however, quite killed. For this reason many Jews were dragged by horses and hanged in London immediately after Easter.[5]

---

[2] *Foedera*, I, p. 571   [3] 25 July.   Authorities disagree on this date.
[4] 31 March   [5] 2 April

distracti et suspensi sunt.ᵃ Facta est mutacio monete in
Anglia quadrante trigono in rotundum permutato, nec
tamen adhuc pristina racionabilis moneta inter nouam
discurrere prohibebatur.ᵇ Vltra uero consuetum obolis
penitus suspensis factus est unus denarius magnus
equipollens iiii. denariis communibus.ᶜ Iohannes
Dublinensis electus consecratus est in archiepiscopum
apud Waltham vi. Kal. Septembris ᵈ a Iohanne archiepiscopo Cantuariensi astantibus sibi Nicholao
Wintoniensi, Roberto Bathoniensi et Wellensi
et Willelmo Norwicensi episcopis. Robertus de
Kilwardeby cardinalis quondam Cantuariensis archiepiscopus ueneno ut dicitur extinctus in fata decessit.
Dominus rex constituit, prouidit et ordinauit quod
religiosi de cetero terras siue tenementa non adquirant.

Iohannes electus sancti Eadmundi expeditis negociis
suis in curia Romana benediccionemque suam a manu
f. 167ᵛ domini pape Nicholai consecutus, / recepta eciam baronia
sua a domino rege aliisque omnibus tam suam quam
conuentus porcionem contingentibus,[1] die sanctorum
Innocencium in ecclesia sua solempniter est receptus;
cuius expense in ipso itinere ad m.dc.lxxv. marcas x.
solidos ix. denarios excreuerunt.ᵉ

Ricardus Lincolniensis episcopus uite terminum
fecit; cui successit magister Oliuerus de Sutton',
eiusdem loci decanus. Dominus rex Natale Domini
apud Winton' celebrauit.ᶠ

ᵃ Apud Norhamton' . . . sunt *marked* uacat MS²
ᵇ prohibe MS²; *final three letters erased and* -batur *in margin in pencil* MS²;
perhibetur M
ᶜ denariis communibus *corr.* MS²   ᵈ Decembris *Oxenedes*
ᵉ *Lacuna of 1 line* M   ᶠ *Lacuna of 1 line* MS (3 M)

[1] The royal mandate to John de Berwick, keeper of the abbey, to restore
the temporalities is dated 5 November 1279; *CPR, 1272–81*, p. 331.

There was an alteration of the coinage in England. The triangular farthing was replaced by a round one. Nevertheless the old coin, which until then had been lawful, was not forbidden to circulate with the new. Another innovation was the total abolition of halfpennies and the minting of a new large penny equivalent to four [ordinary pennies]. John, archbishop-elect of Dublin, was consecrated at Waltham on 27 August by John, archbishop of Canterbury, assisted by Nicholas, bishop of Winchester, Robert, bishop of Bath and Wells, and William, bishop of Norwich. Cardinal Robert de Kilwardby, formerly archbishop of Canterbury, died, it was said by poison. The king established, provided and ordained that henceforth the religious orders should not acquire lands or tenements.

When John, the abbot-elect of Bury St Edmunds, had brought his business at the Roman court to a successful issue and obtained his blessing by the hand of Pope Nicholas [III], and received from the king his barony and everything else appertaining both to his and to the convent's portion,[1] he was solemnly admitted to his church on the feast of the Holy Innocents. The expenses of his journey to Rome amounted to 1,675 marks 10s. 9d.

Richard, bishop of Lincoln, died and was succeeded by Master Oliver de Sutton, dean of Lincoln. The king kept Christmas at Winchester.

1280

Robertus prior sancti Eadmundi cum per *[a]* aliquod tempus paralisi laborasset, debilitate sua tandem considerata, die sancti Pauli [1] sponte cessit prioratui; cui successit Stephanus de Ikewrthe, eiusdem loci supprior. Nicholaus Wintoniensis episcopus vi. Idus Februarii obiit.[2] Quo mortuo postulatus est in episcopum Wintoniensem Robertus Batoniensis et Wellensis episcopus; cuius postulacione in curia Romana cassata dominus papa liberam contra spem conuentui Winton' eligendi concessit facultatem, elegeruntque *[b]* sibi *[c]* magistrum Ricardum de Mora, eiusdem loci archidiaconum. Iohannes Londoniensis episcopus obiit vi. Idus Februarii; post quem electus est dominus Fulco Luuel archidiaconus Colecestriensis quo statim resignante magister Ricardus de Graueshende archidiaconus Norhamton' electus successit eidem.   Facta est eclipsis lune uniuersalis nocte sancti Eadwardi regis et martyris [3] luna per duarum fere horarum spacium colore infecta sanguineo. Symon sacrista sancti Eadmundi sacristie cessit, cui subrogatus est Willelmus del *[d]* Hoo camerarius. *[e]* [4]   Ricardus abbas Westmonasterii thesaurarius regis factus est.   Magister Thomas Bec thesaurarius garderobe regis electus est in episcopum Meneuensem, consecratusque est Lincoln' f. 168 die sancte Fidis [5] / a domino Iohanne Cantuariensi archiepiscopo.   Quo eciam die sanctus Hugo quondam

---

[a] cum per *corr. MS²*; per *om. M*
[b] elegerunt *corr. and* que *added MS²*; que *om. M. (and Oxenedes)*
[c] igitur *M (and Oxenedes)*   *[d]* de *M*
[e] Facta est eclipsis lune . . . camerarius *marked* uacat *MS²*

[1] 25 January
[2] This date, 8 February, is wrong. It is the date given below for John bishop of London's death. Nicholas died on 12 February 1280; *Wav.*, p. 393, *Wig.*, p. 477.

1280

Robert, prior of Bury St Edmunds, after he had suffered from paralysis for some time, at length on the feast of St Paul [1] voluntarily resigned his office, having consideration for his infirmity. He was succeeded by Stephen de Ixworth, subprior of Bury. Nicholas, bishop of Winchester, died on 8 February.[2] On his death Robert, bishop of Bath and Wells, was postulated to the see of Winchester, but his postulation was quashed in the Roman court and the pope granted the convent of Winchester the unhoped-for power of free election. The convent elected the archdeacon of Winchester, Master Richard More. John, bishop of London, died on 8 February. Fulk Lovel, archdeacon of Colchester, was elected to succeed him, but he immediately resigned and Master Richard de Gravesend, archdeacon of Northampton, was elected as his successor. There was a total eclipse of the moon on the night of the feast of St Edward, king and martyr [3]; the moon was the colour of blood for nearly two hours. Simon, sacrist of Bury St Edmunds, resigned from office and was replaced by William de Hoo, the chamberlain.[4] Richard, abbot of Westminster, was made the king's treasurer. Master Thomas Bek, the treasurer of the king's wardrobe, was elected bishop of St David's and consecrated at Lincoln on St Faith's day [5] by John, archbishop of Canterbury. On the same day St Hugh, formerly bishop of Lincoln,

---

[3] 18 March
[4] William de Hoo, sacrist 1280-94. His formulary and letter-book (Brit. Mus. MS Harley 230) were published by me for the Suffolk Records Society in 1963.
[5] 6 October

Lincolniensis episcopus in presencia domini regis Anglie
aliorumque magnatum solempniter est translatus. Die
sanctorum Iohannis et Pauli incepimus nouam monetam
fabricare.¹ In crastino sancti Petri ad Vincula ² et die
nocteque sequentibus facta est tanta pluuie inundacio
tantaque secuta est aquarum uehemencia quod homines
et mulieres [senes] ª cum iunioribus et pecora campi,
molendina, pontes, domos et arbores submersit, fena et
blada [per loca] ᵇ pleraque asportauit. Regi Anglie a
magno Tartarorum rege nuncii amicabiliter sunt directi.
Inhibitum est ne quis ultra diem Assumpcionis ³ de
ueteri moneta negociaretur. Facti sunt noui oboli
rotundi. ᶜ Walterus episcopus Exoniensis uite terminum
fecit, successit magister Petrus de Exon' eiusdem loci
canonicus. Radulphus abbas Croylaundie in fata
decessit. Tot fulgura tantaque tonitrua audita sunt
per plura loca Anglie uigilia sancti Martini, quod domos
arboresque prostrauerunt et multiplici ᵈ admiracione
uidentes terruerunt. A clero Anglie concessa est regi
quinta decima bonorum spiritualium secundum taxacionem Walteri ᵉ Norwycensis episcopi per tres annos.
Magnus rex Norwagie uite terminum fecit. Dominus
rex celebrauit Natale Domini apud Burgum in Norfolchia. ᶠ Undecimo Kal. Septembris castro Suriano in
fata decessit Iohannes ⁴ papa uacauitque sedes mensibus
vi. diebus xiiii. Iohannes archiepiscopus Cantuariensis

ª Supplied from M (and Oxenedes); om. MS
ᵇ per loca supplied from M (and Oxenedes); om. MS
ᶜ In crastino sancti Petri . . . rotundi marked uacat MS²
ᵈ multi M   ᵉ + quondam M (and Oxenedes)
ᶠ Dominus rex celebrauit . . . Norfolchia erased P; below after in principio
subsequentis Oxenedes, Cotton

¹ 26 June. cf. Brit. Mus. MS Harley 645 (' Kempe ' register from
Bury), ff. 79ᵛ, 80, for a note concerning this grant.

was solemnly translated in the presence of the king and the magnates of England. On the feast of SS John and Paul we began to mint a new coinage.[1] On the morrow of the feast of St Peter ad Vincula [2] and on the following day and night there was such a torrent of rain, and the force of the rushing flood which resulted was so strong, that men and women, the old and the young, and cattle in the fields were drowned, mills, bridges, houses and trees submerged, and hay and corn in many places washed away. Ambassadors were sent by the great king of the Tartars on a friendly mission to the king of England. Everyone was forbidden to buy and sell with the old currency after Assumption day.[3] New round halfpennies were minted. Walter, bishop of Exeter, died and was succeeded by Master Peter of Exeter, a canon of that place. Ralph, abbot of Crowland, died. There was a great storm with thunder and lightning in many parts of England on the eve of Martinmas. Many houses and trees were destroyed and those who watched were struck with great terror and awe. The clergy of England granted the king a fifteenth of revenues from spiritualities for three years according to the assessment of Walter, bishop of Norwich. Magnus, king of Norway, died. The king kept Christmas at Burgh in Norfolk. Pope John [4] died on 22 August in the castle of Soriano. The Holy See remained vacant for six months and fourteen days. John, archbishop of Canterbury, held a visitation of the

---

[2] 2 August [3] 15 August
[4] This should be Nicholas, not John.

uisitauit episcopatum Norwycensem uidelict Norfolch'
in fine istius anni et Suffolch' in principio subsequentis. *a*

1281

Dominus rex moram fecit in Norfolch' usque post festum
Purificacionis. *b*　Facta est eclipsis lune uniuersalis Non.

f. 168ᵛ Marcii.　Symon de Turon' sancte Cecilie pres/biter cardinalis in summum pontificem est electus, dictusque est
Martinus tercius.[1]　Facta est eclipsis lune pridie Kal.
Septembris luna per tempus non modicum in colore
cinereo permanente.　Henricus Leodiensis episcopus [2]
in Alemannia dignitate episcopali, eo quod proletarius
extiterat in ultimo concilio Lugdunensi spoliatus,
sexaginta enim et unum, ut dicebatur, filios et filias
genuerat, viii. Idus Septembris noctanter superueniens
successorem suum Iohannem manu propria interfecit.[3]
Magister Hugo de Euesham tituli sancti Laurencii
factus est presbiter cardinalis. *c*

Impetrata est a domino rege de nouo separacio inter
bona abbatis et conuentus sancti Eadmundi, ita quod de
cetero nullo casu confundantur, appensis domino regi
mille libris [4] excepto auro regine ad tantam pecunie
summam pertinente, aliisque expensis a latere prouenientibus que in inmensum accreuerent.　Huius carte tenor
in fine rotuli de cartis de anno eiusdem regis nono
continetur.[5]　Dominus rex celebrauit Natale Domini
apud Wigorniam. *d*

---

a Lacuna of *1* line MS; undecimo Kal. Septembr' . . . subsequentis om.
and lacuna of *9* lines M

b Dominus rex moram fecit . . . Purificacionis marked uacat MS²

c Facta est eclipsis lune . . . cardinalis marked uacat MS²

d Lacuna of *1* line MS (*7* M)

[1] Recte Martin IV

bishopric of Norwich, that is of Norfolk, at the end of this year, and of Suffolk at the beginning of the next.

1281

The king stayed in Norfolk until after Candlemas. There was a total eclipse of the moon on 7 March. Simon of Tours, cardinal-priest of St Cecilia, was elected pope and took the name Martin III.[1]   There was an eclipse of the moon on 31 August and the moon stayed the colour of ashes for some time.   Henry, bishop of Liège,[2] in Germany, who had been deprived of his episcopal rank in the last council of Lyons because he was a father and had (so it was said) begotten sixty-one sons and daughters, came upon his successor John on the night of 6 September and murdered him with his own hand.[3]   Master Hugh de Evesham was made cardinal-priest of the title of St Lawrence.

The king was asked for a new charter separating the property of the abbot and of the convent of Bury St Edmunds so that henceforth they would never by any chance be confused;   1,000 marks were paid to the king,[4] excluding the gold due to the queen in respect of this large payment and other expenses incurred in addition which amounted to a considerable sum.   The tenor of this charter is to be found at the end of the Charter Roll for this the ninth year of this king's reign.[5] The king kept Christmas at Worcester.

---

[2] For the deposition of Henry de Gueldre, bishop of Liège 1247–74, see Potthast, II, no. 20777.

[3] For a different account of the death of John de Enghien, bishop of Liège 1274–81, see Thilrode's chronicle, *Mon. Germ. Hist., Scriptores*, xxv, p. 561.

[4] See Pipe Rolls, 8 Edward I, E.372,124 membrane 3[d] (P.R.O.).

[5] *Cal. Charter Rolls, 1257–1300*, p. 259

1282

Die Purificacionis beate Marie celebrauit missam
episcopus Sidonensis [1] in ciuitate Ierosolem ubi per
multa retroacta tempora propter Sarracenorum
dominium a diuinis penitus fuerat cessatum. [a]

Liwelinus princeps Wallie inmemor pacis et federis [2]
inter dominum regem Anglie et ipsum dudum initi
preuaricator una cum Dauid germano suo eidem
domino regi fit rebellis. Castrorum igitur domini regis
in Wallia et in marchia uigilia Palmarum [3] quedam
subuertens quedam succendens aliisque enormibus intendens fidelium domini regis multitudinem copiosam
interfecit atque domino Rogero de Clifford utpote
f. 169 diluculo in lecto suo reperto secum in Wal/liam abducto
cum preda non modica ad propria repedauit. Unde
dominus rex in ulcionem iniuriarum sibi illatarum
excercitum dirigens in Walliam in subsidium guerre sue
sub mutui specie a singulis ciuitatibus suis et burgis
necnon a ciuitatibus et burgis uirorum ecclesiasticorum
in sue guerre cepit subsidium. Ad cuius quidem rei
execucionem missus est per totam Angliam dominus
Iohannes de Kirkeby archidiaconus Couentriensis qui a
London' viii. millium marcarum modo predicto cepit
contribucionem. Visitatis igitur primo de Gernemuta et de
Norwico burgis et burgensibus acceptisque a Gernemuta
mille marcis et a Norwic' libris quingentis tandem apud
sanctum Eadmundum declinauit, ubi burgensibus ad
quingentas marcas taxatis, [4] seruientum ipsius curie
monachorum taxacionem ut a burgensibus, quod nunquam hactenus contigerat, minime taxarentur eiusdem

---

[a] Die Purificationis . . . cessatum *marked* uacat *MS*[2]

[1] Adam, bishop of Sidon 1278?–1305

1282

On Candlemas day the bishop of Sidon[1] celebrated
mass in the city of Jerusalem, where divine services had
been altogether suspended for a long time because of
the rule of the Saracens. Llewelyn, prince of Wales,
ignoring the peace and in violation of the treaty[2]
formerly concluded between the king of England and
himself, rebelled together with his brother David against
the king. On the eve of Palm Sunday[3] he destroyed
some of the king's castles in Wales and in the Marches,
burnt others and engaged in other outrages. He killed
numerous liege men of the king, and finding Roger de
Clifford in bed early in the morning, carried him off to
Wales and returned home with considerable booty.
The king in revenge for the injury done to him led his
army into Wales. In aid of the war he raised a subsidy
in the form of loans from all his cities and boroughs,
and from the clergy. To put this into effect John
Kirkby, archdeacon of Coventry, was sent all over
England. He took a contribution of 8,000 marks from
London in the aforesaid way. Then he first visited the
boroughs of Yarmouth and Norwich and took 1,000
marks from the burgesses of Yarmouth and £500 from
those of Norwich. At length he went to Bury St
Edmunds and assessed the burgesses at 500 marks.[4]
The assessment of the servants of the monks' household
was entrusted to the prior of Bury so that they should
not be assessed by the burgesses, which had never

---

[2] i.e. the treaty of Conway; cf. above, p. 64, under 1277
[3] 21 March
[4] cf. *Cal. Chancery Rolls, Various, 1277–1326*, pp. 241–2

loci priori commisit, quorum taxacio ad summam xxvi.
marcarum accreuit. Fraternitas eciam Duodene [1] uille
sancti Eadmundi per eundem priorem ad xii. marcas fuit
taxata. Ab abbate uero et conuentu sancti Eadmundi
c. marcas sub eodem extorsit colore. Interim Alienora,
filia domini Symonis de Monte Forti, quondam comitis
Leicestrie, nupta Liwelino principi Wallie, filiam
pariendo superstitem Wenlianam [a] nomine, die sanctorum Geruasii et Prothasii [2] diem clausit extremum,
sepultaque est apud Landwairs [3] in domo Fratrum
Minorum. [b] In expedicione igitur supradicta dominus
rex cepit pro singulis seruiciis militaribus l. marcas,
mitius tamen cum abbate sancti Eadmundi agendo
ccc. libras pro seruicio suo cepit ab eodem. In ista
eciam expedicione Willelmus filius et heres domini
Willelmi de Valenc' et quidam alii cum eo in West
Wallia, domini Lucas de Tany, Rogerus de Clifford
iunior, Willelmus de Lindeseye, Willelmus de Audedelee
f. 169ᵛ et plures / alii cum illis in Nord Wallia absque aliquo
Wallensium detrimento, quidam fugiendo aquis inter-
cepti et submersi, quidam ceciderunt gladio. Rebus
igitur sic se habentibus, Liwelinus princeps Wallie iiii.
Idus Decembris feria vi.[4] ab excercitu regis Anglie in
Suth Wallia interceptus, uita capiteque priuatus est.
Cuius capud in crastino ad regem in Nord Wallia est
allatum. Qui statim illud excercitui suo in Angleseye

---

[a] Wencianam *MS*, *M*
[b] Visitatis igitur primo (*p. 74 above*) . . . Minorum *marked* uacat *MS²*

[1] A guild of secular clerks; Lobel, pp. 46, 73. Traditionally the guild
originated from the twelve secular clerks whom Cnut replaced by monks
as guardians of St Edmund's body: Brit. Mus. MS Harley 3977, f. 25,
25ᵛ; J. Battely, *Antiquitates S. Edmundi Burgi ad annum 1272 perductae* (1745),
p. 36.
[2] 19 June
[3] Llanfaes, near Beaumaris, Anglesey. The birth of Gwenllian and

happened before; the servants' tax amounted to 26 marks. The prior assessed the ' guild of the twelve ' [1] of the town of Bury St Edmunds at 12 marks. 100 marks were extorted from the abbot and convent of Bury on the same pretext. Meanwhile Eleanor, daughter of Simon de Montfort, formerly earl of Leicester, and wife of Llewelyn, prince of Wales, died on the feast of SS. Gervase and Prothase [2] while giving birth to a daughter named Gwenllian, who survived her. She was buried in the house of the Friars Minor at Llanfaes.[3] The king levied 50 marks from every knight's fee for the Welsh campaign. But he treated the abbot of Bury St Edmunds more leniently for he raised only £300 from him for the service owed by the abbot. On this campaign died William, the son and heir of William de Valence, and others who were with him in west Wales, and Luke de Tany, Roger de Clifford the younger, William de Lindsey, William de Audley and many others with them in north Wales; some were drowned while taking flight and others perished by the sword. The Welsh suffered no losses. While events were thus progressing Llewelyn, prince of Wales, was intercepted by the army of the king of England on Friday, 10 December,[4] in south Wales, and so lost his head and his life. On the next day his head was carried to the king in north Wales. The king immediately sent it to his army in Anglesey; when the

---

death of Eleanor are noticed in *Brut y Tywysogyon*, ed. Thomas Jones (Board of Celtic Studies, University of Wales History and Law series, no. xi, 1952), p. 117.

[4] Friday, 11 December is the correct date; J. E. Lloyd, ' The Death of Llywelyn ap Gruffydd,' in *Bull. of the Board of Celtic Studies*, v (May 1931), p. 349.

commoranti destinauit, cuius conspectu satiatis *ᵃ* Angle-
siensibus statim London' iussum est deportari. In
cuius occursum in crastino sancti Thome Apostoli, ¹
exeuntes Londonienses, cum tubis et cornibus, illud per
omnes uicos London' cum clangore mirabili, condux-
erunt. Quo facto collistrigio suo toto illius diei residuo
illud defixerunt. Aduesperascente uero die, ad Turrim
London' est deportatum et in excelsa trabe transfixum.
Corpus uero principis trunctum et lacerum in abbacia
de Cumnir ² de ordine Cisterciensi est sepultum.

Pirate quidam de Selland' et Holland' circa
Gernemut' et Donewic' tyrannidem excercentes pirati-
cam quecumque sibi obuiancia depredabantur, homines
trucidabant, naues *ᵇ* non nullas cum contentis secum
abduxerunt. Florencius comes Holland' in ulcionem
mortis Willelmi patris sui dudum a Frisonibus interfecti ³
et inter ipsos ignominiose sepulti gloriose triumphans,
quindecim milia Frisonum interemit, non nullique metu
comitis patriam deserentes spontaneumque exilium
subeuntes ad alia se loca diuersa transtulerunt. Corpus
igitur patris sui apud Frisones paucis arbitris inglorie
tumulatum ad propria cum solempni transtulit apparatu
et cum honore non modico honeste in partibus suis
f. 170 *ᶜ* tradidit sepulture.*ᵈ* Ricardus ar/chidiaconus Wintoniensis, dudum loci eiusdem electus, in manum summi
pontificis resignauit electionem de ipso factam *ᵉ* ad
episcopatum ecclesie memorate, quem statim dominus
papa contulit magistro Iohanni de Punteyse archidiacono

ᵃ Paragraph mark erased MS   *ᵇ + -que M (and Oxenedes)*
ᶜ Grotesque griffin at foot of page in pen and ink MS
ᵈ Pirate quidam de Selland' . . . sepulture marked uacat MS²
ᵉ facte MS, MP, P; factam Cotton

¹ 22 December

men of Anglesey had seen enough of it he ordered it to be carried to London. The Londoners came out to meet it on the morrow of St Thomas the Apostle [1] with trumpets and horns, and conducted it through all the streets of London with a great din. After this they fixed the head to their pillory for the rest of the day. At sunset it was taken to the Tower of London and fastened to a high beam. The headless and mutilated body of the prince was buried in the Cistercian abbey, Cwmhir.[2]

Pirates from Zeeland and Holland ruled the sea as tyrants round Yarmouth and Dunwich; they raided whatever ships they met, killed the crews and sailed off with not a few boats and their cargo. Florence, count of Holland, in revenge for the death of his father William, who had long before been murdered by the men of Frisia [3] and ignominiously buried in their land, won a glorious victory over them. He killed fifteen thousand Frisians; some from fear of the count fled the country and went into voluntary exile elsewhere. The count then took his father's body, so shamefully buried among the Frisians in the presence of only a few people, and carried it home in solemn procession and gave him a decent burial with full rites in his own country. Richard, archdeacon of Winchester, who had formerly been elected bishop of Winchester, surrendered to the pope his election to the see, as recorded above. The pope immediately gave the see to Master John de Pontissara, archdeacon of Exeter. The king of the

---

[2] Cwmhir, Radnorshire. There is no other evidence that Llewelyn was buried there; R. H. Morris, ' Burial of Llewelyn ap Gruffydd,' in *Archaeologia Cambrensis*, 6th series, XI (1911), pp. 26ff.

[3] William was killed in 1256 (see above, p. 21).

Exoniensi. Rex Tartarorum una cum Hospitalaribus
cum soldano dimicauit. In quo conflictu cesis paganis
captus est ipse soldanus et apud Babiloniam arctiori
custodie commendatus.¹ Alienora regina Anglie apud
Rothelan filiam peperit quam uocauit Elizabeth.ᵃ
Isabella comitissa de Arundel diem claudens extremum
apud Marham sepelitur. Magister Thomas de
Cantilupo episcopus Herefordensis in curia Romana
defungitur; cui per eleccionem successit magister
Ricardus de Swinefield, archidiaconus Londoniensis.
Hertmannus ᵇ filius regis Alemannie, qui filiam regis
Anglie fuerat desponsaturus, incaute super glaciem
gradiens, gelu dissoluto glacieque interrupta, aquis
interceptus atque suffocatus est.² Die sancti Francisci ³
natus est Iohanni de Hastingge filius suus primogenitus
quem uocauit Willelmum. Dominus Thomas Leneband archidiaconus Suffolch' uigilia sancte Lucie ⁴ apud
Horham diem clausit extremum. Dominus rex celebrauit Natale Domini apud Rothelan in Wallia.ᶜ

1283

Tocius Anglie communitas tricesimum denarium
omnium mobilium suorum in subsidium guerre sue,
equitatura, armatura, thesauro et garderoba dumtaxat
exceptatis, domino regi concesserunt. In cuius pecunie
contribucione ᵈ allocari fecit rex totam pecuniam anno
precedente sub mutui specie uel colore ubicumque
receptam. Idem rex dominica in media Quadragesima,

ᵃ Om. and a lacuna of 1¼ in. M; on erasure Oxenedes; Walkinianam Cotton
ᵇ Corr. by erasure from Hertinannus MS; Hertinannus P, Oxenedes, Cotton
ᶜ Die sancti Francisci . . . Wallia marked uacat MS² and a lacuna of 1 line
MS (4 M)
ᵈ -taxat exceptatis . . . contri- mainly on erasure MS

Tartars joined with the Hospitallers to fight the sultan. In the war infidels were slain and the sultan himself captured and closely guarded in Cairo.[1] Eleanor, queen of England, gave birth to a daughter at Rhuddlan, whom she named Elizabeth. Isabel, countess of Arundel, died and was buried at Marham. Master Thomas de Cantilupe, bishop of Hereford, died at the Roman court. Master Richard de Swinfield, archdeacon of London, was elected to succeed him. Hartmann, son of the king of Germany, who was to marry the king of England's daughter, walked incautiously on some ice, and as there was a thaw and the ice was broken, he was swept away by the water and drowned.[2] On the day of St Francis[3] a first son was born to John de Hastings; he called him William. Thomas Leneband, archdeacon of Suffolk, died on St Lucy's eve[4] at Horham. The king kept Christmas at Rhuddlan in Wales.

1283

The whole commonalty of England granted the king as an aid for his war a thirtieth on all their movables, excepting only horses, arms, the treasury and wardrobe. The king allowed all sums of money which he had received the year before with the appearance or under the pretence of a loan to be counted as part of the contribution to this tax. On the Sunday of mid-Lent,

---

[1] Probably a muddled reference to the battle of Homs, 30 October 1281, for which see R. Grousset, *Histoire de Croisades*, III, pp. 699–701.

[2] A better authority says that he was shipwrecked on the Rhine and drowned on 20 December 1281; *Regesta Imperii, 1198–1254*, ed. J. F. Böhmer (1849), p. iii.

[3] 4 October   [4] 12 December

f. 170ᵛ / que tunc v. Kal. Aprilis euenit, totum thesaurum
domini pape de decimis in subsidium Terre Sancte
concessum, per diuersa loca Anglie depositum, seruris
diruptis, cepit, abduxit et iuxta sue uoluntatis arbitrium
de eodem disposuit. Iohannes episcopus Rofensis uite
terminum fecit, cui successit magister Thomas de
Ingoluestorpe, decanus sancti Pauli London', consecratus Cantuar' die sanctorum Cosme et Damiani.[1]
Post mortem Liwelini principis Wallie, eiusdem fratre
Dauid fuga lapso ceterisque Walensibus omnibus tam
nobilibus quam ignobilibus domini regis uoluntati ultro
se committentibus, idem rex totam Walliam usque ad
mare Hybernicum, uniuersis castellis et municionibus
sibi contraditis, subiugauit. Leges Anglicanas imposuit
atque iusticiarios aliosque ministros ad pacis custodiam
ibidem constituit; scaccariumque Wallie scaccariique
ministros apud Cestram collocauit. Interea Dauid
supradictus omni excercitu suo destitutus, per incertas
sedes uagabundus et errans, tandem ad quandam
casulam delitescendi gratia ad sui confusionem diuertens,
per aliquos de excercitu regio circumuentus, cum uno
de filiis suis et aliis decem, captus atque coram rege
uigilia sancti Albani [2] est adductus, cuius precepto in
castello Cestrie arctiori custodie est commendatus.
Igitur in parleamento generali die sabbati in crastino
sancti Leodegarii [3] apud Salop' habito,ᵃ Dauit frater
Liwelini quondam principis Wallie, qui se pro principe
post mortem fratris sui gesserat, in ipsa domini regis
curia, presidente in iudicio auctoritate regia domino

ᵃ Interea Dauid supradictus . . . habito *marked* uacat *MS*²

[1] 27 September. 26 November is the correct date; Peckham's *Register*,
ed. C. T. Martin (RS, 1882), ii, pp. 592–3.
[2] 21 June
[3] 3 October. An error as Saturday was on 2 October.

which fell on 28 March, the king seized all the pope's
treasure from the tax of a tenth, which had been granted
in aid of the Holy Land and deposited in various parts
of England.   He broke open the coffers, carried off the
money and disposed of it as he thought fit.   John,
bishop of Rochester, died and was succeeded by Master
Thomas de Ingoldsthorpe, dean of St Paul's, London,
who was consecrated at Canterbury on the feast of SS.
Cosmas and Damian.[1]   After the death of Llewelyn,
prince of Wales, his brother David took to flight and all
the other Welshmen, of both noble and humble rank,
submitted voluntarily to the king's mercy;   thus the
king subdued the whole of Wales as far as the Irish sea,
and every castle and fortified place was surrendered to
him.   He imposed on Wales the laws of England and
instituted justices and other officials for keeping the peace
there.   He set up an exchequer for Wales with its
officials at Chester.   Meanwhile the aforesaid David,
who had lost all his army, wandered aimlessly like a
vagabond through little-known regions and at length
turned aside to hide in a small cottage, to his own
undoing;   for he was surrounded by men of the royal
army and captured together with one of his sons and
ten other men.   On the eve of St Alban [2] he was brought
before the king and by his command sent to Chester
castle for closer confinement.   Then in a general
parliament held at Shrewsbury on a Saturday, the
morrow of St Leger's day,[3] David, the brother of
Llewelyn, lately prince of Wales, who acted as prince
after his brother's death, was brought before the king's
court, under the presidency of John de Vaux, sitting as

Iohanne de Vallibus, de prodicione, regie maiestatis lesione ac sacrilegio conuictus, corporis detraccioni atque f. 171 suspensioni, capitis detrunccacioni, combustioni atque / membrorum adiudicatus est deseccioni. Cuius capud London', corpus uero per quatuor partes desectum, Wincestr', Norhampton', Cestr' atque Eborac' est transmissum. Viscera uero eiusdem propter frequentem ecclesiarum combustionem, ad sacrilegii facinus puniendum, combustioni ibidem sunt adiudicata; cum quo eciam senescallus eiusdem, Mabadinda nomine, factis pocius quam nomine barbarus, super prodicione conuictus, equis distractus et suspendio demum est interemptus. *a*

Robertus Dunelmensis episcopus obiit, cui successit dominus Antonius Bek', eiusdem loci archidiaconus. Nicholaus abbas sancti Augustini Cantuarie, simulata peregrinacione ad sanctum Nicholaum ad Barum,[1] curiam domini pape adiit atque baculo et anulo dignitatis sue in manum domini pape resignauit. Quo facto ordini se transtulit Cartusiensium. Abbaciam uero contulit dominus papa cuidam Thome de Findon', eiusdem monasterii monacho. *b*

Petrus rex Arragonie in terris Sicilie, Calabrie et Apulie, racione uxoris[2] sue utpote filie Manfredi, filii Fredericii quondam Romanorum imperatoris, qui ipsis terris, ut asseruit, saisitus obiit et uestitus, ius sibi uendicans hereditarium ipsarum terrarum proceres tum promissis tum donis sibi alliciens cunctorum magnatum terrarum memoratarum assensu et fauore omnia castella et municiones Karoli regis Sicilie arte siue dolo una die

---

a cum quo eciam . . . interemptus *marked* uacat *MS²*
b Nicholas abbas . . . monacho *marked* uacat *MS²*
[1] St Nicholas of Myra, at Bari   [2] Constance

judge with royal authority.   There he was convicted of
treason, lèse-majesté and sacrilege, and condemned to
be drawn, hanged, beheaded, burned and quartered.
His head was sent to London and the four quarters of
his body to Winchester, Northampton, Chester and
York.   His bowels were condemned to the flames to
punish his crimes of sacrilege, for he had often set fire
to churches.   His steward called Mabadinda (even
more barbarous in deed than in name), was also convicted of treason.   He was drawn by horses and finally
put to death by hanging.

   Robert, bishop of Durham, died and was succeeded
by Anthony Bek, archdeacon of Durham.   Nicholas,
abbot of St Augustine's, Canterbury, on the pretext of
going on a pilgrimage to St Nicholas at Bari,[1] went to
the papal court and resigned his staff and ring of office
into the pope's hands.   Then he joined the Carthusian
order.   The pope gave the abbacy to a certain Thomas
de Findon, a monk of the same monastery.

   Peter, king of Aragon, vindicated his hereditary
claim to the lands of Sicily, Calabria and Apulia by
right of his wife [2] as the daughter of Manfred, son of
Frederick, who was formerly the emperor of the Romans
and who had died, as [Peter] said, seised and in possession of these lands.   Peter won the support of the chief
men of these lands with promises and bribes, and, with
the consent and approval of all the magnates of the
said lands, in a single day occupied by cunning or
trickery every castle and fortified place of Charles,
king of Sicily.   He slew the men he found in them,

occupauit, uiros inuentos trucidauit, thesauros sibi
appropriauit, nauigium suum, hominibus cesis, penitus
destruxit; terrasque illas Karolo rege expulso pre-
occupans filium suum manu imperatoris Constantino-
politani,[a][1] cuius consilio et auxilio omnia predicta
presumpserat corona regni Sicilie fecit coronari.

    Hoc anno et duobus precedentibus fructus omnium
f. 171ᵛ gardinorum per Angliam / fere defecerunt.[b] A clero
prouincie Cantuar' concessa est domino regi in subsidium guerre sue uicesima omnium prouentuum
ecclesiasticorum per duos annos secundum taxacionem
Walteri quondam Norwicensis episcopi. Ricardus
abbas Westmonasterii domini regis thesaurarius prima
die mensis Decembris obiit, terciaque post hec die apud
Westmonasterium sepulture commendatur. Cui successit Walterus de Wenloch eiusdem loci monachus.
Dominus rex Natale Domini apud Rothelan in Wallia
celebrauit. Soldanus Babilonie defungitur.[2] London'
et per non nulla [c] loca Anglie [d] tante uise choruscaciones,
tantaque die sancti Stephani audita sunt tonitrua, quod
audientibus et uidentibus terrorem et horrorem non
modicum incusserunt. Estas tota cum maxima
autumpni sequentis parte uehementer et continue
pluuiosa omnem fere spem satorum in uiridi delusit in
arido.[c][3]

1284

Frater Iohannes de Derelington' de ordine Fratrum
Predicatorum archiepiscopus Dublinensis non procul a

---

[a] -nopoli *corr. MS²*
[b] ipsarum terrarum proceres . . . defecerunt *seems to be marked* uacat
[c] + Esexie M   [d] *Added MS²; in text P; om.* M
[e] Soldanus Babilonie . . . arido *marked* uacat *MS²; lacuna of 1 line MS.*
Mends at this point, 5 lines from foot of folio.

took over the treasure and completely wiped out
Charles's navy and killed the crews. When he had
driven out King Charles he occupied the lands, and then
had his son crowned king of Sicily by the hand of the
emperor of Constantinople,[1] with whose advice and aid
he had undertaken this whole enterprise.

In this year and in the two previous years the fruit
in every garden in England failed almost completely.
The clergy of the province of Canterbury granted the
king in aid of his war a twentieth of all ecclesiastical
revenues for two years according to the assessment of
Walter, formerly bishop of Norwich. Richard, abbot
of Westminster, the king's treasurer, died on 1 December
and was buried at Westminster on the third day after
this. He was succeeded by Walter de Wenlock, a monk
of Westminster. The king kept Christmas at Rhuddlan
in Wales. The sultan of Cairo died.[2]   In London and
in many parts of England on St Stephen's day such
bright flashes of lightning were seen and such loud
thunder heard, that those who saw and heard were
filled with great terror and awe. The heavy and per-
sistent rains of the whole summer and most of the
following autumn completely belied at harvest time the
hopes the farmers had had when the corn was green.[3]

1284

Brother John de Darlington, a member of the order of
Friars Preachers, archbishop of Dublin, died not far

---

[1] Michael Paleologus, emperor 1260–82
[2] Probably a reference to Abaqa Khan, who died on 1 April 1282.
[3] cf. Luke 23:31

ciuitate London' v. Kal. Aprilis in fata decessit, sepultusque est in noua ecclesia Fratrum Predicatorum in castello
Bainardi London'. Die Pasche uidelicet v. Idus Aprilis
apud sanctum Eadmundum, circa horam diei primam,
tam subita tamque repentina fulminum choruscacio,
tam eciam continuatus cum fulgure tonitrui fragor
contigit inmoderatus, quod uix qui audierunt pedibus
stare potuerunt. Et cum tanta tunc ibidem contigisset
tempestatis uehemencia dampnum nullum per patriam
fecit aut permodicum. Eandem tempestatem eisdem
die et hora in partibus transmarinis audiuimus contigisse. *a* Di esancti Marci ewangeliste[1] apud Kayrnerwan
f. 172 in Wallia / natus est domino regi Anglie filius dictusque
est Eadwardus. Robertus Sari[sburiensis] episcopus
obdormiuit in Domino; cui successit magister Walterus
Scamel, eiusdem loci decanus. In Alemannia quidam
trufator[2] subito se palam manifestans Fredericumque
quondam Romanorum imperatorem, qui superius anno
Domini M.CC.L. uite terminum fecerat, se esse simulans
multam et frequentem familiam necnon eciam tocius
pene regionis habens fauorem excercitum coadunauit
copiosum, regeque Radulpho non contradicente, immo
pocius rem dissimulante, se ut dominum et imperatorem
ab omnibus fecit uenerari. Dominus Aldephonsus
domini regis Anglie filius apud Windlishores die sancti
Magno martyris[3] diem clausit extremum. Qui uigilia
Decollacionis sancti Iohannis Baptiste[4] apud Westmonasterium solempni traditus est sepulture. In
crastino sancte Fidis[5] apud sanctum Eadmundum ante
horam diei primam subite facte sunt choruscaciones et
tonitrua tam uehemencia tamque terribilia ut audienti-

---

a Die Pasche uidelicet . . . contigisse *marked* uacat *MS²*

from London on 28 March and was buried in the new church of the Friars Preachers in Baynard's castle in London. At Bury St Edmunds on Easter Sunday (that is on 9 April) about the first hour of the day there were such sudden and unexpected lightning flashes and such a loud and prolonged crash of thunder accompanied by lightning, that those who heard could hardly stand upright. But though the fury of the storm was so great at Bury it did no damage to the countryside, or practically none. We heard that the same storm affected lands across the sea on the same day and at the same hour. On the feast of St Mark the Evangelist [1] a son was born to the king at Caernarvon in Wales and he was called Edward. Robert, bishop of Salisbury, fell asleep in the Lord. He was succeeded by Master Walter Scamel, dean of Salisbury. In Germany an impostor [2] suddenly appeared and pretended he was Frederick, the former emperor of the Romans, who had already died in the year of the Lord 1250. He collected a large crowd of regular followers, became popular in most of that region and united a considerable army. He made everyone honour him as lord and emperor; meanwhile King Rudolf did not oppose him but virtually ignored the affair. Alfonso, son of the king of England, died at Windsor on the feast of St Magnus martyr.[3] He was buried with full rites at Westminster on the eve of the Decollation of St John the Baptist.[4] At Bury St Edmunds on the morrow of St Faith's day [5] before the first hour there were such violent and terrifying flashes of lightning and thunder claps, that those who heard

---

[1] 25 April   [2] Dietrich Holzchub   [3] 19 August
[4] 28 August   [5] 7 October

bus et uidentibus maximum incuterent terrorem. Apud Donewicum v. Kal. Decembris ab hora die tercia usque ad horam sextam uisum est mare flamma quadam non perlucida sed flaua pocius concremari.[a] Dominus papa ob culpam rebellionis contumacem et inobedientem Petri dudum regis Arragonie regnum suum Philippo regis Francie filio contulit et heredi, reddendo sedi apostolice pro dicto regno centum libras annuas. Idem Philippus duxit in uxorem heredem regni Nauarre.[1] Iohannes Cantuariensis archiepiscopus uisitauit episcopatum Lincolliensem extenditque uisitacionem suam usque ad Passionem Domini in anno subsequente. Illa pars ecclesie sancti Petri Rome ubi fuit altare apostolorum cum precipuis et principalibus eorundem yconiis subita coruit et inopinate. Hugo de Liziniato rex Cypri[2] cum filio suo et aliis quibusdam de familia sua per fratres milicie Templi ueneno sunt extincti. In / ecclesia beate Marie de Arcubus London' quidam de Londoniis Laurencius dictus per quosdam maligne mentis homines de ciuitate supradicta uulneratus, demumque in trabe ecclesie laqueo est suspensus.[3] Super quo rex Anglie non modicum conturbatus, quosdam minus tamen nocentes sed minime locupletes equis distrahi tandem laqueo iussit suspendi, nocenciores uero sed locupleciores pena mulctari censuit pecuniaria.[b] Dominus rex celebrauit Natale Domini Bristoll'.

f. 172ᵛ

---

[a] In Alemannia quidam trufator . . . concremari *marked* uacat *MS*²
[b] Idem Philippus . . . pecuniaria *marked* uacat *MS*²

[1] Joanna, daughter of Henry I, king of Navarre 1270–4
[2] Hugh III of Lusignan, king of Cyprus 1267 to 26 March 1284. There seems to be no evidence that he and his son were poisoned by the Templars. His younger son Bohemond died on 3 November 1283.
[3] Laurence Duket; for slightly different accounts of his death see *Ann. Lond.*, p. 92; *Croniques de London*, ed. Aungier, p. 19.

and saw them were stricken with great terror. At
Dunwich on 27 November, from the third hour of the
day until the sixth hour, the sea seemed to burn with a
flame of a lurid yellow light rather than a clear one.
Because of the disloyal crime of obstinate rebellion the
pope gave the kingdom of Peter, formerly king of Aragon,
to Philip, the king of France's son and heir, who was to
pay the Holy See 100 livres a year for the kingdom.
The same Philip married the heiress to the kingdom of
Navarre.[1] John, archbishop of Canterbury, visited the
diocese of Lincoln and prolonged his visitation until
Passion Sunday in the following year. That part of the
church of St Peter's at Rome where the altar of the
apostles stood, with their celebrated and far-famed
statues, suddenly and unexpectedly collapsed. Hugh
of Lusignan, king of Cyprus,[2] his son and others of his
household were killed by poison by the Knights of the
Temple. In the church of St Mary le Bow in London a
certain Londoner called Lawrence was wounded by
some evilly disposed men of the aforesaid city and
finally hanged by a noose from a beam in the church.[3]
The king of England was not a little perturbed about
this; he ordered that some who were less guilty but
least able to pay should be torn asunder by horses and
then hanged with a rope, and those who were more
guilty, but richer, should be punished with a fine. The
king kept Christmas at Bristol.

1285

Karolus rex Cicilie apud Barlettum in Apulea uigilia
Epiphanie uite terminum fecit,[a][1] post cuius decessum
Siculi fouentes partem Petri de Arrogon', qui eciam
uiuente dicto Karolo regimen Cicilie contra ecclesiam
Romanam occupauerat, tenentes in custodia sua
Karolum [b] principem de la Moree [2] dicti regis filium in
guerra ab eisdem captum cum triumpho redierunt ad
propria.

Iohannes Cantuariensis archiepiscopus episcopatum
Eliensem uisitaturus, in ipso Eliensi monasterio omnes
maiores amouit obedienciarios priore dumtaxat excepto. [c]

Dominus rex Anglie una cum regina et tribus filiabus
suis uota in guerra sua Wallie facta Deo et sancto
soluturus Eadmundo x. Kal. Martii cum magna
deuocione et reuerencia ibidem accessit, iter in crastino
uersus Norfolchiam, ubi moram per totam traxit
Quadragesimam sequentem, arepturus. Qui quidem
suorum diuersorumque progenitorum suorum muni-
mentis in nullo deferendo, pondera, mensuras et ulnas
uille sancti Eadmundi per marescallum suum mensurarum, quod tempore patris sui hoc semel factum
fuerat tantum allegando, fecit examinari. Emolumentum
tamen ex illo uisu omniumque uisuum in aduentibus
suis et heredum suorum proueniens reparacioni et
decorationi feretri sancti concessit Eadmundi et carta
sua confirmauit.[3] Et quia sacrista et balliui sui per

---

[a] *Lacuna of 1 line MS*   [b] -ū *corr. MS²*   [c] -to *corr. MS²*

[1] 5 January. *Les Grandes Chron.*, VIII, p. 100, and Nangis, *Chron.*, I,
p. 262, give 7 January and say he died at Foggia.

[2] Charles II, count of Anjou and Maine 1285–90, king of Naples
1285–1309. For his title as prince of the Morea (Achaia) see the *Cambridge
Medieval History*, IV, p. 446.

[3] *CPR, 1281–92*, p. 178, ibid., *1292–1301*, p. 183

1285

Charles, king of Sicily, died at Barletta in Apulia on the vigil of Epiphany.[1] After his death the Sicilians supported Peter of Aragon, who, while Charles was still alive, had taken over the government of Sicily in opposition to the Roman Church, and returned triumphantly to their own land holding captive Charles, prince of the Morea,[2] the king's son, whom they had captured in battle.

John, archbishop of Canterbury, set out to hold a visitation of the bishopric of Ely, and removed all the important obedientiaries from office in the monastery of Ely except the prior.

The king of England, with the queen and his three daughters, in order to fulfil a vow made to God and St Edmund during his Welsh campaign, arrived at Bury St Edmunds on 20 February with deep devotion and reverence; then on the next day he set out for Norfolk, where he stayed for the whole of the following Lent. The king, without respect for the charters of privileges granted by him and his predecessors, had the weights, measures and ell-measures of the town of Bury St Edmunds inspected by his marshal of measures, merely alleging that this had once been done in the time of his father. He granted, however, and confirmed by charter that the profits accruing from this view and from all views held when he and his heirs should visit Bury, should be used for the upkeep and decoration of St Edmund's shrine.[3] And since the sacrist and his bailiffs

f. 173 burgenses *a* uille allegantes quod in / aduentu tantum regio huiusmodi uisus fieri debuerat hactenus prepediti extiterint a mensurarum uisu faciendo, ordinatum est per consilium domini regis et sacriste sub periculo libertatis uille in manum domini regis capiende quatinus *b* singulis annis bis huiusmodi examinacionem faciendo burgenses aliosque de uilla ad corporale prestandum compellat sacramentum, contradicentes primo per pecuniam, secundo, si maior extiterit contumacia, per incarceracionem donec super eorum transgressione rex consulatur puniendo.[1] Domino rege, ut dictum est, in partibus Norfolch' moram faciente, tota communitas uille Gipuyc' apud ipsum *c* regem super diuersis facinoribus acusata et in magna parte conuicta in maxima pecunie summa est condempnata. Et preterea xiii. de melioribus tocius uille per dimidium annum per diuersa Anglie loca carcerali sunt custodie deputati.[2]

Philippus rex Francie circa mediam Quadragesimam exercitum contra regem mouit Arragon', qui tam terrestri et nauali prelio quam eciam inedia quampluribus suorum consumptis thesaurique sui non modica parte amissa et ab emulis suis occupata tandem apud ciuitatem Parpelonam dissinterie incomodo uiam uniuerse carnis ingressus est. Corpus uero regis apud sanctum Dionisium cum progenitoribus suis die sancti Martini solempniter est tumulatum.

Thomas prior ecclesie Christi Cantuariensis uigilia Palmarum[3] apud Bellum locum regis monachum induit Cisterciensem; cui successit Henricus eiusdem loci

---

a burgensenses *MS, P*
b fieri debuerat . . . quatinus *seems to be marked* uacat *MS*²
c pecuniam, secundo, si maior . . . ipsum *seems to be marked* uacat *MS*²

had hitherto been prevented from holding an assize of measures by the burgesses, who alleged that such a view should be held only on the occasion of a royal visit, it was decreed with the counsel of the king and sacrist, under peril of the king taking the liberty of the town into his own hands, that [the sacrist] should compel the burgesses and other people of the town to take a corporal oath when he held this inspection twice each year. Those who refused were to be punished first by a money fine and second, if they persisted in their obstruction, by imprisonment until the king had been consulted about their transgression.[1] As has been said, the king stayed some time in Norfolk. The whole commonalty of the town of Ipswich was accused before the king of various crimes, convicted on most counts and fined a huge sum of money. Moreover thirteen of the most eminent men of the town were sent for imprisonment for half a year to different places in England.[2]

Philip, king of France, about the middle of Lent led his army against the king of Aragon. A great number of Philip's men died in battle on land and at sea as well as from lack of food. No small part of his treasure was lost and captured by his opponents. He himself died of dysentery at the city of Perpignan. His body was buried with his ancestors at St Denis with full rites at Martinmas.

Thomas, prior of Christ Church, Canterbury, assumed the habit of a Cistercian monk at the royal abbey of Beaulieu on the vigil of Palm Sunday.[3] He was

---

[1] Lobel, pp. 37–8; Brit. Mus. MS Harley 645, f. 49
[2] cf. *Cal. Charter Rolls, 1257–1300*, p. 402
[3] 17 March

thesaurarius. Dominus papa apud Perusium iiii. Kal. Aprilis [1] uite terminum fecit, sepultus ibidem primo die mensis eiusdem. Vacauitque sedes diebus . . . [a]; cui successit dominus Iacobus de Sabell', sancte Marie in Cosmidin diaconus cardinalis, dictusque est Honorius. Dominus rex cepit scutagium xl. solidorum super scutum pro exercitu Wallie ultimo preterito. Dominus rex cum capite sancti Dauid qui et Dewy et aliis reliquiis f. 173ᵛ secum apportatis / a Wallia a Turri London' usque ad Westmonasterium solempnem fecit processionem.[2] Due lune viii. Idus Maii [b] in Suffolchia acies bellatrices in aere apparuerunt.[c][3] Habito parlamento apud Westmonasterium in festo sancti Iohannis, dominus rex multa ordinauit et pupplicari fecit statuta inter que nonnulla ut pluribus uidetur sunt ordinata iurisdictionem ecclesiasticam in magna sui parte euacuantia. Ille trufator qui se Fredericum nominauit super heresi aliisque criminibus conuictus, presentibus archiepiscopis et episcopis Teutonicis quibusdam, ii. Idus Iulii igni traditus incendio consumptus est.[d][4] Willelmus Eboracensis archiepiscopus apud Pontiniacum in partibus decessit transmarinis, cui successit magister Iohannes dictus Romanus ecclesie Lincolniensis precentor. Maria filia regis Anglie die Natiuitatis beate Marie apud Aumbrisbere in sanctimonialem est uelata.[5] Alexander rex Scocie filiam comitis de Drues regis Francie con-

---

[a] *Lacuna* ½ *in. long MS*
[b] + apparuerunt *exp. and a paragraph mark erased MS, which is corrupt here*; + apparuerunt *and a paragraph mark* Oxenedes
[c] Due lune . . . apparuerunt *marked* uacat *MS²*
[d] Ille trufator . . . est *marked* uacat *MS²*

[1] He died on 28, not 29, March; Potthast, II, p. 1794.
[2] As St David is not in the calendar of Westminster abbey it seems likely that Edward I took his relics to the royal chapel at Westminster.
[3] Paraselenae and aurorae must have caused the phenomena; C. E. Britton, *A Meteorological Chronology to A.D. 1450* (1937), p. 122.

succeeded as prior by Henry, the treasurer of Christ
Church.   The pope died at Perugia on 29 March [1] and
was buried there on 1 April.   The Holy See remained
vacant for . . . days;   then Jacopo Savelli, cardinal-
deacon of St Mary in Cosmedin, succeeded and took
the name Honorius IV.

The king took a scutage of 40s. on each knight's fee
to pay for the army of the last Welsh campaign.   The
king led a solemn procession from the Tower of London
to Westminster bearing the head of St David (also
called Dewy) and other relics which he had brought
from Wales.[2]   On 8 May there was an appearance of
two moons and in Suffolk armies appeared fighting
in the sky.[3]   In a parliament held at Westminster on
St John's day the king enacted and published many
statutes, among them some which seemed to many
people to reduce the liberties of the Church to almost
nothing.   That same impostor who called himself
Frederick was convicted of heresy and other crimes and
was committed to the flames and burnt on 14 July in
the presence of certain of the archbishops and bishops
of Germany.[4]   William, archbishop of York, died
abroad at Pontigny and was succeeded by Master John,
called le Romeyn, precentor of the church of Lincoln.
Mary, the king of England's daughter, took the veil at
Amesbury on the feast of the Nativity of the Blessed
Virgin Mary.[5]   Alexander, king of Scotland, married

---

[4] O. Lorenz, *Deutsche Geschichte im 13 und 14 Jahrhundert* (1864–7), II, p. 402,
accepts the date 7 July, not 14 July, for Dietrich's death.

[5] 8 September.   This date is wrong.   Mary took the veil on 15 August,
the Assumption of the Virgin;   *CPR, 1281–92*, p. 190; *Wig.*, p. 491.

sanguineam duxit in uxorem.[1] Facta est itineracio
iusticiariorum in comitatu Norhamtonie sub iusticiariis
dominis Iohanne de Wallibus, Willelmo de Saham,
Iohanne de Metingham, Rogero Loueday et aliis. Et
in Esexia sub iusticiariis dominis Salomone de Rofcestr',
Roberto de Redingge, Ricardo de Boyland, Waltero de
Stirchele et aliis. Dominus rex celebrauit Natale
Domini apud Exoniam in Deuonia.[a]

1286

Facta est itineracio iusticiariorum in comitatu Norfolch'
in crastino sancti Hyllarii [2] sub iusticiariis dominis
Salomon' de Roff', Roberto Fulcon', Ricardo de
Boylund, Waltero de Styrchele, Waltero de Hopeton',
Thome de Sudend' et aliis. Philippus filius Philippi die
Epiphanie Remis in regem Francie coronatus est.
f. 174 / Domino rege magnum parlamentum apud Westmonasterium post Purificacionem tenente, parlamento
interfuerunt nuncii regis Francie, dominus videlicet
Mauricius de Croun, comes Burgund' [3] et dominus
Iohannes de Acra de proceribus regni Francie. Alex-
ander rex Scocie uiam uniuerse carnis ingressus est [b]
xiiii. Kal. Aprilis. Dominus rex post festum Pasche
mense Mayo transfretauit cum rege Francie collocuturus
et parlamento Francie circa dies Rogacionum habito
Parisius sui presenciam exhibiturus et ipsi regi Francie
de terris quas clamat de eo tenere homagium facturus.[c][4]
Quinto Idus Iunii Hugo Elyensis episcopus apud
Dunham [5] manerium suum in insula Elyensi diem

---

[a] *Lacuna of 2 lines. Change of handwriting*; *the text from the top of the page
to* Deuonia *seems to be marked* uacat *MS*[2]
[b] *Corr. MS*[2]
[c] Dominus rex post festum . . . facturus *marked* uacat *MS*[2]

the count of Dreux's daughter; she was a relative of the king of France.[1]   An eyre was held in the county of Northampton by the justices John de Vaux, William de Saham, John de Mettingham, Roger Loveday and others, and an eyre was held in Essex by the justices Solomon de Rochester, Robert de Reading, Richard de Boyland, Walter de Stirchley and others.   The king kept Christmas at Exeter in Devon.

1286

An eyre was held in the county of Norfolk on the morrow of St Hilary's day [2] by the justices Solomon de Rochester, Robert Fulk, Richard de Boyland, Walter de Stirchley, Walter de Hopton, Thomas de Southend and others. Philip, the son of Philip, was solemnly crowned king of France at Rheims on the feast of the Epiphany.   The king held a great parliament at Westminster after Candlemas and there were present ambassadors of the king of France, namely the Lord Maurice de Craon, the count of Burgundy,[3] and Lord John d'Acre, from the nobles of the kingdom of France.   Alexander, king of Scotland, died on 19 March.   During the month of May, after Easter, the king crossed the channel in order to consult with the king of France and appear at a parliament held in Paris some time about Rogationtide and do homage for the lands which he claimed to hold of the king of France.[4]   On 9 June Hugh, bishop of Ely, died at his manor of Downham [5] in the Isle of Ely.   He

---

[1] Joleta, daughter of Robert IV, count of Dreux 1246–82
[2] 14 January
[3] Ottoninus, count of Burgundy 1279–1303
[4] *Foedera*, I, p. 665
[5] According to the *Historia Eliensis*, in H. Wharton, *Anglia Sacra* (London 1691), I, p. 637, he died on 16 June at Doddington in the Isle of Ely.

clausit extremum, cui successit dominus *a* Iohannes de
Kyrkebi domini regis Anglie thesaurarius uigilia Natalis
Domini sollempniter intronizatus. Willelmus Rames'
abbas paralisis laborans incomodo sue resignauit dignitati,[1] cui successit Iohannes de Sauter', eiusdem loci
monachus. Prioratus canonicorum de Westacre [2] cum
ecclesia omnibusque aliis suis officinis circa Natiuitatem
beate Marie igne consumptus est. Alyenora mater
regis Anglie mense Iulio apud Aumbrisbyr' sanctimonialis habitus uelamen sibi imposuit. Walterus *b* Sar'
episcopus uita decessit, cui successit magister Henricus
de Branteston', eiusdem loci decanus. Dominus
Willelmus de Warenn' filius et heres Iohannis de
Warenn' comitis Suther' in torneamento apud Croinden'
a suis emulis, ut dicebatur, mense Decembris interceptus *c* et crudeliter interemptus est.*d* Dominus rex
apud insulam de Olyrun *d* in Guascon' Natale Domini
celebrauit.*e*

1287

f. 174ᵛ Nocte dominice Circumcisionis tam uenti uehementia
quam maris uiolentia multa apud Gernem', Dunewyc'
et Gypwicum, sed et per alia diuersa loca Anglie
aliarumque regionum mari contiguarum prostrata sunt *d*
edificia. Et precipue *f* in illa parte Anglie que Meris-
landia[3] dicitur tota fere prouincia in stagna aquarum
conuersa hominum multitudo intollerabilis aquis inter-
cepta est et necata. In crastino octauarum Epiphanie
parum ante auroram subite choruscaciones apud sanctum
Eadmundum apparentes, uidentes non modicum terru-

---

a -e- *corr. MS²*   *b* Waltero *MS, P*
c -ceptus *corr. MS²*   *d Corr. MS²*
e Lacuna of 2 lines MS   *f* precipua *before corr. MS²*

was succeeded by John de Kirkby, the treasurer of the king of England, who was solemnly enthroned on Christmas eve. William, abbot of Ramsey, who suffered from paralysis, resigned from office [1] and John de Sawtry, a monk of Ramsey, succeeded him. The priory of the canons of West Acre,[2] including the church and all the other buildings, were burnt down about the time of the feast of the Nativity of the Blessed Virgin Mary. Eleanor, the king of England's mother, took the veil at Amesbury in the month of July. Walter, bishop of Salisbury, died and was succeeded by the dean, Master Henry de Brandeston. William de Warenne, son and heir of John de Warenne, earl of Surrey, was intercepted and cruelly killed by his enemies, so it was said, at a tournament held at Croydon in the month of December. The king kept Christmas on the island of Oléron in Gascony.

1287

On Sunday night on the feast of the Circumcision a violent gale and a stormy sea destroyed buildings at Yarmouth, Dunwich, Ipswich and many other places in England and in coastal districts elsewhere. Especially affected was that part of England known as the Marshland [3]; nearly all that region became a lake and innumerable people were cut off by the water and drowned. A little before dawn on the morrow of the octave of Epiphany there were sudden flashes of lightning at Bury St Edmunds, which terrified spectators not a

---

[1] He resigned some time in 1285; *Chron. Abbatiae Rameseiensis,* ed. W. D. Macray (RS, 1886), p. 344.

[2] West Acre, Norfolk, priory of Austin canons

[3] The Marshland; the Fens round Wisbech and in Norfolk, see below p. 126.

erunt.*a* In crastino sancti Hyllarii [1] sederunt apud
Catishale iusticiarii itinerantes qui supra. In quo
quidem itinere implacitauerunt nos domini I[ohannes]
de Creyk, Godefrid' de Beaumund, Radulf' de Berners
de maneriis nostris de Semere et Groten'; cuius quidem
cause facta discussione tandem patriam habentes sus-
pectam utpote aduersariis nostris familiarem et affinem *b*
ius nostrum per duellum decreuimus *c* esse defendendum.
Die igitur a die Pasche in unum mensem ad Bancum
apud Westmonasterium partibus assignata sic saltem eo
tempore negocium est protelatum. Cuidam pugili de
partibus Lincoll' qui dicebatur Rogerus Clericus contulit
abbas de proprio premanibus xx. marcas, xxx. marcas
post duellum recepturas ab eodem. Idem uero pugil
toto expectacionis tempore una cum magistro suo apud
nos quamuis sub calumpnia est commoratus.[2] In
uilla siquidem sancti Eadmundi sederunt iusticiarii
nostri domini H[enricus] de Gildeford' et H[enricus] de
Schineholt et *d* Ricardus Weyland' senescallus terrarum
domini abbatis. Qui duo primi quamuis clerici fuerunt
iusticiarii in itinere supradicto, nichil tamen iusticiarii
supradicti de uilla ipsa se intromiserunt, sed mere ad
instantiam nostram dicti clerici dictum negocium sunt
executi. Dominus papa feria iiii.[3] in septimana Palmarum in crastino dominice Annuntiacionis *e* [4] apud
Sanctum Petrum Rome in fata decessit, sepultusque
f. 175 est / ibidem die [5] ueneris Parasceue sequente; et uacauit

---

a Nocte dominice . . . terruerunt *marked* uacat *MS²*
b af- *corr. MS²*   *c* -ec- *corr. MS²*   *d Added MS²*
e ii. Non. Aprilis die Parasceu ii *in margin MS²*

[1] 14 January
[2] For this late instance of a judicial duel see V. H. Galbraith, 'The
Death of a Champion (1287),' in *Studies in Medieval History presented to
F. M. Powicke*, ed. R. W. Hunt, W. A. Pantin, R. W. Southern (1948),
pp. 293ff.

little. On the morrow of St Hilary's day [1] the afore-
mentioned justices in eyre sat at Cattishall. In this
eyre John de Creyk, Godfrey de Beaumont and Ralph
de Berners sued us for our manors of Semer and Groton.
When the case had been investigated we at length
declared that we would defend our right by judicial
combat, as we suspected that the surrounding district
supported and was in league with our opponents.
Accordingly a day one month after Easter was assigned
for the parties to appear before the King's Bench and
the case was adjourned until then. The abbot paid a
certain champion called Roger Clerk, who came from
the district of Lincoln, 20 marks in advance from his own
money. After the duel Roger was to receive 30 marks
more from him. The champion during the whole time
of waiting stayed with us, accompanied by his trainer,
although under challenge.[2] Our justices, Henry de
Guildford, Henry de Schineholt and Richard Wayland,
the steward of the abbot's lands, sat in the town of
Bury St Edmunds. Although the first two were clerks
engaged on the aforesaid eyre, the judges did not meddle
with the town itself in any respect, but the clerks carried
through the business entirely at our request. The pope
died on the fourth day [3] in Holy Week, which was the
morrow of Lady day,[4] at St Peter's in Rome. He was
buried there [5] on the following Good Friday. The

---

[3] This should read the fifth day as he died on Thursday, 3 April.

[4] This seems to be an error for the feast of the Annunciation is on
25 March. The morrow of the feast of St Mary the Egyptian (2 April)
would be correct.

[5] 4 April. He died at St Sabina and was buried in St Peter's.

sedes mensibus xi., diebus xxiiii. Iudei per totam
Angliam cuiuscumque etatis aut sexus die ueneris in
crastino apostolorum Philippi et Iacobi [1] secure sunt
custodie mancipati. Qui tandem dominum regem de
xii. libris ei soluendum certificantes ad propria quique
redierunt. In octauis apostolorum Petri et Pauli [2]
Stephanus prior sancti Eadmundi uiam uniuerse carnis
ingressus est, cui successit W[illelmus] de Rokelund,
eiusdem loci camerarius in crastino sancti Iacobi [3] per
uiam scrutinii electus. Tercio Kal. Augusti inter Romane
ecclesie et Francorum ex una parte et imperatoris
Consta[nt]inopolis fouentis partes regis Arragonie [a] [4]
excercitus ex altera mirabilis in mari factus est conflictus.
In quo Grecis cum parte sua triumphantibus non nulli
de tocius excercitus nobilioribus captis atque reliquis
crudeliter iugulatis uictoria parti [b] cessit aduersariorum.
Magna Suth Walensium pars duce quodam Reso
Mereducii [c] filio regis Anglie fit rebellis. Qui tandem
non absque tam nobilium quam ignobilium strage
permaxima de gente Anglorum facta aliasque [d] expensas
inutiles dampna multimoda et pericula non modicum
inutilia fuga lapsus, quo tunc aliquandiu delituit penitus
ignorabatur. Et sic ipso Reso tanquam nusquam com-
parente excercituque Anglicano ad propria redeunte
siluit terra et quieuit. Facta est eclipsis lune uniuersalis
nocte sanctorum Romani et Seuerini.[5] Die sancti
Kalixti [6] preualentibus aduersariis nostris pugilique
nostro in duello London' interfecto, maneria nostra de
Semere et Groten' amisimus sine aliqua spe rehabendi.[7]

---

[a] Arragor MS, P [b] parte *corr.* MS²
[c] *Corr.* MS² [d] -s- *interlin.* MS²

[1] 2 May [2] 6 July [3] 26 July

Holy See was vacant for eleven months and twenty-four days. The Jews throughout England of every age and both sexes were thrown into prison on Friday, the morrow of the feast of the Apostles Philip and James.[1] They returned home only after they had undertaken to pay the king £12,000. On the octave of the feast of the Apostles Peter and Paul,[2] Stephen, prior of Bury St Edmunds, died; he was succeeded by William de Rockland, chamberlain of Bury, who was elected by the method of scrutiny on the morrow of St James's day.[3] On 30 July there was a tremendous battle at sea between the army of the Roman Church and the French on the one side, and the army of the emperor of Constantinople, who was a supporter of the king of Aragon,[4] on the other. In the battle the Greek side was triumphant; many of the greatest men in the whole army were captured and the rest cruelly slain, and victory went to the enemy. Most of south Wales rebelled against the king of England's son under Rhys ap Maredudd. Rhys took flight after causing a great slaughter of Englishmen, both nobles and commoners, and much futile expense, damage and danger. He hid for some time but where he hid was not known. And so Rhys never reappeared and the English army returned home leaving the country peaceful and quiet. There was a total eclipse of the moon on the night of the feast of SS. Romanus and Severinus.[5] On St Calixtus's day [6] our enemies were victorious and our champion slain in judicial combat in London. And so our manors of Semer and Groton were lost without any hope of recovery.[7] On 3 November,

---

[4] Alfonso III, 1285–91   [5] 23 October   [6] 14 October
[7] In fact the abbey regained both manors in 1290 (*CCR, 1288–96*, p. 126), so the chronicler must have written his entry before that date.

Tercio die mensis Nouembris presentante W[illelmo] de
Hoo sacrista receptus fuit ad officium monetarie
exequendum Ricardus de Lothebyr' aurifaber de
London'[1] et cuneus de nouo incisus. Stephanus
Cycestriensis episcopus uite terminum fecit, cui successit
magister G[ilbertus] de sancto Leophardo. Mare mense

f. 175ᵛ Decembris proprium litus egressum in partibus / Northf'
et Suthf' et precipue Gernemut' multorum extitit causa
incommodorum. Domino regi Anglie in partibus
Wasconie commoranti a rege Tartarorum sollempnes
directi sunt nuntii ad antiquas amicitias inter ipsum
dominum regem et predecessores suos [et] reges Tartarorum renouandas et firmius coroborandas.ᵃ Idem
dominus rex celebrauit Natale Domini apud Burgedalim
in Gasconia.ᵇ

1288

Tercio Non. Februarii in crepusculo noctis subito et ex
inopinato apud sanctum Eadmundum nullis penitus
signis preambulatis sub uno et eodem momento apparuit
choruscacio cum non dico tonitruo sed fragore quodam
terribili fetoreque subsequente intollerabili. Concomit-
abantur eciam dictam tempestatem scintille ignis mani-
feste oculos uidentium horribiliter concutientes. Huius
siquidem tempestatis uehementia turri ecclesie de
Bernewelle succensa aliisque dampnis conuentui dicti
loci illatis tercia fere pars ipsius uille igne consumpta
est.[2] Refectorio eciam sancti Eadmundi aliquantulum
adhesit ignis ille sed celerrime a monachis eidem est

ᵃ Tercio Kal. Augusti . . . coroborandas *marked* uacat *MS*²
ᵇ *Lacuna of 1 line MS*

[1] The Memoranda Rolls (P.R.O.), K.R., 15–16 Edward I, membrane
1ᵈ, headed ' Communia de termino Sancti Michaelis Anno xv finiente,'

on the presentation of William de Hoo, sacrist [of Bury
St Edmunds], Richard de Lothbury, a goldsmith of
London,[1] was received in the office of moneyer, and
a new die was cut. Stephen, bishop of Chichester, died
and was succeeded by Master Gilbert de St Leofard.
In December the sea overflowed its shores in Norfolk
and Suffolk and caused great hardship, particularly at
Yarmouth. The king of England was staying in
Gascony when ambassadors were sent to him by the king
of the Tartars to renew and strengthen the long-standing
friendship of the king and his predecessors with the
Tartar kings. The king kept Christmas at Bordeaux
in Gascony.

1288

At nightfall on 3 February, suddenly, without any
warning or previous sign, there was a flash of lightning
at Bury St Edmunds and at the very same moment a
terrific crash (I could not call it thunder) followed by an
unbearable stench. With the storm came bright sparks
of fire which dazzled the eyes of beholders. The violence
of the storm set fire to the tower of the church at
Barnwell, and did other damage to the convent there;
moreover nearly a third of the town was burnt down.[2]
The refectory at Bury St Edmunds caught fire for a
short time but the monks quickly came to the rescue.

---

record that Hoo presented Richard to the barons of the Exchequer 'ad
custodiendum cuneum abbatis sancti Edmundi in villa predicta.' The
barons admitted him. For a letter of Hoo to the lord treasurer and barons
of the Exchequer, asking them to admit Lothbury 'ad officium monetar'
faciend' de cuneo nostro' on the presentation of Simon de Kingston, see
Brit. Mus. MS Harley 230, f. 10ᵛ.
   [2] The fire is noticed in *Liber Memorandorum Ecclesie de Bernewell*, ed J. W.
Clark (1907), p. 220.

subuentum. Dompnus Ieronimus episcopus cardinalis Penestrinus *a* de ordine Fratrum Minorum die sancti Petri in Cathedra[1] in summum pontificem est electus, dictusque est Nicholaus quartus. Henricus Sar[isburiensis] episcopus in fata decessit, quo defuncto electi sunt duo magistri, videlicet Willelmus de la Cornere et Laurentius Hakebrun', eiusdem loci canonici, sed L[aurentio] statim defuncto, iterum electus est magister W[illelmus] supradictus. Pridie Non. Iunii[2] habito conflictu inter ducem Brabantie[3] ex una parte et archiepiscopum Coloniensem[4] et comitem de Gelre[5] ex altera utriusque eciam partis procerum cesa multitudine copiosa. Archiepiscopus Coloniensis et comes de Gelre capiuntur et in custodia ducis Brabantie retruduntur. Sicque Brabantini optata potiti sunt uictoria.*b* Maxima*c* / pars nundinarum sancti Botulfi una cum domibus Fratrum Predicatorum in crastino sancti Iacobi[6] igne consumpta est. Willelmus Norwycensis episcopus ultimo die mensis Augusti apud Therlinge manerium suum in Essex' diem clausit extremum. Qui Norwyc' delatus, ii. Idus Septembris ibidem est sepultus; cui successit magister Radulfus de Walepol archidiaconus Elyensis. Iohanne *d* de Hemmigeston' priore Elyensi defuncto, successit Iohannes de Schepreth' eiusdem loci monachus. Quinto Idus Octobris facta est eclipsis lune pene uniuersalis durauitque fere post noctis medium usque ad aurore exortum.*e* Dominus rex apud Belegarde in terra Biern' Natale Domini celebrauit.*f*

f. 176

---

a episcopus cardinalis Penestrinus *in margin MS*
b Pridie Non. Iun' . . . uictoria *marked* uacat *MS*[2]
c scrib *in margin in pencil with a tie-mark which may refer to a similar mark kelow by* Iohanne de Hemmigeston' *MS*[2].   *d Corr. MS*[2]
e Quinto Idus Octobris . . . exortum *marked* uacat *MS*[2]
f Lacuna of 1 line MS; apud Belegarde in terra Biern' (*on erasure*) . . . celebrauit] Natalem Domini apud Olirun in Gascon celebrauit *Oxenedes*

Gerolamo, cardinal-bishop of Palestrina of the order of Friars Minor, was elected pope on the feast of St Peter in Cathedra [1] and took the name Nicholas IV. Henry, bishop of Salisbury, died. On his death two masters were elected, that is William de la Corner and Lawrence Hakebrun, canons of Salisbury. But Lawrence immediately died and Master William was elected again. On 4 June [2] there was a battle between the duke of Brabant [3] on the one side and the archbishop of Cologne [4] and the count of Geldres [5] on the other; a great many of the most important people on both sides were killed. The archbishop of Cologne and the count of Geldres were captured and committed to the custody of the duke of Brabant. And so the men of Brabant obtained the desired victory. The greater part of the fair at Boston and the buildings of the Friars Preachers were burnt down on the morrow of St James's day.[6] William, bishop of Norwich, died at his manor of Terling in Essex on the last day of August. He was carried to Norwich and buried there on 12 September. Master Ralph de Walpole, archdeacon of Ely, succeeded him. John de Hemingstone, prior of Ely, died and was succeeded by John de Shepreth, a monk of Ely. On 11 October there was a total eclipse of the moon, which lasted approximately from midnight to daybreak. The king kept Christmas at Bellegarde in Béarn.

---

[1] 22 February
[2] On 5, not 4, June; O. Lorenz, *Deutsche Geschichte*, pp. 374–5.
[3] John I, 1261–94   [4] Siegfried, 1275–97
[5] Rainald I, 1271–1326   [6] 26 July

1289

Mense Februarii circa festum sancti Petri in Cathedra [1]
Reginaldus abbas de Waltham [2] uite terminum fecit,
sepultusque est apud Waltham in crastino sancti Mathie
apostoli [3]; cui successit *a* Robertus de Elingtone, eiusdem
loci canonicus. Quinto Kal. Marcii Willelmus prior
Norwycensis uite terminum fecit; cui successit Henricus
de Lakenham, eiusdem loci sacrista. Dominus rex et
regina quarto a transfretacionis sue anno pridie Idus
Augusti apud Douoram applicauit in Anglia moraque in
Cancia et postea in Esex' aliquantulum protracta die
sancti Lamberti [4] ad sanctum accessit Eadmundum, in
crastino partes Norfolch' petiturus. Vnde per insulam
Elyensem nauigio procedens Londoniamque tendens
diem Translacionis sancti Eadwardi [5] apud Westmonas-
etrium solempniter celebrauit. *b*

Dominus Thomas Weylaund, capitalis regis iusticiarius, in Banco regio inferiori [6] super retentacione *c*

f. 176ᵛ quorundam / de suis, qui quendam nuper interfecerant,
indictatus per inquisicionem conuictus, et se gratie
regis committere formidans, Fratribus Minoribus apud
sanctum Eadmundum commorantibus se contulit. Vbi
rege precipiente per aliquot dies a patria diligenter
custoditus, cum minus sperabatur habitum sumpsit
eorundem. Quo audito rex quendam de suis collater-
alibus militem una cum toto comitatu ad dictam
custodiam securius firmandam destinauit. Tandemque
dictus dominus Thomas post duorum mensium obsi-

---

a Change of handwriting MS
b Dominus rex et regina . . . celebrauit marked uacat MS²
c reteccacione MS, P; recepcacione Oxenedes

[1] 22 February   [2] Abbey of Austin canons, Essex
[3] 25 February   [4] 12 September   [5] 13 October

1289

In February, about the feast of St Peter in Cathedra,[1] Reginald, abbot of Waltham,[2] died and was buried at Waltham on the morrow of St Matthias's day.[3]   He was succeeded by Robert de Ellington, a canon of Waltham. On 25 February William, prior of Norwich, died and was succeeded by the sacrist of Norwich, Henry de Lakenham.   The king landed with the queen in England at Dover on 12 August, four years after he had set sail from England.   He stayed a while in Kent and then in Essex, and on St Lambert's day [4] came to Bury St Edmunds on his way to Norfolk next day.   From Norfolk he went by boat through the Isle of Ely towards London.   He solemnly kept the feast of the Translation of St Edward [5] at Westminster.

Thomas Wayland, the king's chief justice, was indicted before a lower royal court,[6] on a charge of having harboured some of his own men who had murdered a man, and was convicted by a jury.   He feared to put himself at the king's mercy and fled to the house of the Friars Minor at Bury St Edmunds.   There by the king's order he was besieged for several days by men of the neighbourhood; when there was little hope left he assumed the friars' habit.   On hearing this the king sent a knight from his familiar circle to make the guard even more secure in collaboration with the officials of the country.   At length, after two months' siege and when

---

[6] For the special tribunal set up to try the justices see Powicke, *Thirteenth Century*, p. 362.

dionem dispersis primo per loca fratribus fere uniuersis ipso habitu relicto *a* et seculari assumpto exiuit et ad regem adductus in Turri London' saluo deponitur custodiendus.

Dominus papa Karolum principem de la Muree Karoli dudum regis Sicilie filium regno Sicilie sublimauit et ipsius dyademate die Pentecost' solempniter coronauit.[1] Ciuitas Tripolitana cum uniuersis urbibus et uiculis necnon tota patria adiacente interfecta Christianorum multitudine permaxima a Sarracenis capta, destructa et subuersa est.

Dominus rex Natale Domini apud Westmonasterium solempniter celebrauit.[b]

1290

Habito parleamento apud Westmonasterium et a die Circumcisionis Domini usque post festum sancti Valentini protracto super diuersis diuersorum iusticiariorum transgressionibus ibidem uentilatis pro diuersis causarum meritis diuerse a domino rege et eius consilio sentencie sunt prolate. Inter quas dominus Thomas Weylaund omnibus bonis suis mobilibus et immobilibus sempiterno confiscatis absque spe remeandi exilio deportatus est.[2] Multique de iusticiariis tam de Banco quam de itineracionibus preteritis saluo custodiendi ad Turrim sunt transmissi. Inter quos principales fuerunt domini Iohannes de Luuethot', Willelmus de Brunton', Rogerus de Leyc' et Robertus de Lithleber' et hii quidem de Banco. De itinerantibus fuerunt domini Salomon

---

a incipe rel *in margin faintly in pencil MS*[2]
b *Lacuna of 1 line MS*

[1] 29 May
[2] Wayland appears among the French civilians and canonists who

nearly all the friars had dispersed in various directions, Thomas took off his friar's habit, put on secular clothes and came out, and was taken to the king and imprisoned in the Tower of London.

The pope raised Charles, prince of the Morea, son of Charles formerly king of Sicily, to the throne of Sicily and crowned him with his father's crown on Whit-Sunday.[1] The city of Tripoli, all the towns and villages and surrounding countryside were captured, destroyed and razed to the ground by the Saracens and a very great number of Christians slaughtered.

The king kept Christmas with full rites at Westminster.

1290

A parliament was held at Westminster and sat from the feast of the Circumcision until after St Valentine's day. There they discussed the wrongdoings of the different justices; and according to their different deserts the king and his council passed different sentences. Among them Thomas Wayland had all his property, both movable and otherwise, confiscated forever and was exiled without hope of returning.[2] Many justices of the King's Bench and justices in eyre were imprisoned in the Tower. The most important of these were the justices of the King's Bench, John de Lovetot, William de Brunton, Roger de Leicester and Robert de Littlebury. Of the justices in eyre were Solomon de Rochester,

---

advised Edward I in 1291 on the law of succession to the throne of Scotland; see A. Gransden, *EHR*, LXXII (1957), p. 271: Wayland was an important landowner in East Anglia and held the manor of Onehouse from the abbot of Bury; *CCR, 1288–96*, pp. 106–7.

de Rof', Ricardus de Boylaund, Thomas de Sudendon', Walterus de Hopet' et Ricardus [1] de Preston'. Sed
f. 177 primis in fine istius parleamenti/redempciope necuniaria non modica interueniente dimissis, ultimi rege alias se transferente in ipsa Turri remanserunt. Qui tamen incontinenti non absque coniuencia regia sed eo precipiente more priorum ad propria *a* sunt reuersi.

Iohannes Elyensis episcopus, domini regis thesaurarius, in crastino Annunciacionis beate Marie apud Ely diem clausit extremum; cui, die Cene [Domini] proximo ibidem honorifice tumulato, successit magister Willelmus de Ludo archidiaconus Dunhelmensis et decanus sancti Martini Magni London', dominique regis de garderoba sua thesaurarius electus iiii. Idus Maii. Gilbertus de Clare comes Glouernie duxit in uxorem dominam Iohannam dictam de Acre, quia apud Acconem nata est, filiam regis Anglie *b* ultimo die mensis Aprilis apud Westmonasterium. Eodem die in mari Armorico iuxta sanctum Matheum inter Baionenses, Quinque Portenses et Gernemutenses ex una parte et Flandrense nauigium ex altera exortum est nauale bellum seuissimum. Vbi de Flandrensium multitudine permaxima tum aqua, tum igne iniecto, tum eciam armis iugulata, nauibus eciam eorum plerisque submersis, aliquibus uero concrematis, aliisque sibi fuge presidio consulentibus uictoria potita est pars aduersa. *c* Dominus rex regem patrem suum apud Westmonasterium intumulatum nocte dominice Ascensionis subito et inopinate amoueri fecit et in loco excelsiore iuxta sanctum Eadwardum collocari.[2]

---

a more . . . propria *corr. MS²*
b *Lines ruled in pencil in margin as though for an addition MS*
c *Change of handwriting and in margin lines are ruled as though for an addition MS*

[1] An error for ' Robert '? See *CPR, 1281–92*, p. 202.

Richard de Boyland, Thomas de Southend, Walter de Hopton and Richard [1] de Preston. While the first mentioned obtained their freedom at the end of this parliament by paying a considerable money fine, those mentioned last remained in the Tower and the king went away. But they returned to their homes almost immediately with the king's consent, and indeed by his command, in the same way as the others.

John, bishop of Ely, the king's treasurer, died at Ely on the morrow of Lady day. He was honourably buried there on Maundy Thursday. Master William de Louth, who was archdeacon of Durham, dean of St Martin le Grand in London and treasurer of the king's wardrobe, was elected on 12 May to succeed him. On the last day of April at Westminster Gilbert de Clare, earl of Gloucester, married the king's daughter, the Lady Joan, called of Acre because she was born there. On the same day there was a fierce battle at sea off the coast of Brittany by the Pointe Saint-Mathieu, between the men of Bayonne, the Cinque ports and Yarmouth on the one side and the Flemish fleet on the other. A great many men of Flanders were killed, some by drowning, some when their ships were fired and some in combat. Many of their ships were sunk, some were burnt and some sought safety in flight. And so the victory went to their adversaries. The king had his father's tomb at Westminster suddenly and unexpectedly moved on the night of the feast of the Ascension and put in a higher place next to the tomb of St Edward.[2]

---

[2] 11 May. Henry III was buried at first in the grave of Edward the Confessor before the high altar. Henry's funeral effigy was completed in 1290 and his grave was moved to the sanctuary behind the altar.

Bellum seuissimum et cruentum inter Norwagie[1] et
Dacie reges,[2] in quo apud Schonore[3] in Dacia de
Norwagiensibus cesa sunt xxv. millia Dacorum exercitu
non multo uiolato.[a] Rogerus Bigot comes Norf' et marescallus Anglie traduxit Aliciam filiam Iohannis de Aueynes
comitis Agennogie.[4] Iohannes filius et heres Iohannis[b]
ducis Brabanc', patre suo cum infinita procerum multitudine presente, Margaretam filiam regis Anglie vii.
Idus Iulii apud Westmonasterium sollempniter desponsauit. Omnes fructus per totam Angliam tam
gardinorum quam eciam sepium, pomis tamen glandibus
utcumque exceptis, defecerunt.[c] Willelmus, Elyensis
electus, ix. Kal. Decembris[5] in sacerdotem ordinatus,
primo die mensis Octobris apud Ely in ecclesia beate
f. 177ᵛ Marie pa/rochiali a domino Iohanne archiepiscopo
Cantuariensi cum sollempnitate precipua in episcopum
Elyensem est consecratus. In cuius sollempnitatis
crastino celebrauit ibidem concilium suum archiepiscopus supradictus cum suffraganeis suis et aliis de clero
ibidem conuenientibus. In quo concilio concessa est
domino regi a clero decima omnium bonorum
spiritualium per unum annum, ita tamen ut non
colligatur decima ista ante festum sancti Michaelis
anno proximo uenturo. Accepta a tocius Anglie communitate omnium bonorum temporalium quintadecima,
dominus rex omnes cuiuscumque sexus aut etatis per uniuersam Angliam habitantes Iudeos absque spe remeandi
perpetuo dampnauit exilio. Rogerus abbas sancti
Albani circa festum Omnium Sanctorum in crastino

---

^a Bellum seuissimum . . . uiolato *marked* uacat *MS*²
^b *Corr. MS*²; Walteri *Oxenedes*
^c Omnes fructus . . . defecerunt *marked* uacat *MS*²

[1] Eric II, 1280–99   [2] Eric IV, 1286–1320
[3] Skanör, Malmöhus, Sweden. This is probably a reference to the

A most cruel and bloody war raged between the king of Norway [1] and the king of Denmark. [2] At Skanör [3] in Denmark two thousand, five hundred Norwegians were killed while the Danish army hardly suffered at all. Roger Bigod, earl of Norfolk and marshal of England, married Alice, the daughter of John d'Avênes, count of Hainault. [4] John, son and heir of John duke of Brabant, in the presence of his father and a gathering of innumerable nobles, married with full solemnity Margaret, daughter of the king of England, on 9 July at Westminster. There was a dearth of all fruit throughout England, both in gardens and in fields, except apples and acorns. William, bishop-elect of Ely, was ordained priest on 23 November [5] and was consecrated bishop of Ely on 1 October in the parish church of St Mary at Ely by John, archbishop of Canterbury, with great pomp. On the day after this ceremony the archbishop held a council at Ely with his suffragans and other members of the clergy gathered together there. In this council a tenth of all spiritual revenues for one year was granted to the king, but it was not to be collected before Michaelmas in the next year. The king accepted from the commons of England a fifteenth of the revenues from all temporal property. Then he exiled without hope of return all Jews of both sexes and every age living in England. Roger, abbot of St Albans, died at All Saints' tide (on the morrow

---

Norwegians' attempt to capture Skanör in July 1289; J. H. S. Birch, *Denmark in History* (1938), p. 86.
    [4] Count of Hainault 1280–1304
    [5] This must be wrong. According to *Historia Eliensis*, in H. Warton, *Anglia Sacra*, 1, p. 639, he was ordained on 16 September.

Animarum [a][1] in fata decessit; cui successit Iohannes de
Berchamstede,[b] eiusdem loci monachus. Robertus
abbas de Radingg' sue cessit dignitati; cui successit
Willelmus de Sutton', eiusdem loci camerarius.
Margareta, filia Irici regis Norwagie et Margarete
filie Alexandri regis Scocie superius sine herede de se
defuncti [2] et Margarete regine filie Henrici tertii regis
Anglorum et sororis Eadwardi regis, eiusdem regis filii,
cui tanquam propinquiori sanguine regni Scocie ius
competebat hereditarium, que eciam dispensacione in
curia Romana iam prehabita Eadwardo supradicti
regis Eadwardi filio nupciali federe sperabatur fuisse
copulanda, in insula de Orkeneya defungitur.[c] Alienora
regina Anglie, domini regis consors, iiii. Kal. Decembris
apud Herdeby in comitatu Lincoln' uite terminum fecit.
Sepulta autem est apud Westmonasterium cum apparatu
celebri et sumptuoso xvi. Kal. Ianuarii. Quo facto
dominus rex uersus Ayisrigge [3] heremitorium comitis
Cornubie Natale dominicum celebraturus diuertit.[d]

1291

f. 178 Collecta est quintadecima superius regi concessa / [e] unde
ne ministri regii in preiudicium libertatum ecclesie
sancti Eadmundi aliquid attemptare contingeret, abbas
et conuentus loci eiusdem pro quintadecima bonorum
suorum burgensium uille sancti Eadmundi et natiuorum
suorum pro mille marcis cum domino rege finem

---

[a] in crastino Animarum *added* MS[2]
[b] Berahamstede *before corr.* MS[2]
[c] Margareta filia Irici . . . defungitur *marked* uacat MS[2]
[d] *Lacuna of 1 line* MS   [e] *Change of handwriting* MS

[1] 3 November. Confirmed by *Gesta Abbatum Monasterii S. Albani*, ed.
H. T. Riley (RS, 1867–9), I, p. 485.

of All Souls' day) [1] and was succeeded by John de Berkhampstead, a monk of St Albans. Robert, abbot of Reading, resigned from office and William de Sutton, chamberlain of Reading abbey, succeeded him.

The death took place in the Orkney islands of Margaret, the daughter of Eric, king of Norway, and Margaret. The latter was the daughter of Alexander, king of Scotland (who had died previously without an heir of the body),[2] and Queen Margaret, daughter of Henry III, king of England, and sister of King Edward, that king's son. To [Margaret, daughter of Eric] belonged the hereditary right to the throne of Scotland as the nearest to it in blood. It had been hoped that she would marry Edward, son of the aforesaid King Edward, and a dispensation had already been sought in the Roman court. Eleanor, queen of England, the king's consort, died at Harby in Lincolnshire on 28 November. She was buried at Westminster with a magnificent procession and great pomp on 17 December. After this the king travelled to the earl of Cornwall's hermitage at Ashridge [3] to keep Christmas.

1291

The fifteenth previously granted to the king was collected. The abbot and convent of Bury St Edmunds paid a fine of 1,000 marks to the king instead of paying a fifteenth on their own property and that of the burgesses of the town of Bury and of their villeins, lest the royal officials should try to do anything which would prejudice the

---

[2] Alexander III, king of Scotland 1241–85, died on 19 March 1286 (see above, p. 86).

[3] Ashridge, Bucks. Edmund, earl of Cornwall, founded a college of Bonhommes there in 1283; VCH, Bucks., I, pp. 386–90.

fecerunt.[1] Quo facto burgus sancti Eadmundi nullo penitus alio mense intromittente per predictorum abbatis et conuentus ministros in forma communi est taxatus.[2] Facta est eclipsis lune xv. Kal. Martii. Sexto Idus Februarii London' circa horam primam subito et inopinate intonuit de celo Dominus [3] tam uiolenter et acerbe quod audiencium corda mirabiliter sunt perterrita.

Inter ecclesiam Romanam et Karolum regem Sicilie ex una parte et Petrum regem Arragonie ex altera, regem Francie ex una parte et regem Arragonie ex altera, item regem Francie ex una parte et regem Ispanie ex altera, multimodis dampnis, cedibus et calamitatibus hinc inde precedentibus, rege precipue Anglie se intromittente, et nuncios suos sollempnes ad pacem procurandam et formandam ad partes trans-marinas transmittente, pax et concordia facta est et confirmata. Que tamen breui post tempore Petro uidelicet Arragonie rege mortuo Iacoboque fratre suo regnum Sicilie uiriliter occupante infirmata est et ad nichilum redacta. A magno et summo Tartarorum rege [4] tam domino pape quam Francie et Anglie regibus pro amicicia renouanda et confirmanda et pro Christiane fidei sacramento suscipiendo necnon et pro subsidio Terre Sancte conferendo solempnes sunt nuncii directi.[a] Iohanna comitissa Glouernie, domini regis Anglie filia, die ueneris iiii. Non. Maii apud Winche-cumb' peperit filium suum primogenitum quem uocauit

---

[a] Facta est eclipsis lune . . . directi *marked* uacat *MS*[2]

[1] Quittance for the fine is enrolled in the Pipe Rolls, 23 Edward I, membrane 24: 'pro habenda acquietancia quintedecime omnium bonorum suorum temporalium et bonorum conuentus sui et uillanorum suorum et hominum tocius uille sancti Edmundi, salua Regi quintadecima bonorum omnium aliorum liberorum tenencium ipsius Abbatis et conuentus predicti.'

liberties of St Edmund's church.[1] When this had been done the borough of Bury St Edmunds, before another month was out, was assessed in the usual way by the official of the aforesaid abbot and convent.[2] There was an eclipse of the moon on 15 February. On 8 February in London at about the first hour of the day, suddenly and unexpectedly 'the Lord thundered in the heavens'[3] so violently and loudly that the hearts of those who heard were filled with awe and terror.

As there was a state of war between the Roman Church and Charles, king of Sicily, on the one side and Peter, king of Aragon, on the other, between the king of France and the king of Aragon, and between the king of France and the king of Spain, in which damage, loss of life and disaster of every kind befell all parties, the king of England took special pains to intervene, sending his solemn envoys overseas to bring about peace and shape its terms; and so peace and concord were achieved and established. But after a short time, when Peter, king of Aragon, had died and his brother James had courageously seized Sicily, the peace was weakened and then brought to nothing. The great and supreme king of the Tartars [4] sent ambassadors both to the pope and to the kings of France and England to renew and strengthen their friendship, to discuss his adoption of the Christian faith and to offer aid for the Holy Land. Joan, countess of Gloucester, daughter of the king of England, on Friday 4 May at Winchcombe gave birth to her eldest

---

cf. Memoranda Rolls (P.R.O.), L.T.R., 18–19 Edward I, membrane 5.
    [2] See *CPR, 1281–92*, pp. 414–15, for the royal grant to the abbey of the right to levy the fifteenth due from them, the town, etc. for their own use.
    [3] Ps. 17:14
    [4] Arghun Khan 1284–91; cf. *Foedera*, I, p. 742.

Gilebertum. Dominus Thomas Rofensis episcopus die
sancti Pancracii [1] apud Rof' in senectute bona obdormiuit in Domino; cui successit Thomas, eiusdem
ecclesie prior. Alienora, domini regis Anglie mater, in
crastino sancti Iohannis apud Aumbrebyr' in mortem
impingens, tercio die post Natiuitatem beate Marie [2]
concurrentibus tam Anglie quam Francie proceribus
potissimis solempniter est tumulata.

f. 178ᵛ Mortuo totaliter / et consumpto tam semine quam
sanguine Alexandri regis Scocie ultimo defuncti ceperunt
quidam in regno Scocie ius sibi hereditarium uendicare.
Quod considerans rex Anglie suppremum ius regni
eiusdem asseruit sibi competere. Ad quod luculencius
declarandum apud Norham in marchia Scocie accedens
uiros religiosos de nonnullis Anglie ecclesiis cum
cronicis suis conuocauit ibidem.ᵃ Quibus diligenter
coram toto consilio suo inspectis, scrutatis et consideratis
uniuersis patuit et singulis regni Scocie ius suppremum
ad ipsum spectare et pertinere debere.[3] Que omnia
cum coram maioribus Scocie tam episcopis quam
comitibus et aliis nonnullis essent recitata et diligenti
examinacione ponderata, non habentes Scotti quid pro
se allegarent, ipsum tanquam dominum suppremum
susceperunt. Cui eciam tanquam domino castella
Scocie tam citra mare Scoticum quam ultra una cum
sigillo Scocie commendauerunt sibique fidelitatem
iurauerunt et per litteras suas patentes sibi securitatem
prestiterunt et ut illi qui in regno Scocie ius sibi uendicauerant iudicio curie regis Anglie stare deberent

---

ᵃ Added MS²; in text P

[1] 12 May. The chroniclers disagree on the date.
[2] The chroniclers disagree on the date.
[3] For Edward's appeal to chronicle evidence see F. Palgrave, *Documents*

son, whom she named Gilbert. Thomas, bishop of
Rochester, died at a good old age on St Pancras's day [1]
at Rochester. He was succeeded by Thomas, prior of
Rochester. Eleanor, the king's mother, who died on
the morrow of St John's day at Amesbury, was buried
with full rites three days after the Nativity of the Blessed
Virgin Mary [2] in the presence of a great gathering of
the most influential men of England and France.

As all the descendants and blood-relatives of
Alexander, the late king of Scotland, were dead and the
line extinct, certain men in Scotland undertook to
claim their hereditary right to the throne. The king
of England saw this and asserted that the overlordship
of the kingdom belonged to him. In order to establish
his claim with more support, he went to Norham in the
Marches of Scotland and summoned monks from some
of the churches in England to come there with their
chronicles. The chronicles were inspected, investigated
and discussed before all the king's council; and it was
clear to one and all that the overlordship of Scotland
belonged and ought to belong to the king. [3] When all
this had been recited before the notables of Scotland,
that is before the bishops, earls and others, and
the evidence carefully weighed, since the Scots had
nothing to say they accepted the king as overlord.
They entrusted to him as their lord the castles of Scotland, both this side of the Scottish sea and beyond it,
together with the seal of Scotland, and swore fealty to
him. They gave security by letters patent and declared
that those who had claimed the throne of Scotland should

---

illustrating the History of Scotland, I, pp. 56–137; *Foedera*, I, p. 769; V. H.
Galbraith, *Historical Research in Medieval England* (1951), pp. 34–5.

adiudicarunt. Quo facto dominus I[ohannes] de
Bailiool' et dominus R[obertus] de Bruis aliique quidam
inferius nominati ᵃ pro iure suo uendicando se optulerunt. Qui tandem in hoc consenserunt ut xl. uirorum
legalium de utroque regno ex una parte et similiter xl.
ex alia parte necnon et xx.¹ ex parte regis Anglie
arbitrio se committerent ut uidelicet singulorum ration-
ibus et iuribus coram ipsis allegatis suam super hoc
sententiam in crastino sancti Petri ad Vincula ² promul-
garent et puplicarent. Quo facto rex Anglie episcopum
de Chatenes' ³ cancellarium Scocie constituit. Cui
eciam unum de clericis sue cancellarie Anglie Walterum
de Amundham dictum ⁴ associauit, cuius consilio et
assensu omnia forent facienda et exequenda. Castell-
orum uero custodiam fidelibus suis, prout sibi uidebatur,
distribuit. Pacis eciam et tranquillitatis custodes
aliosque regalium negociorum executores tam citra
mare quam ultra constituit. In crastino igitur sancti
Petri supradicto comparentibus coram domino rege
supradicto utriusque terre proceribus apud Berewich'
omnibusque qui in regno Scocie ius sibi uendicauerant
consilio communi consideratum est omnium calumpniam
irritam esse debere et inanem preterquam dominorum
I[ohannis] de Bailiol' et R[oberti] de Brus et I[ohannis]
de Hasting' et aliorum qui inferius nominantur.ᵇ
De quorum iure discuciendo assignatus est partibus
dies apud Berewich' in crastino sancte Trinitatis ⁵
f. 179 proximo uenturo / coram domino rege Anglie aliisque

ᵃ aliique quidem inferius nominati *in margin MS²*; *in text P* (*and Oxene*des)
ᵇ et aliorum . . . nominantur *in margin MS²*; *in text P* (*and Oxenedes*)

¹ Twenty-four is the correct number; see *Foedera*, I, p. 766. Bruce
chose forty of the assessors and Baliol the other forty.
² 2 August
³ Alan, bishop of Caithness 1282–92; *Foedera*, I, p. 757

abide by the judgment of the king of England's court. Then John de Baliol, Robert de Bruce and the others listed below presented themselves to vindicate their claim. At length they agreed to submit to the judgment of forty lawful men of each kingdom for the one party, and likewise forty for the other party, and twenty men [1] representing the king of England, with the intention that after the arguments and claims of each individual had been put before them, they should pronounce and publish their decision on the morrow of the feast of St Peter ad Vincula.[2] When this was done the king of England made the bishop of Caithness [3] chancellor of Scotland and appointed one of the clerks of the chancery of England called Walter de Amersham [4] to help him, stipulating that everything was to be done with Walter's advice and consent. The king distributed the responsibility for the castles among his liege men as suited him. He also appointed keepers of the peace and of good order and others to carry out the king's business, to act on both sides of the Scottish sea. So on the morrow of St Peter's day, as aforesaid, important men of both kingdoms and all those who had presented a claim to the throne of Scotland appeared before the king at Berwick. It was decided with common counsel that all the claims were invalid and of no weight except those of John de Baliol, Robert de Bruce, John de Hastings and the others named below. The morrow of the next Trinity Sunday [5] was assigned to the parties for the hearing of their claims at Berwick in the presence of the king and some of his liege men, who were to meet him

---

[4] Usually called Agmodesham, Amundesham, etc., i.e. Amersham.
[5] 2 June

suis fidelibus ibidem sibi occursuris. Hiis ita gestis
Florencius comes Holland', Robertus de Bruys dominus
de Valle Anandi, Iohannes de Baillol' dominus de
Galeweya, Iohannes de Hasting' dominus de Bergeueny,
Iohannes Cumin dominus de Badenough', Patricius de
Dunbar comes March', Iohannes de Vescy pro patre
suo, Nicholaus de Soules et Willelmus de Ros, in quibus
uel in quorum aliquo ius regni Scocie quiescere crede-
batur de iuris seu iurium assercionibus et allegacionibus
contra diem sibi superius prefixum deliberaturi ad
propria redierunt.ᵃ   Vnde dominus rex considerans et
perpendens per tenorem cronicarum uirorum religiosorum ius suum in regno Scocie non modicum fuisse
declaratum, uolensque huius facti sui reique geste
memoriam perpetuis temporibus fore duraturam maioribus Anglie domibus scripsit in hac forma: ' Eadwardus
Dei gratia rex Anglie, dominus Hibernie et dux
Aquitannie dilectis sibi in Christo abbati et conuentui
de sancto Eadmundo ᵇ salutem.   Mittimus uobis sub
sigillo scaccarii nostri presentibus appenso transscripta
quarundam litterarum que in thesauraria nostra resident
tenorem qui sequitur continentes: " A ceus qui cete
lettre uerrunt u orrunt, Florenz counte de Hoylaund,
Robert de Bruys seyngnur del ual d'Anaunt,
Iohan de Baillol ᶜ seyngnur de Gaweye, Iohan de
Hasting' seyngnur de Bergeueny, Iohan Comin seyngnur
de Badenough', Patrich de Dumbar counte de la
Marche, Iohan de Vescy pur sun pere, Nichole de
Soules e Williame de Ros, saluz en Deu.   Cum nus

ᵃ contra diem . . . redierunt *in a triangle in margin MS*
ᵇ sancti Petri de Burg' *in margin MS²*; Sancti Petri de Burg' *in text instead of* de Sancto Eadmundo P
ᶜ -l *interlin. MS²*

there. When this had been arranged Florence, count of Holland, Robert de Bruce, lord of Annandale, John de Baliol, lord of Galloway, John de Hastings, lord of Abergavenny, John Comyn, lord of Badenoch, Patrick de Dunbar, earl of the March, John de Vescy, on behalf of his father, Nicholas de Soules and William de Ross, in whom or in one of whom the right to the throne of Scotland was believed to rest, returned home to await the day fixed for the presentation and discussion of their claims to such right or rights. As the king considered that the gist of the monastic chronicles made his rights over the kingdom of Scotland perfectly clear and as he wished to put what he had done on permanent record for all time, he wrote in the following form to the most important religious houses in England: 'Edward, by the grace of God, king of England, lord of Ireland and duke of Aquitaine, to the abbot and convent of Bury St Edmunds, his beloved in Christ, greetings. We are sending you under the seal of our Exchequer appended to these presents copies of certain letters which are in our treasury; the contents are as follows: " To those who see or hear this letter we, Florence, count of Holland, Robert de Bruce, lord of Annandale, John de Baliol, lord of Galloway, John de Hastings, lord of Abergavenny, John Comyn, lord of Badenoch, Patrick de Dunbar, earl of the March, John de Vescy, on behalf of his father, Nicholas de Soules and William de Ross, give greetings in the Lord. Because we believe that we

entendums auer dreit el reaume de Escocie e ço dreit
mustrer, chalanger e auerrer deuaunt celi qui plus de
poer, iurisdicciun e resun eust de trier nostre dreit e le
noble prince sire Eadward, par la grace de Deu roys de
Engletere, nus eyt enformez par bones et suffisauntes
reysuns que a luy apent e auer deit la suuereyne
seyngnurie del dit reaume de Escoce e la conuysaunce ᵃ
de oyr, trier e terminer nostre dreyt; nus de nostre
propre uolonté, saunz nule manere de force u destresce,
uolums, otriums e grauntums de receyuere dreyt
f. 179ᵛ deuaunt luy come souerayn seyngnur de la terre. / E
uolums ia le meyns e promettums que nus averums e
tendrums ferm e estable sun fet e que celuy enportera
le reaume a qui dreit le durra deuaunt luy.   En testmoine
de cete chose nus auums mis nos seals a cest escrit.   Fet
e duné a Norham le maredy procheyn après l'Ascensiun,
l'an de grace mil cc. nonaunte primereyne.¹ "   " A tuz
ceus qui cete presente lettre uerrunt u orrunt, Florenz
counte de Hoylaund, Robert de Bruys seyngnur del ual
d'Anaut, Iohan de Bayllol' seyngnur de Gaweye, Iohan
de Hasting' seyngnur de Bergeueny, Iohan Comin
seyngnur de Badenough', Patrik' de Dumbar cunte de
la Marche, Iohan de Vescy pur sun pere, Nichole de
Soules et Wiliame de Ros, saluz en Deu.   Cum nus
eyums otrié e graunté de nostre bone uolenté e commun
assent, saunz nule destresce, al noble prince sire
Eadward, par la grace de Deu rei de Engletere, qu'il
comme suuerayn seyngnur de la terre d'Escoce puisse
oyr, trier e terminer nos chalangers e nos demaundes que
nus entendums mustrer e auerrer pur nostre droit el
reaume d'Escoce e dreit receyuere deuaunt luy cum

ᵃ *MS repeats* de Escoce et la conuysaunce

¹ *Foedera*, i, p. 755

have a right to the throne of Scotland and mean to
show, justify and assert this right in front of him who
has the greatest power, jurisdiction and right to hear
our claims, and because the noble Prince Edward, by
the grace of God king of England, has informed us with
good and adequate arguments that the supreme overlordship of Scotland belongs to him, together with
responsibility for the kingdom and the right of hearing,
trying and deciding the right of our claims, we of our
own free will, without being forced or in any way
compelled, wish and undertake to accept judgment of
our case from him as overlord of the land. And we
wish and promise to ratify and uphold his decision and
that the kingdom of Scotland shall be handed to him for
whom judgment is given in the king's presence. In
witness of these things we have put our seals to this letter,
made and given at Norham on the Tuesday after
Ascension day in the year of grace 1291." [1] " To all
those who see or hear this letter we, Florence, count of
Holland, Robert de Bruce, lord of Annandale, John de
Baliol, lord of Galloway, John de Hastings, lord of
Abergavenny, John Comyn, lord of Badenoch, Patrick de
Dunbar, earl of the March, John de Vescy, on behalf of
his father, Nicholas de Soules and William de Ross,
give greetings in the Lord. Since we of our own free
will and common assent, without any coercion, have
granted and conceded to the noble Prince Edward, by
the grace of God king of England, that he as overlord of
the land of Scotland may hear, try and decide our claims
and demands, which we mean to show and assert,
concerning our right to the throne of Scotland, and to

suuereyn seyngnur de la terre, promettaunz ia le meyns
que sun fet auerum ferm e estable e que celuy enportera
le reaume a qui dreyt le dorra deuaunt luy, mes pur ço
que l'auaunt dit roy de Engletere ne poet tel manere de
conuysaunce fere ne acumplir saunz jugement, ne jugement ne dreit estre saunz execucion, ne execucion ne
poet il fere duement saunz la possession e seysine de
memes la terre e des chasteus; nus uoloms, otriums e
grauntums qu'il, comme souereyn seyngnur a parfere
les choses auaunt dites, eyt la seysine de tute la terre
e des chasteus de Escoce, taunt que dreyt soyt fet e
parfurni e demaundaunz, en tel manere que, auaunt ço
f. 180 qu'il eit la / seysine auaunt dite, face bone suerté e
suffisaunte as demaundaunz e as gardeins e a la commune
del reaume de Escoce a fere la reuersiun de memes le
reaume e des chasteus oue tute la reauté, digneté,
seyngnurie, fraunchises, custumes, dreytures, leys, usages
e possessiuns e tute manere de apurtenaunces en memes
l'estat qu'il estoyent quant ᵃ la seysine luy fu baillé e
liueré, a celuy qui le droit enportera par jugement de
la reauté, sauue al rey de Engletere le humage de celuy qui
serra roy.   Issint que la reuersiun seit fete dedenz les
deus moys aprés le iur que le dreit serra trié e afermé, e
que les issues de memes la terre en le meen tens recewes
seient sauuement mis en depos e ben gardees par la
meyn le chaumberleyn de Escoce qui ore est e de celuy
qui serra assigné a luy de par le roy de Engletere e
desuz lur seaus, sauue resunable sustenaunce de la terre
e de chasteus e de ministres del reaume.   En testmoine
de cete ᵇ choses auaundites nus auums mis nos seals a
cest escrit.   Fet e doné a Norham le mekerdi aprés

accept judgment before him as overlord of the land, and have promised to uphold his action and that the kingdom shall be handed to him for whom judgment is given in the king's presence, but as the king of England cannot hold this sort of responsibility without the power of judgment, nor judgment nor right without the power of execution, and he can have no power of execution without the possession and seisin of the land itself and its castles, we wish, concede and grant that he, as overlord responsible for carrying out the above-mentioned duties, should have seisin of all the land and castles of Scotland. In order, however, that justice be done to the claimants, he should, before he has seisin as aforesaid, give good and sufficient security to the claimants, guardians and whole community of the realm of Scotland to return the same kingdom and castles with all the royal power, dignity, lordship, franchises, customary liberties, privileges, laws, customs, possessions and everything belonging to the kingdom, in the same condition as they were when seisin was entrusted to him. He should also deliver the realm to him in whose favour the law of the kingdom by royal judgment should decide, saving the right of the king of England to the homage of him who will be king. The kingdom should be returned within two months after the day when the lawful claim is investigated and affirmed. In the meantime the revenues of the land should be safely deposited and carefully kept by the chamberlain of Scotland, whoever he is, and by he who shall be assigned to the chamberlain by the king of England, under their seals, except only a reasonable sum to be spent for the maintenance of the land, castles and the officials of the kingdom. In witness of these things we have put our seals to this letter. Made and

l'Ascensiun, le an de grace M.CC. nonaunte primerein." [1]
Vnde uobis mandamus quod eadem faciatis in cronicis
uestris ad perpetuam rei geste memoriam annotari.
Teste magistro W[illelmo] de Marchia thesaurario nostro
apud Westmonasterium ix. die Iulii, anno regni nostri
decimo nono per breue de priuato sigillo.' [a]

Rodulphus Alemannie et Petrus Arragonnie [2] reges
mortis fatum experti sunt. Submerso in mari patriarcha
Ierosolimitano Nicholao non nullis Christianis fuga
elapsis plerisque eciam gladio trucidatis, ciuitas Accon-
ensis cum contentis a soldano Babilon' [3] eiusque excercitu
paganis capta et funditus est euersa. De suis tamen
pagani multitudinem incredibilem amiserunt. Petrus
Exoniensis et Willelmus Sar' episcopi uite terminum
fecerunt. In Exoniensi magister Thomas de Bitton',
decanus Wellensis, in Sar' dominus Nicholaus
Lungespeye, euisdem ecclesie thesaurarius, successerunt. Post mortem Rodulphi Alemannorum regis,
dissidentibus electoribus, Iohannes de Aueynes comes
Hagenogie a quatuor, et Reginaldus [b] comes de Gelres a
tribus electoribus, sunt electi. [c]

f. 180ᵛ

1292

A uigilia Natalis Domini usque ad diem sancti Siluestri [4]
utrobique tamen exclusiue sol, luna stelleue non
comparuerunt, nix, grando, glacies, pluuia, uentusue
non extiterunt quin pocius utinam felici auspicio omnia
pariter elementa quasi quodam letali sopita uinculo

---

[a] + *material relating to the succession to the Scottish throne inserted at the order
of Edward I*: Hyring fuit primus rex . . . recitabantur (*Thorpe, pp. 250–63*) P.
[b] *Corr.* MS²   [c] *Lacuna of* 1 *line* MS

[1] *Foedera*, I, p. 755

given at Norham on Wednesday after Ascension day, in the year of grace 1291." [1] We command you, therefore, that you have these letters recorded in your chronicles so that these events are remembered forever. Witnessed by Master William de March, our treasurer, at Westminster on 9 July in the nineteenth year of our reign by writ under the privy seal.'

Rudolf, king of Germany, and Peter, king of Aragon,[2] died. After Nicholas, patriarch of Jerusalem, had been drowned at sea, and many Christians had taken flight and many more had fallen by the sword, the city of Acre, with everything in it, was captured and razed to the ground by the infidel sultan of Cairo [3] and his army. An extraordinary number of infidels was, however, slain. Peter, bishop of Exeter, and William, bishop of Salisbury, died. Master Thomas de Bitton, dean of Wells, succeeded to the see of Exeter and Nicholas Longespée, treasurer of Salisbury, to the see of Salisbury. After the death of Rudolph, king of Germany, there was disagreement among the electors and four elected John d'Avênes, count of Hainault, and three elected Reginald, count of Geldres.

1292

From Christmas eve till St Silvester's day,[4] not counting these days themselves, neither sun nor moon nor stars were visible. There was no snow, hail, frost, rain or wind; it was as if—and would that it were a favourable omen—all the elements were equally quiet, imprisoned

---

[2] The death of Alfonso (not Peter) III has already been noticed at the beginning of the annal (p. 97 above).

[3] Khalil, sultan 1290–3   [4] 31 December

quieuerunt.[a] Dominus rex apud Westmonasterium et Gilbertus comes Glouernie cum comitissa sua, regis Anglie filia, apud Clare Natale Domini solempniter celebrauerunt.

Dominus papa domino regi Anglie [b] decima omnium prouentuum ecclesiasticorum omnium eciam bonorum uirorum religiosorum quoruncunque, Hospitalariis tamen et Templariis exceptis, per vi. annos in subsidium contulit terre Ierosolimitane. Facta est igitur noua taxacio bonorum nostrorum spiritualium et aliorum per dominum Ricardum rectorem ecclesie de Snailwell' dominumque Ricardum rectorem ecclesie de Sutton'. Bonorum autem nostrorum spiritualium per taxatores supradictos talis facta est descripcio.[1]

Taxacio bonorum nostrorum spiritualium facta per dominos Ricardum et Ricardum de Snailwell' et de Sutton' rectores anno Domini M.CC.XCI. [c]:

Bona celerarii spiritualia				*Decima*		
	m.	*s.*	*d.*	*m.*	*s.*	*d.*
Pakenham	xxxii.				xlii.	viii.
Berton'	xxx.			iii.		
Horningesh' parua	i.					xvi.
Mildenhale	xlv.			iiii. et di.		
Porcio abbatis de						
Bello	xx.			ii.		
Ecclesia sancti						
Laurencii in						
Norwyc'		xl.			iiii.	
SUMMA	vi.xx.xi.		SUMMA	xiii.		xvi.

[a] Quo facto dominus I. de Bailiool' et dominus R. de Brius aliique quidam inferius nominati (*p. 99*) . . . quieuerunt *marked* uacat *MS*²
[b] *Added MS*²; *in text P.*   *Change of handwriting MS*
[c] M.cc.x.cii. *H*

[1] For the assessment of the sexennial tenth (imposed in 1291) see above, p. xxvi.

in a deathlike sleep. The king kept Christmas at Westminster, and Gilbert, earl of Gloucester, and his countess, the king of England's daughter, kept it at Clare.

The pope granted [the king of England] a tenth of all revenues from spiritualities and of all the revenues of the religious orders, excluding the Hospitallers and Templars, for six years in aid of the land of Jerusalem. A new assessment was made, therefore, of our spiritual and other revenues by Richard, rector of the church of Snailwell, and Richard, rector of the church of Sutton. The returns relating to our spiritual revenues made by the aforesaid assessors were as follows [1]:

The assessment of our spiritual revenues made by Richard, rector of Snailwell, and Richard, rector of Sutton, in the year of the Lord 1291:

The cellarer's revenues from spiritualities				*The tenth*		
	mks	*s.*	*d.*	*mks*	*s.*	*d.*
Pakenham	32				42	8
Barton	30			3		.
Little Horningsheath	1					16
Mildenhall	45			4½		
The portion of the abbot of Battle	20			2		
The church of St Lawrence in Norwich		40			4	
TOTAL	131			TOTAL	13	16

f.181 *Bona spiritualia sacriste*   *Decima*

	m.	*s.*	*d.*	*m.*	*s.*	*d.*
Ecclesia sancte Marie	xxxvi.			iii.	viii.	
Ecclesia sancti Iacobi	xxxi. et di.			iii.	ii.	
Ecclesia de Rudham		xx.			ii.	
SUMMA	lxix.			SUMMA vi.	xii.	

Bona spiritualia camerarii   *Decima*

	m.	*s.*	*d.*	*m.*	*s.*	*d.*
Rutham	vi.				viii.	
Broch	l.			v.		
SUMMA	lvi.			SUMMA v.	viii.	

Bona spiritualia elemosinarii   *Decima*

	m.	*s.*	*d.*	*m.*	*s.*	*d.*
Hildercle	ii.				ii.	viii.
Stanton' Omnium Sanctorum	iii.				iiii.	
Redgraue	iii.				iiii.	
Sancte Marie et sancti Iacobi	xl.			iiii.		
SUMMA	xlviii.			SUMMA iiii.	x.	viii.

Wlpet in uniuerso	xx. [a]					
SUMMA	xx.			SUMMA ii.		

SUMMA tocius taxacionis	ccc.xxiiii.			SUMMA tocius decime	xxxii. v.	iiii [b]

---

[a] port' infirmar' pitanc' et hostil' sū lxvi. li. xi. s. iiii. d. (?) *in margin* MS[2]

[b] + et facit xxi. li. xii. s. H

The sacrist's revenues from spiritualities	mks	s.	d.		*The tenth* mks	s.	d.
The church of St Mary	36				3	8	
The church of St James	31½				3	2	
The church of Rougham		20				2	
TOTAL	69			TOTAL	6	12	

The chamberlain's revenues from spiritualities	mks	s.	d.		*The tenth* mks.	s.	d
Rougham	6					8	
Brooke	50				5		
TOTAL	56			TOTAL	5	8	

The almoner's revenues from spiritualities	mks	s.	d.		*The tenth* mks	s.	d.
Hinderclay	2					2	8
Stanton All Saints	3					4	
Redgrave	3					4	
The churches of St Mary and St James	40				4		
TOTAL	48			TOTAL	4	10	8

	mks				mks	s.	d.
Everything from Woolpit	20						
TOTAL	20			TOTAL	2		

	mks				mks	s.	d.
TOTAL of the whole assessment	324			TOTAL of the tenth	32	5	4

Taxatio bonorum spiritualium ad hospitalem sancti Saluatoris pertinencium facta per eosdem qui supra:

	m.	s.	d.		m.	s.	d.
						Decima	
Pake[n]ham	iiii.					v.	iiii.
Haregraue	i.						xvi.
Horningg' magna		xx.				ii.	
Neweton'	iii.					iiii.	
Elmeswelle	i.						xvi.
Culeford'		x.					xii.
Eluedene		xx.				ii.	
Chelewrth'		xxx.				iii.	
Meleford'	lxx.				vii.		
Cokefeld'	iii.					iiii.	
Redgraue		v.					vi.
Saham monachorum	ii.					ii.	viii.
Wirlingwrth'	iiii.					v.	iiii.

f. 181ᵛ beside Wirlingwrth'

	li.	s.	d.		li.	s.	d.
SUMMA	lxii.	xviii.	iiii.	SUMMA*a* vi.	v.	x.	

Taxacio bonorum temporalium eiusdem hospitalis per magistrum Ricardum de Sancta Fredeswida archidiaconum Bukingham' et dominum R[obertum] Luyterel *b* canonicum Sar' facta:

	li.	s.	d.		li.	s.	d.
						Decima	
Ikelingham	xii.						
Sancti Eadmundi	viii.	xiii.	viii.				
Culeford'		ii.	vi.				
Fornham sancti Martini		vii.					
Fornham sancti Genouef'		xi.	v.				
Westowe	vii.	xvii.	iiii.				
SUMMA	xxix.	xi.	xi.	SUMMA	lviii.	viii.ob.	

SUMMA
utriusque decime ix.   iiii.   viii.ob.*c*

a Supplied from H
b R. Luyterel interlin. MS²; Robertum in text H
c viii. d.ob.] vi. d. H

The assessment of the revenues from spiritualities belonging to the hospital of St Saviour made by the above-named assessors:

	mks	s.	d.	The tenth mks	s.	d.
Pakenham	4				5	4
Hargrave	1					16
Great Horningsheath		20		2		
Newton	3			4		
Elmswell	1					16
Culford		10				12
Elveden		20		2		
Chelsworth		30		3		
Melford	70			7		
Cockfield	3			4		
Redgrave		5				6
Monk Soham	2			2		8
Worlingworth	4				5	4
	£	s.	d.	£	s.	d.
TOTAL	62	18	4	6	5	10

The assessment of the revenues from the temporalities of the same hospital made by Master Richard of St Frideswide's, archdeacon of Buckingham, and Robert Lutterel, canon of Salisbury:

	£	s.	d.	The tenth £	s.	d.
Icklingham	12					
Bury St Edmunds	8	13	8			
Culford		2	6			
Fornham St Martin		7				
Fornham St Genevieve		11	5			
West Stow	7	17	4			
TOTAL	29	11	11		58	8½

TOTAL of both tenths 9 4 8½

Contulit eciam idem dominus papa domino regi supradicto decimam omnium prouentuum de temporalibus omnium religiosorum, Templariis dumtaxat et Hospitalariis exceptis. Ad quorum taxacionem ordinatis per totam Angliam, Scociam, Hyberniam et Walliam taxatoribus, ad nostras eciam partes magistri Ricardus de sancta Fredeswyda archydiaconus Bukyngham' et Robertus Luterel canonicus Sar' sunt directi. Quibus modum intaxando excedentibus retaxata sunt omnia per uenerabiles patres dominos Wintoniensem et Lincolliensem episcopos dicti negocii executores principales et in hunc modum redacta.

Taxacio bonorum temporalium conuentus sancti Eadmundi per Wyntoniensem et Lincolliensem episcopos facta:

Taxacio bonorum celerarie

	li.	s.	d.
Mildenhal'	iiii.xx.xix.	xiiii.	x.ob.
Berton' parua	xiiii.	viii.	iii.ob.
Heringewelle	xvii.	iiii.	x.ob.
Saham		xiii.	vi.
Eluedene	xvi.	xix.	viii.
f. 182 Wepstede	xxxvii.	xvii.	ii.
Horingesh' utraque	xxxvi.	viii.	ob.
Ryseby	xvi.	xiii.	vi.
Newetone	xxii.	x.	i.ob.
Grangie celerarii cum pertinenciis	lxx.	iiii.	viiii.
Gnatishal'		v.*a*	
Ingham	xvii.	xv.	viii.
Rucham	xxxix.	iii.	iiii.qu.
Falisham [et] Geddinge	viii.		
Ametone		viii.	ii.
Fornham sancti Martini	xv.		xxii.
Thymeworthe		xliii.	i.
Bradefeld' monachorum	xxxiiii.	viii.	vi.

a + Ixwrthe ix. li. xvii. s. vii. d. *del. MS*

The pope also granted to the king a tenth of all revenues from the temporal property of all the religious orders except the Templars and Hospitallers. Assessors were appointed throughout England, Scotland, Ireland and Wales to make the assessment for this tenth. Master Richard of St Frideswide's, archdeacon of Buckingham, and Master Robert Lutterel, canon of Salisbury, were sent to our district. But since they exceeded all bounds in their assessment everything was reassessed by the reverend fathers the bishop of Winchester and the bishop of Lincoln, the principal agents for the tax. Their assessment was as follows:

The assessment of the revenues from the temporalities of the convent of Bury St Edmunds made by the bishop of Winchester and the bishop of Lincoln:

The assessment of the cellarer's revenues

	£	s.	d.
Mildenhall	99	14	10½
Little Barton	14	8	3½
Herringswell	17	4	10½
Monk Soham		13	6
Elveden	16	19	8
Whepstead	37	17	2
Both Horningsheaths	36	8	½
Risby	16	13	6
Newton	22	10	1½
The cellarer's grange and its appurtenances	70	4	8
Knettishall		5	
Ingham	17	15	8
Rougham	39	3	4¼
Felsham and Gedding	8		
Ampton		8	2
Fornham St Martin	15		22
Timworth		43	1
Monks' Bradfield	34	8	6

		li.	s.	d.
Pakenham		lxii.	xiiii.	ob.
Bertone		xlvii.	iii.	iii.
Beketone			xi.	iiii.
Tothstok'			vi.	viii.
Grotene		vii.	xiiii.	ix.ob.
Semere		xv.	xiii.	
Chelesworth'		xxii.	xix.	iiii.
Cokefeld'		xlii.	vi.	v.
Fresingfeld'		xii.	vii.	vii.
Westowe			xxx.	
Wadewelle'			xx.	vii.ob.
Gasebec			vi.	viii.
Ixworth'			x.	
Berdewell'			iii.	iiii.
	Summa	dc.lxv.	vii.	iiii.qu.
	Decima	lxvi.	x.	viii.ob.qu.

f. 182ᵛ *In Norfolch'*

		li.	s.	d.
Suthereye		xiiii.	viii.	ii.ob.
Upwelle			xii.	
Helegeie			lx.	
Parua Walsingham			x.	
	Summa	xviii.	x.	ii.ob.
	Decima		lvii.	ob.

Summa tocius taxacionis bonorum
  temporalium celerarii in Suff' et Norf' dcc.iii.   xv.   i.ob.qu.
Decima inde   lxx.   vii.   vi.
                et ultra   i.ob.qu.

In aliis comitatibus

	i.	s.	d.
Wrabenesse	lvii.	viii.ᵃ	
Sebrithewurth		c.ᵇ	
Grantebrig'	xix.	vii.	
Werketon'	xxix.	vi.	iii.
Wayneflech		xlvi.	x.
London'		x.	
Bomstede		xv.	

ᵃ vii. li. viii. s. *MS*²   ᵇ c. s. *MS*²; *and* lxxviii. s. iii. d. *added in pencil MS*²

		£	s.	d.
Pakenham		62	14	$\frac{1}{2}$
Barton		47	3	3
Beyton			11	4
Tostock			6	8
Groton		7	14	$9\frac{1}{2}$
Semer		15	13	
Chelsworth		22	19	4
Cockfield		42	6	5
Fressingfield		12	7	7
West Stow			30	
Wordwell			20	$7\frac{1}{2}$
Gosbeck			6	8
Ixworth			10	
Bardwell			3	4
	TOTAL	665	7	$4\frac{1}{4}$
	The tenth	66	10	$8\frac{3}{4}$

In Norfolk

		£	s.	d.
Southery		14	8	$2\frac{1}{2}$
Upwell			12	
Hilgay			60	
Little Walsingham			10	
	TOTAL	18	10	$2\frac{1}{2}$
	The tenth		57	$\frac{1}{2}$

TOTAL of the assessment of the revenues from the
   cellarer's temporalities in Suffolk and Norfolk   703   15 $1\frac{3}{4}$
The tenth   70   7   6
                                        and in addition $1\frac{3}{4}$

In other counties

	£	s.	d.
Wrabness	7	8	
Sawbridgeworth		100	
Cambridge		19	7
Warkton	29	6	3
Wainfleet		46	10
London		10	
Bumpstead		15	

	m.	*s.*	*d.*
Thethingworth et Hegethorp' in comitatu Leyc'	ii.		
Wysebech' de una piscaria		v.	
Ely de una piscaria	ii.et di.		
Dudinton' de temporalibus		xvi.[a]	

Bona sacriste

	li.	*s.*	*d.*
Ikelingham	xvii.	xviii.	vii.
Dunham		lxvi.	iiii.
Westle	vi.	xii.	iii.
Aldhag'	ix.	xiii.	v.ob.
Cauendisch			xii.
Cokefeld'		xxx.	
Brethenham			vi.ob.
Thrillawe parua		xiii.	iiii.
Hauekedone			xv.
Stanefeld			iii.ob.
Hauerhille		ii.	vi.
Hemegraue		l.	
Haustede		xx.	
Villa sancti Edmundi	iiii.xx.ii.	v.	
Melles		iii.	i.
Totstok'			ii.ob.
SUMMA	cxxv.	xvii.	x.
Decima inde	xii.	xi.	ix.ob.

f. 183 (marginal note beside Hemegraue)

In Northfolch'

	li.	*s.*	*d.*
Northreppes		vii.	iii.qu.
Fincham		viii.	
Bradefeld		xliii.	i.ob.
Meringthorp		iiii.	vi.
Freton		iiii.	iiii.
Illington'		ii.	
Aylesham	xxvi.	xix.	iiii.qu.
Banigham		xxxiiii.	ix.ob.
Iteringham		xxvii.	vii.

[a] Thethingwurth . . . xvi. s.] *MS²*

	mks	s.	d.
Theddingworth and Hothorpe in the county of Leicester	2		
From one fishpond at Wisbech		5	
From one fishpond at Ely	2½		
From temporalities in Doddington		16	

The sacrist's revenues

	£	s.	d.
Icklingham	17	18	7
Downham		66	4
Westley	6	12	3
Oldhall	9	13	5½
Cavendish			12
Cockfield		30	
Brettenham			6½
Little Thurlow		13	4
Hawkedon			15
Stanningfield			3½
Haverhill		2	6
Hengrave		50	
Hawstead		20	
The vill of Bury St Edmunds	82	5	
Mellis		3	1
Tostock			2½
TOTAL	125	17	10
The tenth	12	11	9½

In Norfolk

	£	s.	d.
Northrepps		7	3¼
Fincham		8	
Bradfield		43	1½
Morningthorpe		4	6
Fritton		4	4
Illington		2	
Aylsham	26	19	4¼
Banningham		34	9½
Itteringham		27	7

	li.	*s.*	*d.*
Aleby			i.
Erpingham			iiii.
Tutington'		xxxii.	x.
Ingwrthe		xxvii.	v.
Botone			xii.
Burg'		iii.	
Dunham			v.
Plumstede		iii.	xi.ob.qu.
Mathelask'		iii.	vi.
Summa	xxxvii.	iii.	vi.qu.
Decime inde		lxxiiii.	iiii.qu.

	li.		*d.*
Summa taxacionis bonorum temporalium sacriste in Suthff' et Norf'	c.lxiii.		xvi.qu.
Decima inde	xvi.	vi.	i.ob.
		et ultra	i.qu.

Bona camerarii

	li.	*s.*	*d.*
Stanton'	x.	x.	iii.
Wathlesfeld	iiii.		ix.
f. 183ᵛ Hyldercle	xxiiii.	xvi.	x.ob.
Truston'		iii.	
Hepewrthe		ii.	vi.
Rinkinghale		xxiiii.	
Rucham		xx.	vi.
Beckles cum Endegate	xix.	xiii.	vi.
Werlingham utraque		xxvi.	viii.ob.
Ringesfeld		xiiii.	ii.
Westone		xxix.	viii.
Elith		iiii.	
Badewelle		ii.	ix.
Summa	lxv.	ix.	
Summa decime	vi.	x.	x.ob.qu.

	£	s.	d.
Alby			1
Erpingham			4
Tottington		32	10
Ingworth		27	5
Boughton			12
Burgh		3	
Downham			5
Plumstead		3	11¾
Matlask		3	6
TOTAL	37	3	6¼
The tenth		74	4¼

TOTAL of the assessment of the revenues from the
sacrist's temporalities in Suffolk and Norfolk   163   16¼
The tenth therefrom   16 6 1½
and in addition 1¼

The chamberlain's revenues

	£	s.	d.
Stanton	10	10	3
Wattisfield	4		9
Hinderclay	24	16	10½
Troston		3	
Hepworth		2	6
Rickinghall		24	
Rougham		20	6
Beccles and Indgate	19	13	6
Both the Worlinghams		26	8½
Ringsfield		14	2
Weston		29	8
Eleigh		4	
Bardwell		2	9
TOTAL	65	9	
The tenth	6	10	10¾

Bona camerarii in Norfolch'

	li.	s.	d.
Porringlond		vii.	
Castre	xi.	iiii.	x.qu.
Biskele		ii.	
Geluerton'		ii.	iii.ob.qu.[a]
Brok' [b]	xxxv.	xiii.	v.ob.
Schtisham		lxxvi.	xi.
Howe			
Langhale et Kyrkestede	iiii.		ix.ob.qu.
Hemenhale		xxxviii.	iiii.
SUMMA	lvii.	iii.	iiii.ob.
Summa decime		c.xiiii.	iiii.

	li.	s.	d.
SUMMA taxacionis omnium bonorum temporalium camerarii in Suff' et Norf'	c.xxii.	xii.	i.ob.
Summa tocius decime prouenientis ex eadem	xii.	v.	ii.ob.

Bona pitantiarii

	li.	s.	d.
In Watlesfeld'		xx.	
In uilla sancti Edmundi	vii.	x.	iii.
In Clopton'		lxi.	x.
f. 184 In Mendham		v.	
SUMMA	xi.	xvii.	i.
Summa decime		xxiii.	viii.ob.

Bona elemosinarii

	li.	s.	d.
In uilla sancti Edmundi	ix.	ii.	viii.
In Wlpit		lix.	iiii.
In Liuermere magna			xviii.
In Drenkestone		xvi.	ob.
SUMMA	xii.	xix.	vi.ob.
Summa decime		xxv.	xi.ob.

[a] *Supplied from H (sum erased MS)*   [b] Breckles *del. MS.*; Brok *MS²*

The chamberlain's revenues in Norfolk

	£	s.	d.
Porringland		7	
Caister	11	4	10¼
Bixley		2	
Yelverton		2	3¾
Brooke	35	13	5½
Shottisham		76	11
Howe			
Langhale and Kirkstead	4		9¾
Hempnall		38	4
TOTAL	57	3	4½
The tenth		114	4

	£	s.	d.
TOTAL of the assessment of all revenues from the chamberlain's temporalities in Suffolk and Norfolk	122	12	1½
Total of the tenth therefrom	12	5	2½

The pittancer's revenues

	£	s.	d.
In Wattisfield		20	
In the vill of Bury St Edmunds	7	10	3
In Clopton		61	10
In Mendham		5	
TOTAL	11	17	1
The tenth		23	8½

The almoner's revenues

	£	s.	d.
In the vill of Bury St Edmunds	9	2	8
In Woolpit		59	4
In Great Livermere			18
In Drinkstone		16	½
TOTAL	12	19	6½
The tenth		25	11½

Bona infirmarii

	li.	*s.*	*d.*
In uilla sancti Edmundi	vi.	xviii.	i.
In Schropham		v.	
SUMMA	vii.	iii.	i.
Summa decime		xiiii.	iii.ob.qu.

Bona minorum obedientiariorum in uilla sancti Edmundi

	li.	*s.*	*d.*
Bona subcelerarii		xvi.	
Bona subsacriste		xxxv.	viii.
Vestiarius		c.	
Hostilarius monachorum		xv.	
Hostilarius exterior		xlii.	
SUMMA	x.	xi.	viii.
Summa decime		xx.	x.qu.
		et ultra	i.ob.

Obuenciones feretri sancti Edmundi

	li.	*s.*	*d.*
SUMMA	xl.		
Summa decime	iiii.		

Bona precentoris

	li.	*s.*	*d.*
In Westowe		xiii.	iiii.
SUMMA		xiii.	iiii.
Summa decime			xvi.

f. 184ᵛ *Bona hospitalis*

	li.	*s.*	*d.*
In Ikelingham		xii.	
In Culeforde		ii.	vi.
In uilla sancti Edmundi	vii.	xix.	ii.
In Fornham sancti Genouefe		v.	vi.
In Westowe	iiii.	xii.	viii.
In Meleford		viii.	vi.
SUMMA	xxv.	viii.	iiii.
Summa decime		l.	x.

The infirmarer's revenues

	£	s.	d.
In the vill of Bury St Edmunds		6	18	1
In Shropham			5	
TOTAL		7	3	1
The tenth			14	3¾

The revenues of the minor obedientiaries in the town of
   Bury St Edmunds

	£	s.	d.
The revenues of the subcellarer			16	
The revenues of the subsacrist			35	8
The keeper of the vestry			100	
The guestmaster of the monks			15	
The exterior guestmaster			42	
TOTAL		10	8	8
The tenth			20	10¼
and in addition				1½

Offerings from the shrine of St Edmund

	£	s.	d.
TOTAL		40		
The tenth		4		

The precentor's revenues

	£	s.	d.
In West Stow			13	4
TOTAL			13	4
The tenth				16

The revenues of the hospital

	£	s.	d.
In Icklingham		12		
In Culford			2	6
In the vill of Bury St Edmunds		7	19	2
In Fornham St Genevieve			5	6
In West Stow		4	12	8
In Melford			8	6
TOTAL		25	8	4
The tenth			50	10

SUMMA taxacionis omnium bonorum temporalium singulorum
obedientiariorum sancti Edmundi in Suff' et Norf':

	li.	s.	d.
	m.iiii.xx.xviii.	viii.	viii.
Decima	c.ix.	xvi.	x.ob.qu.
	et ultra	i.	

SUMMA taxacionis bonorum temporalium eorundem in aliis
comitatibus: li. s. d.

                                                            li. s. d.
SUMMA utriusque *a*

Radulfus Karleolensis episcopus obiit; cui successit
Iohannes canonicus et celerarius loci eiusdem.
Iohannes prior Elyensis uite terminum faciens appositus
est ad patres suos uigilia sancti Georgii, cui successit
Iohannes Salomonis supprior eiusdem loci de Ely
oriundus. Dominus papa quarto die mensis Aprilis die
uidelicet Parasceue Rome in fata decessit uacauitque
sedes mensibus tribus et diebus ix.*b* Dominus rex
uigilia Translacionis sancti Eadmundi [1] ueniens apud
sanctum Eadmundum cum filio suo et filiabus festum
cum omni sollempnitate celebrauit. Fecitque moram
tum ibidem tum apud Culeford, manerium abbatis a
sancto Ædmundo per tria distans miliaria, per x. fere
dies continuos. Vltraque procedens Walsingham teten-
dit uersus Scociam iter suum dirigens. In recessu
siquidem suo cartam nobis dedit ne de cetero pretextu
alicuius usurpacionis preterite aliquis iusticiariorum
suorum occasione aliqua infra banleucam sancti Edmundi
f. 185 sedere / presumat.[2] Resus filius Mereduc' quidam inter
Wallenses prepotens, nemorum opacis se committens,

a Facta est igitur noua taxacio bonorum nostrorum spiritualium (*above*,
p. *104*) . . . utriusque *marked* uacat *MS²*
b *Lacuna* 2 *in. long MS*; mensibus tribus et diebus ix. *at foot of page MS²*

TOTAL of the assessment of all the revenues from the
temporalities of every obedientiary of Bury St
Edmunds in Suffolk and Norfolk

	£	s.	d.
	1,098	8	8
The tenth		109	16	10¾
	and in addition	1

TOTAL of the assessment of their temporalities in
other counties   £   s.   d.

TOTAL of both   £   s.   d.

Ralph, bishop of Carlisle, died and was succeeded
by John, canon and cellarer of Carlisle.   John, prior of
Ely, died and was laid with his fathers on the eve of
St George's day.   He was succeeded by John Salomon,
subprior of the abbey and a native of Ely.   The pope
died in Rome on 4 April, that is on Good Friday, and
the Holy See was vacant for three months and nine days.
The king with his son and daughters came to Bury St
Edmunds on the eve of the Translation of St Edmund [1]
and celebrated the feast with full rites.   For ten days he
divided his time between Bury and Culford, the abbot's
manor three miles from Bury.   Then he started for
Scotland, travelling through Walsingham.   On leaving
he granted us a charter forbidding that in future any of
his justices should dare on any occasion to sit within the
banlieu of Bury St Edmunds on pretext of any former
usurpation.[2]   Rhys, son of Maredudd, the leader of the

---

[1] 28 April
[2] *CPR, 1281–92*, p. 488; notification that the session of the king's
justices at St Edmund's shall not be a precedent to the prejudice of the
abbot and convent, dated 28 April at Bury St Edmunds.

sedicionemque contra regis Anglie pacem excitans
predacionibus eciam latrociniis atque homicidiis in-
sistens, per quosdam regis supradicti fideles captus est.
Qui ad regem per medium Anglie ad Eboracum per-
ductus per totam ciuitatem distractus, demum laqueo
suspensus, interiit.ᵃ In quindena Pasche¹ super com-
potu W[illelmi] de Redham uicecomitis Norf' et Suff'
allocate fuerunt carte libertatum nostrarum ad
scaccarium libertatesque in illis cartis contente que
hactenus remanserant indiscusse ecclesie nostre imperpetuum extiterunt adiudicate.ᵇ Cuiusmodi sunt communia ammerciamenta in itinere iusticiariorum tam de
homageriis nostris quam alienis quibuscumque infra
libertatem, de nostris uero ubicumque inuentis, mur-
drum, uastum, diem et annum, quare non uenit, quare
sepeliuit, amerciamenta eciam hominum nostrorum
coram quibuscumque iusticiariis regis assignatis quocumque locorum fuerunt amerciati, catalla felonum et
fugitiuorum annum et uastum et cetera huiusmodi.
Vnde statim de hiis ᶜ que hactenus extiterant indiuisa
dc. et xl. libre abbati fuerunt allocate.

Occurrentibus domino regi Anglie proceribus regni
Scocie, prout anno precedenti condictum fuerat in
crastino sancte Trinitatis² apud Berewych', de negocio
regni Scocie res est ita protelata quod in quindena
sancti Michaelis proximo subsequentis anni ᵈ per ante-
dictos ipsius negocii arbitros aut alicui certe persone
ipsius regni dominium ᵈ adiudicabitur aut ad ipsius

ᵃ Dominus rex vigilia Translacionis . . . interiit *marked* uacat MS²
ᵇ allocaciones adiudicate sunt abbati *in margin* MS²
ᶜ statim de hiis *corr.* MS²   ᵈ *Corr.* MS²

¹ 20 April   ² 2 June

Welsh, hid himself in the woods.   He stirred up sedition against the king of England's peace and devoted himself to robbery and murder.   Finally he was captured by some of the king's liege men and led across England to the king at York.   He was dragged all through the city and perished by hanging.   On the quindene of Easter [1] the charters of our liberties were recognised as valid in the Exchequer when William de Redham, sheriff of Norfolk and Suffolk, presented his account.   It was decreed that the liberties specified in the charters, which had hitherto remained undisputed, were to belong to our church forever.   Included among these liberties were the following: the right to the common amercements taken by justices in eyre from our liege men within the Liberty and from strangers staying there, and from our men wherever they might be, the right to murder fines, a year and a day, waste, the writs of ' quare non venit ' and ' quare sepelivit,' amercements taken from our men before any of the king's justices, wherever they might be amerced, the chattels of felons, a year and waste of fugitives and all the other liberties of this kind.   In respect of these amercements, which up till now had remained undivided, £640 was credited [at the Exchequer] to the abbot immediately.

When the leaders of the realm of Scotland had met the king of England, as arranged in the previous year, on the morrow of Trinity Sunday [2] at Berwick to discuss the affairs of Scotland, the matter was postponed until the quindene of Michaelmas next following on the understanding that on that day either the arbitrators would award the lordship of the kingdom to some specific

regni regimen per regis Anglie consideracionem prouide-
bitur. Venientibus igitur eo tempore illis superius
nominatis quibus illud negocium commissum fuerat
discutiendum una cum tribus illis fratribus [1] superius *a*
nominatis in regno Scocie ius sibi uendicantibus plane
determinatum est ab eisdem dominorum R[oberti] de
Brus et I[ohanis] de Hasting' calumpniam irritam esse
debere et inanem, dominoque Iohanni de Baylloll'

f. 185ᵛ tanquam / sanguine propinquiori ius ipsius regni competere denuntiarunt. Quapropter fidelitate domino
regi Anglie de tota terra Scocie die sancti Eadmundi
regis et martyris [2] prius facta *a* idem dominus I[ohannes]
cum omnimoda sollempnitate iuxta consuetudinem
antiquitus constitutam apud Scone *b* in presencia dominorum I[ohannis] de Warenn' et H[enrici] Lincoll'
comitum ex parte domini regis Anglie ibidem acceden-
tium die sancti Andree apostoli in solio regni Scocie
sollempniter est collocatus, homagium nichilominus de
toto ipso regno cum pertinenciis predicto domino regi
Anglie tanquam domino suppremo facturus.*c*

Octauo Kal. Iunii [3] tota ciuitas Karleol' cum
suburbio sed et ipsa cathedralis ecclesia igne consumpta
est. Cassata in curia Romana electione facta de
Iohanne comite Hagenog' et Reginaldo comite Gelrensi
ad regnum regni Alemannie electus est Adoilphus
comes *d* de Ansou et in regni solio sublimatus.[4] Die
sanctorum Crispini et Crispiniani [5] dominus *e* Robertus

---

a Corr. MS²   *b* Eadmundi . . . facta corr. MS²
c Occurrentibus domino regi (*p. 114*) . . . facturus marked uacat MS²
d Comes added MS²
e die sanctorum . . . dominus on erasure MS

[1] These three competitors were cousins, not brothers: Baliol, grandson
of the eldest daughter of David, earl of Huntingdon, the brother of William
the Lion, Bruce, the son of the second daughter, and Hastings, grandson
of David's third daughter.

individual, or that the king of England would make such provision as he thought fit for the government of it. On the day specified, therefore, the above-named, who had been authorised to discuss the matter, met and were joined by the aforesaid three brothers [1] who laid claim to the realm of Scotland. The arbitrators determined definitely that the claims of Robert de Bruce and John de Hastings were without foundation and invalid and declared that the right to the kingdom belonged to John de Baliol as the nearest in blood. John de Baliol, therefore, first swore fealty to the king of England for the whole land of Scotland on the feast of St Edmund, king and martyr.[2] Then with every solemnity, according to ancient custom, he was installed at Scone on the throne of the kingdom of Scotland in the presence of the earls John de Warenne and Henry, earl of Lincoln, who had come to represent the king of England, on St Andrew's day. John de Baliol had still to do homage for the whole of the kingdom and its appurtenances to the aforesaid king of England as overlord.

On 25 May [3] the whole city of Carlisle, including the cathedral church and the suburbs, was burnt down. The elections of John, count of Hainault, and Reginald, count of Geldres, to the kingdom of Germany having been quashed in the Roman court, Adolph of Nassau was elected and raised to the throne.[4] On the feast of SS. Crispin and Crispinian [5] Robert Burnell, bishop of

---

[2] 13 October
[3] Confirmed by *Chron. de Lanercost*, ed. J. Stevenson (1839), p. 147.
[4] *Cassata in curia . . . sublimatus:* Liebermann in *Mon. Germ. Hist. Scriptores*, xxviii (1888), p. 595, *n.* 5, says that he does not know the authority for this passage.
[5] 25 October

Burnellus episcopus Bathonensis et Wellensis, domini regis cancellarius, uite terminum fecit; cui successit magister Willelmus de Marchia, domini regis Anglie thesaurarius.[a] Dominus Iohannes archiepiscopus Cantuariensis vi. Idus Ianuarii uiam uniuerse carnis ingres[sus] est. Dominus rex Natale Domini apud Nouum Castrum super Thynam celebrauit, ubi occurrit ei Iohannes rex Scottorum, qui in crastino festi de regno Scocie eiusque pertinenciis quibuscumque homagium fecit eidem.[a]

1293

Dominus rex edicto publico statuit et ordinauit ut omnes xl. libratas terre optinentes infra xii. dies Natali consequentes militaribus accingerentur.[1] Magister Robertus de Winchelse archidiaconus Esexs' in ecclesia sancti Pauli London' ad archiepiscopatum Cantuariensem est electus. Magister Thomas Bek' Meneuensis episcopus obiit; cui successit quidam clericus eiusdem loci canonicus dictus magister Dauid filius Martini. Offensus in Antonium episcopum Dunelmensem Iohannes archiepiscopus Eboracensis, eo quod se et capitulum suum Dunelmense idem Antonius uisitari a se ut a suo primate non permisit, excommunicacionis sentenciam in ipsum Dunelmensem omnesque cum eo communicantes / publice et sollempniter fulminauerat. Dominus igitur rex tum quia familiaris suus Dunelmensis extitit tum eciam quia personam suam et filiorum suorum contra priuilegium sibi a curia Romana indultum a sentencia lata, ut asseruit, non exceperat, in Eboracensem seuire disposuit. Quo comperto saluo iure ecclesie sue Eboracensis actioneque sua contra

f. 186

Bath and Wells, the king's chancellor, died and was succeeded by Master William Marsh, the king's treasurer. John, archbishop of Canterbury, died on 8 January. The king kept Christmas at Newcastle-on-Tyne. John, king of Scotland, met him there and on the day after Christmas did homage for the realm of Scotland and its appurtenances.

1293

The king established and ordained by public edict that everyone holding forty librates of land should receive knighthood within the twelve days following Christmas.[1] Master Robert de Winchelsey, archdeacon of Essex [and canon of] St Paul's, London, was elected archbishop of Canterbury. Master Thomas Bek, bishop of St David's, died and was succeeded by a clerk and canon of St David's called Master David, son of Martin. John, archbishop of York, was angry with Anthony, bishop of Durham, because Anthony refused to allow him as his primate to visit him and his chapter of Durham. So Archbishop John solemnly and publicly pronounced the sentence of excommunication on the bishop of Durham and everyone having anything to do with him. The king was furious with the archbishop of York, partly because the bishop of Durham was his friend and partly because he and his sons were not excepted, it was said, from the sentence, though according to the privilege granted to him by the Roman court they should have been. When this became public the archbishop of York made his peace with the king and bought his goodwill

---

[1] cf. *Parl. Writs*, I, p. 257

Dunelmensem domini regis gratiam et pacem tribus librarum milibus [1] mediantibus redemit.[a]

Factum est prelium magnum nauale et horribile prope sanctum Matheum inter Anglorum, Hyberniensium et Baionensium ex una parte et Normanorum ex altera nauigia Idibus Iunii feria vi. proxima ante festum Pentecosten,[2] in quo Normannis et eorum copiis usque ad internicionem, tum aqua tum ferro cesis, submersis et consumptis, ingenti preda[b] uictoriaque triumphali absque aliquo sui excercitus dampno potiti sunt Angli. Nouies enim uiginti naues de Normannis in eo conflictu capte et inter uictores sunt distribute. Vnde in sortem Gernemut' triginta naues cessere et apud Gernemut' cum ingenti preda spoliorum nomine sunt adducte. Relique uero inter reliquos pro numero bellatorum et auxilio sunt disperse. In isto siquidem conflictu de Baionensibus tres tantum naues extitere. Subsecutum est bellum in mari multo priore seuius, in quo Teutonicorum, Flandrensium et eciam Lombardorum copias cum nauibus quam pluribus contraxerant Normanni. Quibus occurrentibus Quinque Portensibus, Baionensibus et Hyberniensibus in primo congressu multi ex parte ceciderunt Anglorum. Qui tamen tandem uiribus resumptis partem aduersariorum cum suis copiis usque ad internicionem combusserunt, prostrauerunt, contriuerunt. Sicque non absque graui excercitus sui dampno, uictoria quamuis cruenta potita est pars Anglorum. Acta sunt hec die martis vii. Kal.

---

[a] Offensus in Antonium . . . redemit *marked* uacat *MS*[2]
[b] predan *MS*

[1] The fine was for 4,000 marks; *Rot. Parl.*, 1, p. 104.
[2] Friday before Pentecost was on 15 May, so the chronicler probably wrote June by mistake for May.

for £3,000,[1] without prejudicing, however, the rights of his church of York or of his case against the bishop of Durham.

On 13 June, which was the Friday before Pentecost,[2] a fierce and terrible battle was fought at sea off the Pointe Saint-Mathieu between the English, Irish and men of Bayonne on one side and the Normans on the other. The Normans and their forces having been wiped out, some by drowning in the water, some felled by the sword, the English won a triumphant victory and took a huge spoil without any loss to their army. Nine score Norman ships were captured in the battle and distributed among the victors. Thirty of these ships were allotted to Yarmouth and were taken there laden with immense booty by way of prize. The rest of the ships were divided among the other belligerents according to their number and the amount of help they had supplied. Only three ships from Bayonne took part in the battle. An even fiercer sea-battle followed. The Normans allied themselves with German, Flemish and Lombard forces and their numerous ships. In the first clash between them and the men of the Cinque ports, Bayonne and Ireland many fell on the English side. But the soldiers at length recovered their strength and burnt, battered and trampled on the enemy forces so that they were utterly destroyed. And so the English side was victorious, though the victory was a bloody one and the English army suffered great loss. This took place on Tuesday, 26 May, the feast of St Augustine;

Iunii die sancti Augustini et sic Martis die Martium opus in mari consummatum est.[a]

Magna pars uille Grantebrig' cum ecclesia beate Marie vii. Idus Iulii [1] igne consumpta est. Willelmus abbas de Torn' in fata decessit; cui Odo eiusdem loci monachus et elemosinarius successit. Alienora regis

f. 186ᵛ Anglie filia primogenita nupsit domino Henrico / comiti de Baroduc' [b][2] apud Bristoll' [c] uigilia sancti Mathei apostoli die dominica.[3] Habita uictoria de paganis in mari Mediteraneo quidam pirata de Ianuensibus, Benedictus Zacharie [4] dictus, eorumque spoliis potitus cuilibet quinque regum Christianorum uidelicet Francie, Anglie, Alemannie, Hyspannie [5] et Cypri,[6] duodecim paganos transmisit captiuos.[d] Domini reges Anglie apud Cantuar' et Francie apud Boloniam supra mare Natale Domini celebrauerunt.[e]

1294

Dominus rex die sancti [7] Edwardi regis et martyris cum magna deuocione apud sanctum accessit Edmundum ubi per unam tantum noctem moram faciendo eiusdem loci conuentum in crastino laute et copiose immensa procurauit. Edwardus rex Anglie ac si alter Salomon in omnibus agendis suis hactenus strenuus, magnificus et gloriosus, Blanchie consanguinee sue, sororis uidelicet Philippi regis Francie, in secundo consanguinitatis

---

[a] isto siquidem conflictu . . . est *marked* uacat *MS²*
[b] *Final -a erased MS*   [c] *Final -o erased MS*
[d] Habita uictoria . . . captiuos *marked* uacat *MS²*
[e] *Lacuna of 1 line MS*

[1] Confirmed by *Liber Memorandorum Ecclesie de Bernewelle*, ed. J. W. Clark, p. 230.
[2] Henry, son of Thibaud, count of Bar, succeeded his father in 1296 or 1297. Either the chronicler, by calling him count in 1293, muddled his

thus on Mars's day a Martian feat was accomplished at sea.

A great part of the town of Cambridge, including St Mary's church, was burnt down on 9 July.[1] William, abbot of Thorney, died and was succeeded by Odo, monk and almoner of Thorney. The king of England's eldest daughter, Eleanor, married Henry, count of Bar,[2] at Bristol on Sunday, the eve of the feast of St Matthew the Apostle.[3] After a pirate from Genoa called Benedict Zacharias[4] had won a victory over the infidels in the Mediterranean and taken possession of their spoils, he sent twelve captive infidels to each of the five Christian kings, of France, England, Germany, Spain[5] and Cyprus.[6] The king of England kept Christmas at Canterbury and the king of France kept it at Boulogne-sur-Mer.

1294

The king came with pious devotion to Bury St Edmunds on the feast of St Edward the king and martyr.[7] He stayed only one night and on the morrow entertained the convent with great magnificence and generosity. Up till now Edward, king of England, had in all his acts shown himself energetic, generous and triumphant, like another Solomon. But he became infatuated with an unlawful love for his relative Blanche, the sister of Philip, king of France. She was related to him in the

---

facts, or he was writing after Henry's succession. The same error occurs below, p. 120, under 1294.
    [3] 20 September
    [4] For Benedetto Zaccaria see R. S. Lopez, *Genova Marinara nel Duecento: Benedetto Zaccaria Ammiraglio e Mercante* (1933).
    [5] Sancho IV, king of Castile 1284–95
    [6] Henry II, 1285–1324   [7] 18 March

gradu sibi propinque,[1] amore infatuatus illicito super
matrimonio cum eadem contrahendo a curia Romana
secum dispensari petierat et impetrauerat. Cuius rei
gratia omnes terras suas Aquitannie et Gwasconie cum
omnibus suis pertinenciis ipsas terras cum dicta Blanchia
quasi denuo *a* in liberum ut sperabat matrimonium
recepturus regi Francie, proprie tamen uoluntatis ductus
arbitrio et absque aliquo fidelium suorum consilio, bona
fide resignauit. Et fuit facta ista resignacionis littera
apud sanctum Edmundum rege tunc ibidem existente
cancellarioque ad hoc tamen cum sigillo a London' a
rege uocato in Quadragesima.[2] Accessit et alia iuxta
quorundam assercionem priuacionis terrarum supra-
dictarum occasio *b*; cum enim rex Anglorum ipsas terras
de rege Francie tanquam de domino capitali pro certo
seruicio sibi faciendo teneret et ad faciendum quod
pro ipsis terris de iure antiquo facere tenebatur ad
curiam Francie sepe sepius fuisset uocatus nec se nec
per aliquem alium responsalem sufficientem, ut asserebant Franci, aliquando comparuisset tandem habito
f. 187 prius et deliberato legittimo processu super / negocio
memorato per tocius curie Francie consideracionem *c*
post Pascha Parisius tanquam contumax et rebellis rex
Anglie pro se et heredibus suis a terris supradictis
sentencialiter forisiudicatus est, spoliatus, frustratus et
priuatus.[3] Subornatur tamen aliter *d* ab aliquibus ista
temeraria presumpcio quod uidelicet terrarum suarum

a de- *added MS²*
b quorundam . . . occasio *on erasure MS*
c *Corr. from* consedicionem (?) *MS²*
d *Added MS² ; in text P*

[1] Blanche, daughter of Philip III, was Edward's first cousin once
removed.
[2] P. Langtoft, *Chron.*, ed. T. Wright (RS, 1866–8), ii, p. 198, mentions
Edward's letter, already sealed. A mandate among the Chancery warrants

second degree.[1] Edward asked for and obtained a dispensation from the Roman court to contract a marriage with her. For the sake of this he resigned in good faith all his lands in Aquitaine and Gascony with all their appurtenances (as though he could expect to receive them back together with Blanche in free marriage) to the king of France of his own free will without the advice of his liege men. The letters of resignation were drawn up at Bury St Edmunds, where the king was still staying, and the king summoned the chancellor in Lent to come with the seal from London.[2] The loss of these lands was attributed by some to another cause. Now the king of England held these lands from the king of France as his lord-in-chief in exchange for certain services which he owed to [the king of France], and in order to perform the services due from those lands by ancient custom he had been summoned time and time again to attend the court of France, but (as the French asserted) had never appeared either in person or by adequate attorney. At last, therefore the whole court of France tried the case and carefully considered the matter and pronounced judgment on Edward in Paris after Easter: the king of England, for himself and his heirs, as contumacious and rebellious, forfeited by judicial sentence the lands in question. And so he was plundered and robbed and his plans frustrated.[3] Some people, however, put forward a rash theory, that by entering into such an agreement, in view of the oath he had taken to go on the

---

orders the chancellor to bring as secretly as possible the great seal and a trustworthy clerk to the king at the manor of the abbot of Bury St Edmunds near Bury by 16 March 1294; *Cal. Chancery Warrants, 1244–1326*, p. 40.
   [3] *Foedera*, I, pp. 793ff.; Rishanger, pp. 140–1

transmarinarum ut pote qui iter suum in obsequium Crucis salutifere deuouerat huiusmodi federe contracto maiori rex Anglie securitati prouideret et quieti. Habita igitur libera, plenaria et pacifica possessione et disposicione terrarum earundem Anglorumque rege non tam uoluntarie quam temerarie et inconsulte sic cedente a dicte perturbacionis muliere ipsi Anglorum regi dirigitur in mandatis se nulli hominum et presertim tante etatis uiro aliquando uelle maritari. Et sic optato sed illicito merito frustratus matrimonio antiquo predecessorum suorum prothdolor priuatus est patrimonio. Tandem uero idem rex Anglie ad cor rediens factique tam presumptuosi quamuis sero penitens contractis finitimorum tam regum quam aliorum potentum copiis iniuriam sibi taliter illatam uindicaturus terrasque suas tam fraudulenter occupatas uendicaturus et terrestrem et naualem copiosum congregauit excercitum. Cuius rei gratia Adulphum regem Alemannie omnesque eiusdem terre magnates ut pote archiepiscopum Coloniensem,[1] Siefred' episcopum Traiectensem [2] aliosque tam reges quam episcopos ducesque comites atque omnes potentes Alemannorum imperio subiacentes hos premiis illosque federibus amicitiisque contractis ad suam partem allexit atque transire coegit.[3] Regem eciam Arragonie [4] sibi amicissimum cum ducibus et comitibus Prouincie et Sabaudie et eorum uiribus de Lombardia quoque aliarumque nacionum gentibus maximum coadunauit belli munimentum. In expedicione eciam ista Iohannes dux Brabantie, Constantius comes Holond' et Seland' [5] et Henricus comes de Baroducis [6] cum suis in multi-

---

[1] Siegfried, archbishop of Cologne 1275–97
[2] John (not Siegfried), bishop of Utrecht 1291–6
[3] *Foedera*, I, p. 812
[4] James II, king of Aragon 1291–1327

Crusade, the king was taking thought for the greater peace and security of his overseas territories. When, however, the king of England, not so much voluntarily as thoughtlessly and ill-advisedly, had thus handed over the free, full and peaceful possession and control of his lands, the woman who was the cause of the trouble wrote and informed him that she did not wish ever to marry any man, especially such an old one. And so the illegal marriage which Edward had desired was deservedly frustrated and, alas, he was deprived of the ancient inheritance of his forebears. The king of England at last came to himself and repented, although too late, his rash deed. He gathered together forces from neighbouring kings and rulers and so collected a great army for war at land and sea in order to avenge the wrong done him and liberate his lands, which had been occupied by deceit. To serve his purpose Edward bound to his side by bribes and treaties and mutual friendship Adolph, king of Germany, and all the great men of that country including the archbishop of Cologne,[1] Siegfried, bishop of Utrecht,[2] and the other kings, bishops, dukes and counts and all the important men under German rule, and urged them to join him.[3] He also assembled a powerful military force comprising his great friend the king of Aragon,[4] with the dukes and counts of Provence and Savoy and their forces and men from Lombardy and of other nations. On this expedition also John, duke of Brabant, Constance, count of Holland and Zeeland,[5] and Henry, count of Bar,[6] with

---

[5] Florence (not Constance), count of Holland and Zeeland 1256–96
[6] Henry, son of the count of Bar (1240–96/7); Henry is wrongly called count above 1293, above, p. 118.

tudine innumera conuolarunt. Proceres eciam Anglie tam persone ecclesiastice quam seculares super auxilio sibi in guerra sua in partibus transmarinis patrando f. 187ᵛ conuenti / liberaliter annuerunt dum tamen pro tempore futuro hoc ad consequenciam non traheretur. Omnes eciam uiros ecclesiasticos ut pote archiepiscopos, episcopos et abbates, ueteranos eciam uiduas aliasque dominas et mulieres per seruitium militare de se in capite tenentes scuto cuilibet centum marcas imponens ad redempcionem pecuniarum coegit. Vnde abbas sancti Edmundi pro vi. militibus suis pro quibus regi respondere tenebatur ad dc. marcas taxabatur et sic de ceteris. Solucio tamen usque ad transfretacionem suam differebatur. Quibus ita gestis rex Anglie, Deo et hominibus displicente, et utinam sibi non incongruo fretus consilio, die festo Translacionis sancti Martini ¹ que die contigit dominica una et eadem die et hora ministros suos ad hoc preordinatos subito et ex insperato per totam destinauit Angliam ad querendum, scrutandum et inuestigandum omnes et singulos religiosorum domos sollicite et diligenter tam in ecclesiis quam aliis quibuscumque et singulis eorum officinis non ecclesiarum turribus parcentes nec latrinis, nulli eciam dignitati, excellentie, prerogatiue, exempcioniue deferentes aut fortune. Hec enim perscrutacio siue inuestigacio adeo fuit generalis ut nec cenobiis quidem nec sacris edibus aut eciam domibus leprosorum inferioribus parceretur. Per domos enim loca et hospitia prelatorum, archiepiscoporum uidelicet episcoporum, abbatum, archidiaconorum, prebendariorum in ecclesiis cathedralibus et aliis necnon rectorum seu uicariorum sed et per omnes

---

¹ 4 July. Guisborough, p. 248, agrees with this date but *Flores*, III, p. 274, gives 11 July.

their retinues, congregated in an immense gathering. The chief men of England, both ecclesiastics and laymen, met and generously consented to a grant to help Edward's war abroad. It was stipulated, however, that this was not to be appealed to as a precedent in future. Moreover he compelled all ecclesiastics, that is the archbishops, bishops and abbots, and also old men, widows and other women, both noble and otherwise, who held from him in chief by military service, to pay a money fine, making every knight's fee liable for 100 marks. Hence the abbot of St Edmund's was assessed at 600 marks for his six knights, for whom he was bound to answer to the king, and so with the rest. Payment was put off, however, until his departure. Afterwards the king of England, to the displeasure of God and men (would that he did not rely on such unworthy counsel!), on the feast of the Translation of St Martin,[1] which was a Sunday, sent his officials especially appointed for the purpose, suddenly and unexpectedly and on the same day and at the same hour, to all parts of England to search, examine and investigate with care and diligence every religious house including their churches and each domestic office, sparing neither towers nor privies, without regard to dignity, eminence, privilege, exemption or riches. This survey or investigation was so universal that neither convents, sacred buildings nor the more humble leper-houses escaped. For not only did they go through all the houses, premises and guest-houses of the prelates, that is of the archbishops, bishops, abbots, archdeacons, prebendaries in cathedral and other churches, rectors and vicars, but also all the cities,

ciuitates, burgos, castella, uicos et uillas et personas tam
seculares quam ecclesiasticas, penes quas aliqua sperabatur posse reperiri pecunia, discurrentes omnes serruras
sibi iusserunt reserari, apertasque scrutantes inuenta
sigillauerunt et reposuerunt, non apertas uiolenter fregerunt et inuentarium penes se retinentes. Nichil tamen
penitus apud nos asportantes, illas tamen recludentes
sigillis suis tam apertis quam non apertis appositis
recesserunt. Operi eciam tam nephario scelus inauditum et piis auribus superaccumulantes abhorrendum
monasterium sancti regis et martiris Edmundi cum uilla
adiacente que pro ciuitate refugii a priscis temporibus
fuerant constituta, que nemo hactenus regum attemptare
f. 188 presumpserat, in emunitatis ecclesiastice preiu/dicium
suo uiolenter prophanarunt scrutinio. Et nec regum
collacionibus nec summorum pontificum deferentes sentenciis latis in animarum suarum pernitiem secundum
formam alibi factam et ultra in omnibus processerunt.
Transmarinorum uero mercatorum pecunias aliaque
eorum bona ubicumque inuenta tam in ecclesiis quam
extra ceperunt et ad thesaurum regium portauerunt.
Tallias eciam peccuniarum suarum sibi debitarum in
manus mercatorum de Anglia inuentas retinuerunt et
ad solucionem sibi faciendam ipsos compulerunt.

Petrus quidam Meronensis Appulus genere Frederici
quondam imperatoris aliquando notarius sub pro-
fessione regule sancti Benedicti qui a *a* Cisterciens' ad
uitam migrauerat heremeticam etate centenarius et
ultra [1] in crastino Translacionis sancti Martini [2] apud

---

a + Monte Cassino *in margin MS²*

[1] He was about eighty. Cf. H. K. Mann, *The Lives of the Popes in the Middle Ages* (1902–32), XVII, p. 265.
[2] 5 July

boroughs, castles, villages and hamlets, [visiting] both laymen and clergy, wherever it was hoped that any money could be found, and ordered all locks to be opened for them.   They examined unlocked repositories, sealing and putting back what they found.   Those that were locked they broke open forcibly, locking them again, and kept an inventory with them.   They took nothing at all from us but opened the repositories and imprinted their seals on both locked and unlocked ones before they left.   To this evil business they added another unheard-of crime, most offensive to all good men: for by their investigations they violently desecrated, to the prejudice of ecclesaistical immunity, the monastery of St Edmund the king and martyr, together with the adjoining town, which had been privileged as a city of refuge from the earliest times, and no previous king had dared attack it.   And taking heed neither of royal grants nor of papal sentences promulgated, they proceeded, to the damnation of their souls, to follow the same routine as was followed elsewhere, only taking things even further.   They also seized the money and other property of foreign merchants wherever they found them, whether in churches or not, and carried them to the royal treasury.   They kept the tallies which they found in the hands of the English merchants for money owed them, and forced the merchants to make payment to them.

Peter de Morrone, an Apulian born, formerly a notary of the Emperor Frederick and subject to St Benedict's rule, who had left the Cistercian order to become a hermit, was elected pope at Perugia on the morrow of the feast of the Translation of St Martin [2] when he was a hundred years old or more.[1]   Before his election

Perusium in summum pontificem est electus, ante cuius
electionem uacauerat sedes apostolica anno uno,
mensibus tribus et diebus nouem; dictusque est
Celestinus quintus qui pridie Idus Septembris consecratus, sollempniterque est intronizatus.

Fames et inopia pregrandis per totam Angliam;
quarterium enim *a* frumenti quod uix et difficulter
inueniebatur ad xxiiii. solidos per aliqua loca uendebatur. Sed et mensis Augusti cum Septembre
subsequente in tantum ymbribus continuis madidus fuit
et pluuiosus quod usque ad festum sancti Michaelis
parum aut nichil de nouo grano potuit reperiri.

Rex Anglie uniuersas per totam Angliam religiosorum domos capitulis transmarinis subiectas cum eorum
bonis undecumque prouenientibus in manu sua cepit *b*
atque earundem cura ministris et custodibus suis
commendata religiosis per ipsas domos degentibus
certam constituit annonam videlicet cuilibet monacho
per ebdomados xviii. denarios. *c* *1*   Quod dum *d* super-
habundauit sumptibus sue guerre deputauit. Cister-
cienses tamen super hoc non sollicitauit, Cluniacensibus
quidem seu Premonstracensibus aut aliis quibuscumque
non pepercit, sed eorum bonis taliter confiscatis in
tristicia eos uiuere compulit egestate et merore.   Insuper
omnes pensiones annuas suis principalibus domibus
annuatim debitas ad suum thesaurum iussit deportari.
Idem rex parleamento die et in crastino sancti Michaelis
f. 188ᵛ / apud Westmonasterium habito tum precibus tum
exhortacionibus tum eciam comminatoriis premissis

---

a Added MS²   *b Corr. from* receipt *MS²*
  c uidelicet cuilibet . . . xviii. d. *in margin in pencil overwritten in ink with*
tie-marks MS²
  d Corr. from cum (?) *MS²*

the Holy See had been vacant for one year, three months
and nine days.   He took the name Celestine V and on
12 September was consecrated and solemnly enthroned.

There was a famine and great want throughout
England.   A quarter of corn, which was hardly obtain-
able at all, cost 24s. in some places.   Worse still, during
August and the following September there was a continuous drenching downpour of rain, so that very little
or none of the new crop could be harvested before
Michaelmas.

The king of England took into his hands all religious
houses throughout England which were subject to a
chapter abroad, together with all their revenues, from
whatever source.   He put his officials and keepers in
charge of them and ordered a fixed allowance to be
given to the monks who remained in these houses, that
is 18d. a week for each monk.[1]   What was left over from
their resources he allotted to his war.   He did not,
however, molest the Cistercians, but the Cluniacs,
Premonstratensians and all the other orders were not
spared; he confiscated their property and so forced them
to live in misery, poverty and sorrow.   Moreover he
ordered that all annual payments due every year to the
principal houses should be diverted to his treasury.
The king held a parliament at Westminster on Michaelmas day and on the following day.   After beginning
with prayers, entreaties and even threats, he compelled

---

[1] This sum is confirmed by the copy of a royal mandate relating to French
monks in England, in Cotton, p. 300.

uniuersos et singulos Anglie prelatos cum suo clero nec non et religiosos omnes possessiones optinentes ad ipsum parlamentum uocatos ad prestacionem medietatis omnium bonorum suorum *a* spiritualium et temporalium iuxta taxacionem pro decimis proximo prehabitam sibi patrandam et ad tres terminos ipso anno durante soluendam compulit et uiolenter induxit. Cuius quidem prestacionis summa ad c.i. millia libras excreuisse refertur. Nostra siquidem prestacio ad dc.lv. libras xi. denarios, ob. qu. excreuit.

Interim magister Iohannes de Saunford' archiepiscopus Dublinensis qui una cum domino Antonio Dunelmensi episcopo aliisque non nullis regis Anglie fidelibus pro negociis guerre sue regem Alemannie ipsiusque terre proceres cum apparatu non modico adierat Angliam rediens et apud Gernemut' ueniens post paucos dies ibidem defungitur cui successit frater Willelmus de Hodom de ordine Predicatorum.*b* In parlamento supra proximo habito magister Willelmus de Monte Forti decanus sancti Pauli London' qui negocii decime regi Anglie in subsidium Terre Sancte dudum concesse in curia Romana procurator et precipuus negociorum ipsius regis in subuersionem libertatum ecclesie Anglicane executor extiterat et promotor, subito et inopinate in conspectu ipsius regis sibique assistentium subita percussus passione ultimum in terram corruens spiritum efflauit. Elatusque est apud sanctum Paulum et *c* ad patres suos appositus.*d* Walenses tempus aptum et oportunum se inuenisse arbitrantes

---

a Added MS²; in text P

b cui successit . . . Predicatorum *as p. 123, n. c in margin in pencil overwritten in ink with tie-marks MS²*

c Added MS²

d In parlamento supra . . . appositus *marked* uacat *MS²*

and forced each and every prelate and their clergy and all the religious who owned property, whom he had summoned to this parliament, to make him a payment of half of all their spiritual and temporal revenues according to the assessment made recently for the tenth, to be paid in three instalments during this year. The sum total of the contribution is said to have amounted to £101,000. Our contribution was £655 0s. 11¾d.

In the meantime Master John de Sandford, archbishop of Dublin, who had accompanied Anthony, bishop of Durham, and other faithful subjects of the king of England, with a considerable retinue, to negotiate with the king of Germany and the chief men of that land about the king of England's war, on his return to England came to Yarmouth and died after he had spent a few days there. He was succeeded by Brother William de Hothum, of the order of Friars Preachers. When parliament was held William de Montfort, dean of St Paul's, London, who was the procurator in the Roman court for the business connected with the tenth previously granted to the king of England for the defence of the Holy Land, and also the principal agent and promoter of the king's schemes for the overthrow of the liberties of the English Church, was suddenly and unexpectedly struck with pain in the presence of the king and his court and unexpectedly gave up the ghost. He was brought for burial to St Paul's and laid with his forebears. Considering the time propitious, the Welsh,

duce quodam Mereduco Abliwelini regi Anglie facti
rebelles et *ª* Snowdon' inuadentes multos de regis Anglie
fidelibus ibidem inuentos trucidauerunt et male tractauerunt castella subuerterunt aliaque deformia et
enormia in contemptum et dispendium ipsius regis per
totam Walliam operati sunt. In crastino sancti Martini
apud Westmonasterium concessa est regi *ᵇ* populo
laicali decima omnium bonorum suorum in subsidium
guerre sue tam Gallice quam Wallice. In ciuitatibus
uero burgis aliisque regis dominicis habitantes ad
sextum, aliique mercatores alibi commorantes ad
septimum, communitas uero reliqua ad decimum
f. 189 taxati sunt denarium. Villa / eciam sancti Edmundi in
qua hactenus nullus minister regis a tempore libertatum
primo nobis concessarum aliquam excercere presumpsit
iurisdictionem, per communes patrie taxatores in tolhus
publico uidelicet uille loco residentes et burgensibus
iuratis articulos contradentes est taxata. A quorum
communitate seruientes nostros neque prece neque
precio prothdolor ullatenus potuimus uellicare. Sic
tamen quieuit res ut pro tempore futuro quantum ad
libertates nostras has et alias hactenus habitas et usitatas
per hoc in posterum nequaquam aliquale nobis preiudicium generetur et super hoc carta nobis concessa
est specialis. Excercitus naualis regis Anglie nuper
Gasconiam directus castellis et terris aliquibus uiriliter
captis et subiugatis mirabiliter in breui profecerunt. *ᶜ*
Rex Anglie in expedicione sua Wallica apud Aber-
conewei Natale Domini celebrauit.

Celestinus V papa status et etatis sue considerans
impotentiam statutum edidit et mox a fratribus approba-

ª Added MS²   *ᵇ -a added MS²*
ᶜ Villa eciam sancti Edmundi . . . profecerunt marked uacat MS²

led by a certain Madog ap Llewelyn, rose in rebellion
against the king of England.   They invaded Snowdonia
and killed and maltreated many of the king's subjects
whom they found there.   They destroyed castles and
committed other outrages throughout Wales against
the king's honour and to his great expense.   On the
day after Martinmas the laity granted to the king at
Westminster a tenth of all their revenues in aid of both
his French war and his Welsh one.   The inhabitants
of the cities, boroughs and other royal demesnes were
assessed for a sixth penny, and merchants living elsewhere for a seventh, but the rest of the community paid
the tenth.   The town of Bury St Edmunds was assessed
by the ordinary tax-assessors of the region, who sat in
the toll-house, that is in the town hall, and delivered
their articles to burgesses who were on oath.   Never
before, since our liberties were first granted to us, had
any royal official dared exercise any authority in the
town.   Nor alas! were we able by prayer or price to
save our servants from being classed with the townsmen.
It was, however, settled that in future this action should
in no way prejudice us in respect of these and our other
liberties which we had hitherto enjoyed.   A special
charter was granted to us to this effect.   The king of
England's army which had sailed to Gascony bravely
captured and subdued castles and lands and made
remarkable progress in a short time.   The king of
England kept Christmas during his Welsh campaign at
Aberconway.

Pope Celestine V, thinking of his weakness caused by
his age and condition, decreed and obtained the approval
of his brethren that whoever was Roman pontiff at the

ri procurauit quod Romano pontifici qui pro tempore
fuerit si sibi utile uisum fuerit et oportunum sue dignitati
resignare et ad arcioris instituti contemplacionisue otium
siue requiem liceat transmigrare.[1]   Quo facto cum per
quinque menses et dies xxi. summi pontificatus apicem [a]
gubernasset die sancte Lucie uirginis [2] apud Neapolim
facta prius resignacione ad dilectum sibi sue pristine
solitudinis locum remeauit. Eo igitur sic cedente
uacauit sedes Romana diebus undecim. Vndecimo
igitur die uigilia uidelicet Natalis Domini proximo
sequente electus est dominus Benedictus de Anagnia
oriundus tituli sancti Nicholai in Carcere Tulliano
diaconus cardinalis, dictusque est Bonefacius octauus.[b]

1295

Magister [c] Robertus archiepiscopus Cantuariensis
secundo die mensis Ianuarii [3] a curia rediens Romana
apud Gernem' applicuit.   Quartodecimo Kal. Februarii
una cum nocte et die subsequentibus uento flante
imbriumque instancia uehementi concomitante facta
est tam terribilis elementorum concussio quod centenarii
ipsam tempestatem tunc uidentes consimilem se uidisse
f. 189ᵛ minime recoluerunt ; / unde uniuersa tam Holandie
quam Merslandie semina hyemalia aquis pene sunt
consumpta.[d] Bonefacius octauus in summum pontificem electus xi. Kal. Februarii in urbe est coronatus;
qui statim predecessorum suum acciuit ipsumque certe
custodie honeste tamen in curia sua commendauit.
Vltimo die mensis Februarii in castello de Windleshor'

---

[a] quinque menses . . . a[picem] *on erasure and in margin MS*²
[b] de Anagnia . . . octauus *on erasure*; *lacuna of 2 lines MS*
[c] *Change of handwriting.   P ceases to follow our MS closely.*
[d] Quartodecimo Kal. Febr' . . . consumpta *marked* uacat *MS*²

time could, if it seemed to him right and opportune, resign from office and change to the leisure or peace of the more strictly contemplative life.[1]   When this was done and he had been pope for five months and twenty-one days he resigned at Naples on the feast of St Lucy the virgin.[2]   Then he returned to the spot dear to him, his former place of solitude. After his resignation the Holy See was vacant for eleven days.   On the eleventh day, which was Christmas eve, Benedict was elected. He was born at Anagni and was cardinal-deacon of the title of St Nicholas in Carcere Tulliano.   He took the name Boniface VIII.

1295

Master Robert, archbishop of Canterbury, landed at Yarmouth on 2 January[3] on his way back from the Roman court.   On 19 January and all that night and the next day a hurricane blew accompanied by a heavy, continuous downpour; the storm was so terrible that the centenarians who saw it could remember nothing similar.   All the winter seed both in Holland and in the Marshland was almost totally destroyed by the rain. Boniface VIII, who had been elected supreme pontiff, was crowned in the city on 22 January.   He immediately summoned his predecessor and put him under safe, though honourable, guard in his court.   On the last day of February a fire suddenly burst out in Windsor

---

[1] The text of Celestine's resignation is unknown. His successor, Boniface VIII, issued a decree, in *Liber Sextus*, i, 7, 1, to the effect that a pope may resign.

[2] 13 December

[3] Other authorities state that he touched Yarmouth on 1 January 1295; *Wig.*, p. 518, and the continuator in *Gerv. Cant.*, ed. W. Stubbs (RS), II, p. 311.

ignis subito succensus quam plurimas eiusdem castelli officinas consumpsit non nullas eciam de egregiis edificiorum picturis denigrauit et deformauit.ᵃ ¹ Domini Berardus Albanensis episcopus cardinalis qui fuerat Lugdonensis archiepiscopus ² et Symon Penestrinus episcopus cardinalis qui fuerat archiepiscopus Biturnensis ³ a domino papa directi uenerunt in Angliam Londonieque cum sollempnitate precipua sunt recepti. Qui ex parte summi pontificis habito tractatu cum rege Anglie super statu guerre sue inter ipsum et Francie regem inite pacisque reformacione, statim infra octabas Assumpcionis ⁴ regem Francie adituri et super eodem negocio ipsum conuenturi mare petierunt et transfretauerunt.

Rex Anglie subacta Wallia London' reuertitur, cui die ueneris proxima post festum sancti Petri ad Vincula ⁵ nunciatum est Francos cum nauibus et galeis numerosis apud Doueram die martis precedente hostiliter applicuisse, ipsamque uillam aliqua sui parte igne appetito mutilasse, prioratum inuasisse, unum uel duos de monachis ⁶ una cum aliis quibusdam de uilla trucidasse predam eciam copiosam abduxisse sicque non absque graui excercitus sui dampno ad loca de quibus aduenerant redisse, filium enim comitis Attrabacensis ⁷ ibidem ferunt interisse. Dominus Robertus archiepiscopus Cantuariensis secundo die mensis Octobris in sede sua pontificali domino rege cum suis proceribus et eciam fere

---

ᵃ Vltimo die mensis . . . deformauit *marked* uacat *MS*²

¹ The other chronicles do not mention this fire. A royal order to repair the houses, tower, etc. of Windsor castle is dated 12 November 1296 at Bury St Edmunds; *CCR, 1288–96*, p. 498.

² Berard de Gout, archbishop of Lyons 1289–94, cardinal-bishop of Albano 1294–7

³ Simon de Beaulieu, archbishop of Bourges 1281–95, cardinal-bishop of Palestrina 1295–7

castle. It destroyed many of the castle's domestic offices and charred and spoilt some of the wonderful paintings in the building.[1] Berard, cardinal-bishop of Albano, who had been archbishop of Lyons,[2] and Simon, cardinal-bishop of Palestrina, who had been archbishop of Bourges,[3] were sent by the pope to England and were received with great magnificence in London. They discussed on the pope's behalf with the king of England the state of the war which had been declared between the king of England and the king of France and the possibility of making peace. They went to the coast and embarked immediately afterwards on the octave of Assumption day [4] to meet the king of France on the same business.

When the king of England had subdued Wales he returned to London. On the Friday after the feast of St Peter ad Vincula [5] it was reported to him that the French had come on the previous Tuesday on a hostile expedition with sailing-ships and numerous galleys and landed at Dover. They had damaged the town by setting fire to part of it, attacked the priory, butchered one or two of the monks [6] and some townsmen and carried off much loot. Then they returned to where they came from, only, however, after considerable loss to their army: it is said that the son of the count of Artois [7] was killed. Robert, archbishop of Canterbury, was enthroned with full rites on his pontifical throne on 2 October in the presence of the king and the chief men

---

[4] 22 August   [5] 5 August in 1295
[6] A monk called Thomas de la Hale was killed; Rochester chronicle, in Brit. Mus. MS Cotton Nero D ii, f. 187; see C. R. Haines, *Dover Priory* (1930), p. 244.
[7] Son of Robert II, count of Artois (1250–1302)

tocius archiepiscopatus sui suffraganeis presentibus sollempniter est intronizatus.

Dominus Thomas de Turblevile miles quidam de Marchia oriundus domesticus et precipuus regis Anglie familiaris cum ipsius regis excercitu anno precedente ad Guasconiam est directus ubi cum non nullis sue milicie commilitionibus in quodam conflictu a Francorum exercitu captus est et arciori custodie sub eorundem potestate commendatus. Interim siquidem de rege Anglie tradendo et per consilium eius seducendo inter f. 190 ipsum et regem Francie / est tractatum. Quo facto quasi furtim a carcerali elapsus custodia Angliam rediit regem adiit et gratanter ab ipso rege est admissus. Conuenerat siquidem cum rege Francie quod totam Angliam, totam Hyberniam et totam Scociam et Walliam uno et eodem tempore sub guerra constitueret generali, ut uidelicet rege Anglie tam multipliciter occupato naualis exercitus regis Francie ad quemcumque eligeret Anglie portum nullo resistente uel impediente posset applicare et de ipsa terra pro sue uoluntatis arbitrio disponere et ordinare. Pro huiusmodi tradicionis mercede pollicitus est eidem rex Francie principatum Wallie [a] sibi et heredibus suis se daturum. Sed quia nichil occultum quod non reueletur [1] signis quibuscumque precedentibus aliquibus regis fidelibus et eciam ipsi regi de prodicione fit suspectus. Quo male sibi conscio et se a curia subtrahente mittitur circumquaque ad eum querendum et reducendum. [b] Rege igitur apud Cantuar' tunc agente captus est idem proditor in Cancia et London' adductus, super quem inuenta

[a] Corr. MS²
[b] Conuenerat siquidem cum rege ... reducendum marked uacat MS²

[1] Matt. 10:26, Luke 12:2

of the realm and also nearly all the suffragans of his province.

Thomas de Turberville, a knight and native of the Marches and a personal servant and close friend of the king of England, had been sent with the same king's army in the previous year to Gascony.   There, together with some other soldiers of his company, he was captured in battle by the French and when in their power was put under close guard.   During this time a plot was hatched between him and the king of France to deceive the king of England and betray him by his counsel. When this had been arranged he escaped as if by stealth from his imprisonment and returned to England.   He went to the king and was joyfully received by him.   He had agreed with the king of France that he would raise all England, Ireland, Scotland and Wales in war at one and the same time, so that while the king of England was engaged on all sides the French army could put ashore at whatever English port it chose without any difficulty or resistance, and rule and organise the country as it wished.   The king of France promised to give the principality of Wales to Turberville and his heirs as a reward for his treachery.   But as ' there is nothing hid that shall not be revealed ' [1] by some sign or other, some of the king's faithful subjects and even the king himself began to suspect a plot because of certain indications. Turberville, having a bad conscience, left the court, so the king sent everywhere to look for him and bring him back.   The traitor was captured in Kent while the king was at Canterbury and was conducted to London.   They found on him letters from the king of France to him and

sunt breuia tam sibi a rege Francie quam transcripta breuium ab ipso regi Francie transmissorum tanquam predicionis huiusmodi instrumenta ipsumque factum luce clarius uerificancia. Vigilia igitur sancti Dionisii[1] apud London' equis distractus est, capud eius ad Turrim transmittitur sicque [a] consumptus interiit.

Rogerus Cestrie[2] episcopus in fata decessit, cui successit Walterus de Langeton'.[b]   Willelmus Batonensis et Wellensis episcopus summus regis Anglie ad scaccarium thesaurarius non sine regis et suorum offensa grauiori a sue dignitatis officio ignominiose summotus pacem regiam duobus librarum millibus sibi redemit numeratis cui substituit rex dominum Walterum de Langeton' garderobe sue thesaurarium.[c]   Rex Anglie circa festum sancti Andree[3] parlamentum suum tenuit apud Westmonasterium in quo ordinauit quod in subsidium guerre sue de burgis et dominicis suis septimum caperet denarium.   De ceteris uero undecimus sibi denarius est concessus.   Collectores in Suffolch' fuerunt domini P[etrus] de Melles miles et R[adulfus] Bomund clericus [d][4]: ut autem ad spiritualia uentum est responsum accepit a clero quod ipse per statuta sua Deo et ecclesie detestabilia / multa contra statum et in preiudicium ipsius ecclesie nuper ordinauerat, ea igitur conuencione ut errata corrigerat et statuta tam crudelia reuocaret et sanctam ecclesiam suo pristino statui restitueret concessa est ei a clero decima omnium bonorum suorum tam temporalium quam spiritualium.

f. 190ᵛ

---

[a] *Added MS²*
[b] cui successit Walterus de Langeton' *inserted in a contemporary hand in lacuna and* cui successit Walterus de Langeton' Angl' thes' *in margin MS².*
[c] Willelmus Batonensis . . . thesaurarium *marked* uacat *MS²*
[d] Collectores in . . . clericus *marked* uacat *MS²*

[1] 8 October

copies of the letters he had sent to the king of France, the means of his treason and proof clearer than day of what he had done. Therefore he was drawn by horses in London on the vigil of the feast of St Denis [1]; his head was sent to the Tower and thus he perished.

Roger, bishop of Chester,[2] died and was succeeded by Walter de Langton. William, bishop of Bath and Wells, the high treasurer of the king of England's Exchequer, was removed from the dignity of his office in disgrace and not without the grave displeasure of the king and his court. He bought the king's peace for £2,000 in cash and the king made treasurer in his place Walter de Langton, treasurer of the king's Wardrobe. About the time of St Andrew's day [3] the king of England held his parliament at Westminster, at which he ordered that a seventh penny should be taken from his boroughs and demesnes in aid of his war. The others granted him an eleventh penny. The tax-collectors in Suffolk were Peter de Melles, knight, and R[alph] Bomund, a clerk.[4] When it came to ecclesiastical property he received the reply from the clergy that in his statutes, hateful to God and the Church, he had lately enacted much contrary to the dignity of the Church and to its prejudice. So by an agreement that the king should mend his ways and revoke his cruel statutes and restore the Holy Church to its former state, the clergy granted him a tenth of all their revenues, both temporal and

---

[2] i.e. of Coventry and Lichfield; the term ' of Chester ' was sometimes used of the bishops of Coventry and Lichfield until the creation of the see of Chester in 1541; see *Handbook of British Chronology*, ed. F. M. Powicke and E. B. Fryde (1961), p. 232 *n.*

[3] 30 November

[4] cf. *Parl. Writs*, pp. 45–6

Ita tamen quod tam taxacio quam collectio per ecclesiasticos non regios ministros ordinaretur. Qui etsi
donum qualiterqualiter acceptasset promissum tamen
non dum adimpleuit huius concessionis, in episcopatu
Norwicensi collectores sunt constituti de sancto Edmundo
in Suffolch' et de Wimundham in Norfolch' priores ut
ante.[1]

Gylebertus comes Glouern' et Hertford' in crastino
sancti Nicholai [2] diem clausit extremum. Qui apud
Theskesbiri tumulatus iuxta progenitorum suorum
monumenta decenter est sepultus. Rex Anglie Natale
Domini apud sanctum Albanum celebrauit. Stola
naualis exercitus regis Anglie Gasconiam petiturus
ducibus dominis Eadmundo fratre suo et H[enrico] de
Lacy comite Lincoln' apud Plummeth' in Cornub' mari
se contulerunt die sancti Stephani. In isto exercitu
ccc. et lx. naues fuerunt numerate uigintique nautarum
milia.[a]

1296

Rex Anglie ad sanctum Eadmundum in crastino sancti
Mauri [3] accessit et in crastino eiusdem loci conuentum
laute et copiose pauit et procurauit. Nauigium regis
Anglie Gasconiam profecturum in festo commemora-
cionis sancti Pauli in Britann' applicuit.[4] Rex Anglie a
sancto Eadmundo diuertens uersus Scociam sibi iam
factam rebellum cum magno diuertit excercitu.[b]

---

[a] *Lacuna of 2 lines MS*

[b] *The text in MS ends 6 lines from the end of the page and recommences in another
hand and a browner ink at the head of f. 191; added in a mid-fourteenth-century charter-
hand at the foot of f. 190ᵛ is the note:* Anno Domini M.CCC.LII. die sancte
Katerine que fuit in die dominica circa horam nonam inopinate crescente
uento nimis magno cum tonitruo ultra modum horribili et coruscacione
ualida uno et eodem momento subito uidebatur et nocte precedenti uentus
nocte media horribilis et cito pertransiens audiebatur. Illo tempore

spiritual. It was stipulated, however, that the assessment and collection should be done by ecclesiastical and not by royal officials. Although the king had accepted the gift on these conditions he had not yet fulfilled these promised concessions. In the bishopric of Norwich the prior of Bury St Edmunds in Suffolk and the prior of Wymondham in Norfolk were made collectors as before.[1]

Gilbert, earl of Gloucester and Hertford, died on the morrow of the feast of St Nicholas.[2] He was honourably buried in his family tomb at Tewkesbury. The king of England kept Christmas at St Albans. The king of England's fleet, bound for Gascony under the leadership of the king's brother, Edmund, and Henry de Lacy, earl of Lincoln, set sail from Plymouth in Cornwall [sic] on St Stephen's day. There were three hundred and sixty ships in this force and twenty thousand sailors.

1296

The king of England arrived at Bury St Edmunds on the morrow of the feast of St Maurus's day[3] and on the next day at his own expense he feasted the convent lavishly and generously. The king of England's fleet, bound for Gascony, put in at Brittany on the feast of the Commemoration of St Paul.[4] The king of England left Bury St Edmunds and set out with a large army for Scotland, which had now rebelled against him.

---

crastino Omnium Sanctorum uenit Bancus regis Anglie apud Sanctum Edmundum et sedit hic illo termino tunc iusticiariis Willelmo de Scharishill' et W. Basset. *In margin in pencil is* xxii. ann' pre' an' euang' annum Dionys'.

[1] For their appointment, dated 11 December 1295, see *CPR, 1292–1301*, p. 173. Possibly ' ut ante ' refers to the fact that they were deputy collectors of the papal sexennial tenth of 1291; Lunt, *Financial Relations*, p. 633.
[2] 7 December   [3] 16 January   [4] 25 January

f. 191   Anno Domini M.CC.XCVI. dies Pasche fuit viii. Kal. Aprilis et annus bisextilis.   Littere dominicales A et G.

Iohannes dictus Romanus[1] Eboracensis archiepiscopus uiam uniuerse carnis ingressus; cui successit magister Henricus de Newewerk[2] eiusdem loci decanus. Rex Anglie ut supra Scociam tendens die ueneris in septimana Pasche tercio Kal. Aprilis quamdam famosam uillam Scocie Berwik dictam potenti sibi uirtute subiugauit, ix. milibus de Scotis neci traditis; sed econtra uersipelles Scoti subdola conspiracione concepta partes Northanumbrorum atque Comberland' grandi depopulacione uastauerunt. Ecclesiis seu rebus ecclesiasticis non parcentes, plusquam c.xx. uillas diro incendio consumpserunt. Prioratum eciam de Exselpham cum tota uilla combusserunt: ubi ferunt quamdam crucifixi saluatoris ymaginem terribili uoce uindictam exclamasse cum quidam Scoticus laminas eius pedibus affixas irreuerenter eius pedibus abstrahebat. Dehinc uero perpessi sunt stragem non modicam in obsidione castri de Dunbar, ubi fuga uniuersaliter contenti ab Anglis tanquam uenacione ferali exagitati sunt atque stupendis ludibriis deputati. Ibi iugulati sunt viii. milia hominum: ibi eciam occubuit dominus Patricius[3] qui flos milicie dicebatur.

Petrus Meronensis[4] qui quondam summi pontificatus insignitus honore eidem dignitati cesserat et honori in senectute bona obdormiuit in Domino.

Hybernenses[5] et Walenses uocati ingenti numero uenerunt ad dominum regem ad adiutorium prestandum; qui perfusi super faciem terre sicut locuste omnem resistentem potestatem loris arcioribus con-

[1] John Romanus or le Romeyn, archbishop of York 1286–96, died 11 March

In the year of Our Lord 1296 Easter was on 25 March. It was a leap-year and the Dominical letters were A and G.

John called le Romeyn,[1] archbishop of York, died and was succeeded by Master Henry de Newark,[2] dean of York. On Friday in Easter week, 30 March, the king of England, who as mentioned above had set out for Scotland, captured by his military skill the famous town of Berwick in Scotland and slaughtered nine thousand Scotsmen. But the cunning Scots made a clever plot and plundered and sacked the regions of Northumberland and Cumberland. They spared neither churches nor ecclesiastical property and burnt down over a hundred and twenty townships. They even set fire to the priory and town of Hexham; it is said that a statue of the crucified Saviour there cried vengeance in a terrible voice when a Scotsman irreverently tore away the pedestal attached to the feet. Afterwards the Scots suffered a serious defeat at the siege of Dunbar castle. They fled headlong all together, hunted by the English like wild beasts amid general derision. Eight thousand men were killed and Patrick [3] who was called ' the flower of knighthood ' fell.

Peter de Morrone,[4] who had previously been distinguished with the honour of supreme pontiff and had resigned from that honour and dignity, died at a great old age.

The Irish [5] and the Welsh were summoned and came in great numbers to help the king. They poured over the face of the earth like locusts. They bound tightly

---

[2] Henry Newark, consecrated 15 June 1298
[3] Patrick Graham; cf. Guisborough, p. 278
[4] Peter de Morrone, Celestine V   [5] *Dunst.* pp. 403-4

stringebant aut trucidabant, non nullos uero exulari proscripcione cohercuerant. Est quidem in prouincia

f. 191ᵛ quadam Scocie que Lochenes [1] dicitur castellum pre-/ cipuum et robustissimum, utpote in eminentis rupis uertice constitutum omni castrensi robore munitissimum, Puellarum siue Edineburth [2] dictum. Ad huius castri refugium propter sui securitatem et firmitatem multi de Scotis confugerant. Obsesso igitur castro per Anglorum excercitum uidebatur quasi inexpugnabile. Angli tamen condensauerunt pregrandem terre cumulum quasi montulum, super quo machinis compositis massis plumbeis tamquam pro lapidibus ad loci predicti confusionem caucius et directius [a] iacerent. Ecce nunc loca feriantur concaua, nunc subteranea. Eya cuncta regi nostro applaudenter subministrant elementa. Aer inportabilibus massarum iactibus quibus transuerberantur muri, nec loca tutaminis inclusos tueri preualebant. Terra[m] uero tamquam insolidam se prestitit dum numquam suis Scoticis uel pedem contulit in bello solidatum, uel solum quondam proprium bellantibus Anglis non euacuatum. Fuit eciam predicto castello fons quasi perpetuo scaturiens qui tunc exsiccatus ita fuerat ut nec inclusis tuta fuerit interioris tuicionis. Obrui igitur [b] omnem locum munitum Scocie sub inestimabilis breuitatis compendio consecutus est rex Anglie.

Constantinus comes Holandie et Selandie [3] quorundam domesticorum suorum fraudibus et insidiis

---

[a] directiuus MS

[b] interioris tuicionis obnui; igitur . . . *The passage appears to be corrupt MS*

[1] Loch Ness: presumably an error for Lothian
[2] cf. the account of the capture in Guisborough, p. 279, and Rishanger, p. 160.
[3] The name of the murdered count of Holland was not Constantine but Florence. The same mistake occurs above, p. 120.

with thongs or killed everyone who resisted them, and denounced some so that they were forced to go into exile. In the province of Scotland called Loch Ness [1] there is a famous and mighty fortress, built on the top of a high rock and strongly fortified with every military defence, called Maidens' Castle, otherwise Edinburgh.[2] Many Scotsmen fled to the shelter of this citadel because of its safety and strength. When the English army besieged the fortress it seemed impregnable. The English, however, heaped together a great mound of earth like a small mountain and on it put their machines, so that they could hurl carefully and accurately lumps of lead instead of stones, to the confusion of the citadel; low-lying places and even underground ones could be struck. See how all the elements combined admiringly to serve our king!—the air with an insupportable rain of metal which battered holes in the walls so that no place of safety could protect the besieged; the very ground did not seem solid and offered no firm foothold to the Scotsmen in battle, nor was there any land which once had been theirs now free of the warring English; there was a spring in the fortress which flowed continually, which now had dried up, so that there would be no safety for the besieged even in the innermost places of the castle. And thus the king of England succeeded in destroying every fortified place in Scotland in an extraordinarily short time.

Constantine, count of Holland and Zeeland,[3] was trapped by the treachery and plots of some of his

circumuentus uigilia sancti Botulphi [1] gladiis confossus est.

Iohannes nuper rex Scocie uigilia sancti Iohannis Baptiste regie clemencie se submisit ad uillam sancti Iohannis que precipua est tocius Scocie quam rex sibi subiugauerat. Rege igitur Scocie libere custodie deputato assignati sunt ei delectandi limites in canibus et auibus in prouincia que comitatui Londoniensi adiacet circumquaque per xx. miliaria. Ceteri uero regni potentes circumquaque per ciuitates Anglie carceribus includuntur. Rex igi/tur Anglie omne regnum Scocie dominacioni sue subdidit et regimini. Vnde ex Anglia, Scocia et Wallia monarchiam quondam tocius Britannie per multa tempora decisam et truncatam occupauit. Tanta peracta uictoria sub tante celeritatis compendio in tante necessitatis articulo uix recolitur a quoquam regie dignitatis uiro. Creata sunt enim contra eundem regem bella debacancia in Vasconia, in Wallia, in Scocia; et nauali bello per maria ubique tamen fide et ueritate seruata felicius dimicauit, cum tamen hostes marini nauigium suum in decuplum numerositate superabant. Ex Wallia uno capto principe, altero subacto [2]: ex Scocia siquidem, ut dictum est, nobiliter triumphauit. Rex igitur Anglie totam Scociam legibus suis Anglicanis adductam per ministros suos fore decreuit custodiendam et regendam. Hiis ergo rite peractis et expeditis idem rex cum excercitu suo Angliam peciit, uersus sanctum Edmundum iter suum dirigens; ibidemque parliamentum suum cum proceribus et magnatibus regni instituit celebrandum.

f. 192

---

[1] 16 June

[2] Madog, leader of the men of north Wales, surrendered to Edward on 31 July 1295 (*Wig.*, p. 522), and Morgan, leader of the men of Glamorgan, some time in the summer of 1295 (Guisborough, p. 252).

servants and stabbed by their swords on the eve of
St Botolph's day.[1]

John, formerly king of Scotland, submitted to the
king's mercy on the eve of the feast of St John the
Baptist at Perth, the largest town in the whole of
Scotland, which the king had conquered. The king of
Scotland was put under open arrest; the area within a
twenty-mile radius of the county of London was assigned
to him for hunting and hawking. The other magnates
of Scotland were put in chains in cities throughout
England. Thus the king of England reduced the whole
kingdom of Scotland to his power and rule, and so
obtained absolute power over England, Scotland and
Wales, the former kingdom of Britain long torn and
divided. Such a victory by any person of royal rank,
achieved so swiftly in such a short time and in so great
an emergency, could hardly be recalled. For savage
wars raged against the king in Gascony, Wales and
Scotland, and he fought engagements at sea to a happy
issue everywhere and preserved faith and truth, even
though his enemies outnumbered his ships by ten to one.
In Wales he captured one prince and subdued another.[2]
In Scotland, as has been said, he triumphed nobly: the
king of England put all Scotland under his English laws
and ordained that it should be watched over and
governed by his officials. When he had successfully
accomplished this he left with his army for England and
directed his journey to Bury St Edmunds. There he
ordered his parliament to be held with the chief men
and magnates of the realm.

Mortuo comite Glouernie Gilberto [1] adhesit quidem iuuenis nomine Radulphus de marchia oriundus cognomine Monthermer [2] a secretis comitisse; quo militaribus a rege peticione dicte comitisse accincto sollempnitate tepide uel publice non promulgata dictam comitissam desponsauit. Quo audito rex militem incarcerauit. Comitissam filiamque suam curtatis libere condicionis habenis in abbacia sanctimonialium de Ambreberi inclusit. Sed post hoc agente ecclesia que iusti fouet contractum matrimonii uirum suum recepit. Ipsa quoque ad peticionem comitum et baronum a custodia reuocata in terris suis restituta est. Rex tamen totum

f. 192ᵛ honorem Tunbregie retinu/it, sed postea dicto comiti resignauit.[3] Dominus Robertus de Wer comes Oxonie [4] migrauit ad Dominum in crastino sancti Bartholomei apostoli. Rex parleamentum suum tenuit apud sanctum Edmundum in crastino Animarum a clero et a cetero populo subsidium terre sue specialiter petiturus. Quo accedens extra scepta monasterii in domum cuiusdam Henrici de Len declinauit; ibique quamdiu in uilla commoratus est pernoctabat. Quod quidem hospicium multis cessit in offendiculum tamquam regie excellencie inhonestum et regibus preteritis temporibus inusitatum. Ne archiepiscopi Cantuar' suspecta presencia in crucis baiulacione et benedicionis largicione priuilegiis siue exempcioni ecclesie sancti Edmundi derogaret, litteras suas patentes manu publica conscriptas priusquam eiusdem ecclesie exemptos limites subintraret tam pro se quam pro successoribus suis

---

[1] Gilbert de Clare, 6th earl of Gloucester 1262 to 22 December 1295
[2] Joan of Acre married Ralph de Monthermer, a member of the late earl's household, early in 1297; G.E.C., *Complete Peerage*, v, p. 709.
[3] cf. Rishanger, p. 173; Guisborough, p. 259; *Dunst.*, p. 407. The honour of Tonbridge was restored by Letters Patent in November 1301;

After the death of Gilbert, earl of Gloucester,[1] a young man called Ralph, surnamed Monthermer,[2] a native of the Marches, became intimate with the countess. At her petition the king knighted him. Ralph then married the countess with little ceremony and no public announcement. When the king heard this he imprisoned the knight and immured the countess and her daughter with restricted freedom in the convent of Amesbury. But then through the agency of the Church, which supports a true contract of marriage, she got back her husband. The countess was also released from custody at the petition of the earls and barons and her lands restored. The king, however, kept all the honour of Tonbridge but afterwards relinquished it to the said earl.[3] Robert de Vere, earl of Oxford,[4] died on the morrow of the feast of St Bartholomew the Apostle. The king held his parliament at Bury St Edmunds on the morrow of All Souls' day especially to ask the clergy and the rest of the people for an aid to help his country. When he arrived he went to the house of Henry de Lynn, outside the limits of the monastery; he slept there as long as he remained in town. Many people were offended by this form of hospitality as unworthy of royalty and not usually offered to kings in former times. Lest the archbishop's presence, which was regarded with mistrust in respect of the bearing of his cross and his bestowal of benediction, should detract from the privileges and exemption of St Edmund's church, the king granted letters patent formally drawn up before he entered the exempt limits of this church, making them

---

Cal. of Chancery Warrants, I, p. 147.
      [4] Robert de Vere, 5th earl of Oxford 1263–96. The date of his death, 25 August, was unknown to the editors of G.E.C., *Complete Peerage*, x, p. 218.

perpetuo munimine eidem fecit ualituras. Quique domini regis peticioni super ante petito *a* obtemperare distulisset, aut quantum ad ipsum fuit denegasset ab eodem rege lacessitus publice iniuriis sine honore derelinquitur. Plebs laicorum breui prehabito consilio xii. denarios omnium bonorum, et burgenses vii.[1] denarios regi concesserunt. Archiepiscopus cum clero consilium suum tenuit apud sanctum Edmundum in quo nouam constitucionem papalem publicauit que precise prohibet ne quis ecclesiastica persona potestati *b* seculari inconsulto summo pontifice aliquid quoquo modu seu quouis colore exquisito contribueret. Hec est bulla domini pape: 'Bonefacius etc. Ad perpetuam rei memoriam: clericis laicos infestos opido tradit antiquitas

f. 193 etc.'[2] Habita igitur disputacione su/per pretacta constitucione, uiam per quam regie uoluntati condescendere possent sine periculo non inuenerunt. Archiepiscopus igitur pro se et pro toto clero illud idem regi innotuit. Quibus intellectis dominus rex archiepiscopum ceterosque prelatos ac totum clerum Anglie ab illo die grauare et molestare decreuit clero prefigens diem ulteriorem in octauis sancti Hillarii[3] apud Londoniam. Interim rex cum proceribus regni sollempniter celebrauit et pacem indixit ecclesie. Rex festum sancti Edmundi[4] conuentum pauit.

Nuncii regis Anglie ad parliamentum regis Francie transfretauerunt. Resus[5] quidam filius Resi, uir potens

---

a petitis *MS*   *b* potestate *MS*

[1] According to Guisborough, p. 286, and Rishanger, p. 165, the burgesses granted an eighth.   [2] *Foedera*, I, p. 836
[3] 20 January. See F. M. Powicke, *The Thirteenth Century* (1953), p. 675
[4] 20 November
[5] Apparently the brother of Maelgwn, who was the son of Rhys Fychan ap Rhys ap Maelgwn (G. T. O. Bridgeman, *History of the Princes of South Wales* (1876), p. 209 and the text on p. 207). Maelgwn was the leader of

binding for its perpetual protection, both for himself and for his successors. Whoever should have hesitated to comply with the king's demand mentioned above or refused as much as he could, was publicly attacked by the king and dishonoured. After a brief consultation the laity granted the king a twelfth penny of all revenues and the burgesses granted a seventh penny.[1] The archbishop held his council with the clergy at Bury St Edmunds. In it the new papal constitution was made public. It definitely forbade any ecclesiastical person to pay anything to the secular power in any manner or under any pretext whatever, however elaborate, without consulting the pope. This is the papal bull: ' Boniface etc. In perpetual memory of this affair; past history teaches us that the laity are very hostile to the clergy. . . .'[2] After a debate on this constitution they could find no way by which they would be able to concede to the king's wish without danger. So the archbishop, speaking for himself and the whole clergy, informed the king of this. When the king heard this he decided that from a given day he would harass and molest the archbishop and other prelates and all the clergy of England: he fixed the day for the clergy['s decision] as the octave of the feast of St Hilary,[3] in London. Till then he declared peace between himself and the Church. The king solemnly kept the feast of St Edmund [4] with the chief men of the realm and entertained the convent.

The king of England's ambassadors crossed the sea to [attend] the parliament of the king of France. Rhys,[5]

---

the Welsh of west Wales, and no doubt his brother Rhys had been ' on the run ' since the collapse of the rising in the summer of 1295. No other chronicler mentions the surrender of Rhys, news of which seems to have reached the king while he was staying at St Edmunds. Rhys and another brother Griffith suffered a long imprisonment in Norwich castle (*CCR, 1307–13*, pp. 12, 33, ibid., *1318–23*, p. 65).—V. H. G.

Wallie potestate constipatus ac hostis Anglorum quasi
munitus die sancti Edmundi hora qua rex ibidem
instabat missarum sollempniis una cum complicibus
suis regie paci se sponte conformauit, eiusdemque
subieccioni collum suum mansuete subiugauit. Super
quo idem rex martiri ubique mirifico grates persoluens
debitas oblaciones suas eidem humili deuocione destinauit.

Rex cum moram fecisset apud sanctum Edmundum
per tres septimanas,[1] iter arripuit uersus Clare; set ante
dissessum suum illud altare quod extra septa monasterii
fecerit speciali priuilegio ne ex consequenti preiudicium
ecclesie generaret in frustra concidit et particulatim
diuisit. Rex Natale Domini apud Gipiswicum celebrauit. Nuncii regis Anglie omni spe pacis frustrati a
curia Francorum reuertentes in Angliam redierunt.

1297

Hoc anno sequenti fuit littera dominicalis F.

Margareta [2] filia regis Anglie et ducat[iss]a Brabancie
die sancti Sebastiani [3] portum peciit ad partes tendens
Brabancias. Elisabeth filia regis Anglie nupta est
f. 193ᵛ comiti Hoyland '.[4] Nota / quod filia regis senior
Elienora dicta nupsit comiti de Bars [5]: altera uero
Iohanna comiti Glouernie Gilberto: tercia Margareta
duci Brabanico ut dictum est: quarta Elisabeth comiti

---

[1] From 8 or 9 November to 29 November 1296
[2] Margaret married John II, duke of Brabant 1294–1312, in 1290.
[3] 20 January
[4] John I, count of Holland and Zeeland 1296–9. He married Elizabeth
in 1296.
[5] Eleanor, widow of Alfonso III of Aragon, married Henry III, count
of Bar 1296–8, in 1293.

son of Rhys, a powerful man backed by the strength of Wales and apparently a strongly entrenched enemy of the English, voluntarily submitted with his confederates to the king's peace on the feast of St Edmund at the hour when the king was attending high mass at Bury. He bowed his neck in dutiful subjection to the king. Because of this the king gave due thanks to the martyr, whose miraculous power is universal, and made offerings with humble devotion.

After the king had stayed at Bury St Edmunds for three weeks [1] he set out for Clare. Before he left he dismantled and broke into small pieces the altar which he had erected by a special dispensation outside the boundaries of the monastery, lest as a result it should be prejudicial to the church. The king kept Christmas at Ipswich. The king of England's ambassadors left the French court after they had lost all hope of peace and returned to England.

1297

In the following year the Dominical letter was F.

Margaret,[2] the king of England's daughter and duchess of Brabant, set sail for Brabant on St Sebastian's day.[3] Elizabeth, the king of England's daughter, was married to the count of Holland.[4] It should be remembered that the king's eldest daughter, called Eleanor, married the count of Bar.[5] His second daughter, Joan, married Gilbert, earl of Gloucester. The third, Margaret, was married to the duke of Brabant, as has been said. The fourth, Elizabeth, was married to the

Hoyland': quinta [1] sanctimonialis facta est apud Ambrebir'. Comes Flandrie nuncios una cum litteris suis obligatoriis domino regi Anglie super federe cum eodem prelocuto sollempniter destinauit [a]; et sic nauale bellum inter Anglicos et Flandrenses sedauit et facti sunt amici qui prius fuerant detestabiles inimici.

Generalis conuocacio cleri facta est apud Londonias in octauis sancti Hillarii [2] ad tractandum de pace sancte ecclesie Anglicane et regis comminacionibus et de pressuris uoluntariis obuiando. Sic communi omnium assensu plus regem eternum timencium quam momentaneum et animarum periculum quam lapsum rerum temporalium decretum est sacra summi pastoris uniuersalis ecclesie decreta feruenti debere constancia ab omnibus illibata custodiri et incontaminata. Et hoc per sollempnes nuncios ipsius cleri una cum periculis in constitucione papali iminentibus regi demandatum est. Ad quod quidem rex motus inauditam duriciam contra sanctam ecclesiam excercere disposuit ut ipsam dominam et mundi reginam citra iuste tuicionis obumbracionem derelictam faucibusque sceleratorum et diripiencium expositam ab omni priuaret proteccione curiali [et] conueniencia, quinpocius uideretur eius infestatoribus exasperacionum calcaria ministrare. [3] Preterea secundum quosdam mandauit edictum ne laycos clericis infestos equisque supra quadraginta solidos appreciatis spoliantes censura iusticie curialis cohiberet. Die uero quo rex hanc miseram contra

---

[a] defuit MS

[1] Mary, born 1279, took the veil at Amesbury, Wilts, at the age of 17, along with her grandmother Eleanor, wife of Henry III, and thirteen others: later, a nun at Fontevrault. Margaret's marriage, which is only

count of Holland.   The fifth [1] became a nun at Amesbury.   The count of Flanders sent formal ambassadors
with letters of alliance to the king of England concerning
the treaty he had already discussed with him.   Thus he
calmed the strife at sea between the English and the men
of Flanders; those who before had been bitter enemies
were made friends.

A general convocation of the clergy met in London
on the octave of the feast of St Hilary [2] to discuss the
peace of the Holy English Church and the king's threats
and how to resist ' voluntary ' prises.   As the assembly
feared the Eternal King more than him who was king
for the time and the peril of their souls more than the
hazards of worldly affairs, it was ordained by the
common assent of everyone that the holy decree of the
chief shepherd of the universal Church ought to be
maintained with passionate constancy inviolate and un-
touched.   This was announced to the king by formal
messengers, together with the punishments threatened
in the papal decree.   At this the king was angry and
determined to treat Holy Church with unheard-of
rigour, to the extent of depriving the lady and queen of
the world, abandoned without a shadow of rightful
protection and exposed to the fangs of wicked men and
robbers, of the help and protection of the law courts;
indeed he seemed rather to spur on her enemies.[3]
Moreover according to some he published an edict
that the censure of the courts of law should not extend
to laymen attacking clerks and robbing them of horses
worth more than 40s.   On the day when the king issued

---

a matter of hearsay (' ut dictum est ') here, was fully recorded and dated
under 1290, above, p. 95.—V. H. G.

[2] 20 January   [3] cf. *CPR, 1293–1301*, p. 239
   (2,683)   21

clerum tulit sentenciam quamplures de nobilioribus sui
excercitus in Wasconia in prelio contra Francos cecid-
f. 194 erunt.[1] / Quidam capti fuerunt ex quibus dompnus
Iohannes de sancto Iohanne nuper regis senescallus in
Wasconia [2] unus erat, et multi alii. Hostes etenim in
insidiis latitantes inopinato inpetu numerositate
triumphabant. Plures de clero proprie salutis in-
memores et terrena tantum sapientes mentes amplectantes
uacillando femineas, ueluti regis secretarii et aulici [3]
primitus cum dicto rege pacem pepigerunt; statuta
papalia penitus postponentes summam quinte partis
omnium bonorum suorum tam spiritualium quam
temporalium regi concesserunt. Rex omnia laica feoda
archiepiscoporum, episcoporum, religiosorum et aliorum
clericorum cuiuscunque gradus et condicionis qui proteccionem non acceperant, necnon et omnia bona
eorundem ubicumque extra scepta ecclesiastica inuenta
in manu sua seysiri fecit.[4] Ob quam causam predicta
bona sic capta graui depopulacione confiscantur.
Dompnus rex parliamentum suum cum laicis ad hoc
tantum uocatis apud Sar[isberiam] in die Cinerum [5]
tenuit de expedicione guerre suo contra regem Francie
tractaturus. Vnde dompnus rex quosdam de comitibus
uidelicet constabularium [6] et mariscallum [7] Anglie
admonuit ut secum transfretarent aut saltem Wascon'
peterent; cuius uoto non annuentes nec posse nec uelle
uerbis excusatoriis terram propriam tot inimicis cir-

---

[1] Guisborough, p. 287, says the same thing, though less positively; cf.
Flores, III, p. 100.

[2] John de St John, Edward I's lieutenant in Gascony 1293, seneschal and
chief counsellor of John of Brittany when lieutenant of Aquitaine 1294,
captured by French near Bellegarde 1297, died 1302 (*DNB*).

[3] cf. *Flores*, III, p. 291: 'falsi clerici, aulici curiales . . . qui postulatis
consilium dederant et fauorem.'

[4] For Edward I's instructions to the sheriff of Worcester see *Wig.*, p. 580.

this cruel sentence against the clergy, many of the nobles in his army fell in a battle against the French in Gascony.[1] Some men were captured, among whom was John de St John, formerly the king's seneschal in Gascony,[2] and many others, for the enemy triumphed by weight of numbers after lying in ambush and attacking suddenly. Many of the clergy forgot their own salvation and were but worldly-wise; they acted with the weakness of women, as for instance the king's clerks and courtiers [3] who immediately tried to make peace with the king. They put the papal statute wholly on one side and granted the king a fifth part of all their revenues both spiritual and temporal. The king seized into his hands all the lay fees of the archbishops, bishops, the religious orders and the other clergy of every rank and condition who had not accepted protection, and all their property wherever it was to be found outside ecclesiastical boundaries.[4] For the aforesaid reason the property which had been taken in this way was confiscated and suffered grave pillage. The king held his parliament, with the laity who alone had been summoned, at Salisbury on Ash Wednesday [5] to discuss the question of his military expedition against the king of France. There the king asked certain earls, that is the constable [6] and marshal [7] of England, to cross the Channel with him or at least go to Gascony. They did not consent to his request and explained firmly by way of excuse that they neither could nor would quit their own country when it was surrounded by so many

---

[5] 27 February
[6] Humphrey de Bohun, 7th earl of Hereford 1275–98, hereditary constable of England
[7] Roger Bigod, 5th earl of Norfolk 1270–1306, hereditary marshal

cumuallatam exire et desolatam relinquere expresse
pandebant. Rex uero responsa eorum ab illo die tacite
gestabat.

Memorandum quod die Cinerum confiscata sunt
omnia bona et omnia maneria seisita abbatis et
conuentus sancti Edmundi una cum burgo sancti
Edmundi. Tercio congregatus est totus clerus apud
f. 194ᵛ London' circa mediam Quadragesimam de innumer/is
exaccionibus et contumeliis ac iniustis dampnis ecclesie
sancte et clero indies illatis exquisite tractaturus. Cum
per octo dies disputando laborassent adhuc aliquam
uiam regie potestati sine periculo complacendi super
contribucione petita non inuenerunt. Et hoc regis
consilio finaliter responderunt. In eodem consilio
quidam frater ¹ de ordine predicatorum affirmabat
publica uoce coram omnibus regis peticionem iustam
esse, cuius se iusticiam coram summo pontifice defen-
surum irreuerberata fronte protestatus est. Item, rex
diem indixit citra quem de clero qui proteccionem
non haberent omnia mobilia in maneriis inuenta forisfacta
iudicabantur, nullumque seruicium a laicis haberent.
Rex eciam possessiones eorum pro uelle suo distribueret.
Et si quandoque extra consilii tuicionem inuenti
fuerint quasi hostes puplici ergastulo punirentur.

Obiit episcopus ² Sar[um] cui successit magister
Symon de Gaunt euisdem loci canonicus.

Anno Domini M.CC.XCVII. Littera dominicalis F et
dies Pasche fuit xviii. Kal. Mai.

Memorandum quod secunda nocte post dominicam

---

¹ cf. *Flores*, III, pp. 100, 294: 'quidam causidici et duo de ordine
praedicatorum, temporalem et regalem fauorem quaerentes, insistunt
argumentis probare clerum ipsi regi in tempore belli, non obstante consti-
tutione apostolica de suis facultatibus, posse licite subuenire.' William
Hothum, prior provincial of the Friars Preachers, was made archbishop

enemies and leave it deserted. From that day the king bore their reply in mind without saying anything.

It must be remembered that on Ash Wednesday all the goods of the abbot and convent of Bury St Edmunds were confiscated and all their manors together with St Edmund's borough. The whole clergy met for the third time in London about the middle of Lent to discuss in detail the innumerable exactions, injuries and unjust losses daily inflicted on the Church and clergy. When they had argued this way and that for eight days over the contribution requested, they still did not find any way of complying with the royal authority without peril. Finally they gave this answer to the king's council. In this council a friar [1] of the Preaching order publicly affirmed before everyone that the king's request was just and declared with shameless effrontery that he would defend its justice before the pope. The king named a day after which all the chattels found on the manors of those of the clergy who would not have protection should be adjudged forfeited, and they should have no service from laymen. The king would distribute their property as he wished. If even they were found without the protection of the council they were to be punished by imprisonment as public enemies.

The bishop of Salisbury [2] died and was succeeded by Master Simon de Gaunt, a canon of Salisbury.

In the year of the Lord 1297 the Dominical letter was F and Easter day was on 14 April.

It should be recorded that on the second night after

---

of Dublin soon afterwards; see below, p. 150, for his death (30 August 1298).—V. H. G.

[2] Nicholas Longespée, bishop of Salisbury 1291–7

Palmarum [1] ante matutinalem sinaxin [2] facta fuit horibilis elementorum concussio, tonitrua, fulgura, ignis et grando inauditoimpetu in inuicem conflixerunt. Erat autem pregrandis grando experimento mirifica que uirilis pol[l]icis coequebatur circumferencie. Et post nocturnos ymnos facta est eclipsis lune iteratoque consimilis tempestas uti resumptis uiribus ualide perstrepuit. Item, die translacionis sancti Edmundi [3] ante solis ortum est terre motus magnus per plura loca Norfolchie. Quidam monachus de Waldena, Symon dictus, habundanter sciencie clericalis fonte potatus in uniuersitate Cantebrigie incepit et docuit iura canonica.[4]

Rex indixit parliamentum apud Lincolniam in octauis sancti Iohannis Baptiste [5] in quo orta est dis-
f. 195 sen/sio inter ipsum et quosdam comites et barones regni quod tam clerum quam populum intollerabili onere conabatur obprimere. Petebat enim iterato a clero medietatem omnium bonorum suorum, a laicis uero sextum denarium et a burgis tercium denarium. Responderunt ergo comites et barones sine assensu archiepiscopi Cantuar' et tocius cleri tam onerosam et inportabilem exactionem se nullo modo subire, sed petebant instanter bona pocius ecclesie sancte et sua iniuste a regiis ministris comuniter capta indilate restitui, et articulos et punctos in magna carta contentos de cetero obseruari. Quorum iustis postulacionibus rex non adquieuit sed ulterius dissimulando negocium pro-

---

[1] 9 April
[2] *synaxis:* a gathering of monks for praying or saying the psalms (Du Cange)   [3] 9 June
[4] For the Black Monks to go to the university was still something of a novelty—especially at Cambridge. It was during John de Northwold's abbacy that Gloucester college was founded at Oxford for the Benedictines. —V. H. G.
[5] 1 July. Cotton, p. 325, supports this date, but Lincoln is a mistake

Palm Sunday[1] before matins[2] there was a terrible storm; thunder, lightning, fire[-balls] and hail came in turn with unheard-of violence. The hailstones were immense and astonishing to witness, for their size was as big as a man's thumb. After the night hymns there was an eclipse of the moon and then the storm started again, raging with renewed violence. On the feast of the Translation of St Edmund[3] there was a big earthquake in many parts of Norfolk before sunrise. A certain monk of Walden named Simon, having drunk deep at the fount of ecclesiastical learning, incepted at the university of Cambridge and taught canon law.[4]

The king summoned a parliament at Lincoln on the octave of the feast of St John the Baptist.[5] In it a dispute arose between him and some of the earls and barons of the realm because he had tried to lay an unbearable burden on both the clergy and the laity. For he had again asked the clergy for half of all their revenues, the laity for a sixth penny and the boroughs for a third penny. The earls and barons replied without the consent of the archbishop of Canterbury and all the clergy that they would on no account submit to such a heavy and unbearable exaction, but rather they earnestly asked that the property of Holy Church and their own, which together had been unjustly seized by the royal officials, should be restored without delay, and that henceforth the clauses and terms contained in Magna Carta should be observed. The king did not agree to these just demands but artfully postponed the question.

for London. The famous 'By God, Sir King, I shall neither go nor hang' incident had occurred at the Salisbury parliament held the previous February: and a section of the baronage were in open revolt. The king, who was unable to enforce their obedience ('responsa eorum tacite gestabat') now hastened to make peace with the Church.—V. H. G.

telauit. Rex in se tandem reuersus leuiori spiritu inspiratus omnes de gremio ecclesie statuta papalia obseruantes nec transsitoriam regis tirannidem metuentes ad pacem et proteccionem suam per litteras suas uoluntarie reconciliauit. Archiepiscopus tenuit generale concilium cleri apud Londonias dominica [1] proxima post diem sancti Laurencii adhuc specialiter tractaturus de contribucione facienda quam rex tociens postulauerat set semper lesionem consciencie allegantes dissenserunt. Rex uigilia sancti Bartholomei [2] misit se in mare apud Winchilse et tercia die applicuit in Flandria apud le Swine, ubi Portuenses xvii. naves [3] de Gernemutis ignibus combusserunt et nautas [a] crudeli cede interemerunt. Hoc audiens rex tacite rem gestabat. Die sancti Egidii [4] fulminata est generalis sentencia ab uniuersis et singulis archiepiscopis, episcopis et Anglie in dyocesis suis auctoritate apostolica super omnes ecclesias et ecclesiasticas libertates nuper uiolenter

f. 195ᵛ et contra / iura ecclesiastica intrantes et in locis sacris scrutinium facientes et super omnes alios quocumque modo eisdem consencientes.

In crastino [5] exaltacionis sancte Crucis insurrexerunt Scoti contra Anglicos cum certificati fuerunt de transfretacione regis Anglie, in quo conflictu dominus Hugo de Cressingham [6] nuper factus thesaurisarius regis Scocie, captus est et capite truncatus. Comites et barones tenuerunt parliamentum suum apud Norhamton' super discordia orta inter regem et ipsos die sancti

---

[a] nautos MS

[1] 11 August; *Wig.*, p. 522, and Cotton, p. 532, give the day of St Vincent (10 August).
[2] 23 August
[3] Twenty-five according to Rishanger, p. 177. See above, p. xxxiii.
[4] 1 September

At last the king, moved by a kindlier spirit, came to himself; he freely restored to his peace and protection by royal letters all those who from the bosom of the Church had observed the papal statutes and not feared the transient tyranny of the king.   The archbishop held a general council of the clergy in London on the Sunday [1] after the feast of St Laurence, especially to discuss making the grant which was repeatedly sought by the king, but against which the clergy always protested, alleging that it hurt their consciences.   On the eve of St Bartholomew's day [2] the king put to sea from Winchelsea and three days later reached the Zwyn in Flanders.   There the Portuguese burnt seventeen ships [3] from Yarmouth and cruelly butchered the sailors.   When the king heard this he pondered it in silence.   On St Giles's day [4] a general sentence of excommunication was fulminated by each and every bishop of England in their dioceses by papal authority against everyone who previously forced their way contrary to canon law into churches and ecclesiastical liberties and made a scrutiny of the sacred places, and against all those who had in any way tolerated them.

On the morrow [5] of the feast of the Exaltation of the Holy Cross the Scots rose against the English because they had been informed that the king of England had crossed the channel.   In the clash Hugh de Cressingham,[6] who had previously been made treasurer of Scotland, was captured and beheaded.   The earls and barons held their parliament at Northampton on St

---

[5] 15 September.   This date is too late, for the battle of Stirling was on 11 September.
[6] Hugh Cressingham, treasurer of Scotland 1296–7

Mathei.[1] Edwardus filius regis tenuit parliamentum suum apud London' in festo sancti Michaelis de pace et concordia inter regem patrem suum et barones tractaturus; ubi ex communi assensu consilii regis commorantis in Anglia, archiepiscoporum, episcoporum, comitum, baronum renouata fuit magna carta Anglie et in eadem quedam addiciones apposite et munita sigillo regis de scaccario[2] et singulorum maiorum de consilio regis, et cum magna festinacione domino regi in partibus transmarinis degenti eam transmiserunt. Quam dominus rex suscipiens cum suis magnatibus ibidem presentibus habito tractatu factum commendauit, et magno sigillo suo apposito perpetuo munimine coroborauit. Quam cartam per solempnes nuncios ad barones in Anglia celebri uoto remandauit. Inter hec Scotici duce quodam Maleis[a][3] cum Willelmo Walensi fere totam terram de Northumbria, Cumberlondia, Coupeland'[4] et Westmerlond' peruagantes, rapinis et incendiis deuastarunt. Senes cum iunioribus, matres cum puerulis letali morte trucidarunt. Quos tandem compatriote resistentes in propriam patriam compulerunt remeare. Ferunt quidam tunc septingentas et f. 196 quindecim uillas / et uiculas esse uastatas. Treuge capte sunt inter reges Francie et Anglie a festo sancti Andree usque ad Carnipriuium.[5] xviii. Kal. Ianuarii

---

a maleis *MS*

[1] 21 September. The Close Roll under date 16 September refers to this gathering, with instructions for keeping the town and castle safely: *CCR, 1296–1302*, p. 129.—V. H. G.

[2] The king had taken the Great Seal to Flanders, leaving to the regent ' the Seal which was wont to be used in England while the king was in Gascony '; *Foedera*, I, p. 876.—V. H. G.

[3] The leaders of ' the army of the kingdom of Scotland ' were Andrew of Moray and William Wallace; Guisborough, p. 306. The MS reads ' Maleis,' which may be a corruption for ' Waleis,' Wallace; but it seems probable that the author meant to refer to Moray.

Matthew's day [1] to discuss the quarrel which had arisen between the king and themselves. Edward, the king's son, held his parliament in London on Michaelmas day to discuss a peace and agreement between his father, the king, and the barons. There by the common consent of the king's council remaining in England, and of the archbishops, bishops, earls and barons, the Great Charter of England and certain additions which had been made to it were renewed and confirmed by the king's Exchequer seal [2] and the seals of all the chief men of the king's council. They sent the charter in great haste to the king, who was occupied across the seas. The king received it, and after talking the matter over with his magnates, who were there with him, approved what had been done and gave it permanent force by applying his great seal. He returned the charter to the barons in England by formal messengers with a noteworthy promise.

Meanwhile the Scots, led by a certain Moray[?] [3] accompanied by William Wallace, overran nearly all Northumberland, Cumberland, Copeland [4] and Westmoreland and laid them waste by fire and robbery. They butchered old men and young, women and children. But the local inhabitants resisted and at last forced them to return to their own country. Some say that on this occasion seven hundred and fifteen towns and villages were devastated. A truce was made between the kings of France and England from St Andrew's day to Ash Wednesday.[5] On 15 January

---

[4] Copeland Forest, Cumberland
[5] 26 February

translatus fuit sanctus Lodewicus apud Parisium, quondam rex Francie de quo in uita beati Thome martiris legitur. Rex celebrauit Natale Domini in Gaunt in Flandria.

1298

Littera dominicalis E.

Quedam elongaciones treugarum inter reges affirmantur a festo Epiphanie per duos annos firme durature. Et interim missi sunt sollempnes nuncii ad curiam Romanam domino pape cuius ordinacioni et disposicioni de discordia orta inter eos totaliter se submiserunt. Quoniam rex Anglie arduis in Anglia occupatus negociis tarde in Flandriam applicuit, Francorum excercitus Flandrensibus magna dampna intulerunt. Ceperunt etenim nobiles uillas de Bruges, Dam, Ilde [1] et Curterai aliisque nonnullis flammis consumptis. Rex cum parua milicia transfretauit [2] hostesque suos astucia celebri preteriuit. Proposuerunt namque Franci ipsum in primo littoris appulsu campestri bello excepisse. Cum rex inter prudentes prudentissimus Walenses suos usque ad xxx.m. erectis lanceis signisque affixis premisit; unde exploratores Francie tot signis perteriti, eciam supra uires perteriti, tantam Anglorum regis crediderunt fuisse potenciam, quantam uexillorum numerositate conceperunt. Rex circumuallatus periculo a tergo uidit intensis manibus suis quo doluit, preuidit hostes in patulo quo timere debuit, lateraque sua quasi militum

---

[1] Ilde *sic* MS: Lille? For Philip le Bel's capture of Lille see Nangis, *Chron.*, I, p. 301.

[2] The king's crossing to Flanders has already been mentioned above, p. 141.

St Louis, the former king of France, was translated at Paris: concerning him is to be read in the life of St Thomas the martyr. The king kept Christmas at Ghent in Flanders.

1298

Dominical letter E.

Certain extensions of the truces between the kings were declared; they were definitely to last for two years from Epiphany. Meanwhile formal ambassadors were sent to the pope at the Roman court, and the kings submitted completely to his decision and judgment concerning the dispute which had arisen between them. As the king of England was occupied with pressing business in England he arrived late in Flanders and the French army inflicted great loss on the Flemings, for they captured the noble towns of Bruges, Damme, Lille [1] and Courtrai and burnt down many others. The king crossed the sea with a small force [2] and escaped his enemies by remarkable astuteness, for the French planned to capture him in person in open battle when he first touched the shore. Since the king [was] extraordinarily clever he sent in advance his Welshmen, numbering up to thirty thousand, with lances erect and pennons attached. Therefore the French scouts were terrified by so many colours, even more terrified than the strength of the force justified, and believed that the force of Englishmen was as large as they supposed it to be from the number of banners. The king was surrounded with perils: behind him he saw danger, by which he was troubled, since his troops were closely engaged; in front of him he saw the enemy in open country, which ought to frighten him; as for his flanks,

nuda cateruis. Nil tamen tremefactus per omnia, ciuitatem de Brugis intrauit. Cito tamen inde recessit f. 196ᵛ ad urbem munitissimam de / Gaunt quoniam auditis quibusdam sinistris rumoribus Francorum ibidem euentum expectare noluit, unde iter[um] agente fraude ciuium Brugis capta fuit a Francis. Morante rege apud Gaunt quadam die exiit delectandi gracia cum magnatibus, quo egresso ciues portas ciuitatis obstruxerunt et Anglis inclusis bellicose mortem inferre ceperunt. Eleuatis igitur hinc inde tediosis clamoribus, arreptis armis relicti Anglici uiriliter prospereque resistebant, unde suorum quibusdam cesis grauem in opido cedem excercuerunt. Obserrati siquidem erant uici inmensis ex transuerso cathenis ac repagulis ut uix posset ex Anglis alter alteri parare suffragium. Interea iugulatus est quidam Anglicus in conspectu quorundam ᵃ Wallicorum qui in suburbio erant. Vnde quidam eorum arepta costa sua flumine transnatato, paloque transito in hostes ruit inopinatus tribus cesis fluuio renatato, illesus ad socios suos remeauit. Quapropter rex precepit sibi dari c. solidos ob signum uirtutis et audacie. Est autem Gaunt urbs fortissima, ciuitas munitissima, castrum inuincibile, refugium indomabile, muris fossatis palis aquisque circumcincta mirificis. In ciuitate mille turres eminent defensabiles totaque castrensi robore premunitur. Obsidionem non timet nisi excercitus in quatuor partibus diuidatur. Nec potest pars parti subuenire propter magnas uariasque intricaciones aquarum nisi circumgirato xv. dierum spacio. A Gayo

---

ᵃ quidam *MS*

they were almost bare of troops. But he was not frightened for a moment and entered Bruges. However he quickly left it for the mighty city of Ghent, because he had heard some ominous rumours and was unwilling to await the arrival of the French there. Thereupon the city of Bruges was once again captured by the French through the treachery of the citizens. One day while the king was staying at Ghent he left the city with his nobles for the sake of amusement. When he had left the citizens barred the city gates and began ferociously to kill the English, who were shut in. Terrible screams rang out on all sides; the remaining English seized their weapons and fought back bravely and successfully. Some of their men fell but they carried out a great massacre in the town. The streets were shut off by huge chains and bars fastened across them so that one Englishman could hardly bring help to another. Meanwhile one Englishman was slain in full view of certain Welshmen who were in the city suburbs. And thereupon one of them snatched up his tunic and swam across the river. He crossed the palisade and unexpectedly rushed at the enemy, killing three of them. Then he swam back over the river and rejoined his fellows unhurt. On account of this the king ordered 100s. to be given to him as a token of his courage and daring. Ghent is a very strong and heavily fortified city, an impregnable fortress and an invincible place of refuge, surrounded by remarkable walls, ditches, palisades and moats. A thousand defensive towers dominate the city and the whole is fortified like a citadel. A siege causes no alarm unless the army is divided into four parts; and then one part cannot help another without winding in and out for fifteen days on account of the variety and numerous

Iulio Cesare quondam fundata unde a Gayo Gaunt
nuncupatur. Interim inter reges, homines et con-
federatos capte sunt quedam hostilitatis sufferentie seu
treuge a die Epiphanie per duos annos.[1] Regesque
submiserunt se in viii. arbitros quorum sentenciis et
diffinicionibus auctoritate domini pape roboratis pax
f. 197 inter eos perpetue soliditatis nancisseretur funda/mentum.
Maturato igitur diffinitores apostolorum petunt limina;
ex parte regis Francorum,[2] archiepiscopus Remensis,
episcopus Li[n]g[on]ensis, comites de Artoys et de
Britannia [3]: ex parte regis Anglorum archiepiscopus
Dublinensis,[4] electus Eboracensis,[5] comes de Saueia et
dominus Oto de Grandasumma.[6]

Preterea Flandrenses qui regi Francie destinauerant
regem Anglie cui se dederant fraudibus et insidiis
multigenis circumuenire conati sunt pro incontinencia,
ut ferunt, uxorum filiarumque ac famularum suarum ab
Anglis stupratarum. Quapropter die sancti Blasii [7]
preconceptam in Anglos aggredi temptauerunt maliciam; sic per totam patriam ex industria quieuerunt
sonitus campanarum ut cum compatriote primam
tintillacionem in ciuitate de Gaunt perciperent mox de
uilla in uillam conclangerent sicque consono impetu
omnes Flandrensium copie uillam de Gaunt circum-
uallarent. A summo igitur mane obseratis ianuis
ciuitatis, balistis machinisque bellicis desuper dispositis

---

[1] Already mentioned; above, p. 143.

[2] Philip IV, king of France 1285–1314

[3] Peter Barbette, bishop of Rheims 1274–98; John de Rochefort, bishop
of Langres 1296–1305; Robert II, count of Artois 1250–1302; John II,
duke of Brittany 1286–1305

[4] William de Hothum, archbishop of Dublin 1296–8

[5] See *Foedera*, I, p. 887, where Anthony, bishop of Durham 1283–1310/11,
appears in place of Henry of Newark, the elect of York, and Hugh de Vere
is listed after Otto de Grandison.

intricacies of the moats.   The city was originally founded
by Gaius Julius Caesar and was called Ghent after Gaius.
Meanwhile between the kings, their men and allies a
respite from hostilities or truce was agreed on for two
years [1] from the feast of Epiphany.   The kings submitted
to the judgment of eight men, by whose verdict and
decisions, supported by papal authority, the peace
between the kings should obtain a foundation of lasting
strength.   The arbitrators, therefore, hastened to the
Apostolic See.   Representing the king of the French [2]
were the archbishop of Rheims, the bishop of Langres,
the count of Artois, and the count of Brittany [3];
representing the king of the English were the archbishop
of Dublin, [4] the archbishop-elect of York, [5] the count of
Savoy and Otto de Grandison. [6]

Moreover the men of Flanders had planned to hand
over the king of England, to whom they had allied
themselves, to the king of France.   They attempted to
deceive him by various tricks and plots, because it is
said, their wives, daughters and maidservants had been
debauched by the English.   So on the feast of St Blaise [7]
they attempted to carry out the wicked plan they had
conceived against the English.   Thus throughout the
countryside they had silenced the bells on purpose so
that when their fellow countrymen heard the first tinkle
in the city of Ghent they would at once clang every bell
from town to town; at this unison of bells all the forces
of Flanders would rush to surround the town of Ghent.
At the break of day, therefore, the city gates were barred
and above them placed ballistic machines and other

---

[6] Amadeus, count of Savoy 1285–1323, and Otto de Grandison, keeper
of the Channel Islands 1275–1328, died 1335.

[7] 3 February

excluserunt pedites et Wallicos qui hospitabantur in
ciuitatis proastio [1] ne regi periclitanti subuenirent.
Sicque omnibus Anglorum cedibus extirpatis miser
utrimque eiulatus attollitur. Intus etenimque ruebant
iugulati extraque morticinis fratribus subuenire non
poterant. Tandem Anglici et Wallici qui seclusi erant
conglobatis uiribus urbis portas iniectis flammis prostrauerunt. Mirum dictu et res grandis: cum enim
inter stridentem flammam atque portarum uiuaces
carbones adustarum licet periculosior immineret
introitus cateruatim insilierunt per medium ignis.
Sequitur ergo dira ruina in ciuitate tam in cede ciuium
quam in conflagracione nobilium memorialium. His
rex Anglie expergescens iniuriis ad sedandum malorum
insolenciam stipatus milite processit armatus in publico
cui ferunt balistis tela inmissa fuisse. Flandrenses
f. 197ᵛ tamen ulterius fortu/ne ponderositatem non ferentes
leoninam superciliositatem in uulpinam conuertentes
astuciam, ueniam regiis uestigiis inclinati simulatione
tamen postulauerunt. Quapropter quodam die martis
hostilem iterato fabricauerunt rebellionem. Quorum
insolenciam rex uirilius repressit. Iterum implorant regis
graciam et optinuerunt. Quod indignati Anglorum
pedites egre ferebant. Vnde post pacem preconizatam
magnam opidi substanciam expoliauerunt, aurum uidelicet, argentum, arma et pannos preciosos. Super quibus
conuicti multi pedites de Anglia suspensi fuerunt. Et
nisi dominus Antonius de Bek Dunelmensis episcopus

---

[1] *proastium:* suburbs (Du Cange)

military engines. They shut out the foot-soldiers and Welshmen, who were lodging in the city suburbs,[1] so that they could not come to help the king in his peril. And so all the English were wiped out in a great massacre; cries of distress rose on either side, for those inside were falling dead and those outside could not bring help to their dying brothers. At length the English and Welsh who were shut out concentrated their forces and threw firebrands at the city gates and destroyed them. It was a great and astonishing feat. When an entrance, though a dangerous one, offered between the leaping flames and glowing ashes of the burning gates, the companies of troops leapt through the middle of the fire. A terrible devastation of the city followed, comprising both the slaughter of the citizens and the conflagration of the noble monuments. The king of England was stirred by these outrages and, in order to stay the insolence of the rabble, appeared armed in public with a bodyguard of knights; it is said that the ballistic machines threw missiles at him. But the men of Flanders no longer had the balance of fortune on their side, so they changed the arrogance of the lion into the cunning of the fox; they deceitfully bowed down at the king's feet and asked for pardon. Thereupon on a certain Tuesday they again engineered a hostile rebellion, but the king manfully suppressed their insolence; again they implored the king for mercy and obtained it, which vexed and angered the English foot-soldiers. After peace had been proclaimed they plundered the great riches of the town, that is the gold, silver, arms and precious stuffs. Many of the English foot-soldiers were convicted of this and hanged. If Anthony de Bek, bishop of Durham, who often found

qui plerumque compatriotis promtis ac piis compatitur
uisceribus, cuiusdam magnatis Angligeni extruncasset
maliciam, omnes fere pedites de Anglia fuissent morte
turpissima condempnati. Nec pretereundum cum rex
noster per plateas incederet inmensam cathenam ex
transuerso protensam sonipede calcaribus exacuato
ualido congressu protriuerit, tam suum quam equi sui
paruipendens discidium.

Ad resecandum Scottorum audaciam qui *ᵃ* fines
Anglie inuaserant conducti sunt a filio regis cum manu
forti marescallus et Herfordie comites. Ad quorum
expedicionem clerus decimas bonorum spiritualium et
temporalium contradidit preter penam statuti papalis
hiisdem indicto mandato ab archiepiscopo ne hiis
sumptibus ultra fines Anglie hostes insequerentur. Ista
concessio cleri sussurrum excitabat inter quosdam, quia
hoc anno sponte contulit quod anno alio eciam coactus
recusabat. Ad quod dicendum est quod hic committitur
bellum licitum quod pro tuicione regni ac rei publice
que maxima sui parte per hostiles inuasiones mutilantur,
conseritur, quampocius ubi iminet regni subuersio in
quo proprium cuiuslibet interesse conspicitur, ui et
manu liceat obuiare. Secus est enim aliena con-
cupiscere et propria contueri.

f. 198   Interea obiit dominus Willelmus / de Bello Campo
comes Warwyci.[1] Rex applicuit apud Sandwicum
rediens de Flandria in crastino sancti Gregorii pape [2]
ubi in propria persona citauit Portenses peremtorie ut

ᵃ quib3 *MS*

[1] William de Beauchamp, 9th earl of Warwick 1268–98
[2] 13 March

pity in his heart for his quick-witted and devout country-men, had not cut short the malice of a certain English magnate, nearly all the foot-soldiers of England would have been condemned to a shameful death.   Nor must it be omitted that when our king was riding through the streets he trampled down a huge chain stretched across a street by clapping his spurs to his charger and rushing at it, not caring about the downfall of himself and his horse.

To stop the audacity of the Scots, who had invaded English territory, the king's son assembled the earl marshal and the earl of Hereford with a strong force. The clergy handed over a tenth of their spiritual and temporal revenues for the expedition, despite the penalty of the papal statute; a mandate had been addressed to them by the archbishop forbidding these resources to be used for pursuing the enemy beyond the border of England.   This grant of the clergy gave rise to comment among certain people because this year they had con-tributed voluntarily what another year they had refused even under compulsion.   To this may be answered that on this occasion the war undertaken is lawful because it is fought for the safety of the kingdom and common weal, which is greatly damaged by enemy incursions, and it is even more lawful to resist by force of arms threats to overthrow the realm in which the property of everyone is obviously involved, for to covet other people's possessions is quite different from guarding our own.

Meanwhile William de Beauchamp, earl of Warwick,[1] died.   The king, returning from Flanders, landed at Sandwich on the morrow of the feast of St Gregory the pope.[2]   There he issued a peremptory summons to the men of the Cinque ports to appear

assisterent coram eo London' dominica Palmarum responsuri super despectu et indignacione dampnis et insolenciis sibi et suis transmare illatis. Magister Willelmus de Luze episcopus Eliensis[1] uita discessit vi. Kal. Aprilis.

Anno M.CC[XC]. octauo dies Pasche fuit viii. Idus Aprilis.

Dicti Portenses iterato coram rege uocantur apud Sanctum Albanum[2]; ibidem osculati sunt Gernemutos ipsoque die in mensa communicantes pacifice repatriauerunt. Ignis apud Westmonasterium plura edificia consumpsit.[3] Rex uenit apud sanctum Edmundum vii. Idus Maii[4]; in crastino die sabati conuentum pauit. Et cito post maturato itinere boriales tendebat in partes uocatoque apud Eboracum parliamento in crastino Trinitatis iiii. Non. Iunii. Ibi quoque rex Anglie quam proceres summotis cunctis intestine prohibiteque contumelie scrupulis mutuis debitarum amiciciarum se confederauerunt nexibus. Rex eciam spondebat se formam magne carte in omnibus obseruaturum; sicque contra Scociam in suos iterum cornua erigentem hostilia excercitum mouit.

Instante scilicet die eleccionis sancti Dunstani[5] Elienses cenobite in eligendo sibi episcopum dissenserunt. Vnde pars una elegit priorem eiusdem ecclesie, pars altera dominum Iohannem de Langeton' domini regis cancellarium, utrosque uiros prouidos et discretos et quantum spectat ad morem personarumque circum-

---

[1] William of Louth died 25 March 1298.

[2] In 1297 the men of the Cinque ports had burnt some ships from Yarmouth in the Zwyn; above, p. 141. For grants made by the king at St Albans in April to the Cinque ports and Yarmouth see *CPR, 1293–1301*, pp. 348–9, *CCR, 1296–1302*, pp. 204, 205.

[3] cf. *Flores*, III, p. 104; *Wig.*, p. 536. A ' confederation ' made between St Edmund's and Westminster between 1215 and 1222 is printed in R.

in person before him in London on Palm Sunday to answer for the lack of respect and impertinence, the insults and arrogance, with which they had treated the king and his men when abroad.

Master William de Louth, bishop of Ely,[1] died on 27 March.

In the year 1298 Easter day was on 6 April.

The aforesaid men of the Cinque ports were summoned again to the king's presence at St Albans.[2] There they kissed the men of Yarmouth, dined with them on the same day and returned home in peace. A fire at Westminster burnt many buildings.[3] The king came to Bury St Edmunds on 9 May [4] and entertained the convent on the next day, which was Saturday. Soon afterwards he hastened northwards, having summoned a parliament to meet at York on the day after Trinity Sunday, that is on 2 June. There both the king and the chief men were joined to each other by mutual bonds of rightful friendship, all anxiety about unlawful faction in their midst having been removed. Moreover the king promised to observe Magna Carta in everything. And so he marched his army against Scotland, which once again was gathering its fighting strength against his men.

On the very day of the election of St Dunstan [5] the monks of Ely disagreed on the election of their bishop. One party elected the prior of that church and the other John de Langton, the king's chancellor. Both men were wise and judicious and fit for such a high office as far

---

Widmore, *An Inquiry into the Time of the First Foundation of Westminster Abbey* (1743), p. 232.—V. H. G.

[4] Gough's *Itinerary* confirms that Edward was at Bury on 9 May, and on Saturday, 10 May.

[5] 19 May

stancias ad tantam dignitatem peridoneos.[1] Septimo
Kal. Iunii mortuo quodam prediuite Londoniarum ciue
nocte dominica post gallicinium urbis plateis per
pauperes ut agapem acciperent constipatis subito insil-
uerunt inter eos filii Belial cupientes / denarios de
manibus executorum defuncti abripere. Quorum
cassatis conspiracionibus horrendum egenis furorem
infuderunt c.xx. et nouem trucidatis xxx.que submersis.
Occasio autem huius cedis fuit quod mendicus quidam
die altero latenter eorum secretis participans consiliis
in plebe diuulgauit: ipsi uero celeratissimi ut hunc
egenum inter ceteros interimerent tot suam mortibus
iniuriam uindicarunt Herodiana nimirum inflammati
nequicia qui Christum persequi condiram innocentum
necem cumulauit. Archiepiscopus tenuit consilium
Londoniis in crastino [2] sancti Iohannis Baptiste ubi
accessit filius regis sub patris nomine a clero quatuor
peticiones postulaturus. Primo, ut pro eo orarent.
Secundo, ut publice excomunicatos denunciarent ecclesiarum inuasores et incendiarios et maxime Scottos.
Tercio, ut placeret clero regi concedere residuum
pecunie comitibus concesse. Quarto, ut si cogeret
necessitas placeret eidem clero ipsum regem respicere
auxilio pecuniari. Affuerunt interea quidam aulici
clerici uolentes elata fronte archanis eorum se inmiscere
tractatibus quos archiepiscopus sub excomunicacionis
interminacione expulit de sinodo. Tractabantur autem

f. 198ᵛ

---

[1] cf. *CPR, 1292–1301*, p. 352; a special note is made that John Langton,
the chancellor, handed over the Great Seal to keepers while he left the court
on 6 June to consult with the archbishop about his election. Three
further entries in the chronicle deal with this matter.—V. H. G.

[2] 25 June. See Wilkins, *Concilia*, ii, p. 236

as behaviour and rank were concerned.[1]   On Sunday
night, 26 May, a certain rich citizen of London died
and on the following morning after cock-crow the streets
of the town were crowded with the poor waiting to
receive alms; thereupon some sons of the devil suddenly
leapt upon them, wishing to snatch the pennies from
the hands of the dead man's executors.   Their plot was
brought to naught and in their fury they fell on the poor
people, slaying a hundred and twenty-nine and drowning thirty.   The reason for this massacre was that a
certain beggar on a previous day had been admitted
secretly to their innermost councils and had then
revealed them to the mob.   Therefore they speedily
revenged the wrong the beggar had done them by a
great slaughter so that this poor man would perish with
the rest.   There is no doubt that they were inflamed
with wickedness like Herod, who to persecute Christ
massacred a great number of innocent people.   The
archbishop held a council in London on the morrow [2]
of the feast of St John the Baptist.   The king's son
attended in order to present four requests to the clergy
on behalf of his father: first that they should pray for
him;   second that they should publicly denounce as
excommunicate those who broke into and burnt
churches, and especially the Scots;   third that the
clergy should be willing to grant the king the rest of the
sum of money granted by the earls;   and fourth that if
necessary the clergy should be willing to show their
regard for the king with a pecuniary aid.   Meanwhile
some clerks of the king's court who were present, having
the effrontery to wish to take part in the secret dis-
cussions, were expelled from the synod by the archbishop
under threat of excommunication.   In fact some very

ibi quedam secreciora negocia que usque ad diem prefinitum ad aures communes peruenire non poterant.

In festo sancte Marie Magda[le]ne [1] conuenit tota uirtus Scocie apud Faukirke ad dimicandum campestri bello contra regem Anglie. Qui tandem a facie Anglorum fugati usque ad sexaginta milia ceciderunt. Gawelenses uero commiscuerant plures lanceas cautissime immixtas et circumligatas quod uocatur cheltz, quo diu equitibus Anglie restiterunt. Ex parte Anglorum cecidit magister Adrianus [2] le Iay, magister Templi f. 199 in / Anglia.

Memorandum quod die sancti Pantaleonis martiris [3] et in uigilia ab hora meridiana mira prenosticacio apparuit in sole et luna, utrique enim ita rubicundi seu sanguinei apparuerunt ut nichil terris radiorum preter rubicundum et sanguineum emitterent. Memorandum quod die sancti Magni martiris [4] furtim ablata fuerunt omnia coquilaria refectorii sancti Edmundi una cum duabus peciis argenteis et quinque salsariis argenteis lugubri infortunio sub speciali clausura uespere non obserrata. Super cuius facti fautores et auctores sceleris in pleno capitulo ab uniuersis et singulis sacerdotibus de conuentu stolis indutis candelisque accensis lata fuit publice sentencia in presencia omnium seruiencium de curia. Frater Willelmus de Hothum' de ordine Predicatorum archiepiscopus Dublinensis ac nuncius regis Anglie in partibus transmarinis uita discessit. Item, Aelianora comitissa de Bars et filia regis Anglie mundo ualefecit. Bone memorie Humfridus de Boun comes de

---

[1] 22 July

[2] *Recte* Brian Jay. P. Langtoft, *Chron.*, ed. T. Wright, II, p. 314, *Croniques de London*, ed. Aungier, p. 27

[3] 28 July   [4] 19 August

private business was discussed there which could not be made known to the public ear until an appointed day.

On the feast of St Mary Magdalen [1] the whole strength of Scotland met at Falkirk to fight a pitched battle against the king of England. They fled at length in the face of the English and as many as sixty thousand men fell. The men of Galloway assembled a great many lances packed close together very securely and fenced about to form what is called a schiltron: this withstood the cavalry of England for a long time. Master Adrian [2] le Jay, the master of the order of the Temple in England, fell on the English side.

It should be recorded that on the feast of St Pantaleon martyr [3] and on the vigil at midday an extraordinary omen appeared on the sun and moon; they both appeared so red or rather blood-coloured that they gave forth no rays to the earth except red or blood-coloured ones. It should be recorded that on the feast of St Magnus martyr [4] all the cooking utensils in the refectory of Bury St Edmunds, together with two pieces of silver and five silver salt-cellars, were stolen by stealth; by a sad piece of ill luck they had not been locked in the special safe in the evening. The sentence of excommunication was publicly pronounced against those who had committed the crime and those who had helped them, in full chapter by each and every priest of the convent, wearing stoles and with lighted candles, in the presence of all the domestic servants. Brother William de Hothum of the order of Friars Preachers, archbishop of Dublin and an ambassador of the king of England, died abroad. Eleanor, countess of Bar, the king of England's daughter, died. Humphrey de Bohun, earl of Hereford,

Hereford obiit in uigilia [1] Circumcisionis Domini; sepultus apud Waldene. Et sequente dominica ante diem terre motus magnus factus est.

1299

Circa Purificacionem apparuit cometa densos radios emittens uersus orientem, alte aparens in firmamento ad austrum declinans. Dompnus Iohannes de Langeton' regis cancellarius appellauit ab archiepiscopo Cant' ad curiam Romanam super lite mota inter ipsum et priorem Eliensis ecclesie alterumque eiusdem ecclesie electum. Ideo ambo electi personaliter Romam adeunt.

Rex uocauit parliamentum [2] suum apud London' media Quadragesima a quo clam discessit quia noluit f. 199ᵛ magnam / cartam confirmare. Nec tamen minus lata est sentencia in omnes huius carte uiolatores, sicut prius in consilio archiepiscopi fuerat ordinatum. Quod statutum est fieri bis annis singulis, uidelicet die Omnium Sanctorum et die P[asche]. [a]

Anno domini M.CC. nonagesimo ix. dies Pasche fuit xiii. Kal. Maii et littera dominicalis D.

Dompnus Iohannes de Langton' regis cancellarius et electus Eliensis cum magna pompa et gloria Romam ueniens a ciuibus et cardinalibus immo a domino papa celebri iocunditate receptus est. Qui primo die aduentus sui uultui domini pape dulciter presentatur. Et in crastino negocia sua proposuit; animaduertensque sibi in electione ius scincerum non pertinere ipsam palam

---

[a] A lacuna ½ in. long MS

[1] This date is confirmed by *Cal. Inq. Post Mortem, Edw. I*, II, no. 552.
[2] A parliament without either commons or the lower clergy was summoned for 8 March 1299: Stubbs, *Const. Hist.*, II, p. 154; Guisborough, p. 329.—V. H. G.

of worthy memory, died on the vigil [1] of the feast of the
Circumcision of the Lord.   He was buried at Walden.
On the following Sunday before daybreak there was a
great earthquake.

1299

About Candlemas a comet appeared, shooting out a
radiant tail to the east.   It was visible high in the sky
and sank towards the south.   John de Langton, the
king's chancellor, appealed from the archbishop of
Canterbury to the Roman court in the suit between him
and the prior of the church of Ely; they had both been
elected bishop of that church.   So both the bishops-
elect went in person to Rome.

The king summoned his parliament [2] at London in
the middle of Lent.   He left it secretly because he did
not wish to confirm Magna Carta.   Nevertheless the
sentence of excommunication was pronounced on all
violators of this charter, as had been ordained previously
in the archbishop's council.   It was decreed that the
sentence was to be pronounced twice yearly, on All
Saints' day and at Easter.

In the year of the Lord 1299 Easter day was on
19 April and the Dominical letter was D.

John de Langton, the king's chancellor and the
bishop-elect of Ely, came with great pomp and glory
to Rome and was received with much rejoicing by the
citizens and cardinals and the pope himself.   On the
first day of his arrival he was presented in a friendly way
to the pope.   On the next day he stated his business.
Realising that in the matter of his election sound law

in manu domini pape resignauit. Dicitur autem quoniam dominus papa eidem palmam suam dominica Palmarum ad portandum transmiserit. Idem uero cancellarius obtenta super pluralitate beneficiorum dispensatione [1] licenciatus repatriauit uisitata sollempniter curia. Vocatum est parliamentum apud Londoniam post Pascha [2] in quo comites et barones morosis ac superuacuis uerbosisque regis intricacionibus exasperati iam modicum defuit quin ad inpacienciam prorupissent nisi rex salubriori informatus concilio eorum censuisset celerius peticiones esse adinpleturum. Et hoc archiepiscopus cum comitibus et baronibus a rege rogatus manucepit. Ferunt comitem mariscallum ad curiam uenisse cum mille equis. Astat interea prior Eliensis in curia contra monachos aduersariosque suos quasi ad bestias dimicans, multis ab eisdem interceptus obprobriis. Cuius tandem eleccio quatenus minus canonica quassata fuit. Aduersarii enim cum maledic- cione ut dicitur summi pontificis recesserunt. Ac f. 200 dompnus prior [3] spem figens in Domino reman/sit in curia inperteritus. Quo circa per dominum papam magister Radulfus de Walpol [4] episcopus Norwic' ad sedem Elyensem translatus est. Et dictus prior Eliensis ad episcopatum Norwicensem subrogatus. Deinde papa dedit archiepiscopatum Dublinie archidiacono Cantuar' et dictum archidiaconatum domino Iohanni de Langton' cancellario Anglie.

Sollempnes nuncii denique regum Anglie et Francie ut supradictum est summo missi pontifici tales acceperunt

---

[1] For the dispensation, dated 21 April 1299, to Langton to hold a plurality of benefices see *Les Registres de Boniface VIII*, ed. G. Digard, Bibliothèque des Écoles françaises d'Athènes et de Rome, 2 [e] série, no. 4, vol. 2, nos. 3005–8 (cf. no. 3156).

[2] Parliament was called for 3 May 1299.

was not on his side, he resigned his election publicly into the hands of the pope. It is said that the pope sent him his own palm to carry on Palm Sunday. When the chancellor had obtained a dispensation [1] respecting a plurality of benefices and had made his offerings to the court, he received leave to go home. A parliament was summoned in London after Easter.[2] In it the earls and barons were exasperated by the king's irritable and empty words and prevarications. Their impatience was on the point of breaking out when the king, guided by wise counsel, agreed that their demands should be quickly fulfilled. At the king's request the archbishop [of Canterbury] stood surety for this undertaking with the earls and barons. It is said that the earl marshal came to the court with a thousand horse. Meanwhile the prior of Ely was at the Roman court fighting his opponents, the monks, as if they were wild beasts and sustaining many jibes from them. At last his election was quashed as uncanonical and his adversaries left, with the curse, it is said, of the pope, but the prior [3] put his faith in the Lord and remained undaunted at the court. Thereupon the pope translated Master Ralph de Walpole,[4] bishop of Norwich, to the see of Ely and promoted the said prior in his place to the bishopric of Norwich. Then the pope gave the archbishopric of Dublin to the archdeacon of Canterbury and the said archdeaconry to John de Langton, chancellor of England.

The ambassadors of the king of England and the king of France, who had been sent to the pope, as mentioned above, agreed between themselves to the

---

[3] John Salmon, prior of Ely 1291–9, bishop of Norwich 1299–1325
[4] Ralph Walpole, bishop of Norwich 1289–99, bishop of Ely 1299–1302

inter se pacis et concordiarum condiciones, uidelicet quod Anglie rex nubet Margaretam sororem regis Francie; et super consanguinitatis obiectu papa dispensat. Wasconia cum pertinenciis sine diminucione regi Anglie reddetur. Idem eciam rex Anglie a iuramenti periculo quo regem Francie diffidauit absoluitur. Vt omnis igitur auferatur inter eos hostilitatis occasio rex Anglie regi Francie in dampnorum recompensacionem magnam summam pecunie promisit. Igitur dominus Iohannes de Sancto Iohanne absolutus a carcere repatriauit, cum ceteris concaptiuis preter dominum I[ohannem] de Cretinges [1] qui inter mercatorum solidos irretitur. Regina Anglie Margareta applicuit apud Doueram die martis ante Natiuitatem beate Marie [2] quam filius regis et comes mariscallus cum ruta ualida de naui susceperunt. In crastino ducitur Cantuar[i]e. Feria quinta summo mane celebrantur sponsalia: continuo post missam rex recessit pransurus extra ciuitatem. Regina uero et filius regis in magna aula archiepiscopi regalia celebrauerunt conuiuia, ubi inter prandendum equitauerunt quam plurimi comites et barones.

Hoc anno obiit magister Henricus de Newerk archiepiscopus Eboracensis: cui successit magister Nicholaus de Colcherche.[3] Circa festum sancti Michaelis obiit frater Willelmus de Wodeforde abbas de Burgo, cui successit frater Godefridus de Cruland.[4]

[1] Son and heir of Adam de Cretinges. The chronicler's interest in him is explained by the fact that he held lands in Barrow, Saxham and Fornham (*CCR, 1296–1302*, p. 384). He was at first believed to have been killed in France, but by 24 September 1298 the news had come through that he was alive and well ' in the prison of the king of France '; *CCR, 1293–1301*, p. 175, and many other references.—V. H. G.

[2] The Nativity of the Blessed Virgin Mary, 8 September, was in fact on a Tuesday. For confirmation of this date see the continuator in *Gerv. Cant.* II, p. 317.

terms of peace and reconciliation: it was stipulated that the king of England should marry Margaret, the sister of the king of France (the pope should issue a dispensation from the objection of blood relationship); Gascony with its appurtenances intact should be returned to the king of England. The king of England was freed from the peril which he had incurred as a result of his vow, renouncing his allegiance to the king of France. In order that all cause of hostility between the kings should be removed, the king of England promised the king of France a huge sum of money as recompense for damages. John de St John was released from prison and returned home together with the rest of his fellow captives except J[ohn] de Cretinges,[1] who was entangled in money dealings with merchants. Margaret, queen of England, landed at Dover on the Tuesday before the Nativity of St Mary.[2] She was received from the boat by the king's son and the earl marshal with a gallant band of soldiers. On the next day she was taken to Canterbury. The wedding was celebrated on Thursday morning. Immediately after mass the king left to dine outside the city. The queen and the king's son feasted in royal style in the archbishop's great hall, where during the meal a great many earls and barons rode on horseback.

In this year Master Henry de Newerk, archbishop of York, died and was succeeded by Master Nicholas de Colcherche.[3] About Michaelmas Brother William de Woodford, abbot of Peterborough, died and was succeeded by brother Godfrey de Crowland.[4] In the same

---

[3] This is an error. Thomas Corbridge was consecrated archbishop on 28 February 1300.
[4] William de Woodford, abbot of Peterborough 1295–9; Godfrey de Crowland, abbot 1299–1321

f. 200ᵛ / Et eodem anno circa festum sancti Edmundi regis obiit
pie memorie magister Oliuerus de Sutton' episcopus
Lincolnie: cui successit magister Iohannes de Alderbi
eiusdem loci cancellarius.¹ Rex interea aripuit iter
uersus Scociam sed primo tenuit parliamentum suum
London'. Comes uero marescallus personalem allegans
excusacionem exercitum suum domino Iohanni de
Segraue commissum regi in expedicione Scocie accomo-
dauit. Rex Scociam ueniens brumali tempore de
hostibus suis plene triumphare non potuit tum propter
aeris intemperiem maxime in illis aquilonaribus regionibus, tum propter niuias ᵃ glacieique timidas et incertas
commeaciones.

1300

Littera dominicalis B.

Liberatis igitur suis qui obsessi erant custodiam
Scocie tradidit domino Iohanni de sancto Iohanne et
sociis sibi assignatis. Ipse uero rediit Angliam estiuo
tempore cum maiori expedicione reuersurus. Rex
tenuit parliamentum ² suum London' media Quadragesima in quo post longam et tediosam moram magnas
habuit inde et graues expensas, uarias et periculosas
contumelias inter regem, comites et barones habitas
pacificati sunt. Et magna carta sigillata est et per
ecclesias cathedrales circumcirca distributa. Ob cuius
fauorem quintusdecimus denarius regi conceditur de
laicis.

Noua gaudia noua felicitas nuper nobis de orientis

ᵃ nimias MS

¹ Oliver Sutton died 13 November 1299. John Dalderby was consecrated 12 June 1300.
² 'The most completely constituted parliament that had been called

year about the time of the feast of St Edmund the king, Master Oliver de Sutton, bishop of Lincoln, of pious memory, died and was succeeded by Master John Dalderby, chancellor of Lincoln.[1] Meanwhile the king set out for Scotland, but first he held his parliament in London. The earl marshal excused himself but lent his army, which he had entrusted to John de Segrave, to the king for his Scottish campaign. The king reached Scotland in the winter and was unable to defeat his enemy completely partly because of the severity of the climate, particularly in those northern regions, and partly because of the snow and ice and the hazardous and uncertain communications.

1300

Dominical letter B.

When, therefore, those of the king's men who were beleaguered had been freed, the king gave the guardianship of Scotland to John de St John and those assigned to him. The king returned to England intending to go back with a larger force in the summer. He held his parliament [2] in London in the middle of Lent. In it, after a long and exhausting delay, which was responsible for very heavy expenses, the various dangerous quarrels existing between the king and the earls and barons were pacified. Magna Carta was sealed and distributed among the cathedral churches. In return for this favour the laity granted the king a fifteenth penny.

New joy, new felicity, had recently broken upon us

---

since 1296' (Stubbs) met on 6 March 1300. It was this parliament that passed the 'articuli super cartas.' Though the general sense is clear the grammar of this sentence is at fault.—V. H. G.

partibus illuxerunt. Sane Cassan [1] rex magnus Tartarorum Cham, id est inperator, constituit regem Hermenie [2] principem et ducem exercitus sui. Vnde ultimo die mensis Decembris inter duas magnas ciuitates Gamel' et Damascum primum contra soldanum Babilonie [3] bellum commisit. Ibidem Saraceni uicti fuerunt et mortui. Soldanus igitur in ciuitatem Gamel' fugit. Quem Tartarorum dominus cum toto exercitu insecutus obsedit et cepit dictam ciuitatem. Soldanus igitur fugit

f. 201 Damascum ubi primo ex utraque parte multa milia / Saracenorum ceciderunt; sed tandem omnes soldani copie fuse fuerunt. Soldanus autem cum quinque tantum sociis fugam iniit per solitudinem Babilonie usque Algar. Soldanus misit post hec imperatori Cassando xxx. equos oneratos auro, mandans ei quod uellet tenere de eo omnes terras suas. Cassan uero aurum retinuit nichil prorsus respondens nunciis, asserens se proprium et non alterius thesaurum recepisse. Eya sic euacuatis inimicis Christianorum et extinctis magnus Cham restituit Christianis omnes terras quas antiquitus possidebant.[4]

Anno Domini M.CCC. fuit annus iubileus siue remissiuus et bisextilis; dies Pasche iiii. Idus Aprilis; littera dominicalis C et B.

Hoc anno omnis sexus et etas ab omni orbe Christiano ad curiam festinauit. Absoluebantur enim omnes peregrini uere confessi et contriti a papa ab omni peccato et pena peccati propter annum iubileum.

---

[1] Ghazan Khan of Persia 1295–1305
[2] Constantine II, king of Armenia 1299–1308
[3] en-Nāsir Mohammad, sultan of Egypt (d. 1341), was restored to the throne in 1299.
[4] This account of Ghazan's victory is a little too optimistic; he suffered a severe defeat from the Egyptians in the spring of 1303. For Ghazan and

from the east.   For the great King Ghazan,[1] khan (that is emperor) of the Tartars, made the king of Armenia [2] the chief and leader of his army.   Thereupon on the last day of December the first battle was fought against the sultan of Cairo [3] at a place between the two great cities of Gamala and Damascus.   There the Saracens were defeated and slain and the sultan fled into the city of Gamala.   The leader of the Tartars with the whole of his army pursued him and besieged and captured the said city.   The sultan, therefore, fled to Damascus, where at first thousands of Saracens on both sides fell but at length all the sultan's forces were routed.   The sultan himself, with only five companions, fled through the wildernesses of Cairo to Algar.   After this the sultan sent thirty horses laden with gold to the Emperor Ghazan and announced that he wished to hold all his territories from him.   Ghazan kept the gold but gave the ambassadors no reply at all, asserting that the treasure he had received was his own and not another's. And lo! when the enemies of the Christians had thus been brought to naught and destroyed, the great khan restored to the Christians all the lands which in former times they possessed.[4]

The year of the Lord 1300 was a jubilee year or year of absolution, and a leap-year.   Easter day was 10 April.   The Dominical letters were C and B.

In this year people of both sexes and every age from all over the Christian world hastened to the Roman court.   For on account of the jubilee year the pope absolved all pilgrims, who had truly confessed and were contrite, from all their sins and punishments for sins.

---

the Egyptians see Makrizi, *Histoire des Sultans Mamlouks de l'Égypte*, French trans. by M. Quatremere, II, pp. 124ff.

Rex deinceps congregauit exercitum uersus Scociam
et uocauit omnes comites et barones ut prompti essent
cum seruiciis suis in die sancti Iohannis Baptiste ad
proficiscendum cum eo. Sed in parliamento habito
apud Eboracum post Pentecosten[1] aliquamdiu reluctatum
est eo quod quidam barones dicerent quod ibidem nullum
deberent seruicium exhibere. Tamen quia in gestis
regum antiquis factas fuisse plures probantur expedi-
ciones ipsa eorum allegacio irrita iudicata fuit [et]
inanis. Quod probatur per cronica Malmesberie et
Mariani Scoti et magistri Henrici Huntedon' et
secundum Houeden.[2]

Rex fuit apud sanctum Edmundum viii. Idus Maii
die dominica supplici deuocione beato martiri uitam
redditurus. Nec nunquam ante uidebatur ecclesie et
conuentui graciosior aparere. Concessit eciam abbati
et conuentui fines siue amerciamenta hominum infra
libertatem et burgum sancti Edmundi qui edictum
regium quantum ad kokedonis[3] in mercando uiolauerant,
iusticiariis suis districcius inhibens ne ecclesie priuilegia
quoquo modo uiolarent, uni eorum specialiter sermonem
f. 201ᵛ dirigens / ait: ' Caue precipio tibi ne sancti Edmundi
ledas munimenta, sine dubio enim credo ipsum in
Scocia affuturum ad mei meorumque proteccionem, et ad
hostium debellacionem uibrantibus armis redimitum,
multo te paratiorem aduenturum.' In crastino conuentum pauit. Ibidem accessit ad regem quidam
episcopus transmontanus de sancto Vincencio[4] nuncius

---

[1] 29 May
[2] A further appeal to the chronicles was made later in this year. On
26 September 1300 writs were addressed to St Albans, Westminster and
many other abbeys (doubtless including St Edmunds) to search their
chronicles and archives for whatever related to the kingdom of Scotland
and forward their returns to the king at Lincoln; Rishanger, p. 455. The

The king assembled his army against Scotland and ordered all the earls and barons to be ready with their knights on the feast of St John the Baptist to set out with him. But at the parliament held at York after Pentecost [1] there was opposition for a time because some barons said that they ought not to perform military service there. As, however, it was proved by the ancient acts of the kings that there had been many such expeditions their allegation was judged invalid and of no force. The point was proved by the chronicles of Malmesbury, Marianus Scotus, Master Henry of Huntingdon and Hoveden.[2]

The king was at Bury St Edmunds on Sunday, 8 May, in order to dedicate his life to the blessed martyr with deep devotion. Never had he appeared more gracious to the church and convent. He even granted the abbot and convent the fines or amercements of men in the liberty and town of St Edmund who violated the royal edict relating to trading with ' kokedones.' [3] He strictly forbade his justices to violate the privileges of the church in any way and specially directed an injunction to one of them, saying: ' I order you to take care not to harm the written privileges of St Edmund, for I believe without doubt that he will be in Scotland to protect me and mine and to conquer the enemy; he will come wearing flashing armour much better prepared than you.' On the next day the king entertained the convent. While the king was at Bury the tramontane bishop of Vicenza [4]

---

information was needed to answer the pope's letter claiming Scotland as a fief of the apostolic see.—V. H. G.

[3] *kokedones :* debased French coins; see J. H. Baxter and C. Johnson, *Medieval Latin Word-List* (1934), *sub* 'cocodonis', and Rishanger, p. 195

[4] Rainald, bishop of Vicenza 1296–1303; cf. Guisborough, p. 331: ' homo ualde literatus et eloquens.' He had visited England in the previous year, 1299.—V. H. G.

regi a domino papa missus, super quibusdam articulis
que publicis auribus non inculcabantur. Dictus episcopus fraternitatem conuentus optinuit. In quo eciam
periit ipsa Romanorum proprietas. Dona enim sibi et
suis oblata renuit. Rex autem recessurus specialiter se
commendauit oracionibus conuentus. Cum enim pale-
frido suo portam curie egressurus insideret bis facie post
tergum conuersa et inclinato capite beato martiri et
sanctis eius deuocius inclinauit. Post aliquot eciam dies
uexillum suum priori et conuentui remandauit supplici-
bus litteris flagitans quatinus super eundem signum
missam de sancto Edmundo celebretur; tunc demum
omnium reliquiarum eiusdem loci tactu insigniretur.
Pulcra sane ac predicanda regis deuocio, qui non in
loricis ferreis nec equitum cateruis spem figebat future
uictorie sed in summo salutis auctore principale sue
expedicionis gerit fundamentum, dum ipsa bellorum
insignia que tantum uentis exponuntur et aeri talibus
uoluit insigniri beneficiis. Filius regis diucius perhen-
dinans loca peciit in eodem monasterio ad immorandum
secreciora frater enim noster factus est in capitulo.
Multum enim sibi placuit loci regalitas et crebra fratrum
solacia. Singulis eciam diebus peciit liberacionem
monachilem, uidelicet sicut in refectorio reficiuntur
fratres sibi exhiberi. Ferunt utique eum dixisse numquam [non] sibi loci magnalia dulciaque fratrum
complacuisse consorcia. Duodecimo tamen die
ualefaciens fratribus ad patrem suum regem properauit.

Memorandum quod primo die Iulii regina genuit

visited him. He had been sent as an ambassador by the
pope about certain matters which were not divulged to
the public ear. The said bishop obtained the con-
fraternity of the convent. Because of him the Romans
lost property, for he declined the gifts offered to him and
his men. Before the king left Bury he particularly
commended himself to the convent's prayers. For when
he was mounted on his palfrey ready to go out of the
gate of the courtyard, he looked behind him twice and
bowed very devoutly to the blessed martyr and his saints,
with his head bent low. After a few days he sent back
his standard to the prior and convent, entreating in an
urgent letter that the mass for St Edmund should be
celebrated over this emblem, and then finally that it
should be touched by all the relics at Bury. What
glorious and laudable devotion of the king! He did not
fix his hope of future victory on coats of mail nor troops
of horse but laid the main foundation of his campaign
on the supreme Author of Salvation. He wished the
very insignia of war, which were exposed only to the
wind and air, to have the advantage of such benefits.
The king's son, who had stayed for a longer time, sought
a more secluded place in the monastery for his visit.
He had been made in chapter one of our brethren, for
the regal dignity of the abbey and the monks' abundance
of spiritual comforts pleased him. Every day he asked
for a monk's allowance, just as the brethren ate in the
refectory, to be given to him. It is said certainly that
he alleged that the grandeur of the place and the
agreeable companionship of the monks always pleased
him. On the twelfth day, however, he said goodbye to
the brethren and hastened to join his father.

It should be recorded that on 1 July the queen gave

filium suum primogenitum in paruo uico qui dicitur
f. 202 Brotherworthe[1] iuxta / Pontem fractum, quem uocauit
Thomam ad honorem beati Thome martiris. Eodem
anno rex duxit exercitum in Scociam et occupauit totam
patriam qui dicitur Galwicum: castella et opida et suos
qui alibi in Scocia obcessi fuerant, liberauit; sed parum
quoad alia expediuit ob penuriam peditum et pecunie
et ideo cito reuersus est. Memorandum quod die sancti
Remigii[2] obiit pie memorie dominus Edmundus comes
Cornubie cuius pater fuit magnus Ricardus quondam
rex Almannie et frater regis Henrici patris nostri
Edwardi; unde quia sine sobole discesserat comitatus
regi Edwardo iure reuoluit, quem dictus comes adhuc
uiuens sibi fecerat heredem. In cuius thesauria inuenta
est quasi infinita summa auri et argenti ac preciosorum
lapidum.

Anno[a] regni regis Edwardi quarti[3] xx. octauo
dominus Iohannes de Euerisden' tunc celerarius sancti
Edmundi ualidam expedicionem fecit in partibus
Norhamton' apud manerium de Werketon' de pastura
qui dicitur Butoneris sicut in registro cantoris continetur.[4]
Preterito tamen anno cum in partes illas perambulacio
foreste fieret apud manerium de Werketon'[5] per vii. dies
perhendinauit ad hoc specialiter agens donis et epulis

---

[1] Thomas of Brotherton. Lord William Howard has expunged
' worthe ' and written ' ton ' over it.
[2] 1 October. For the date of his death see L. M. Midgley, *Ministers'*
Accounts of the Earldom of Cornwall, 1296–7 (Camden 3rd series, LXVI, 1942),
p. xvii, n. 2.
[3] The chronicler is here including the three Anglo-Saxon King Edwards
in his numeration.
[4] Eversden was at Warkton (Northants.) on 14 September 1300, when
the men of Boughton (Boughton Hall and Park lie within a mile of Warkton)
fined with him for the pasture; Brit. Mus. MS Additional 14847, f. 62,
62ᵛ, which contains an account of how the abbot of Bury secured his title

birth to her eldest son in a little village called Brother-worth [1] near Pontefract. She called him Thomas in honour of the Blessed Thomas the martyr. In the same year the king led an army into Scotland and occupied all the region called Galloway. He freed the castles and towns and those of his men who had been captured elsewhere in Scotland. But beyond this his expedition met with little success because of the shortage of foot-soldiers and money, so he quickly returned. It should be remembered that on St Remigius's day [2] Edmund, earl of Cornwall, of pious memory, died. His father was the great Richard, formerly king of Germany and the brother of King Henry, the father of our King Edward. As he died without issue the earldom reverted by law to King Edward, whom the earl while still alive had made his heir. In his treasury what seemed like an almost infinite amount of gold, silver and precious stones was found.

In the twenty-eighth year of the reign of King Edward IV [3] John de Eversden, then the cellarer of Bury St Edmunds, made a successful expedition to the manor of Warkton near Northampton on business concerning the pasture called Boughton, as is recorded in the precentor's register. [4] In the year before, when there had been a perambulation of the forest in this district, John de Eversden stayed for seven days at the manor of Warkton, [5] urging with precious gifts and

---

in Boughton apparently by a fictitious action brought against him by the men of Boughton.

[5] The manor of Warkton was within the boundaries of Rockingham forest. For an inquisition concerning venison held by Warkton and other townships before the royal justice of the forest in 1248 see G. J. Turner, *Select Pleas of the Forest* (Selden Soc., XIII, 1901), p. 89.

preciosis ut dictum manerium cum boscis et pertinenciis suis deforestaretur. Quod et factum est, et hoc iuste cum constet dictum manerium ab antiquo non esse de dominicis regis. Fuit enim magnis retroactis annis[1] eiusdem manerii quidam dominus qui habuit uxorem sibi copulatam, uterque iustus, uterque pius ac operibus misericordie assuetus, quibus inuidens inimicus deceptoriam eisdem sub specie religionis inmisit suggestionem. Inprimis itaque suggessit cordibus innocentum sanctorum uictorias confessorum gloriam ac uirginum triumphalem continenciam, sed demum ostendit coronas excellenciores martirum beatorum ut quanto scilicet cicius peruenerint ad coronam martirii tanto uelocius inducantur ad loca

f. 202ᵛ premii. Ecce martirium comendatur / set modus martirii non distinguitur. Elegerunt ergo uitam mundi finire martirio et formam execrande perdicionis precogitauerunt ut dum in uicino manus non haberent occidencium ne diucius prolongaretur optatum gaudium uterque in corpus proprium seuiendo sibi tamen tantum cognitum sacrilegum precipitauit homicidium. Qui die quadam remotis famulorum intersticiis [a] quisque nefas conceptum precurrit occupare. Sed Deus bonus qui noluit sanctos suos inmisceri eternis ludibriis temptatorem hebetauit et temptatos a proposito nequam tali

---

[a] *Sic for* intestacionibus (?) MS

[1] The story that follows is not found in the earlier records of the abbey; but it is in Bodley MS 240, p. 641 (late fourteenth century), and in St John's College, Oxford MS 209, ff. 67ᵛ–70. The passage in Bodley 240 is marked in the hand of the text ' ex cronic' sancti edmundi ' in the margin. Of Warkton, Northampton, the ' list of benefactors ' says: ' Matildis regina et uxor regis Willelmi primi dedit sancto Edmundo Werketone cum omnibus appendiciis eius consensu et uoluntate ipsius regis set sine carta '; *Pinchbeck Register*, ed. F. Hervey, ii, p. 292. The purpose of the story is to prove that Warkton was not ancient demesne because it had not belonged to the king before the Conquest. In the years following the Barons' War the royal courts sought to establish that royal demesne was inalienable and

sumptuous banquets that the manor and its woodlands
and appurtenances should be disafforested.   This he
did and quite rightly, as it is well known that the manor
from ancient times was not a part of the king's demesne.[1]
For many years ago there lived a certain lord of this
manor.   He was married and both he and his wife were
just and good and busy with charitable works.   But the
enemy of mankind, being jealous of them, sought to
deceive them under the guise of religion.   First he
stirred their hearts with the thought of the victories of
the holy innocents, the glory of the confessors and the
triumphant chastity of the virgins.   But then he pointed
out that the most glorious crowns were worn by the
blessed martyrs, so the sooner they won the crown of
martyrdom, the sooner would they be led to the place of
reward.   Thus he recommended martyrdom without
distinguishing the sort of martyrdom.   The man and
his wife, therefore, decided to be martyrs and so end
their life on earth.   They planned how to carry out this
deplorable scheme of perdition: as there was no-one
in the neighbourhood who would kill them, and so that
their day of joy would not be put off any longer, they
both rashly undertook to commit an accursed murder
known to themselves alone, by savagely attacking their
own bodies.   One day when their household was away
they hurried to fulfil their wicked plan.   But the good
God, who did not wish his saints to be made ludicrous
to all eternity, silenced the tempter and turned those
who were tempted from their evil purpose in the follow-

that the king's rights survived in lands that had been royal property
before the Conquest (the ancient demesne).   The tenants on ancient
demesne stood in direct relation to the king and enjoyed certain privileges;
R. S. Hoyt, *Royal Demesne in English Constitutional History* (1950), *passim.*

modo reuocauit. Mos enim predictis a priscis temporibus inoleuit ut cotidie post prandium in honore gloriosi
regis et martiris Edmundi post gracias Deo solutas
potacionem quam plenum siue plenitudinem sancti
Edmundi uocabant ad gustandum postulare, non, quod
absit, ad gule illecebras excitandas uerum ut uerius
loquar ad Christi pauperes recreandos; prothdolor
dicto die concepti sceleris poculum beati martiris
omiserunt. Nimirum cum totum ad malum aspirabant
bonum non sapiebant. Tandem uero inter densas ac
peropacas tenebras lux exilis emicuit sancte uidelicet
recordacionis Edmundi regis oblita potacio unde dum
plenum sancti Edmundi deportatur suasio diaboli
effugatur. Et dum gustatur potus ob deuocionem
sacratus fugatur hostis excecatus. Quapropter uterque
sceleris precogitati penitens sancto martiri gracias egit
dulcifluas. Qui cicius eisdem regis limina uisitantes
dictum manerium de Werketon' cum omnibus pertinenciis suis ecclesie sancti Edmundi inperpetuum donauerunt.
Ipsi eciam intra cepta eiusdem monasterii quoad
uixerint in quadam aula ueteri que Bradefeld [1] dicebatur
permanserunt. Sed obstat quod dicitur crebro inimicis
publicis regem Willelmum primum uel reginam Matil-
dem uxorem eius dedisse idem manerium sancto
Edmundo. Ad hanc questionem respondendum est
f. 203 quod idem / rex Willelmus Angliam armis adquisiuit,
comites subiugauit, comitatus inuestiuit, indigenas ex-
heredauit, alienigenas infeudauit et ut breuiter replicam,
qui totum adquisiuit partes tocius ubi et quomodo et

---

[1] ' Adjoining to [the infirmary at Bury St Edmunds] was a great hall
called originally "Spane," afterwards called "Bradfield Hall" and
"Bradfield Spane," used first as a place of recreation for the monks, and
afterwards as an addition to the infirmary'; G. M. Hills, ' The Antiquities
of Bury St Edmunds,' in the *Journal of the British Archaeological Association*,
XXI (1865), p. 126.

ing way. For their custom from the earliest times was that every day after lunch, when thanks had been returned to God, a drink called the ' plenum ' or ' brimming cup ' of St Edmund, should be quaffed in honour of the glorious king and martyr Edmund. It was not drunk to indulge the palate, which God forbid, but rather, it would be more accurate to say, to refresh the poor of Christ. Alas! on the day chosen for the crime the man and his wife forgot the cup of St Edmund. Small wonder that as they were bent entirely on evil they could remember nothing good. At last, however, a small ray of light flickered in the darkness and deep shadows; it was the forgotten drink of King Edmund of saintly memory. When the ' plenum ' of St Edmund is fetched the devil's evil influence is put to flight; when the sacred cup is tasted with devotion the enemy flies, blinded. Because of this both the man and his wife repented of the crime they had planned and gave their warmest thanks to the sainted martyr. They hurried to the abode of the royal saint and gave the manor of Warkton with all its appurtenances to the church of St Edmund for ever. They themselves spent the rest of their days within the precincts of the monastery in the old hall called Bradfield.[1] There remains the objection that it is often asserted by notorious ill-wishers that King William I or his wife Queen Mathilda gave this manor to St Edmund. The answer to this is that the said King William acquired England by force of arms; he reduced the earls to obedience; he divided the land into counties; he disinherited the native inhabitants; he enfeoffed foreigners and, to be brief, he who acquired

ad quos uoluit distribuit. Quare sub rege nouo et alienigena quasi seculum nouum exoriri in Anglia uideretur adeo ut nonnulli magnates Angligene grauibus expensis a rege flagitabant ut dominia *a* que antiquitus iure possidebant hereditario sub nouo rege possiderent tamquam per nouum regem de nouo feodati: unde quibus illis in diebus idem rex uel regina aliqua donauit, concessit et confirmauit quasi noui donatoris acceperunt fundamenta. Manerium ergo de Werketon' donum regis uel regine dicitur non quasi ante non datum sed sub specie donacionis de nouo confirmatum. Ad huius rei manifestam noticiam sciendum est quod idem rex spoliauit monasterium de Rameseya de mille septingentis libratis terre quas inter milites suos quos Angliam duxerat inpartiuit.

> Prothdolor *b* [1] interea   dura crescit angaria
> Ad monachos Dunelmie   ob quasdam partes peri-
>   fidie
> In claustro que excreuerant   per quas sancti
>   titubabant.
> Per has partes scinditur   et omnis ordo tollitur,
> Subtilis Christi tunica   scissuram fert et aspera.
> Prior priuatus subiacet   et ordo singultus exibet,
> Ouile Christi faucibus   lupinus patet et canibus.
> Dunelmensis episcopus   fultus prauorum manibus
> Vi uisitare uoluit   conuentum sed non potuit.

---

a Corr. by erasure to omnia (?) *MS*
b The verses are unspaced MS.

[1] See Guisborough, pp. 346–51; H. W. Wharton, *Anglia Sacra*, I, pp. 749ff.; *Camden Miscellany*, XIII (3rd series, XXXIV).—V. H. G.

the whole country allotted its parts where, how and to whom he wished.   It seemed that under this new king and foreigner another era had begun in England; thus some of the English-born nobles pleaded with the king, at great expense to themselves, that they might hold the demesne lands which they had owned by hereditary right from the earliest times, under the new king just as if they had been enfeoffed anew by him.   And so when the king or queen at that time gave, granted and confirmed some properties to the nobles, it looked as though the nobles had in fact received endowments from new donors.   In this way the manor of Warkton is called a gift of the king or queen, not because it had not been given before, but because now it was confirmed afresh with the appearance of a gift.   In proof of this fact it should be noted that the same king robbed the monastery of Ramsey of one thousand, seven hundred librates of land, which the king divided among the knights who had come with him to England.

Alas [1] to Durham's monks there came
Harsh violence and bitter shame,
In cloister flourished evil men:
The very saints were shaken then.
All decent order overthrown,
Christ's glorious tunic slashed and torn,
The prior defeated and deposed,
The brethren grieving and amazed,
The sheep of Christ torn from the fold,
By jaws of wolves and dogs were mauled.
Durham's bishop thus upheld
By wicked men, wished to enforce
A visitation on the house.
But his violent plan was foiled.

Nam prior allegauerat   leges consuetudinarias
Primo debere episcopum   uisitari post subditum.
Sed frustra taliter cauellatur   nam ad arma
                 festinatur.
Predictus enim episcopus   scilicet Antonius
Exercitatus a puero   nil amplius quam prelio.
Plus confidebat in gladio   quam in iure canonico.
Iam cingi iubet prioratum   immunitate decoratum,
Nec erat obcessis monachis   fas uti necessariis.
Sic sic pater ecclesie   pater dictus a Patre,
Pater patrans propere

f. 203ᵛ

Pertractat / suos filios   quos efficit in clericos.
Tandem pro pacis optimo   conceditur episcopo
Vt cum duobus clericis   utriusque iuris sciolis
Ingrediatur capitulum   facturus liti terminum.
Abnuit episcopus   respondens obstinacius
Non secum tam paruulis   adiunctis auxiliis
Eorum proposuerat   inmiscere latebris,
Isdem retorquens plurima   uiciorum uolumina.
Velint nolint ueniet   inducens plures acies.

The prior customs found and laws
To prove the bishop in such case
Must visit not, but be instead
First himself the visited.
In vain he quibbled, for my lord
Put the matter to the sword.
From boyhood Bishop Anthony
Had learned to fight most readily,
And in violence trusted more
Than in the texts of canon law.
Though it was privileged and immune
He had the house surrounded soon
And did to the besieged vouchsafe
The bare necessities of life.
Thus the father of the church
(Who from our Father took the name),
A father acting hastily,
Maltreated men, his very sons,
Whom he had ordained clergymen.
At last the monks in hope of peace
Would let the bishop state his case,
And the chapter entering
Two learned clerics with him bring,
Skilled in law of Church and State,
To make an end of the dispute.
But the bishop would not so,
Saying that he could not go
With so few helpers at his side
Into their snare. So he replied,
Flinging back into their faces
A very library of their vices.
Willy-nilly he will come
With mighty force against their home.

Ad illa pallor facies   inducit uultus macies,
Caterua regularium   pauet ad tale nuncium,
Timens secreta regule   tractari ut res publice,
Cum sicut ait apostolus   ' tractetur opus uilius,
Si surgat in ecclesia   potestate layca.'
Nunc secus factum fuerat   episcopus nam iusserat,
Ut secreta capituli   tractentur uelut seculi.
En obstant fratres uirilius   dantes manus ad
                                         fortius,
Petentes ad hec singula   apellacionum remedia.
Prior uota prosequitur   caterua fratrum sequitur,
Nam ipsum deposuerat   et alterum substituerat.

1301

Rex tenuit parliamentum suum apud Lincolniam in festo sancti Hillarii [1] quod protelata fuit per tres septimanas et plus. Omnis tamen antiqua controuersia inter reges et comites et barones per pacis bonum sedata fuit. Vnde foresta manet in eodem statu sicut per ultimos equites segregata fuit et limitata. Ibidem rex dedit filio suo Edwardo principatum Wallie, comitatum Cestrie et Pontiui.

1313

Anno domini M.CCC.XIII. Isabella regina peperit filium primogenitum apud Windishore xiii. die Nouembris et uocatur Edwardus iii.

[1] 13 January

At this the monks were terrified
Lest to the secular world outside
The secrets of their order be
Known and debated publicly.
The apostle said, ' Worse may be yet
If inside the Church's gate
The laity more power get.'
Now by the bishop's own decree
This had been done most wretchedly,
That secrets of the chapter be
Disposed of by the laity.
The brothers struggle bravely still
To remedy each grievous ill.
The prior and convent make their vows;
The prior himself had been deposed
And another prior they chose.

1301

The king held his parliament at Lincoln on the feast of
St Hilary.[1]   It lasted for more than three weeks.   All
the former disputes between the king and the earls and
barons were settled to restore the blessing of peace.   The
boundaries of the forest were to remain the same as
those drawn and divided off by the last group of knights.
In this parliament the king gave his son Edward the
principality of Wales, the earldom of Chester and
Ponthieu.

1313

In the year of the Lord 1313 Queen Isabel gave birth
to her eldest son at Windsor on 13 November.   He is
called Edward III.

1326

Anno domini M.CCC.XXVI. idem Edwardus coronatus fuit in regem die Conversionis sancti Pauli.

1329

Anno domini M.CCC.XXIX. Petrus de Corbario [1] de ordine Fratrum Minorum in ciuitate Romana in papam se fecit coronari de consilio et auxilio Lodowici ducis Bauar'.[2] Iste antipapa cardinales et alios officiales sicut uerus papa creauit.

f. 204   Anno domini M.[CCC].XXIX. Phi/lippa regina Anglie peperit filium primogenitum apud Wodestok xv. die Iunii et uocatur Edwardus quartus.

1334

Anno domini M.CCC.XXXIIII. in uigilia sancti Andree uentus uehemens et dampnosus prostrauit arbores, edificia et campanaria.

1335

Anno domini M.CCC.XX[X]V. obiit quedam mulier in Northfolchia nomine Ioneta que non commedit nec bibit per xxxi. annos.[a]

[a] Anno Domini M.CCC.LXXXII. regni regis Ricardi secundi quinto xxi. die mensis Aprilis (*probably a mistake for 21 May*; *an earthquake is recorded in most chronicles*) post prandium una hora factus est in regno Anglie uehemens terre motus qui populo terre qui in domibus residebant magnum timorem incussit. Credebant enim propter excessiuam exagitacionem domorum et uelocem tremorem eas super se cadere et ideo de eis uelocissime exierunt. Idem eciam terre motus magnis edificiis et precipue ecclesiis ut ecclesiis Christi Cantuar', sancti Pauli London' et Westmonasterii plurima dampna fecit. Eodem eciam anno et mense uidelicet xxiiii. die circa quartum ictum orologii post mediam noctem factus est eciam terre motus sed non erat ita uehemens sicut primus *in charter-hand of the late fourteenth century and* Wil. con. Willelmus. Hen. Stephanus. Hen.que secundus. Ri. Iohannes.

1326

In the year of the Lord 1326 the same Edward was crowned king on the day of the Conversion of St Paul.

1329

In the year of the Lord 1329 Peter de Corberia,[1] a member of the order of Friars Minor, had himself crowned pope in the city of Rome on the advice and with the help of Ludwig, duke of Bavaria.[2] This antipope created cardinals and other officials just like a true pope.

In the year of the Lord 1329 Philippa, queen of England, gave birth to her eldest son at Woodstock on 15 June. He is called Edward IV.

1334

In the year of the Lord 1334 on the eve of St Andrew's day a violent and destructive gale blew down trees, buildings and bell towers.

1335

In the year of the Lord 1335 a woman called Joneta, who had neither eaten nor drunk for thirty-one years, died in Norfolk.

Henricus. tres Edward. Ri.que secundus. postea regnarunt Hen. quartus. quint. sextus. Ed. quart. Ed. quint. R. tercius. Hen. quoque binus. 20. Hic resident monachi post annos mille viginti. Hic Uuius. Leffstan. Baldwyn. Robertus. Albold'. Anselm' et Ordingus. Hugo. Sampson, Hugo. Ricardus. Henric'. Edmundus. Symon'. Iohannes. Thomas. Ricardus. Willelmus. Ion. Ion. bisbin' Willelmus comitatur. Iohannem sequitur Robertus tuncque Ricardus. Thomas. Willelmus. Iohannes iam dominatur *in charter-hand of the fifteenth century MS*

[1] Peter de Corberia declared Pope Nicholas V on 12 May 1328 (not in 1329 as the chronicle records).

[2] Ludwig, duke of Bavaria 1294–1347, emperor of Germany 1314–47

INDEX

INDEX

Beaulieu Thomas de, bishop of Norwich (1226–36), 6, 7, 9

Boethius, *De Consolatione Philosophiae*, xviii

Bohemia, king of, *see* Przélmilas-Ottokar II

Bohemond, son of Hugh III king of Cyprus, 82n

Bohun, Humphrey de, earl of Hereford (1275–98), 138 and n, 147, 150–1

Bomund, Ralph, tax collector in Suffolk (1295), 129

Bonaventura, Romano, papal legate, 7

Boniface VIII, pope (1295–1303), 126, 143, 151 ; his bull ' clericis laicos ', 135, 138, 147

Bordeaux, 90

Bosco, Richard de, prior of St Edmund's, (1244–52), 12, 14–15, 18

Boston (Lincs.), fire in the fair and house of Dominicans at (1288), 91

Boughton, a pasture, *see under* Warkton

Boughton (Norf.), 110

Boulogne, count of, *see* Reginald

Boulogne-sur-Mer, 118

Bourges, archbishop of, *see* Beaulieu, Simon de

Bouvines, battle of (1214), 2

Boyland, Richard de, justice in eyre, 69, 86, 94

Brabant, 136

— dukes of, *see* John I ; John II

Bradfield (Norf.), 109

— *or* Monks' Bradfield (Suff.), 41, 107

— Hall *or* Bradfield Spane, *see under* Bury St Edmunds, Abbey of

— John de, precentor, then bishop of Rochester (1278–83), 64, 77

Brakelond, Jocelin de, xiv, xv, xvii

Brandeston, Henry de, dean, then bishop of Salisbury (1287–8), 87

Breton, John, bishop of Hereford (1269–75), 58

Brettenham (Suff.), 109

Brienne (*or* Acre), John de, 86

Bristol, 82, 118

Brittany, 7, 130

— dukes of, *see* Arthur ; Geoffrey ; John II

Bromholm (Norf.), 5 and n

Bronescombe, Walter de, bishop of Exeter (1258–80), 72

Brooke (Norf.), manor and church, 43, 105, 111

Brotherton (Yorks.), 158n

— Thomas of, *see* Thomas

Browne, Edward, M.A., xlii and n

Bruce, Robert de, lord of Annandale (1245–95), 99–101, 115 and n

Bruges (Belgium), 143–4

Brunne, Richard de, sacrist of St Edmund's, xxx

Brunton, William de, justice of the King's Bench, 93

Bumpstead (Essex), 108

Burgh (Norf.), 72, 110

— Geoffrey de, bishop of Ely (1225–8), 5, 6

— Hubert de, justiciar, earl of Kent (1227–43), 3, 7–8, 12

— Raymund de, of Dartford, 7

Burgundy, duke of, *see* Robert II ; count of, *see* Ottoninus

Burnell, Robert, bishop of Bath and Wells (1275–92), xl, 56, 65, 68, 70–1, 115–16, 126–7

Burton-on-Trent, Benedictine abbey, abbot of, *see* Insula, Richard de

Bury St Edmunds, 81–2, 87–8, 90 ; ecclesiastical councils at, 37 (1267), 135 (1296) ; parliament at (1296), xxxiii, 133–5 ; royal documents witnessed at, 53, 119, 127n

— Abbey of, xi–xxxv *passim* : during and after Barons' War, xv, xxii–xxv, 31–2, 34–5, 38–9 : bishop of Norwich at, 7 : chronicles of, *Annales Sancti Edmundi*, xvi, xviii, *Chronica Buriensis* written at St Benet of Hulme, xxviii ; chronicle of John de Taxter, *see* Taxter, John de ; *Gesta Sacristarum*, xv : confraternities granted to Edward of Caernarvon, 157, to Rainald, bishop of Vicenza, 157, to Westminster abbey, 148n : friars' disputes with,

Whittlesey, Odo de, almoner, then abbot of Thorney (1293–1305), 118

Wich, Adam de, abbot of Waltham (1264–70), 48

— St Richard, bishop of Chichester (1245–53), 62

Wickhampton, Robert de, bishop of Salisbury (1274–84), 48, 81

Wickwane, William de, archbishop of York (1279–85), 69, 85

William I, king of England (1066–1087), 160

— archbishop of Edessa (Rages), see Geoffrey

— marquess of Montferrat, 57n

— count of Holland (1234–56), 17, 21, 76

— IV, count of Jülich (1218–78), 65

— earl of Ross (1274–1323), 100–101

— 'Blazing' (Willelmus Ardens), a ghost, 55

Winchcombe (Glos.), 97

Winchelsea (Sussex), 141

Winchelsey, Robert de, archdeacon of Essex, then archbishop of Canterbury (1294–1313), 116, 134–5, 140, 141, 147, 149, 152

Winchester, 7, 30, 70, 79; parliament at (1265), xix, 31

— bishops of, see Ely, Nicholas de ; Pontoise, John de ; Raleigh, William ; Valence, Aymer de ; bishop elect, see More, Richard de la ; archdeacon of, see More, Richard de la

— St Swithun's, chronicle of, xvi and n

Windsor, 47, 57, 67, 81, 163 ; ordinances issued at (1265), 32

— castle, xxi, 126–7

Wingham, Henry of, bishop of London (1260–2), 26

Wisbech (Cambs.), 109

Woodford, William de, abbot of Peterborough (1295–9), 153

Woodstock (Oxon.), 164

Woolhampton, Henry de, justice in eyre, 46

Woolpit (Suff.), 43, 105, 111 ; church at, 42

Worcester, 66, 73

— cathedral priory, chronicle of, xliii

— Florence of, chronicle of, xviii

Wordwell (Suff.), 108

Worlingworth (Suff.), 43, 44, 106, 110

Wouldham, Thomas de, prior, then bishop of Rochester (1292–1317), 98

Wrabness (Essex), 108

Wyle, Walter de la, bishop of Salisbury (1263–71), 48

Wymondham (Norf.), Benedictine priory, prior of, see Pulleyn, Adam

Yarmouth, 21, 74, 87, 90, 117, 124, 125 ; attacked by pirates, xxii, 76, 141 ; fleet from 94, 117 ; men of, 148

Yaxley, William de, abbot of Thorney (1261–93), 118

Yelverton (Norf.), 111

York, 114 ; parliaments at, 148 (1298), xxxiv, 156 (1300)

— archbishops of, see Corbridge, Thomas de ; Giffard, Walter de ; Newark, Henry de ; Romeyn, John le ; Wickwane, William de

— cathedral, dean of, see Newark, Henry de

Yorkshire, 69

Zacharias, Benedict, pirate, 118 and n

Zeeland, pirates from, 76

Zouche, Alan de la (d. 1270), 47

— Roger de la (d. 1285), son of Alan, 47

Zwyn (Swine), river (in Flanders), 141

Printed in Great Britain by
Thomas Nelson (Printers) Ltd, London and Edinburgh

Date Due